KERRY'S
Fighting Story
1916 — 21

COUNTY
KERRY

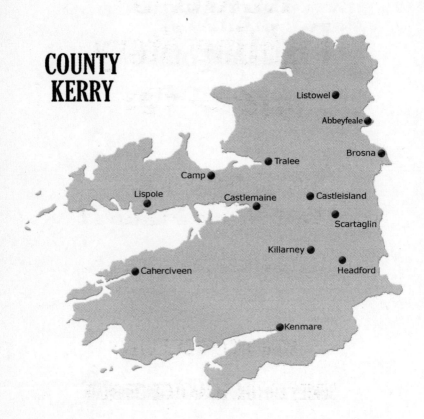

Listowel

Abbeyfeale

Brosna

Tralee

Camp

Lispole

Castlemaine

Castleisland

Scartaglin

Killarney

Caherciveen

Headford

Kenmare

KERRY'S
Fighting Story
1916 — 21

Told By The
Men Who Made It

With a Unique Pictorial Record of the Period

INTRODUCTION BY J.J. LEE

SERIES EDITOR: BRIAN Ó CONCHUBHAIR

MERCIER PRESS
IRISH PUBLISHER – IRISH STORY

MERCIER PRESS

Cork

www.mercierpress.ie

Trade enquiries to CMD Booksource,
55a Spruce Avenue, Stillorgan Industrial Park,
Blackrock, County Dublin

Originally published by *The Kerryman*, 1947

This edition published by Mercier Press, 2009

© Preface: Brian Ó Conchubhair, 2009

© Introduction: J.J. Lee, 2009

© Text: Mercier Press, 2009

ISBN: 978 1 85635 641 1

10 9 8 7 6 5 4 3 2 1

A CIP record for this title is available from the British Library

Printed and bound in the EU.

CONTENTS

PREFACE (2009) BY BRIAN Ó CONCHUBHAIR   9

ACKNOWLEDGEMENTS   14

INTRODUCTION (2009) BY J.J. LEE   15

FOREWORD   23

FORMATION AND DEVELOPMENT OF THE VOLUNTEERS   25

    Tralee   28

    Killarney   44

    Listowel   52

    Dingle   54

    Killorglin   59

    Recruiting in Kerry   62

    Castleisland   66

    Caherciveen   69

    Duagh   72

    Duagh Volunteers   72

THE GERMAN EXPEDITION TO TRALEE BAY   82

KERRY'S PLACE IN THE GENERAL PLAN, 1916   92

CASEMENT AND HIS COMING TO KERRY   103

KERRY IN HOLY WEEK 1916 AND AFTER   117

THERE WAS NO BLUNDER IN KERRY   130

    The O'Rahilly Grave   136

KERRY WAS PREPARED AND READY   138

THE FIRST CASUALTIES OF 1916   142

KERRY HEROES OF THE RISING   149

LET ME CARRY YOUR CROSS FOR IRELAND, LORD!   163

IN MEMORY OF THOMAS ASHE   165

A HOUSE OF MEMORIES   167

CONSCRIPTION AND THE GENERAL ELECTION OF 1918   175
    Irish Republic Established   195

GORTATLEA FIRST BARRACK ATTACK AND CASUALTIES   201

POLICE ATTACKED AND DISARMED AT CAMP   204

A LISTOWEL SENSATION OF 1918   206
    Skilly and Milk   209

ATTACKS ON GORTATLEA, SCARTAGLIN AND BROSNA BARRACKS   211
    Seizures of Arms at Tralee and Glenbeigh   217

CAUSED MUTINY IN LISTOWEL, SHOT IN CORK   220

THE SACK OF TRALEE   228
    American Exiles' Generosity   233

THE MOCK BATTLE OF TRALEE   234

A CHIVALROUS ENGLISH JOURNALIST   239
    Two Black and Tans Shot at Ballybrack   242
    Brave Tommy Hawley   242

THE LISPOLE AMBUSH   245

THE FATAL CHALLENGE OF MAJOR MCKINNON   248
    The Shooting of Major McKinnon   253

MILITARY AMBUSHED AT HEADFORD JUNCTION   255
    How Allman Fell   260

POLICE PATROL ANNIHILATED AT CASTLEMAINE   261
    Daring Coup Frustrated at Castleisland   263

THE CAMPAIGN IN NORTH KERRY   265
    Ballyduff Ambush and its Sequel   265
    Attempted Enemy Round-Up and the Murder of Bob Browne 267
    Commandant Michael Robert McElligott   270

Black and Tans Engaged at Ballylongford   271

Murder of James Kennelly of Moybella   274

Attempted Attack on Lixnaw Station   275

The Murder of Adjutant Willie McCarthy   276

Tarbert Barracks Attack   277

Fight with the Military at Kilmorna   278

Volunteer Officers Murdered at Gortaglanna   281

Lieutenant Jack Sheahan Killed at Coilbwee   284

Attempted Ambush at Knockpogue, Ballyduff   286

Late Captain Michael McElligott of Listowel   287

With the 2nd battalion Kerry No. 1 Brigade   287

Capture of Ballyheigue Coastguard Station   288

Fenit Barracks Attacked   289

Causeway and Abbeydorney Ambushes   290

Ambush at Shannow bridge   292

THE CAMPAIGN IN EAST KERRY   293

Rathmore Barracks Attacked   293

Minor Attacks, Raids and Reprisals   294

Execution of Con Murphy   295

Successful Train Ambush   296

Tureengarriffe Ambush   299

Clonbanin Ambush   300

THE CAMPAIGN IN WEST KERRY   304

Shooting of Paddy Kennedy of Annascaul   307

WORK OF A KILLARNEY INTELLIGENCE OFFICER   310

TRALEE FIANNA ÉIREANN AT WAR   314

BRITISH TRUCE-BREAKERS IN TRALEE   318

BRITISH WARSHIP ENGAGED IN KENMARE BAY   322

Amazing Escape of Military Train   325

IN THE FIGHT WITH CUMANN NA MBAN   327

INDEX   335

PREFACE (2009)

As we approach the centenary of the 1916 Easter Rising and the Irish War of Independence/Anglo-Irish War (1919–1921), interest among scholars and the general public in these historic events gathers unrelenting pace. Recent years have witnessed a slew of books, articles, documentaries and films, emerge at home and abroad all dealing with the events and controversies involved in the struggle for political independence in the period 1916–1922. While many of these projects have re-evaluated and challenged the standard nationalist narrative that dominated for so long, and indeed have contributed to a more nuanced and complex appreciation of the events in question, the absence of the famous *Fighting Story* series – initially published by *The Kerryman* newspaper and subsequently republished by Anvil Books – is a notable and regrettable absence. First published in Christmas and special editions of *The Kerryman* newspaper in the years before the Second World War, the articles subsequently appeared in four independent collections entitled *Rebel Cork's Fighting Story, Kerry's Fighting Story, Limerick's Fighting Story* and *Dublin's Fighting Story* between 1947–49. The choice of counties reflecting the geographical intensity of the campaign as Dr Peter Hart explains in his new introduction to *Rebel Cork's Fighting Story*: 'The Munster IRA … was much more active than anywhere else except Longford, Roscommon and Dublin city.' Marketed as authentic accounts and as 'gripping episodes' by 'the men who made it', the series was dramatically described as 'more graphic than anything written of late war zones', with 'astonishing pictures' and sold 'at the very moderate price of two shillings'. Benefiting from *The Kerryman*'s wide distribution network and a competitive price, the books proved immediately popular at home and abroad, so much so that many, if not most, of the books, were purchased by, and for, the Irish Diaspora. This competitive price resulted in part from the fact that 'the producers were content to reduce their own profit and to produce the booklet at little above the mere cost of production'. Consequently, however, the volumes quickly disappeared from general circulation. Dr Ruán O'Donnell explains in the new introduction to *Limerick's Fighting Story*, 'The shelf life … was reduced by the poor production values they shared. This was a by-product of the stringent economies of their day when pricing, paper quality, binding and distribution costs had to be considered [which] rendered copies vulnerable to deterioration and unsuited to library utilisation.'

The books targeted not only the younger generation, who knew about those times by hearsay only, but also the older generation who 'will recall vividly a memorable era and the men who made it'. Professor Diarmaid Ferriter notes in the new introduction to *Dublin's Fighting Story* that these volumes answered the perceived need for Volunteers to record their stories in their own words in addition to ensuring the proper education and appreciation of a new generation for their predecessors' sacrifices. The narrative, he writes 'captures the excitement and the immediacy of the Irish War of Independence and the belief that the leaders of the revolution did not urge people to take dangerous courses they were not themselves prepared to take'. These four books deserve reprinting therefore not only for the important factual information they contain, and the resource they offer scholars of various disciplines, but also because of the valuable window they open on the mentality of the period. As Professor J.J. Lee observes in the introduction to *Kerry's Fighting Story*, for anyone 'trying to reconstruct in very different times the historical reality of what it felt like at the time, there is no substitute for contemporary accounts, however many questions these accounts may raise. We know what was to come. Contemporaries did not.' The insight these books offer on IRA organisation at local level suggest to Dr Peter Hart 'why IRA units were so resilient under pressure, and how untrained, inexperienced men could be such formidable soldiers … Irish guerrillas fought alongside their brothers, cousins, school and teammates, and childhood friends – often in the very lanes, fields and streets where they had spent their lives together'. In addition these texts reveal the vital roles, both active and passive, women played in the struggle of Irish Independence.

The establishment of Anvil Books in 1962 saw a reissuing of certain volumes, Cork and Limerick in particular. The link between *The Kerryman* and Anvil Books was Dan Nolan (1910–1989). Son of Thomas Nolan, and nephew of Daniel Nolan and Maurice Griffin, he was related to all three founders of *The Kerryman* newspaper that commenced publishing in 1904. His obituary in that newspaper describes how he 'was only a nipper when he looked down the barrels of British guns as His Majesty's soldiers tried to arrest the proprietors of *The Kerryman* for refusing to publish recruitment advertisements. And he saw the paper and its employees being harassed by the Black and Tans.' On graduating from Castleknock College, he joined the paper's staff in 1928 replacing his recently deceased uncle, Maurice Griffin. His father's death in 1939 saw Dan Nolan become the paper's managing director and his tenure would, in due course, see a marked improvement in its commercial performance: circulation increased and ultimately exceeded 40,000 copies per week, and advertisement revenue also increased significantly. Under his stewardship *The Kerryman*, according to Séamus McConville in an obituary in the paper, 'became solidly established as the unchallenged leader in sales and stature among provincial newspapers'. Recognising his talent, the Provincial Newspaper Association elected him president in 1951. Among his projects were the Rose of Tralee Festival, Tralee Racecourse and Anvil Books. Founded in 1962 with Nolan and Rena Dardis as co-directors, Anvil Books established itself as the pre-eminent publisher of memoirs and accounts dealing with the Irish War of Independence. Indeed the first book published by Anvil

Books was a 1962 reprint of *Rebel Cork's Fighting Story* in a print run of 10,000 copies.

Conscious, no doubt, of the potential for controversy the original foreword was careful not to present the *Fighting Stories* as 'a detailed or chronological history of the fight for independence', and acknowledged 'that in the collection of data about such a period errors and omissions can easily occur and so they will welcome the help of readers who may be able to throw more light upon the various episodes related in the series. Such additional information will be incorporated into the second edition of the booklets which the present rate of orders would seem to indicate will be called for in the very near future.' Subsequent editions of *Rebel Cork's Fighting Story* and *Limerick's Fighting Story* did appear in print with additional material as O'Donnell discusses in his enlightening introduction to *Limerick's Fighting Story*, but the proposed *Tipperary's Fighting Story*, as advertised in the Limerick volume with a suggested publication date of 1948 and a plea for relevant information or pictures, never materialised. This 2009 edition adheres to the original texts as first published by *The Kerryman* rather than the later editions by Anvil Books. A new preface, introduction and index frame the original texts that remain as first presented other than the silent correction of obvious typographical errors.

The preface to the final book, *Dublin's Fighting Story*, concluded by noting that the publishers 'would be satisfied if the series serves to preserve in the hearts of the younger generation that love of country and devotion to its interests which distinguished the men whose doings are related therein'. The overall story narrated in these four books is neither provincial nor insular, nor indeed limited to Ireland, but as Lee remarks in *Kerry's Fighting Story*, it is rather 'like that of kindred spirits elsewhere, at home and abroad, an example of the refusal of the human spirit to submit to arbitrary power'. The hasty and almost premature endings of several chapters may be attributed to the legacy of the Irish Civil War whose shadow constantly hovers at the edges threatening to break into the narrative, and in fact does intrude in a few instances. Lee opines that writers avoided the Civil War as it 'was still too divisive, still too harrowing, a nightmare to be recalled into public memory. Hence the somewhat abrupt ending of several chapters at a moment when hopes were still high and the horrors to come yet unimagined.'

Ireland at the start of the twenty-first century is a very different place than it was when these books were first published. Irish historiography has undergone no less a transformation and to bridge the gap four eminent historians have written new introductions that set the four *Fighting Stories* in the context of recent research and shifts in Irish historiography. Yet Lee's assessment in reference to Kerry holds true for each of the four volumes: 'Whatever would happen subsequently, and however perspectives would inevitably be affected by hindsight, for better and for worse, *Kerry's Fighting Story* lays the foundation for all subsequent studies of these foundation years of an independent Irish state.' As we move toward the centenary of 1916, the War of Independence, the Anglo-Irish Treaty and the Civil War, it is appropriate and fitting that these key texts be once again part of the public debate of those events and it is sincerely hoped that as Ruán O'Donnell states: 'This new life of a classic of its genre will facilitate a fresh evaluation of its unique perspectives on the genesis of the modern Irish state.'

Dr Brian Ó Conchubhair
Series Editor
University of Notre Dame
Easter 2009

ACKNOWLEDGEMENTS

I AM GRATEFUL not only to the scholars who penned the new introductions for their time and expertise but also to the following who assisted in numerous ways: Beth Bland, Angela Carothers, Aedín Ní Bhroithe-Clements (Hesburgh Library), Professor Mike Cronin, Rena Dardis, Ken Garcia, Dr Michael Griffin, Alan Hayes, Professor J.J. Lee, Dyann Mahorr, Don and Patrica Nolan, Nora Noonan, Seán Seosamh Ó Conchubhair, Interlibrary Loans at the Hesburgh Library, University of Notre Dame, Eoin Purcell, Wendy Logue and the staff at Mercier Press, the editorial board of *The Irish Sword*, Colonel Patrick Kirby, Dr Pat McCarthy and Dr Kenneth Ferguson. *Táim an-bhuíoch do gach éinne atá luaite thuas, m'athair ach go háirithe as a chuid foighne agus as a chuid saineolais a roinnt liom go fial agus do Thara uair amháin eile a d'fhulaing go foighneach agus an obair seo ar bun agam.*

DR BRIAN Ó CONCHUBHAIR

INTRODUCTION (2009)

DISPARAGING COMMENTS WERE sometimes made about the degree of activity against British physical force in Kerry during the War of Independence, not least by Eoin O'Duffy in his unstable Blueshirt period in 1933, perhaps reflecting the less than hospitable reception he had received in the county. It is certainly still true that Kerry is much better known for the horrors of the Civil War there, which saw some of the worst atrocities of that terrible and tragic period, than for the struggle in the preceding years. Indeed it is likely that reluctance to open up the wounds of the later period led to a neglect of the earlier period for fear of where it might lead. Some who were active in the Civil War carried their silence with them to the grave, or spoke only on condition that their accounts would not become available to the public until after their deaths. *The Kerryman* newspaper therefore rendered an important service to historians when in 1947 it collected some of its earlier reports on the struggle for independence, garnished by recollections of activists of the time. But the Civil War itself was still too divisive, still too harrowing, a nightmare to be recalled into public memory. Hence the somewhat abrupt ending of several chapters in this volume at a moment when hopes were still high and the horrors to come yet unimagined.

Nevertheless the subtitle of the book, 'Told by the men who made it', is a shade disingenuous. For of course only a fraction of those 'who made it' can have contributed to the volume, often under pen-names. It is extremely important as far as it goes, but it is not complete, from even within the IRA, much less from outside it. Ironically, if the title promises rather more than it delivers – much though it does deliver

– in this regard, it actually delivers more than it promises in several important respects, making it even more valuable than appears at first sight.

Firstly, it dates its coverage only from 1916, whereas it really begins in 1913, with the formation of the Irish Volunteers. Indeed, the long first chapter on the spread of the Volunteers in Kerry before the 1916 Rising is among the most valuable in the entire book. It was through the Volunteers that Austin Stack, already renowned as a footballer in a county laying the foundations of its illustrious contribution to the Gaelic Athletic Association (GAA), would like many others rise to prominence in republican ranks. The description of the struggle against John Redmond's National Volunteers after Redmond's call in September 1914 for recruits to fight anywhere in the world for Britain, is particularly useful.

Kerry of course found itself very much in the news on the eve of the 1916 Rising when the saga of the *Aud*, with the German weapons aboard, and of Roger Casement's arrest after coming ashore at Banna Strand on his quixotic mission, directed eyes, as well as squads of soldiers and police, towards strange happenings in the Kingdom. Clearly sensitive to charges of incompetence over the failure to get the guns ashore, contributors seek to refute in detail, in further valuable contributions, charges of local blundering.

Kerry's Fighting Story is not only a record of fighting, useful though that is. In fact most of the account from 1916 to 1918, while paying proper attention to the ordeal in 1917 of Thomas Ashe from Lispole, who died on hunger strike from forced feeding, deals with the political build-up to the 1918 general election, a period full of hard organisational graft whose importance is sometimes overlooked in the light of the more spectacular public events to come, but which was indispensable in laying the basis of a Sinn Féin organisation to supersede the Home Rule/Irish Parliamentary Party.

The title too does not quite reveal the full promise of the contents, in that it contains no reference to women, for its account of Cumann na mBan, though brief, is packed with useful information, to say nothing of the evidence scattered throughout of the involvement of women in a variety of rebel activities.

In short, relevant though all the contents are to the actual fight, over half the text is in fact devoted to the preparations for that fight, rather than to details of the military struggle itself. Far more information has become available since 1947, including notable studies dealing directly with many of the events recorded in the 1947 volume. T. Ryle Dwyer's *Tans, Terrors and Troubles: Kerry's Real Fighting Story 1913-23* (Mercier Press, 2001) carries the story down to the end of the Civil War, and Sinéad Joy's *The IRA in Kerry, 1916–21* (Collins Press, 2005) explores many new sources. Other highly informative contributions include the pioneering studies by Fr Anthony Gaughan, indefatigable biographer of Kerry personalities, two of whom feature frequently here: Austin Stack, and the Home Rule MP for West Kerry, a strong opponent of Sinn Féin and the Volunteers, Tom O'Donnell. Both were published by Kingdom books, in 1977 and 1983 respectively, as was his *Memoirs of Constable Jeremiah Mee* (Kingdom Books, 1975). Some of the personalities who feature in these volumes can also be found, from rather different perspectives, in the letters of a prominent Tralee family, the Moynihan Brothers in *Peace and War 1909–1918*, edited and introduced by Deirdre McMahon (Irish Academic Press, 2004).

Given all the new research contained in these volumes, as well as in other publications of the past sixty years, including good work in local journals, like the *Journal of Cumann Luachra*, one's initial impulse may be to wonder if reprinting the 1947 volume serves any useful purpose. But the initial impulse should be resisted. The volume deserves reprinting for several reasons. In trying to reconstruct in very different times the historical reality of what it felt like at the time, there is no substitute for contemporary accounts, however many questions these accounts may raise. We know what was to come. Contemporaries did not. But they knew, in a way we cannot, what they hoped the sunrise would bring. One has to drink deep from contemporary reports of conflict to capture not only details, however important, but also feelings, one might even say 'all that delirium of the brave', the feelings that accompany awakenings of the spirit, 'Bliss was it in that dawn', etc. Great historians may be able to reconstruct those feelings, or great novelists or poets intuitively divine them, like Yeats at times, as in 'September 1913', or in his Easter 1916 poems. But that is still different from the words of the participants themselves. And in this case, even when the accounts were composed after the Civil War, which estranged so many former comrades, it seems that an attempt was generally made to remain true to the record of the time.

Contemporary newspaper accounts must always be treated with a degree of suspicion until one has winkled out what lies behind them. What were the biases of the editors and reporters? What was their ideological line? How far did they have to write to satisfy the beliefs of their readers – how well did they know, or intuit, what those beliefs were? How did they determine what their readers wanted? How far did they reflect, how far create, public opinion? The critical analysis of newspapers as sources has begun only very recently among students of the Irish media. Interesting here too will be the study of foreign reporting, like that by Hugh Martin of the *Daily News*, whose influential reports from Ireland included accounts of the Black and Tan terror in Tralee in November 1920, cited in *Kerry's Fighting Story*, and whose experience is recorded in Maurice Walsh's *The News from Ireland: Foreign Correspondents and the Irish Revolution* (I. B. Tauris, London, 2008), a book from which students of the Irish media could learn much.

Yet having warned of the pitfalls of over-reliance on contemporary newspapers, some of the issues are fairly straightforward. *The Kerryman* took great pains to list as many of the participants as possible at the musters of the Irish Volunteers. They are unlikely to have been inaccurate, either in terms of inclusion or exclusion. The paper's credibility would have suffered seriously and rapidly if it omitted genuine participants, or included bogus ones. The lists of participants at the various demonstrations and parades in the different towns, which may seem unnecessarily detailed, in fact provide basic raw material about the identity of activists on which further inquiry can be based. So do the long lists of the names of assentors and nominators of Sinn Féin election candidates, including several curates. Students of the priesthood in Kerry will find much to ponder here.

It is often overlooked how much social history can be found in the accounts of political events. The Volunteer gatherings were often festive occasions, enlivening somewhat drab daily routines with their parades, often headed by 'the faithful Strand Street Band' of Tralee, in demand outside as well as inside Tralee, though several other towns had their own bands. The place of music in brightening up sometimes dreary existences deserves much further enquiry in our social history. There could be too a certain grim jocularity to the differences which emerged between the rival Volunteer groups, as in the struggle in Killorglin for control of the town band. What images of communal harmony are called up by the report that on 18 July 1915, the Killorglin brass band 'was for the first time entirely made up of Sinn Féiners', the Redmondites having 'previously failed in an attempt to take possession of the instruments'. On the other hand one may be inclined to wonder how deep the divisions ran in some places, when one finds both groups of Volunteers marching together in Caherciveen in 1915.

It is naturally difficult to recreate accurately historical reality long bathed in a warm retrospective glow. Later generations are more conscious of internal differences and tensions in the Kerry of the time, some of which would explode horribly in the Civil War. Some of these revolved around differences of material interests, which in turn revolved mainly around land issues, thus at times leading to different profiles of rebel activity between broadly North Kerry, with its bigger farms, better land, and higher ratio of landless labourers, and South Kerry. The account here of the disturbance in Listowel in May 1918 concentrates on conflict over land distribution and redistribution, an issue scarcely confined to that locality alone, but which features only fleetingly in many contemporary accounts, anxious to project an image of complete revolutionary solidarity. Other conflicts could, as always, reflect smouldering tensions either within or between families, even more difficult to reconstruct at this distance.

We are sometimes told that those too close to events cannot see them in proper perspective. That can indeed often be the case, but distance from events can in turn lead to distorted disenchantment with some of the more idealised or romantic conceptions of ages of rebellion and revolution, in Ireland as in every other country. For if distance can clarify and illuminate, it can also blur, making it difficult to recapture atmospheres of expectation and excitement, and this in turn can sometimes lead to an excess of cynicism about idealism among those who have never experienced the exhilaration of a new vision of a new earth. It is of course true that a good deal of reading between the lines can be necessary with contemporary recollections, influenced as they often are by personal relations, or factional loyalties, as well as ideological differences. But then later accounts, not excluding those by academics, can be affected by varieties of unscholarly impulses as well, often concealed behind the guise, or disguise, of allegedly academic impartiality. Contemporary and participant accounts therefore provide indispensable raw material for recapturing psychic reality, even if they cannot speak from hindsight. For if they do not enjoy the advantages of hindsight, neither do they suffer the disadvantages.

There are different possible interpretations of these eventful years. Varieties of perspectives on Kerry's fighting story can be found in several other publications. But this *Kerryman* volume remains basic, containing indispensable information that had never been published previously in book form, or some of it in any form, including evocative pictures of many little known, as well as better known, actors in the drama – though one is provoked to wonder at the full story behind the photo of the Boherbee company 1st Tralee battalion, Kerry No. 1 brigade. As the caption coyly comments: 'Its capture by the crown forces, who used it for identification purposes, seriously impaired the fighting powers of a unit from which great things were expected.'

Given the growth in interest in local history, *Kerry's Fighting Story* contains splendid raw material for reconstructing evocative episodes of history in close-knit Kerry communities. There could be few more vivid examples of the potential of local history than the events of these years. Local knowledge of continuity and change, of shops and houses in particular streets, of the bands that played, of the churches where people sought succour and reassurance, of major local events that once transfixed and transformed the participants, and whose anniversaries should surely be celebrated locally, of the terrain of ambush sites, of routes of advance and retreat, of the deeds that were done, the sacrifices made, the defeats and disappointments suffered, the victories won.

Some of the world out of which the resistance fighters came has disappeared for ever. Some of that world can be romanticised in retrospect. But every generation is the richer, and bestows upon later generations a richer legacy – whatever they may do with it – for having in it men and women who refused to bow the knee to those who thought of themselves as the natural born rulers of mankind. Not all of course shared that view. Some may be born to servility, even in Kerry. Some are inevitably eager to ingratiate themselves with their betters, real or presumed. Others reluctantly but inexorably resign themselves to the service of their masters as the best option the accidents of place and date of birth have dealt them. All of that is understandable given human nature. But however mixed the motives of resistance may sometimes be, however unfulfilled some of the dreams, however high the human cost, for themselves and others, Kerry's fight for freedom will always remain, like that of kindred spirits everywhere, at home and abroad, an example of the refusal of the human spirit to submit to arbitrary power.

In the light of the wealth of evidence of the widespread resistance in Kerry recorded here, and despite a fair share of human frailties among the activists, Eoin O'Duffy's comment, as quoted by Ryle Dwyer, that 'Kerry's entire record in the Black and Tan struggle consisted in shooting an unfortunate soldier the day of the Truce', must count among the most fatuous even O'Duffy ever made. Whatever would happen subsequently, and however perspectives would inevitably be affected by hindsight, for better and for worse, *Kerry's Fighting Story* lays the foundation for all subsequent studies of these foundation years of an independent Irish state.

PROFESSOR J.J. LEE
NEW YORK UNIVERSITY
APRIL 2009

FOREWORD

ALMOST THIRTY YEARS ago a small body of men engaged in combat with the armed forces of an empire. Militarily they were weak. Their strength lay in their faith in their cause and in the unflinching support of a civilian population which refused to be cowed by threats or by violence.

For almost two years these men successfully maintained the unequal struggle and finally compelled their powerful adversary to seek a truce. The battles in which they fought were neither large nor spectacular: they were the little clashes of guerrilla warfare – the sudden meeting, the flash of guns, a getaway, or the long wait of an ambush, then the explosive action, and death or a successful decision. And the stake at issue was the destiny of an ancient people.

Before the war years imposed a restriction upon newsprint, as upon other, commodities, *The Kerryman*, in its various Christmas and other special numbers, told much of the story of these men, the men of the flying columns, the Active Service Units of the Irish Republican Army. It now gathers these stories into book form together with others hitherto unpublished. First in the series was *Rebel Cork's Fighting Story*. Now *Kerry's Fighting Story* is presented.

All the stories in these Fighting Series booklets are either told by the men who took part in the actions described, or else they are written from the personal narrative of survivors. The booklets do not purport to be a detailed or chronological history of the fight for Independence, but every effort has been made to obtain the fullest and most accurate information about the incidents described. The Publishers are conscious, however, that in the collection of data about such a period errors and omissions can easily occur and so they will welcome the help of readers who may be able to throw more light upon the various episodes related in the series. Such additional information will be incorporated into the second edition of the booklets which the present rate of orders would seem to indicate will be called for in the very near future.

The publishers believe that the younger generation who know about those times by hearsay only will find these survivors' tales of the fight of absorbing interest, while to the older generation they will recall vividly a memorable era and the men who made it. In short, they feel that *Fighting* series, the story of the Anglo-Irish War county by county, is a series that will be welcomed by Irish people everywhere. For that reason, so that the booklets may have the widest possible circulation, they are being sold at a price within the reach of everyone. To sell these booklets, with their lavish collection of illustrations of unique historical interest, at the very moderate price of two shillings, the publishers were content to reduce their own profit and to produce the booklet at little above the mere cost of production. They will be satisfied if the series serve to preserve in the hearts of the younger generation that love of country and devotion to its interests which distinguished the men whose doings are related therein.

The Editor

FORMATION AND DEVELOPMENT OF THE VOLUNTEERS

by OLD SOLDIER

To PRESENT A clear picture of events in Kerry during the period 1916 to 1921 it is first necessary to trace the trend of developments in the country at large, and in Kerry in particular, from the introduction of the Home Rule Bill of 1912 to the Rising. Under the Home Rule Bill the Irish parliament was to have no influence on foreign affairs, no part in the fixing or collection of customs and excise, very little control over finance and no control over police for six years. Ireland was to have no army or navy of her own. Compared with previous abortive bills of 1886 and 1893, the 1912 measure promised Ireland less immediate financial autonomy, but control of her police at an earlier date. As regards representation at Westminster, she had one hundred and three representatives under the Union, she would have had none at all under the bill of 1886, eighty under the bill of 1893, and under the bill of 1912 forty-two – rather more than half of what would have been appropriate on a reckoning according to population. The Bill, which would never have been accepted as a final settlement of Ireland's national aspirations, passed through the House of Commons by a substantial majority at the beginning of 1913, but having been rejected by the House of Lords it could not pass their veto till the summer of 1914. By that time the situation had been completely changed by Ulster's determination to resist the measure by force of arms. As early as 1912 a solemn covenant had been signed throughout Ulster and drilling by Sir Edward Carson's Ulster Volunteers had begun. In 1913 there were armed parades and the establishment of a Provisional Government with a military committee attached. During the spring of 1914 there was a threat of mutiny by leading British officers if commanded to march against Ulster, and the great gun-running into Larne. Meanwhile, the south had retaliated and the Irish Volunteer movement was launched at the Rotunda Rink, Dublin, on 25 November 1913. Barely a week later the British government issued a proclamation prohibiting the importation of arms into Ireland. For at least twelve months previously the Ulster Volunteers organised by Carson had been receiving large supplies of arms and ammunition, provided and paid for by English Tories, with the openly defiant purpose of opposing the application of the Home Rule measure to Ulster. 'Ulster Unionists', declared the *Irish Times* in its issue of 6 December 1913, 'are convinced that the action of the Government has come too late, and that there are now sufficient arms in Ulster to enable effective resistance to be made to any attempt to force Home Rule on Ulster'.

Two days later the same newspaper, referring to the prohibition of the importation of arms into Ireland, added, 'It, of course, puts an end to the arming of the Irish Volunteers.' Thus the *Irish Times*, despite its feint, summed up accurately the real object of the government's proclamation. In January 1914, the estimated strength of the Irish Volunteers was in the neighbourhood of 10,000. By June of that year more than 100,000 men had attested, but, as was proved by subsequent events, some of these had no intention of fighting, especially against Britain. In the meantime the Defence of Ireland Fund had been launched with the express purpose of arming Ireland's manhood. The fund was intended only to facilitate the purchase of fighting material in quantity, as each Volunteer paid for his own equipment. In London, Roger Casement had gathered around him a small committee of Irish people who by their subscriptions and influence made available a considerable sum of money to supplement the drive for funds in Ireland. One thousand five hundred Mauser rifles and 49,000 rounds of ammunition were purchased by Erskine Childers and Darrel Figgis in Hamburg, and it was decided to land some of the guns at Howth Harbour on 26 July 1914, and the remainder at Kilcool, County Wicklow. Erskine Childers landed 900 rifles and 29,000 rounds of ammunition at Howth, from his yacht, *The Asgard*, which he manned with his wife. The arms and ammunition were handed over to the Irish Volunteers and successfully distributed despite interference by the police and detachments of the King's Own Scottish Borderers. On their return from Howth the Scottish Borderers, under Major Haig, fired on unarmed civilians in Bachelor's Walk, with the result that four people were killed and thirty-eight wounded. A week later the second consignment of arms, which comprised 600 rifles and 20,000 rounds of ammunition, was successfully landed at Kilcool. Thomas Myles and James Creed Meredith were the navigators of the yacht, *Chotah*, which accomplished the gun-running, and Seán Fitzgibbon and Seán T. O'Kelly were in charge of the Volunteer party who took delivery. The arms and ammunition were successfully distributed without serious incident.

Meanwhile, in June 1914, an amending bill had been added to the Home Rule proposals. In principle it meant that there would be no attempt immediately to force Home Rule on north-east Ulster. Whilst Home Rule had been placed on the statute book, it was not to come into force till a year after the Great War, and as a pledge had been given that Ulster was not to be coerced, Carson had won his campaign against the measure.

TRALEE

GREAT MOVEMENTS SOMETIMES spring from small beginnings. When a group of Tralee men gathered in the Irish Club, High Street, one November evening in 1913, few could have guessed that the tiny seed of National Resurgence was about to be sown in the town. A few days previously Matthew McMahon, law clerk of Boherbee, whilst in Dublin with some friends, witnessed the inaugural parade of Volunteers march to the Rotunda Rink. McMahon attended the meeting which followed the parade, made himself known to the organisers, and brought home to Tralee some Volunteer membership cards which he showed to Tom Slattery, of Rock Street. In the Irish Club a few nights later Slattery declared that it was time to form a branch of the Volunteer movement in the town, and he was supported by Jerome Slattery, of Blennerville, who appealed to the young men to rally to the ranks. Chairman of the Irish Club at that time was patriotic Fr Charlie Brennan, then a curate in Tralee, and the name of Austin Stack was also on its membership roll. Following Tom Slattery's address to the members of the club it was decided to make contact with Volunteer headquarters in Dublin, and Diarmuid Crean, now court clerk in Tralee, corresponded with The O'Rahilly, one of the leaders of the movement. Shortly afterwards it was definitely decided to establish a branch of the Volunteer organisation in Tralee, and with that object a public meeting took place in the County Hall. It was presided over by Maurice P. Ryle, and Diarmuid Crean was appointed secretary. Four companies of the Irish Volunteers were formed at the inaugural meeting and these were filled exclusively by the men of Rock Street, Strand Street and Boherbee. An executive was appointed and meetings were held in the Hibernian Hall, then the headquarters of the Tralee John Mitchel Football Club. Fr Brennan and Diarmuid Crean became trustees and the Munster and Leinster Bank were made treasurers of the organisation. Parades took place regularly to the sportsfield, now the Austin Stack Park, and during bad weather the Picturedrome was used for close order drill and lectures. Later, the Rink was acquired and this became the local headquarters of the Volunteers. A period of intensive organisation followed and additional companies were formed inside the Tralee district. Ernest Blythe and Desmond Fitzgerald were then organising branches of the Volunteer movement in West Kerry, and Tralee sent delegates to Dingle to help the work. The Tralee Volunteers were drilled and instructed by two British ex-army men, Edward Leen and John Purtill.

When Volunteer companies had been established in many areas throughout the county it was decided to hold in the Market, Tralee, a mass general parade and review of Volunteers of the town and adjoining districts. This event took place on Sunday, 14 June 1914, when about 2,000 Volunteers paraded, and were inspected and addressed by Captain Maurice Talbot Crosbie of Ardfert. The Tralee companies mobilised in the Town Hall and were there addressed by Fr Charlie Brennan prior to the march to the parade ground. The Strand Street and Boherbee bands headed the battalion, which was under the command of Instructor Edward Leen and his assistants. Big contingents came from Ballymacelligott, Castleisland, Dingle, Knocknagoshel, Brosna, Currans, Cordal, Ventry and Ardfert. Distant districts were debarred from attending because of local parades. Bands accompanied most of the battalions, and the march past from the railway station was followed with the keenest interest by the huge crowd which lined the streets. The Dingle and Ventry contingents were under the command of Instructor Dowling and accompanied by their band. Ardfert was commanded by Instructor Garrett Fernane; Castleisland was commanded by Instructors D. Mahony and J. Cashel. Knocknagoshel with their band were led by Instructor Kerry O'Connor. Cordal was commanded by Instructor Eugene McGillicuddy O'Meara, and Currans by Instructor E. O'Sullivan. Following the parade and review, the assembled Volunteers were addressed by Captain Talbot Crosbie. When the proceedings terminated the various battalions again formed up and marched through the town to Denny Street where the parade was dismissed.

Shortly afterwards Éamonn O'Connor of Ashe Street became secretary to the Tralee Volunteers in succession to Diarmuid Crean, who was appointed to a post in South Africa. The work of organisation went rapidly ahead despite a set-back in the loss of Fr Brennan who was transferred to Millstreet. He was succeeded by Fr Joe Breen, an equally worthy sagart who became treasurer of the organisation. As he bade farewell to Tralee, two hundred Volunteers headed by the Strand Street Band accompanied Fr Brennan to the station. Indicative of the spirit of the time was the presentation made to him by his Tralee comrades-in-arms, a Mauser rifle, fully charged bandolier and haversack.

News of the landing of arms and ammunition for the Volunteers at Howth in July was received in Tralee with jubilation, tempered by sorrow for the fate of the defenceless Dublin people who were brutally murdered by the cowardly Scottish Borderers. Next morning seven hundred men responded to a surprise mobilisation of Volunteers from the town and district, and having formed up outside the Rink, they marched through the streets, headed by the Strand Street Band. The parade was witnessed by an exceptionally large and enthusiastic crowd, and in view of the atrocities in Dublin on the previous evening, there was tension in the atmosphere. Amongst outlying districts represented were Ballyroe, Ballymacelligott, Listellick and Oakpark. The 'Last Post' was sounded at twelve noon by a bugler attached to the Tralee corps. This was timed with the tolling of the Angelus Bell to remind the people to pray for the souls of those callously shot down in the streets of Dublin by the Scottish Borderers. There was an impressive demonstration. A few days later, on the 29 July, Austin Stack led close to five hundred Volunteers from the Tralee district at an enthusiastic county muster in Killarney, on the occasion of the 1914 Oireachtas. The Tralee men were narrowly beaten by the Limerick corps in the Oireachtas competitions for company and section drill. Tralee Signals corps received special praise from Captain Crosbie, who reviewed the troops. The tug-of-war team which represented the Tralee and District Volunteers at the Oireachtas competitions was chosen from: W. Griffin, Dean's Lane; Moss Reidy, Ballymacelligott; Tom Brosnan, Potally; Pat Higgins, Boherbee; Con Healy, Castle Street; Ned Slattery, Bridge Street; John Timoney, Boherbee; Tom Neill, Cross Lane; John McCrohan, Strand Street; Jack McDonnell, Rock Street; Jack Mahony, Connor's Lane; Jack Mahony, Moyderwell; Mick Reardon, Davy's Lane; Pat Sheehy, Rock Street; Pat Barry, Moyderwell.

Early in September 1914, the Tralee Volunteer companies elected the following officers: 'A' company: Matt Walsh, company commander; W. O'Connor, first half company commander; J. Shea, second half company commander; J. Mullins, hon. treasurer; J. Moylan, hon. secretary. 'B' company: D. Healy, company commander; J. Roche, first half company commander; J. Fahy, second half company commander; J. Burke, hon. treasurer; Mort Sullivan, hon. secretary. 'C' company: C. Daly, company commander; P. McGrath, first half company commander; P. Lawlor, second half company commander; Pat Ryle, hon. treasurer; P. Quinlan, hon. secretary. 'D' company: J. Scanlan, company commander; J. McDonnell, first half company commander; D. Mahony, second half company commander; A. Stack, hon. treasurer; E. Barry, hon. secretary. In the same month a Volunteer uniform with accessories, which included the latest pattern American service rifle, exhibited in the display windows of Messrs. Lyons & Co., Drapers, excited a great deal of attention. A house-to-house collection in aid of the Volunteer Armament Fund realised £299 14/-. Further substantial sums were raised by the promotion of concerts and dramatic entertainments. Amongst those who took part in such functions in August and September 1914, were Mrs Redmond Roche, Misses Hanna Spicer, Milly Vale, Bride Murphy, Maud Harris, Pearl Vale and Messrs 'Johnny' Foley, George Reid, Éamonn O'Connor and Denis O'Connor.

Up to that stage the development and organisation of the Volunteer movement had proceeded without a hitch, but following the outbreak of the European War there soon appeared a rift in the lute. There were in the movement Volunteers who believed that Ireland should rally to the Empire's aid in her war with Germany and the other Central Powers. Matters were precipitated by an attempt made by John Redmond, leader of the Irish Parliamentary Party, to gain control of the Volunteers. Immediately the war broke out Redmond declared in the British House of Commons that Britain could withdraw her troops from Ireland, and that the defence of the country could be left safely in the hands of the Volunteers. There followed a good deal of talk about arming the Volunteers with British equipment and at one period it was rumoured in Tralee that 1,500 rifles had arrived in Ballymullen barracks for the local battalion. The British took good care, however, that no arms of theirs would ever reach the hands of the Irish Volunteers, who eventually procured their weapons from other sources. Meanwhile, Redmond had supplemented his parliamentary pronouncement by declaring at Woodenbridge, County Wicklow, that the Volunteers had two duties: one to defend Ireland and the other to defend democracy in Europe. Redmond's statement was in direct contravention of the principles of policy and enrolment of the Irish Volunteers and in a short time led to the 'split', when the Redmondites broke away from the MacNeill (Irish) Volunteers, who were pledged to the cause of Ireland only, the Redmondite Volunteers became known as the National Volunteers. By that time Redmond, who had been promised a nebulous measure of Home Rule as an inducement to support Britain, came out openly as a recruiting agent for the British. With British Prime Minister Asquith, he addressed a meeting in the Mansion House, Dublin, calling for recruits for the British army. In Kerry he had assiduous workers in the same cause in the persons of the Irish Party representatives O'Donnell, Boland and Flavin. The attempts of the Redmondites to make imperial mercenaries of the Volunteers produced many votes of confidence in his policy, but resulted in few recruits.

Following those rapid developments Éamonn O'Connor wrote to Pádraig Pearse explaining that the majority of Tralee Volunteers could not reconcile their ideals with Redmond's policy. In his reply, Pearse counselled patience and advised the Tralee men to bear with things for some time, for the sake of unity. 'The Split', however, was practically at hand and the moment had come for Volunteers throughout the country to make their choice for the Green or for the Empire. It would seem to be the destiny of the Irish nation that just as things are going right a political cataclysm would happen along to overthrow the national fabric which had been slowly and painfully built, By October 1914, the Irish Volunteer movement had become the medium through which Irishmen were afforded an opportunity to express their hatred and contempt for each other. There were two hostile camps; on the one hand the old Provisional Committee, seeking to conserve Ireland's forces for Ireland's benefits, and on the other, the supporters of the Irish Party, led by John Redmond, advocating enlistment in the British army. Stirring scenes were witnessed at the Rink, on Tuesday evening, 13 October, when the Tralee battalion of the Irish Volunteers met to decide whether they would stand by the Provisional Committee, or follow the lead of Redmond. As the issue was put before the men, the Reverend Chairman, Fr Joe Breen, asked all who were not Volunteers to leave the hall. Tom O'Donnell, the Irish Party MP for Tralee and West Kerry, who was not a member of the corps, and who had come uninvited to the meeting, attempted to address the Volunteers on behalf of Redmond, but the men were in no mood to tolerate any such nonsense as recruiting for Britain or an evasion of the issue, and he was requested to leave the premises. Things looked ugly for a while, and several times it seemed as though the 'member' for West Kerry would be forcibly ejected from the hall, but discipline prevailed. Some amusement was caused by a Volunteer who placed a miniature Union Jack on O'Donnell's coat without his knowledge and as he moved about the hall his flag caused great laughter. O'Donnell looked anything but happy amongst his constituents. When O'Donnell left the hall Fr Breen spoke of intrigues against the Volunteers, and advised them to continue their drilling and to perfect themselves in the use of their rifles, until such time as they would be called upon to fight for the dear old cause for which their fathers had shed their blood and given their lives. They had been formed to guard the rights and liberties common to all Irishmen, and they should stick to that. M.J. O'Connor, a member of the committee, then said that the question before them was whether they would stand by the men of Dublin who had the courage to found the Volunteers, and worked hard whilst others, who now sought control of the Volunteers for party purposes, had sneered at them and done their best to kill the movement. He declared that it was open to every man to vote as he thought right. It was a question of standing for Ireland or the Empire; of remaining true to the true ideals of Irish nationality or embracing imperialism; of turning their backs on the principles of those who died for Ireland and accepting the leadership of England's recruiting sergeants. The question of remaining neutral was first put to the men, and by a large majority they decided to have the issue settled there and then. The chairman next asked those who wished to remain true to the original Provisional Committee to move to the right, and those who wished to support John Redmond to move to the left. The scene which followed beggared description. Only twenty men moved to the left. The remainder of the Volunteers, close on three hundred men, moved to the right, holding aloft a green flag which Éamonn O'Connor and Dan Finn had bought in the town that day. The few seceders having withdrawn from the hall, and left behind a Union Jack flag which was derisively flung at them, the companies fell in and were dismissed following a few manoeuvres. The decision of the Tralee Volunteers to support MacNeill, head of the Provisional

Committee, was received with great enthusiasm throughout the town, and the following telegram was immediately dispatched to the Provisional Committee in Dublin:

Owen MacNeill, 41 Kildare Street, Dublin.

Tralee battalion stands firm for the old Constitution and the old Committee.

Éamonn O'Connor, Secretary.

The truth of the old maxim of Napoleon that merchants make bad revolutionaries was as apparent in Tralee as in most other centres. The majority of those who supported the cause of Redmond and the British Empire were men of standing in the town, men 'with a stake in the county'. Some others followed this influential set through fear of losing their jobs, a fear which was well justified, as later on there was a number of instances of victimisation of Irish Volunteers. By and large, Redmond's adherents had sustained a crushing defeat in the town, as Tralee had taken its stand for unqualified support of the movement for Irish freedom, and the ground was then prepared for the great and momentous years which lay ahead.

A meeting of the local Volunteers who followed Redmond's policy was held in the Theatre Royal, Tralee, on Sunday, 24 October 1914. It was addressed by Tom O'Donnell, MP, who referred to England's 'many generosities' to Ireland. 'England,' he said, 'gave us land purchases, labourers' cottages, old age pensions …' – 'And Scottish Borderers,' interjected a voice from the crowd. This remark was greeted with loud applause and an attempt was made to eject the heckler, by two warriors armed with 'Italian Gas Pipes', as the harmless Italian rifles of the Redmondite Volunteers were popularly known. Many Volunteers who had sided with Redmond in the beginning, eventually returned to the fold of the Irish Volunteers.

At a meeting of the Irish (MacNeill) Volunteers held at the Rink, the following Tralee delegates to the County Convention were selected: 'A' company: P.J. O'Connell, Boherbee; 'B' company: P.J. Cahill, Strand Street; 'C' company: T.P. Kennedy; 'D' company: M.J. O'Connor, Rock Street. On Sunday 18 October, the men turned up in large numbers to the Drill Hall where they were presented with new rifles. The work of distributing the rifles was carried out expeditiously, and each Volunteer, as he was handed his rifle, felt that he had the best weapon with which to help Ireland's cause. A route march the same afternoon made a truly impressive sight as the men passed through the principal streets of the town with their magazine rifles, headed by the Strand Street Band under the direction of Michael Landers. A banner with the inscription 'Thou Art Not Conquered Yet Dear Land' was borne aloft by Fianna Éireann as they led the parade. There were scenes of great enthusiasm in the town and the hearts of the people were stirred and the blood tingled in their veins as they watched the armed men of Ireland march by; men who had remained true to the cause of freedom. To quote from *The Kerryman* of the 25 October: 'Corporal Tom O'Donnell's visit did one good thing anyway – it sifted the wheat from the chaff and that was very noticeable on Sunday's march.'

The following Tralee delegates were appointed to a national convention of Irish Volunteers which was held in Dublin on the 25 October: 'A' company: Matt McMahon; 'B' company: Joe Melinn; 'C' company: Éamonn O'Connor; 'D' company: M.J. O'Connor. From that point onwards Austin Stack, who was appointed Kerry delegate to the general Council of Irish Volunteers, became the mainspring of the movement in Kerry, particularly in Tralee, where he received valuable assistance from his friend Paddy Cahill. Although the police began to interfere a good deal, under the Defence of the Realm Act, the work of organisation went ahead steadily. Companies were formed in Blennerville, Ballyroe, Farmer's Bridge, Fenit, Listellick, and Oakpark. Rifle competitions were organised, and on the 13 January 1915, the finals, shot at the Rink in the presence of a large muster of Volunteers, resulted as follows: Michael Hogan,

'A' company (Boherbee), seventeen points; Éamonn O'Connor, 'C' company (Nelson Street), sixteen points; T. Foley, 'D' company, fourteen points; Joe Melinn, 'B' company, fourteen points. In reply to a suggestion in the local unionist paper that money subscribed to the Volunteers on the understanding that the corps was subject to John Redmond should be returned to the subscribers, it was pointed out that the monies were collected for the defence of Ireland and for arming the Irish Volunteers who still existed in the town. The fact that twenty or thirty members deserted to John Redmond had not altered the situation.

Over six hundred Irish Volunteers from Tralee district assembled at the Rink on Monday, 22 November 1914, to pay tribute to Allen, Larkin and O'Brien, who had laid down their lives for Ireland in Manchester, forty-seven years previously. Headed by the faithful Strand Street band and followed by the Boy Scouts who bore aloft their banner, 'Thou Art Not Conquered Yet, Dear Land', they marched to Rath where a beautiful cross is erected to the memory of the Manchester Martyrs. It was a never-to-be-forgotten sight, as the men paraded with military precision, accompanied by a torchlight section. Crowds which thronged the thoroughfares, marched to the cemetery with the Volunteers, and the truly imposing scene stirred the best feelings of all that was patriotic in the town. About 5,000 people were unable to enter the cemetery. As the buglers sounded the 'Last Post', followed by the reverberating echoes of the salvos of the firing party, all present felt that Allen, Larkin and O'Brien had not died in vain for Ireland. The flames from the turf sods held aloft, on Irish pikes caused weird and uncanny shadows to play upon the brown rifles held in the hands of resolute men. The Strand Street Band played Irish martial music as it led the parade back to the '98 memorial in Denny Street, where Instructor Leen, who had been connected with the corps since its inception, informed the assembly of Volunteers that he was compelled by the War Office to break his connection with the movement. He was succeeded by Instructor Cotter.

Following a visit by Pádraig Pearse there was a big increase in the number of recruits admitted to the ranks of the Irish Volunteers in the town, but there still remained some eligible men who, whilst sympathetic to the movement, had not yet joined the ranks. Pearse reviewed over five hundred Volunteers from Tralee, Ballymacelligott, Abbeydorney and Listellick, in the Tralee sportsfield. Headed by the Tralee Pipers' Band, the men marched from the Rink, carrying arms, through the town. En route they were accorded a tremendous ovation by the townspeople. There was a huge attendance on the Review Grounds, and following the parade, Pearse, who was given a most enthusiastic welcome, delivered an address in which he exhorted each Volunteer to play his part in making the Irish Volunteer movement the success it ought to be. When the address concluded the Volunteers returned to their headquarters in the Rink, where the parade was dismissed. On Whit Sunday 1915, Tralee sent a detachment of three hundred fully armed and well-trained Volunteers to a review of the Volunteers of the county and presentation of colours, at Killarney. The salute was taken by Austin Stack, who was then the recognised leader for all Kerry. O'Donovan-Rossa's funeral in August 1915, saw another big muster of Tralee Volunteers. Kerry was not allowed a train to Dublin for the funeral, and as the Volunteers could not make the journey, local celebrations were held at many centres throughout the county, to pay a mark of homage and respect to Rossa's memory. In Tralee three companies, headed by the Boy Scouts and the Strand Street Band, paraded under the command of Captain D. Healy, Captain M. Doyle and Lieutenant W. Farmer. In the parade was Isaac Bernard, an old '67 man, and a friend of Rossa's.

Meanwhile, Tom O'Donnell and other local supporters of John Redmond were busy with recruiting activities, and a number of meetings for that purpose were held in Denny Street. The response was discouraging, to put it mildly, and in their chagrin the local recruiting agents were eloquent in the choice of language applied to all who declined to rally to the Union Jack and leave their bones to bleach on foreign battlefields. Judged from the standpoint of these local gentlemen, Tralee was full of 'dodgers', 'shirkers' and 'slackers', although it was noted that none of the well-paid and loud-mouthed imperialists nor their pals was killed in the rush to join the colours. Such unseemly hesitation was commented upon at a meeting of the Tralee Trades and Labour Councils at the '98 memorial, Denny Street, in December 1915, when Councillor W.T. Partridge declared that there was one policeman in Tralee who ought to be at the front. The gentleman's name was Britten; perhaps he ought to have said 'Great Britten', because he was a district inspector. Partridge understood that he was an Englishman, and one thing that could not be denied was that he did not answer the call of King and country. He happened to be in court some time previously and overheard the district inspector refer to men as 'shirkers', and the thought struck Partridge that while Irishmen were expected to go to the front, they found an Englishman enjoying a good position and a big salary here, insulting men who were not shirkers like himself.

The following letter from Councillor W.T. Partridge, which appeared in *The Kerryman* a fortnight later, provoked much amusement at the expense of District Inspector Britten:

Tralee, December 18th, 1915

Dear Sir,

At a public meeting of protest recently held in Tralee and fully reported in your columns I felt called upon to direct special attention to the fact that your local District Inspector, although an Englishman, had not responded to the call of King and country. It was afterwards pointed out to me by a local JP that Britten may have applied for release in order to serve with the colours, and that probably the necessary permission was refused. Fearing that I might unwittingly be doing even Britten an injustice, I sent the following question to Parliament:

Why the authorities had not granted the request of an English 'gentleman named Britten, residing in the town of Tralee and occupying the position of District Inspector of the Royal Irish Constabulary, to be relieved of his present duties in order to serve with the colours? If they thought the presence of Englishmen in such soft jobs in Ireland had not a deterrent effect on recruiting in Ireland; and, on the score of economy, so essential at present, when such a huge financial strain was taking place, that the duties of District Inspectors could not be more effectively performed by the more experienced Head Constables. The one-hundred-and-fifty-seven, out of the total of one hundred-and-ninety District Inspectors in Ireland who had not Volunteered, could be thus released for active service.

Mr Birrell, in his reply, stated, in effect, that no such application had been received from the Inspector in question, and that out of the one-hundred-and-ninety District Inspectors in Ireland, over one hundred were unfit for active service. I do not know if Britten can be placed amongst the 'crocks' thus referred to. He has the appearance of one physically fit, and therefore, becomes entitled to be styled 'shirker', 'slacker', and all the other nice names they call people who decline to Volunteer to go out and fight for their King and country.

William T. Partridge

Redmond ever had scant reason for enthusiasm about affairs in Tralee, but during 1915 in particular, the wailings of Jeremiah had nothing on the tone of his dispatches from the capital of the Kingdom. The shape of things to come was indicated by the miserable parade of National Volunteers on Saint Patrick's Day, while the 'influentials' of the town remained staunch in their adherence to the Irish Parliamentary Party, the rank and file of the Volunteers were thinning daily, having long previously lost whatever vestige of enthusiasm they ever brought to bear upon the job. Many returned to the fold of the Irish Volunteers. There was a good deal of pro-British and Imperialist sentiment in the town, but it lacked the vitality of the Sinn Féin movement and accomplished nothing. Following upon a summer of inactivity the straits to which the Redmondite Volunteers were reduced in the town by September 1915 was illustrated by a circular which fell into the hands of the Irish Volunteers. The circular, dated the seventeenth of September 1915, was published in *The Kerryman*, under the caption 'THE TWO-PENNY PATRIOTS'! The letter is quoted hereunder, prefixed by *The Kerryman* comment:

THE TWO-PENNY PATRIOTS!

They are going, they are going,

And we cannot bid them stay!

We have been favoured with the following circular which has emanated from the 'headquarters staff' of the Tralee 'army' of 'National' Volunteers, which throws interesting light on the 'patriotism' and 'self-sacrifice' of its members:

I.N.V.
Tralee, 17 September 1915.
To Each Member of the Committee:

Dear Sir,
A meeting of the Committee of National Volunteers, at which you are requested to attend, will be held at the Hall, Edward Street, on tonight – Friday – at 8.30 o'clock.

This Committee consists of twelve members and no more than two or three have attended the meeting summoned during the past six months though circulars have been sent to each member and notice of meeting published in the Press.

For the past seven or eight months the usual weekly contribution of two pence has not been paid by the Tralee Volunteers as they have not attended for drill purposes, with the result that there is no fund to meet the demand for rent and expenses. Under the circumstances the occupation of the Drill Hall for any further period cannot be expected unless something is done by the leaders and public men to re-organise the movement and enlist the support of the public.

Mr Redmond is expected to visit Kerry next month to attend the Convention and review the Volunteers, and if nothing is done in the meantime he will be disappointed at the apathy existing towards the Movement in Kerry.

Yours faithfully, Hon. Secretary, Tralee battalion.

In October 1915, two abortive attempts were made to persuade Redmond to visit Tralee to hold a convention of the 'Party' and to review the National Volunteers – such as were left of them. The business had little appeal for the astute John, who, no doubt, was abundantly aware of the 'sore' straits to which his 'army' had been reduced in Tralee. There were also the unpleasant matters of awkward questions arising from the recruiting activities pursued by himself and his henchmen, coupled to the unpleasant possibility of rough handling by the Sinn Féiners. Despite promises of 'reinforcements' from the Redmondite elements of Cork, Limerick and Waterford, the 'Leader' found convenient and urgent occasion to be elsewhere on the dates fixed for his proposed visits. The collapse of the jamboree arranged for Tralee practically saw the end of organised Redmondite activity in the town, although the futile attempts to recruit for Britain's army continued with unabated persistence. Tom O'Donnell, MP, who remained the prime advocate of the policy in these parts, never let pass an opportunity to point out that 'Home Rule' was an accomplished fact, and the 'Member' would dwell eloquently upon the base ingratitude of the 'shirkers' who refused to dedicate their lives to Mother England. The Home Rule measure, in fact, became the 'cant' of recruiting agents all over the country, despite an ominous note struck by the *British Morning Post* which called forth the following comment from *The Kerryman*:

> In those times, when we are occasionally inclined to feel fatigued by being reminded to an undue and tiresome extent that Home Rule is on the Statute Book, that 'no power on earth' can remove it therefrom and that it will display traces of animation immediately the war ceases, it is good by way of variety, to find that there is another side to the picture. Dull uniformity is impossibly monotonous. Hence, it is refreshing to learn from the English and Tory *Morning Post* that 'there is no such bargain' as that Irish Self-Government will take effect after the war. In effect it says 'we are inclined to agree with the Bishop of Limerick that the Home Rule Bill may never come into operation'. The War, it transpires, has 'so clearly proved the advantages of unity of Government', there is 'likely to be a change of sentiment on this question in both countries after the War'. Now for you! What has anyone to say about broken treaties and 'scraps of paper' after this? And the Irish we discover are fighting not because of any hope of Home Rule, but because they are British subjects and loyal to their King and country. Set down this declaration, beside

the dope handed the public by Redmond and Devlin and Dillon, not forgetting our own Tom O'Donnell – and meditate! There is no need, or, indeed, room for any comment.

Towards the close of 1915 the Royal Irish Constabulary became very determined in their efforts to disrupt the Irish Volunteers. There were many arrests under the Defence of the Realm Act, and one of the first men sentenced was Jack McGaley, who got three months imprisonment. On the 22 November 1915, the Tralee Petty Sessions Court imposed this sentence, and it was subsequently confirmed by the county court on the 15 February 1916. McGaley's crime was to wish damnation upon the English king, and he was convicted on the uncorroborated evidence of a military band sergeant. The bench comprised one nationalist who dissented, the county court judge, and four unionist JPs.

Concerts and dramatic entertainments, promoted in aid of the Volunteers by the Cumann na mBan and Fianna Éireann, were held frequently during 1915 and 1916. Amongst those who participated in a dramatic entertainment held in the Rink, Tralee, on the 15 April 1915, were: Misses K. Lenihan, Nellie Barry, L. O'Brien, Rita O'Connor, N. O'Leary; Messrs Maurice Fleming, F. Walsh, E. Barry, M. Cournane, P. Barry, T. Cournane, T. Gilligan, C. Falvey, M. O'Leary, Joe Melinn, D. Drummond, J. Fleming, senior, J. Fitzgerald, Éamonn O'Connor and M. Walsh. Amongst those who contributed to the success of a similar function on the 27 March 1916, organised by the Tralee Branch of Fianna Éireann were: Miss Nora O'Leary; Messrs T. Gilligan, P. Moriarty, P. Cournane, Joe Sullivan, P. Reidy, Jeremiah Skinner, C. Falvey, L. Regan and D. Barry.

The Tralee '98 Memorial Committee who for many years had charge of the arrangements for the annual commemoration of the Manchester Martyrs, invited Austin Stack, commandant of the Irish Volunteers of Tralee, to organise the 1915 anniversary celebrations. All nationalist bodies in the town received circulars from Austin inviting them to participate in the parade, which moved off from the County Hall in the following order: Ballymacelligott Cavalry, Firing Party, Strand Street Band, Trade and Labour Bodies, Public Bodies, Irish National Foresters, Tralee Catholic Literary Society, Liberal Registration Club, Ballymacelligott Irish Volunteers, O'Dorney Irish Volunteers, Ballyroe Irish Volunteers and Tralee Irish Volunteers. As the parade marched slowly in military formation through the town, the scene was both impressive and inspiring. An officer with drawn sword led the Ballymacelligott cavalry and the horsemen carried pikes. They were followed by eight hundred and seventy Volunteers led by a party with reversed rifles. At Rath the 'Last Post' was sounded and three volleys were fired. It was one of the most remarkable events seen in Tralee for many years and brought with it a spirit of enthusiasm, and a message of hope and courage for the Old Land. Seán Milroy lectured on Wolfe Tone at the Rink on the following Sunday night.

By the early spring of 1916, the organisation and training of the Tralee companies of Volunteers had attained a high pitch of perfection despite the unwelcome attention of the Royal Irish Constabulary, who kept their masters in Dublin Castle fully informed of the course of events. The men would undoubtedly have played a historic part in the general Rising planned to take place throughout the country on Easter Week, but for the confusion which followed the unfortunate arrival of the German arms ship two days ahead of schedule, and the arrest of Austin Stack. Events in Tralee during Holy Week and Easter Week are described elsewhere in this volume.

KILLARNEY

TRUMPETER, WHAT ARE you sounding now? The people of Killarney roused from their peaceful slumber at the unearthly hour of four o'clock on a Sunday morning thirty-four years ago might well have sung or shouted that question. For the cause of their untimely awakening was the almost belligerent blaring of a trumpet. Trumpeter Paddy Wrixon was calling the Volunteers to their first dawn parade, the forerunner of many to follow. This was the awakening of a people not only to a new day but to a new Ireland. The Volunteers were on the march.

That was away back at the close of the year of our Lord 1913, when the world was at peace with itself but when the prostrate Green Isle of Erin was once again commencing to shake the shackles that had been forged on the anvil of Britain's oppressive domination. Another dawn was breaking, shedding an ominous light on the body and soul of a fettered nation. Irish eyes were opening. A new and epic era of history was on the way in.

Killarney rode with the vanguard, leading Kerry into the ranks of that simply named but highly potent movement – the Volunteers. In an obscure, unpretentious, greyish building back of Upper High Street the Young Irelanders of Killarney were meeting frequently in an effort to revive the language. Tutor was none other than 'An Seabhac'. On a bleak and blustery night of November 1913 the lid blew off. The Gaelic League class had a lesson in military drill. That very night a company of Volunteers was formed – the first in Kerry. Appointed section commanders were 'An Seabhac', Michael Spillane, Michael John Sullivan, Seán O'Casey, Pat Horgan and Tadhg Morgan. Secretary was Jim Counihan, post office official, and treasurer William D.F. O'Sullivan. Soldiers without guns, like thoughts without action, were useless, so a gun-purchasing committee was formed. The men selected were 'An Seabhac', Michael Spillane, Jim Counihan, Michael J. O'Sullivan. Weapons took some time to get, but more about that anon. Imbued with a spirit of love of country the company flourished. From the Killarney root came branches that spread themselves over Ballyhar, Fossa, Listry, Beaufort, Glenflesk, Firies and other parts of East Kerry. The trumpeter gave the call. At four o'clock on every Sunday morning the 'Reveille' brought the Volunteers tumbling from the comfort of their beds to line up for a dawn parade and march. The march ended with six o'clock Mass at the friary – but it was only the end of a phase of the day's work. After breakfast the 'missionaries' betook themselves to the country districts organising manpower and showing how. That done, there was another parade in town in the evening. Those who visited the country centres on organisation work each week were M. Spillane, M.J. O'Sullivan, T. Horgan, T. Lyne, C. Fleming, J. Mangan, P. Courtney, J. Hill, S. O'Casey, P. Horgan, 'An Seabhac', J. O'Shea and Chief Instructor McGovern.

Came August 1914, and an event that, locally, was as tremendous as the outbreak of war: the great Oireachtas. This was a week that Killarney will never forget, a week of music, song, dance and parades backgrounded by an industrial exhibition, and burnished with the glitter of a great cultural and political resurgence. On the opening day there was music and there were crowds to beat the band. Puffing trains brought thousands of people into the town and thirty bands from places as far away as Athlone, Dublin, Lusk, Waterford, as well as from the neighbouring counties of Cork and Limerick. Kerry was also well represented in this, the greatest band blitz ever to strike a provincial town in Ireland. Wedged between sidewalks crammed by cheering crowds many hundreds of Volunteers from Killarney and other parts of East Kerry marched between the bands through decorated streets. Right through the week the Oireachtas went on with competitions in dancing, singing, story-telling being watched and listened to by huge crowds. But the third day was the most memorable and colourful of all. That was the day that the growing strength and the ardour of the Irish Volunteers first became really obvious in Kerry. From most parts of Kerry as well as from many other parts of the province of Munster, including the cities of Limerick and Cork, flocked several thousand Volunteers. The streets of the town seethed with life and excitement, the large force of Volunteers on the march attracting considerable attention. The local company stole most of the thunder of the day as they were the only fully armed group in the great assemblage. The slouch-hatted Killarney boys had rifles with bayonets atop jutting out from their shoulders. Here was a real eye-opener for the public and especially for the cynical ones. And, now, where did those boys get those guns and how? Well, it's a case of a picture telling a story. About that time the Kalem film company were 'shooting' an Irish film around Killarney. Rifles and bayonets were part of the 'wardrobe' and some of the Killarney Volunteers were part of the cast. A nod was as good as a wink especially from a Yankee film producer who didn't care a whole lot about the British Bulldog. Little wonder that the Royal Irish Constabulary as well as the crowd stared and blinked. Competitions in signalling and in all forms of drill were held throughout the day and the winning companies were Tralee and Limerick. The 'show' was filmed by the Kalem company.

That was in August of 1914. Two short months later the 'Redmondite split' came. Killarney made use of the diplomatic art to steer itself through the rift. Their purse was in a Redmondite pocket. Tactfully neutrality was engineered and carried. The safety of the funds was assured, but the rift in the national lute and certain local political chicanery sapped the numerical strength of the company. The membership dropped from upwards of one hundred to fewer than twenty. As the year 1915 progressed the drift was, however, arrested, interest and enthusiasm were revived. Concerts and other functions were held to supplement the funds and a couple of hundred pounds realised. Among the artistes who contributed to the success of these shows were: Babs Blennerhassett, Úna McEvoy, Madge Cooper, Molly O'Leary, Michael J. O'Sullivan, Willie Horgan, N. O'Donoghue, Mossie Connor, Seán O'Casey, 'An Seabhac' and the members of the Volunteers' Pipe Band.

On the night of Friday, 7 May 1915, the Killarney Volunteers as a real live fighting force were reborn. The Volunteer Hall in High Street saw a strong muster of men decide unanimously to affiliate with the Irish Volunteers. It was an active night. Shooting practice and drill preceded the great decision. Addressing the men, Captain Michael Spillane said that for certain reasons they had for some time past occupied a neutral position and he thought the time had arrived when they should declare their policy. He felt certain their decision would be the right one. Michael J. O'Connor of Tralee, the next speaker, dealt with the formation of the Volunteers in November 1913, their subsequent history and the events which led up to the unfortunate but inevitable 'split'. He advised that by affiliating with the Irish Volunteers they would only be remaining true to the declaration they made when the Killarney corps was formed. The principles and objects of the Irish Volunteers, he said, remained the same as when the Volunteers were originally established; they had not changed one iota and it was for them now to decide to stick to those principles to secure and maintain the rights and liberties common to all the people of Ireland and to defend their Motherland in her hour of need. Ernest Blythe followed and in a lively address urged the importance and necessity of the corps affiliating with the Irish Volunteer headquarters. He stressed the need for the control and guidance of the men best suited to direct the Volunteer movement, the men who started the organisation and ably conducted it since its formation – Professor MacNeill and his committee. There was, perhaps, no time in Ireland's history, he said, when Ireland's army, the Irish Volunteers, had greater need of capable and able men to steer its course. They, in Killarney, had been neutral since the 'split' but he knew that that would not be said of them in the future and that they would affiliate with the original Volunteers. Captain Dick Fitzgerald, declaring that it was about time they made up their minds, asked those in favour of affiliating with the Irish Volunteers to move to the right side of the hall. And to the right with a cheer went every man present. Then the officers were elected and they were: captain: Michael Spillane, proposed by G. Mahony, seconded by D. Mangan; first-lieutenant: Michael J. O'Sullivan, proposed by

G.M. O'Donoghue, seconded by J.C. Clifford; second-lieutenant: Richard Fitzgerald, proposed by J. Mangan, seconded by P. O'Shea; hon. treasurer: N.F. O'Donoghue, proposed by G. O'Shea, seconded by J. O'Sullivan; hon. secretary: Seán C. O'Casey, proposed by G. McCarthy, seconded by P. Courtney; sergeant: W. McCarthy. Eleven new members were enrolled and the proceedings closed with the singing of *A Nation Once Again* and three ringing cheers for the Irish Volunteers.

Not many weeks later – Whit Sunday 1915, to be exact – Killarney's old cricket field was the scene of a great display of national advancement and solidarity. In a momentous and tense atmosphere, several thousand Volunteers from every nook and corner were reviewed by Eoin MacNeill, the leader of the movement, and presented with their colours, which were blessed by Rev. Ferris. Under the command of Austin Stack the vast assembled force of Kerry's marshalled manhood, fully armed with rifles, provided a striking prelusory picture to the grim and graphic scenes that the future was to etch. This was more than a display of physical strength – it was a living, vivid and forceful symbol of the idealistic trend of Irish thought. Ireland was once more emerging from the mists of English tyranny. And, just like that, the mists had not lifted from the Kerry hills that morning when the men of the 'Kingdom' were leaving their homesteads to converge on Killarney to demonstrate their unanimity and their determination to oust the ancient enemy. From the remote outposts of Dingle and Ballyferriter they came; from Caherciveen and Annascaul; from Tralee, Listowel and Castleisland these men flocked to join their comrades of Killarney and East Kerry in a firm and resolute answer to the nation's call. The scene in the town was as romantic as it was colourful and portentous. Huge crowds, open-eyed with awe and amazement, lined the streets to watch the almost unending procession of bandoliered Volunteers as they marched with heads erect and hearts aflame to the saluting base. The tranquillity of an era of calmly accepted subjection was at an end and fireworks were in the offing. That was the trend of thought that flowed through the minds of the populace. Strength and resoluteness resounded from those marching feet. The atmosphere at the saluting base was electric. 'We have no fear, we have no doubt that the sun is rising for Ireland.' There was a tense and awe-inspiring hush as these prophetic words flowed from the lips of Eoin MacNeill and floated over the vast assemblage. In his hands were the colours – a symbolic sunburst with an old Irish emblem – the work of Kerry hands. In his heart was exultation – the cream of The Kingdom was around him.

We leave that great and glorious day and move along the calendar of 1915 – months that marked steady expansion of the movement – and halt at a date near Christmas of that year. Killarney commemorated the Manchester Martyrs with a display of highly disciplined force. Under the command of Captain Michael Spillane, and Lieutenants Dick Fitzgerald and M.J. O'Sullivan, a great parade of Volunteers moved in procession from the cathedral through the streets of the town. The Volunteers' Pipe Band took the lead and the general public formed a long tail behind the Brass Band of the Temperance Society. The Volunteers with rifles reversed marched in open order. A meeting held at Volunteer headquarters was presided over by Henry Spring, RDC, and addressed by M.J. O'Connor, of Tralee.

Then to the efforts of England to recruit our manhood for the European slaughterhouse. Killarney resisted strongly. Read the summing up of Sir Morgan O'Connell in a letter to *The Times*:

> Mr Redmond has issued a further appeal to the manhood of Ireland to do its duty and fill up the reserves of our gallant Irish regiments. I fear that this appeal will fall on very deaf ears in this county of Kerry. Recruiting in this county, with a population of some 165,000, is dead. The open and avowed pro-German anti-recruiting Sinn Féin element has been allowed to spread and spread until every village in Kerry is rotten with it. In May last I warned the Lord Lieutenant that if meetings openly anti-recruiting in their objects were allowed to be held trouble would surely follow. The reply to that reads: 'If any breach of the Defence of the Realm Regulations occurs it will

be dealt with by a competent military authority.' On 4 February a recruiting meeting was being held in Killarney. A Sinn Féin mob headed by a band marched up and down through this meeting with the usual accompaniment of booing and yelling. This riotous mob was led by one of the Justices of the Peace for Killarney.

And later, at the Rebellion Inquiry, Mr J.C. Percy, JP, stated that he was an honorary recruiting worker and that Killarney was the first place he found Sinn Féin operating against recruiting. He could not get a chairman to preside over the meeting there and had tried the member of parliament, the chairman of the town commissioners and the administrator. 'Then,' he said, 'I went to Sir Morgan O'Connell and he gave me an entirely different reason for refusing. He said there had been a review announced to be held of 5,000 persons from Kerry and this would be an anti-recruiting meeting and would put an end to recruiting in Kerry if it was allowed to be held. He (Sir Morgan) had wired to Mr Birrell and Lord Wimbourne to have it suppressed, but neither of them had moved in the matter. In those circumstances he would not move his little finger to help the British Government.'

The fight against the recruiting campaign was only the lesser part of the operations of the Killarney Volunteers. The big job which they were on was the preparation for the impending Insurrection. The possibility, of landing arms in Kenmare Bay was explored but came to nothing. Mick Spillane and another went to Dublin taking the funds (£200) with them. Theirs was an important mission. To a house in Herbert Park they hied – the house of The O'Rahilly. The £200 went into the hands of The O'Rahilly in exchange for: fifty-two Martini Lee Enfield rifles; two magazine Lee Enfield rifles; 1,700 rounds of .303 ammunition; 10 revolvers; 500 rounds of revolver ammunition. The 'arsenal' was consigned to Killarney as cutlery and arrived safely to the right hands (most of these arms and ammunition were later used by the IRA in barrack attacks and ambushes).

The Killarney Volunteers were all ready to take part in the projected Rising. The story of the cancelling order is old. In May 1916, Mick Spillane, Michael John Sullivan, Patrick O'Shea, Willie Horgan and Dick Fitzgerald, the most prominent of the Killarney group, were arrested. On their release the battalion was reorganised and played an active part in the struggle with the Black and Tans.

LISTOWEL

THE VOLUNTEER MOVEMENT in Listowel may be said to have been initiated in early January 1914, at a meeting held at the old Technical School in Market Street. Little has been recorded of the early activities of the movement in the town, but it is known that the meeting was convened by E.J. Gleeson and that Mr Salmon, instructor to the local Fife and Drum Band, presided. The former read the constitution of the organisation, which was enthusiastically received and adopted. A rifle was procured at Jack McKenna's and all the Volunteers-elect sworn in with it. On the following Sunday the newly-formed company, led by Jack McKenna and E.J. Gleeson, with the band under Salmon marched from the Courthouse out to Finuge and home by Market Street. Later in the same month a further meeting was held in the Gymnasium Hall, at which Thomas Moore was appointed secretary and treasurer. Jack McKenna or Salmon presided at most of these early meetings and urged on everyone to join the organisation in the struggle for the freedom of their country. E.J. Leahy, chief of Fianna Éireann, was active in Volunteer affairs from the very beginning. Early in August 1914, the company paraded before Colonel Scott-Hickie of Kilelton. In charge were Drill Instructors Mortell and Peter Bartishell.

About that time a Volunteer meeting was held at which Rev. Charles O'Sullivan, CC, and Reverend Canon Pattison, rector of

Listowel, were present. Others present were: Michael O'Connell, clerk of the Listowel Union; William McElligott and Jack McKenna, chairman of the Urban District Council. A committee was appointed as follows: Very Rev. D.J. Canon O'Riordan, PP, chairman; Rev. Canon Pattison, Very Rev. J. Breen, STL, president of Saint Michael's College; Jack McKenna and William McElligott. At the time of the Redmondite split, the Listowel Volunteers were almost unanimous in supporting MacNeill, the voting being one hundred and thirty-nine to seven. Following a visit to Listowel by Ernest Blythe in February 1915, the corps was reorganised. Jack Tackaberry was one of the chief movers in this reorganisation, following which a marked improvement was noted. At the same time several new companies were formed in the surrounding districts and field exercises and combined training were carried out extensively. On Saint Patrick's Day 1915, the Listowel Volunteers, under the command of Instructor O'Sullivan, paraded the town after twelve o'clock Mass, headed by the Fife and Drum Band. The officers included Jack McKenna, MCC, CUDC, and E.J. Leahy. All were fully armed with up-to-date rifles and their manly bearing and martial display impressed everybody as they marched with the precision of veterans. Their route march took them through Clieveragh, Bedford and home by Ballygologue where they were dismissed.

Edward J. Gleeson was sentenced to four months imprisonment at Listowel Petty Sessions Court under the Defence of the Realm Act for using words on 21 November 1915, in the AOH Hall in Duagh likely to be prejudicial to recruiting, causing disaffection to His Majesty.

On the eve of the Rising in Easter Week 1916, the Listowel company assembled, fully armed, waiting for the command from headquarters to go into action. Officers included Patrick Landers, James Sugrue, E.J. Gleeson, Jack McKenna, Michael O'Brien and Denis Quille. The command never came, however, and the company was dismissed.

At a meeting of the Volunteers convened by E.J. Leahy and held in the Gymnasium Hall on 6 June 1916, no speeches were permitted and everybody got down to brass tacks without delay. The election of officers and committee resulted as follows: Instructors: Peter Bartishell and William O'Dwyer; Committee: John Moran, of Moran's Hotel, Church Street, treasurer; E.J. Leahy, secretary; L. Buckley, UDC; Thomas Murphy; Patrick Breen, UDC; James Hayes and John Scully.

DINGLE

THE DINGLE VOLUNTEERS came into being in the spring of 1914, following a public meeting held in the town, at which John Curran, Main Street, presided. It was addressed by Desmond Fitzgerald, of Cuan, Ventry, who later enrolled seventy-five recruits. The provisional committee appointed comprised: J. Curran, D. Fitzgerald, P. Devane, J.J. O'Sullivan, P.J. Neligan, D. Corkery, William Kennedy, T. McCarthy, D. McCarthy, J. Kavanagh, J. Moore, RDC, and Jonathan Moriarty, JP. The honorary secretary was J.J. O'Sullivan, and the honorary treasurer, D. Corkery. The corps was most active; drilling and route marches took place weekly, and lectures were given regularly. The men frequently joined forces with the corps of Ballyferriter, Lispole and Annascaul, where the movement was also developing rapidly. A spectator at an early parade of the combined companies in Dingle town was heard to remark that the Ballyferriter men paraded with the precision of the Prussian Guards. Certainly the splendid physique and martial bearing of the gallant West Kerry men was particularly in evidence at the 1914 Oireachtas at Killarney. The corps was not many months in existence before the advent of the Redmondite 'split', which caused the defection of about twenty per cent, of the rank and file, including many of the influential members. On the whole, however, Dingle was overwhelmingly in favour of

Eoin MacNeill's Irish Volunteers. On Sunday, 6 September 1914, there was an important muster of Volunteers in the town; some two hundred men from Caherciveen and Valentia districts, under Commander O'Connor, crossed Dingle Bay in motor trawlers, and were received at the Quay head by units from Dingle, Lispole, Ballyferriter and Dunquin. Headed by the Caherciveen band, the combined forces paraded the streets of Dingle, followed by almost the entire population of the town. In the Mall the parade halted and formed a hollow square for Ernest Blythe who, at the request of the Dingle Committee of Irish Volunteers, extended a hearty welcome to the men from Iveragh. He complimented the various corps on their soldierly appearance and said that, hitherto, a large number of the Volunteers had looked upon their drill as a form of recreation. But they were engaged upon a serious task. They were forming an army to fight for the national freedom of Ireland. They would not fight to hold Ireland for England, but to win Ireland for the Irish people. It had been said that they would fight the Germans if they came to Ireland, but that depended on what the Germans might come for. If the Germans should come with the object of subjugating our country, then they would fight them; but if the Germans should come to Ireland to liberate her from English rule, then the Volunteers would flock to their standards. They should continue their preparations with unabated energy, for it might well be that, in their day and their generation, they should in Ireland see the establishment of a free and independent Irish Republic. Their opportunity might soon come, for in spite of English depreciation it was easily within the bounds of possibility that Germany's fleet should acquit itself as well as her army was doing. John Redmond had stated in the British House of Commons that his Volunteers would defend Ireland against any foreign enemy. Closely analysed that statement might be thought harmless enough, but on the face of it, it implied and was intended to convey, that the Redmondite Volunteers would defend Ireland for England.

Seaghan Óg MacMurchadha Caomhanach, speaking in Irish, said: 'as that district and Iveragh were both Irish-speaking, he would say a few words to them in Irish. He saw before him hundreds of Volunteers, hundreds of the inhabitants of Dingle and of the farmers from the district around it, but what was the good of it all if they came there only to parade and applaud. That was an easy enough thing to do compared with taking their place in the fighting line. Let them get guns; let the man who had a cow sell it and buy a gun for his son (applause). Up to a few days ago their lying venal press had assured them that the Germans were being beaten on land and sea; but today they were almost before the gates of Paris. Now was the day of England's difficulty. They had always heard that England's difficulty was Ireland's opportunity. But how did their leaders propose to take advantage of it? John Redmond, John Dillon, William O'Brien and their miserable little member, Tom O'Donnell, were acting as recruiting agents for the British army. Eternal shame upon the Irishmen who would raise a finger at this juncture to assist the oppressor of his country. And eternal shame upon the man who was not willing to shed his blood for the freedom of Ireland (prolonged applause).' At the conclusion of the proceedings three hearty cheers were given for the Irish Volunteers.

Dingle afforded a hot reception to Tom O'Donnell when he visited the town on 12 September 1914, and made futile efforts to secure recruits for the British army. He also reviewed the Redmondite Volunteers. The Irish Volunteers were very active during the winter and spring of 1915, and there was obviously a much more virile organisation than that of the Redmondite opposition. Nevertheless the Redmondites made a good show when they paraded in uniform but without rifles, on Saint Patrick's Day. They were headed by the Fife and Drum Band, and were again reviewed by Tom O'Donnell, who had with him on that occasion the Marquis MacSweeney of Mashanaglass, inspector-general of the Redmondite Volunteers. Numerically, there were much fewer than the Irish Volunteers whose turn-out the same afternoon made one of the biggest parades of Volunteers ever seen in Dingle. In addition to the Dingle corps contingents paraded from Annascaul, Ballyferriter, Lispole and Ballydavid. Most of the men were armed with rifles, and the parade was headed by the new pipers band. As 1915 wore on the Redmondite influence in the town was completely on the wane, and when Tom O'Donnell again attempted to hold a recruiting meeting on 14 December 1915, there was no man in the district to go on the platform with him. In the course of his speech, O'Donnell referred to strangers who had been visiting the district, and who were paid by German gold to lead the people astray. Having referred to Ernest Blythe and Desmond Fitzgerald, O'Donnell declared that if they ever came round again, he would ask them their real names, what their father's names were and where they came from. According to Tom, 'the people should not turn their backs on tried and trusted leaders like John Redmond who gave them their lands, and, instead, listen to strangers and men like Cotton who came from Tralee to tell them what to do.' The people knew which was the right side, and in case they did not, O'Donnell explained that it was their duty to stand firmly by the Empire. His eloquence was of no avail, for there were no recruits to the Union Jack, and, instead, the influence of the Irish Volunteers and Sinn Féin continued to spread in the town.

The progress, which the Sinn Féin movement had made in Dingle and West Kerry generally, was amply illustrated by a letter written by an English visitor to Dingle to a friend at home in England. Here is an exact reproduction:

Dingle,
Co. Kerry.

A chara,
You will find it hard to understand the above form of address; but I employ it as I am a believer in the old proverb: 'When in Rome do as the Romans do.'

The unfortunate people down here still use the Irish language extensively. This is an extraordinary place and I have many interesting things to tell you about it. Fortunately for my health, I was more or less prepared for the backward state of thought and education here by a very educative gentleman whom I met in Tralee on my way. On his learning that I was about to proceed to Dingle he became very interested. He assured me that there actually were 'Sinn Féiners' in Dingle. Of course, at first remembering that Kerrymen are supposed to be great 'jokers' I thought that he was 'pulling my leg'; but no. He assured me that there were actually several. Having told me that he was himself an Englishman, of course, I was then more or less inclined to believe him. However, my astonishment was great when I got here and discovered that his words were only too true. If you can believe me, I actually met about twenty such ignorant people. This very evening I asked a young chap, who at least looked intelligent, why he did not answer the call of his King and country, and he replied that he had excellent reasons for not doing so. I found out afterwards, that he was born in Dingle. What do you think of that, anyway? It is a shame that something can't be done for these poor people. They are in a frightful state of backwardness. I blame the newspapers for this state of affairs, as they are shamefully ignorant. I don't believe the people down here read the daily papers very much or I suppose they would have learned to understand things better. They actually laugh at the mention of small nationalities! but you can't believe how things really are.

I came to the conclusion that it must have been the priests' fault; but no, they are quite alright and doing their part to educate the people. There was a recruiting meeting here last week (I believe actually the first in the district!) and the local canon presided. Notwithstanding that fact, and powerful speeches made by the local MP not a single man volunteered! Now, you can understand the state of the place. The MP, O'Donnell is his name, took advantage cleverly of the fact that 'Sinn Féiners' cannot seek protection of the law and abused two of them in great style. He seems to be quite a good chap; but the people do not appear to understand him. They tell me that he has more or less 'sprung from the people' and was until recently as bad as any of them, but you should be here to understand things. I will tell you everything when I get back.

Yours very sincerely,
J.H.S.

Ernest Blythe who, since early 1915, had been forbidden to enter

Dingle, revisited the town on 5 February 1916, when an immense gathering turned out to welcome him. He was met by the Dingle Volunteers, all of whom were armed, and was escorted by them through the streets. Tom O'Donnell was not there to question him about his antecedents. Blythe counselled the Volunteers to train conscientiously and to be prepared for the great struggle which lay ahead.

KILLORGLIN

THE VOLUNTEERS WERE not long in existence when corps was formed in Killorglin, and in few other centres was there such marked activity in the early days of the movement. By June 1914, not alone was the work of organisation perfected in the town, but the majority of the surrounding districts and villages also had contributed efficient corps. Representatives of all the Killorglin and district companies assembled in the old town by the Laune for a great meeting in June 1914. Although many who attended the rally seceded to the Redmondite Volunteers when the 'split' came a few months later, it is worth while quoting such of their names as were noted by an enterprising local scribe of the day. The list is a full one, and the number of local districts represented indicates the extent to which the movement had developed in the area. On the platform were the Rev. Fr F. Flynn, CC, and Rev. Fr J. Behan, CC, with Tom O'Donnell MP, J.V. Lillis, BA, P. O'Riordan, D.C. O'Sullivan, S. Coffey, J. O'Brien, W.M. O'Brien, M. O'Doherty and T. Fitzpatrick. The following officers were elected on the committee to take charge of the corps: Tom O'Donnell, MP, D.C. O'Sullivan, T.C. Moore, P. O'Flynn, W. Joy, M. Kennedy, G. Burke, D. Moriarty, P. O'Shea, W. Healy, C. Sheehan and F. Griffin, hon. secretary. Stephen Foley was appointed drill organiser. The various districts were represented as follows:

Killorglin: Messrs E. Collins, MPSI, E. Horgan, C. O'Sullivan, D. Lyne, RDC, J.P. Hartigan, D. O'Sullivan, M. Byrne, D. Coffey, D. O'Donoghue, M.J. O'Sullivan, J.J. O'Sullivan, D.M. O'Sullivan, M. Johnson, J. Johnson, D. Mangan, P. Lane, M. Teahan, S. Coffey, J. Coffey, M. Foley, M. O'Donoghue, W. McSweeney, W. Roche, W.W. Dodd, P. Flynn, J. O'Shea, P. O'Regan, M. O'Doherty, G. Evans, M. Evans, D.J. O'Brien, M.W. O'Brien, P. O'Riordan, J. Kearns, P. Kennelly, W. Clifford, P.T. O'Sullivan, W. Flynn, J. O'Neill, W. Healy, M. O'Connor, J.P. O'Shea, J. O'Connor, J. O'Sullivan, J.J. Houlihan, J. Dee, M. Counihan, J. Healy, T. Linehain, J.J. O'Neill, J. Diggins, P. Downey, P. Heffernan, J. Coffey, T. Scannell, T. O'Riordan, M. O'Riordan, D. O'Neill, D.J. O'Neill, T. Griffin, W. Crowley, M.M. Daly, D. Power, J. Morris, D. Clifford, J. Keane, J. Doyle, T. O'Shea, D. Murphy, M. Moroney, J. O'Neill, J. Diggin, RDC, E. O'Neill, P. Golden, M. Walsh, J. Fitzpatrick, J. Houlihan, P. Flynn, B. O'Riordan, D.J. Clifford, T.J. Clifford, D. Moriarty, D. O'Connor, M. O'Connor, P. Begley, T. O'Callaghan, J. Duffy, P. Sheehan, J. Coffey.

Bansha: Messrs James Foley, Michael O'Sullivan, B. Foley, J. Joy, William Joy, P. Joy, Pat Griffin, M. Sheehan, Ned Langford, John Langford, Pat Sheehan; the Misses Langford, Sheehan and Foley.

Tuogh: Messrs J. Kennedy, M. Kissane, J. Joy, W. Doyle, J.J. Doyle, J.T. Doyle, W. McKenna, W.T. Coffey, J. Coffey, P. O'Sullivan, D. O'Sullivan, M. Foley, J. Foley, J. McSweeney, J. O'Connor, D. O'Connor, E. Mangan, RDC, M. Moriarty, W.J. Moriarty, J. Scully, P. O'Sullivan; the Misses O'Sullivan, Cashman, Doyle, Kennedy, Mason, Johnson, Mangan and Murphy.

Ballymalis: Messrs Pat Butler, John E. Sullivan, Ulick Sullivan, Pat Hannifin, Denis O'Connell, Michael Butler, Timothy O'Sullivan, Frank Butler, Mort Broder, Misses Kennelly, O'Sullivan, Broder, Flynn and Maunsell.

Coolroe: Messrs Denis McGillycuddy, John McGillycuddy, John O'Sullivan, Daniel O'Connor, Charles O'Connor, Arthur O'Connor, Daniel O'Leary, Tom O'Leary, Jim O'Leary, Pat Lyne, Jack McCarthy, Charles McCarthy, John Cantillon; Misses McGillycuddy, O'Connor, O'Leary, Lyne and Hobbins.

Coolbane: Messrs John Golden, John Foley, Michael Foley, Timothy McGillycuddy, Jerry Breen, David Breen, Michael Doyle, Jim Gallivan; Misses Foley, Golden and Breen.

Dungeel: Messrs Tom Johnson, Michael Johnson, Jim Johnson, John Foley, Thomas Kane, J. Kane, Timothy Flynn, James Flynn, John Heffernan; Misses Keane, Johnson, Heffernan, Flynn and Riordan.

Corbally: Messrs George Nagle, Garrett Nagle, John Nagle,

Patrick Teahan, Daniel O'Sullivan, Con O'Sullivan, Jack Ferris, Tim Foley, Tom Foley; Mrs Garrett Nagle.

Doonmaniheen: Messrs Pat Moroney, Jeremiah O'Sullivan, Timothy Kelly, John Harrington, John Sheehy.

Anglont: Messrs Thomas Foley, JP, MCC, Patrick Looney, Mrs Foley, Miss B. O'Sullivan.

Dromin: Messrs P. Mangan, David O'Shea, D. Moriarty, Stephen Kennedy, John O'Connor, John Moriarty, John Mangan, William Mangan, John O'Connor, Maurice O'Sullivan, J. O'Sullivan; Misses O'Connor, Griffin and O'Sullivan.

The first reaction in Kerry to Redmond's parliamentary speech which promised the use of the Irish Volunteers to hold Ireland for the British Empire, took place at a Volunteer concert which was held in Killorglin on 3 September 1914. During the interval, Tom O'Donnell, MP, appeared on the stage and urged upon the audience the necessity for Irishmen to stand by the Empire in her hour of need. Not all of his listeners had realised beforehand that the Irish Parliamentary Party, represented locally by O'Donnell, had moved so completely in favour of the British Empire. There was silence until a young girl in the auditorium jumped to her feet and accused O'Donnell of betraying his country, and pointed out that the purpose of the Volunteers was not to hold this country for Britain, but to strike for freedom at the first favourable opportunity. That opportunity, she informed the flabbergasted O'Donnell, was close at hand. Bedlam broke out in the hall before she had finished speaking, and it was apparent that opinion was fairly evenly divided for and against the Redmondites. O'Donnell had lived in Killorglin for many years, and in the early days of the 'split' he pulled a fair measure of support for the Redmondites. Eventually, however, men, and women, too, began to realise that the decision before them was too great to be decided by reasons of personal friendship, and inside a matter of months there appeared the beginning of a definite swing away from the Redmondite policy. Meanwhile, Tom O'Donnell, who had been entirely disowned by his native West Kerry, concentrated his recruiting activities on his adopted town. Whilst he never had reason to be enthusiastic about the results of his eloquence on the recruiting platform, it was but natural that such a complete swing-over to British imperialism, by one of the founders of the Volunteers in Killorglin, should have a confusing and discouraging effect on the local corps. There was a big falling off in the attendance at Volunteer functions, but the leaders stuck grimly to their guns, and eventually men began to drift back to swell parades and manoeuvres which took place regularly by the banks of the Laune. Hereunder is a ballad which, published in *The Kerryman* of November 1915, did much to debunk O'Donnell, and attract recruits to the Irish Volunteer movement:

RECRUITING IN KERRY

A Kerry Peasant Boy to his Father – November 1914.

'Oh! father, at the Fair of Puck
I heard O'Donnell say
That the Saxon wanted soldiers
And would give the best of pay;
Would give the best of pay, indeed,
And cigarettes galore,
And praises in the newspapers,
What could one wish for more?
And so I was considerin'
If the red coat I'd put on.'

**'Your father was no renegade,
Will you be one, my son?'**

'Ah, father you should have heard him talk
About the big brigade,

That will cover all the country
From Paris to Belgrade;
From Paris to Belgrade, indeed,
That's what he said at Puck;
And he prayed for England's welfare
And the downfall of von Kluck.
And so I was considerin'
If the red coat I'd put on.'

**'Remember '98 my boy
And be your father's son.'**

'He said they gave us Land Acts
And all that we'd require,
And advised us as himself had done,
To work for Saxon hire;
To work for Saxon hire, indeed!
We of the Irish race,
And forget the wrongs of centuries
Which he wants us to efface;
And so I was considerin'
If the red coat I'd put on.'

**'Don't follow his example, boy,
Be true to Ireland, son.'**

'He was ragin' when he spoke about
The "nobodies" who dare
Raise their heads in dear old Ireland
For freedom to declare;
For freedom to declare, indeed,
And said they were a gang
Who desired to smash the Union
And drive out the Englishman;
And so I was considerin'
If the red coat I'd put on.'

'Go join the "nobodies" at once,
Their cause is right, my son.'

'The industries of Germany,
Says Thomas O', says he,
Must be captured by the English
And they have promised me,
And they have promised me, indeed!
That honours are in store
If recruits they are forthcoming,
And we'll bluff the Irish poor;
And so I was considerin'
If the red coat I'd put on.'

'Don't mind the foreign shambles, boy,
Just fight at home, my son.'

'Sure the English want to stay at home
To capture this 'ere trade,
And we're to do the fightin'
Or they'll say that we're afraid
Or they'll say that we're afraid again!
The dirty Hirish dogs
Who're only fit for fightin'
Or slaving in the bogs;
And so I was considerin'
If the red coat I'd put on.'

'Remember Emmet and Wolfe Tone,
And die like them, my son.'

'Ah, father dear how true you are,
Though you are old and worn,
All through the ups and downs of life,
And by its hardships torn;

And by its hardships torn, yes!
But father, don't be troubled,
For I would never join the crew
That pleasant homes have levelled;
And so I was considerin'
The pauper garb I'd first put on.'

'My son, I never doubted you,
You are your father's son.'

'I'll join the Volunteers, tonight,
The Irish Volunteers
Who're out for Irish freedom,
The men who know no fears;
The men who know no fears, my boys!
With no Cockney scum I'll go
To fight a foe not mine at all
But with the boys I know;
And so I was considerin'
That the green coat I'll put on.'

'They're drillin' by the Laune, tonight,
Go, drill with them, my son.'

EEJIT in *The Kerryman*, November 1914.

Recruiting received a further setback in the town during the same month, when a batch of Belgian refugees passed through Killorglin on their way to Glenbeigh. Amongst the Belgian's were some lusty young men who, to all appearances, were well fitted for service at the front. In the next issue of *The Kerryman*, the editor of that journal had some pointed comments on the Belgian drift from the theatre of war, and on the Redmondite policy to replace them in that sector by fighting Irishmen who scarcely knew what the war was all about, beyond what they had heard of the Party prattle about the defence of small nations. Quoth *The Kerryman*:

> That able soldier and strategist, Corporal Tom O'Donnell should know all about it, as I understand that he met the batch of husky refugees on their arrival. It is a matter of surprise that Irishmen should be asked to go out and fight for a country which these men have deserted. John Boland, MP, when inciting, more or less eloquently, young Irish men to take up arms on behalf of 'Gallant little Belgium' and thus prove that Irish chivalry was not dead, should remember that some Belgian refugees are available for the job of 'fighting for Belgium', as it is called. Or perhaps those militant MPs of ours are only preparing a surprise packet for the Kaiser. They may be about to form the Belgian 'Irish Brigade', drilled and instructed by themselves in strategy and on what pertains to the successful bearing of arms. If so, the Germans are indeed done for.

Sinn Féin and the Irish Volunteer movement received great impetus in Killorglin during 1915. A big number of young local men joined on Sunday, 18 July, following a parade of Irish Volunteers under the command of Daniel O'Mahony. They marched through the town several times, headed by the Killorglin Brass Band which, for the first time, was entirely made up of Sinn Féiners. Some of the local Redmondites had previously failed in an attempt to take possession of the instruments. By that time the Redmondite movement was definitely on its way out of town, and Killorglin thus joined with West Kerry in finally rejecting O'Donnell and the policy for which he stood. By 1916 the town and district were solidly pro-Sinn Féin.

CASTLEISLAND

A BRANCH OF the Irish Volunteers were inaugurated in Castleisland on Sunday, 5 April 1914, following a huge public meeting which was addressed from the balcony of the Crown Hotel. Amongst those on the platform were: M.P. McElligott, W.H. O'Connor, RDC,

T.T. O'Connor, Land Leaguer; John Geaney and Jeremiah Kelliher. Kelliher, who was eighty-two years of age at the time, walked about seven miles to be present at the meeting, which was also attended by T. Wren, R. Finn, T.D. Reidy, Denis J. Reidy, Thomas Costelloe, M. Keane, L. Curtin, R.J. Walsh, R.E. Shanahan, C.J. Browne, H. Knight and Jeremiah Laide. W.H. O'Connor presided and M.P. McElligott was appointed secretary to the Volunteers; Denis J. Reidy was instructed to make arrangements for drill. The meeting was addressed by Diarmuid Crean, chairman of the County Board, and by James McDonnell, John Collins and J.M. Collins of the Tralee Volunteer committee.

Great activity followed the inaugural meeting, and drilling, parades and lectures took place weekly. The corps, which was strongly represented at the Killarney Oireachtas in 1914, continued to make progress without set-back of any kind until the Redmondite 'split' in October 1914. On Sunday, 8 November, a huge meeting in support of the Irish Volunteers and Eoin MacNeill took place in the town. There was unbounded enthusiasm, as close on a thousand Volunteers, many of them armed, marched to the meeting place. The Castleisland corps was augmented by contingents from Cordal and Scartaglin, and by a detachment from Tralee accompanied by the Strand Street Fife and Drum Band which led the parade.

A police note-taker from Dublin Castle, who was protected by, a sergeant and some constables of the Royal Irish Constabulary, attended and reported the proceedings, which were marked by a considerable show of police activity, obviously intended to frighten the people. On the proposition of Dan O'Mahony, commander of the Castleisland Volunteers, and seconded by Brian O'Connor, RDC, W.H. O'Connor was appointed chairman and D.J. Griffin, secretary. The gathering was addressed by W.H. O'Connor, Castleisland; B. O'Connor, RDC, Scartaglin; T.T. O'Connor, Cordal; Desmond Fitzgerald, representative of the Provisional Committee; M.J. O'Connor, Tom Slattery and Austin Stack of Tralee. The speakers were given a tremendous reception, and the proceedings were accompanied by great enthusiasm. It was probably the largest and most stirring meeting ever held in the town, which reverberated to the cheers of thousands of The Kingdom's sons and daughters. During the stormy days of the agitation Castleisland proved its metal by its fight for downtrodden tenantry, and against cruel and tyrannical landlordism. Sons of the men who had made history in the 1880s wrote an equally stirring page on that November day; they would not have been true to their sires if they had failed Ireland in her hour of difficulty.

The Castleisland Volunteers trained assiduously during the winter, and presented a splendid appearance when reviewed by Ernest Blythe in the spring of 1915. Contingents from Cordal, Scartaglin and Currans were in attendance with the Castleisland corps when Blythe inspected the men and the rifles. Blythe was assisted by A.W. Cotton, who arrived with a detail of the Tralee cycle corps, and after the review twenty-eight new recruits were enrolled. With the Cordal, Scartaglin and Currans men the Castleisland Volunteers worked hard in preparation for the 1915 Whit parade at Killarney, where the company acquitted itself very well.

On Saturday night, 3 July 1915, Castleisland Volunteers marched to Listowel under most unfavourable weather conditions. They were received by Ned Leahy with other members of the Listowel Volunteer executive, and accommodated in the Gymnasium on Saturday night. Next morning they availed of the Lartigue Railway to travel to Ballybunion, and on the same evening they marched all the way home to Castleisland. One hundred men armed with rifles participated in the march and made a fine appearance. Such movements of Volunteers were planned by the leaders to fit the men for the fight for freedom which they knew was just approaching.

The forty-eighth anniversary of the execution of Allen, Larkin and O'Brien was fittingly commemorated in Castleisland on Sunday, 21 November 1915, when a splendid parade of the Irish Volunteers took place. Many of the men were armed. The procession was led by the Currans band and by a party of torchbearers. Banners with the inscriptions, 'Remember the Manchester Martyrs', 'Remember Ninety-eight' and 'Thou Art Not Conquered Yet, Dear Land', were carried in the parade which marched through the town from the Volunteer Drill Hall, to the graveyard about a mile distant, where an oration was delivered by M.J. O'Connor of Tralee. Dan O'Mahony, captain of the Castleisland Volunteers, and Con Browne also spoke. By 1916 the Castleisland Volunteers were well organised, trained, and ready to play their part in the fight for freedom.

CAHERCIVEEN

OVER THREE HUNDRED men from the Caherciveen district assembled in Daniel Golden's Market Hall, for the formation of the local branch of the Irish Volunteers, on Tuesday night, 18 January 1914. Volunteers were enrolled after the meeting, and the men were given their first drill instruction by John Chapman, who was appointed drill instructor. Following a splendid muster on the occasion of the Oireachtas held at Killarney in 1914, the first big issue which faced the Caherciveen Volunteers materialised with the Redmondite 'split' in October 1914. On the nineteenth of that month the Caherciveen Volunteers assembled in the Carnegie Hall, to decide whether they would follow the lead of Eoin MacNeill and the original Provisional Committee, or whether they would affiliate with the Redmondites. Michael J. Healy, captain of the corps, presided at the meeting, and amongst those who spoke were: Joseph Brennan, William Drummy, Denis J. O'Connell, MCC, Edward Moriarty, James J. O'Shea and John Reidy, MPSI. James O'Shea proposed that the corps remain faithful to the original committee. His proposition was seconded by Jeremiah Kelliher and, following a division, the resolution was carried by thirty-seven votes to twenty-seven. The announcement of the result was received with great acclamation in the town. Although the matter was decided by a vote the minority refused to abide by the decision, and on the following Sunday night another meeting was held in the Carnegie Hall by Volunteers who supported Redmond. Eugene J. Ring, who spoke from the body of the hall in an effort to convince the assembly that the formation of a corps of Redmondite Volunteers was in contravention of the decision of the previous meeting, was refused a hearing. Sixty-three Redmondite Volunteers were enrolled. On the same night the Irish Volunteers held a rifle practice in the Drill Hall of the Caherciveen Market House.

Shortly after the 'split' the Irish Volunteers subscription for the Defence of Ireland fund, met with a splendid response in the town and district. The committee set about the work of collection in a most energetic and systematic manner. They formed a number of squads, and each squad was allocated a certain area inside which it was decided to make a house-to-house collection. Collectors for Ballycarbery, Killehan, Kimego and Clahanelinehan reported that they were received with characteristic generosity. Caherciveen town also did well notwithstanding the seeming apathy of the people. Meanwhile, the rival Volunteer corps pursued their separate paths, until the Saint Patrick's Day Parade of 1915 brought them temporarily together. On that day the Redmondites and the MacNeillites, about five hundred strong, marched in the same procession and behind the same band. The Redmondites, who were unarmed, headed the parade to the west end, and the Irish Volunteers, all of whom were armed with rifles, led the parade on the return journey. There was an enormous crowd of country people in town, and there were never to be forgotten scenes of enthusiasm. When the parade was dismissed, the Volunteers returned to their respective headquarters. The amazing spectacle of the Irish Volunteers and the National Volunteers parading together was again witnessed on 25 July 1915, when they celebrated the anniversary of the successful gun-running at Howth. After nine o'clock Mass, Bugler Moore sounded the 'fall in', and the ranks formed up under the joint command of the officers of both corps. The Irish and Redmondite Volunteers did not maintain separate formation but intermingled and marched, shoulder to shoulder, headed by the brass band. They marched to Foylemore where, after Mass, they were joined by the local Volunteers for drill, which took place in a field lent by P. Lyne. The Volunteers were addressed by J. O'Connell, Michael J. Healy, J.J. O'Shea and J. Brennan.

On the night of 28 November 1915, the streets of the old town again presented an animated spectacle, as they resounded to the measured tread of the martial manhood of Iveragh who mobilised from glen and hillside, from Gleesk and Corobeg, to honour the heroic men whose devoted patriotism and cruel martyrdom will illume for all time the murky skies of Manchester. From the deep glens of Kells; from the slopes of Tyromoyle, Lisbawn and Clahanelinehan; from Letter, Killoe and Ballycarney; from faithful Reenard, and from the gallant little Island of Valentia, came tall, stalwart Iveragh men, despite the bitter winter weather, to show how widespread, deep and sincere were their feelings of veneration for the noble three who so freely and fearlessly gave their lives for Irish freedom. At eight o'clock the procession was marshalled by Captain James J. O'Shea, in front of the Drill Hall of the Irish Volunteers. It was led by the Boy Scouts under Captain Maurice Griffin, who were followed by torch-bearers, standard-bearers, and the Volunteer detachments. The oration was delivered by Micheál Breathnach, Gaelic League organiser. Some days later a sensation was created in town when Thomas Moore, Listowel, and Jeremiah Sullivan, Caherciveen, two young students in the Atlantic Wireless College, were expelled for participating in the Manchester Martyrs commemoration. The order of expulsion was issued by the postmaster general. Other members of the Irish Volunteers lost their employment. But actions of this kind, with the object of breaking up the movement, had the reverse effect, and by the spring of 1916 Sinn Féin and the Irish Volunteers were firmly established and soundly organised in Iveragh.

DUAGH

Soon after the foundation of the Volunteers the greatest aspersion which could be cast upon a Kerry village was to suggest that it had not yet formed its corps of Volunteers. Commenting upon a parade in Listowel town in the spring of 1914, the writer of 'Listowel Notes' in *The Kerryman* referred to the absence of Volunteer activity in a number of North Kerry districts which included Duagh. His colleague who contributed 'Duagh Notes' was up in arms in the issue of the paper which followed, pointing out that Duagh was the first village in North Kerry to form a corps of Volunteers. Arising from the controversy the Duagh Volunteers decided upon a route march to Listowel to display their strength in the North Kerry capital. The parade was headed by about fifty horsemen who made an impressive display in green and gold sashes. Then followed the fife and drum band leading close on two hundred men on foot. They marched through the town in military formation and entered the square, where the band played martial music. The incident was commemorated by a ballad anonymously contributed to a subsequent issue of *The Kerryman*. Here it is:

DUAGH VOLUNTEERS

(Air: 'O'Donnell Abú')

The sun is a-shining in dear old Kilcara,
Where strains of fife music are borne on the gale,
As bravely, Duagh Volunteers are advancing
Forward their march to Listowel by the Feale.
Onward our army then,
Fight for the land again,
Sons of those men who have never known fears,
On 'gainst the Carson crew, noble's the work you do,
Onward to victory, Duagh Volunteers.

Martial the music that's heard ere the sunset,
And cheers of a thousand are thick on the air,
As forward the brave Volunteers are advancing,
And steadily marching, they enter the square.
Onward our army then,
Fight for the land again,
Sons of those men who have never known fears,
On 'gainst the Carson crew, noble's the work you do,
Onward to victory, Duagh Volunteers.

What horsemen are those who so proudly approach us?
Resplendent in sashes of green and of gold,
Led by the banner and band so long famous,
Truly they look like the clansmen of old.
Such is our army then,
Fight for the land again,
Sons of those men who have never known fears,
On 'gainst the Carson crew, noble's the work you do,
Onward to victory, Duagh Volunteers.

In the wake of the horsemen are marching our footmen,
Determined to strive now with might and with main,
To save our dear country, to guard her from danger;
To make of Old Erin a nation again.
Onward our army then,
Fight for the land again,
Sons of those men who have never known fears,
On 'gainst the Carson crew, noble's the work you do,
Onward to victory, Duagh Volunteers.

On their way home they march past Kilmorna,
Where blaze of the bonfires reach high in the sky,
Brave are the days since our boys have been mustered,
Each man determined to do or to die.
Onward our army then,

Fight for the land again,
Sons of those men who have never known fears,
On 'gainst the Carson crew, noble's the work you do,
Onward to victory, Duagh Volunteers.

Soon they are home in their own loved village,
Where hundreds of torches before them are seen,
And as the boys march their band's proudly playing
Erin Mavourneen and Wearin' o' the Green.
Onward our army then,
Fight for the land again,
Sons of those men who have never known fears,
On 'gainst the Carson crew, noble's the work you do,
Onward to victory, Duagh Volunteers.

Brave Volunteers, brave men and noble,
Thousands of others will join in your train,
And march to reawaken the spirit of Erin,
To make of our country a nation again.
Onward our army then,
Fight for the land again,
Sons of those men who have never known fears,
On 'gainst the Carson crew, noble's the work you do,
Onward to victory, Duagh Volunteers.

In the ranks of the Volunteers who participated in the celebrated route march to Listowel was James O'Sullivan, veteran nationalist, who had ever been to the forefront in any movement for the betterment of the country. The drill instructor first in charge of the Duagh corps was Thomas King, who had many years service with the British army in South Africa and in India. He was anxious to apply his experience to preparing Irishmen to fight for the freedom of their country. Although shaken by the Redmondite 'split' Duagh declared her allegiance to the Irish Volunteers. Derrinadaffe and Islandanny districts were up and doing in the autumn of 1914, and made up for the defections of the Redmondites by bringing the strength of the Duagh company to several hundred men. Following the Redmondite 'split' the Duagh corps was drilled by Captain Dillon; Islandanny corps by Captain Keane, and Derrinadaffe by Captain Dowling. The Duagh committee of the Irish Volunteers comprised: J. Moloney, chairman; Thomas O'Brien, John Flynn, Pat Sheehy, Pat McMahon, Thomas Sheehy, Pat Finucane. John P. Sheehy was honorary treasurer and Thomas Stack was honorary secretary. The 1915 Manchester Martyrs' celebration was a big event in the village. Following a parade a meeting was held in the Temperance Hall and presided over by J.J. Sheehy, RDC. It was addressed by E.J. Gleeson, Listowel. Mr Gleeson was shortly afterwards sentenced to four months' imprisonment under the Defence of the Realm Act, because of the speech he made in Duagh. The spirit created in the district by these early activities and the effect of the solid groundwork patiently prepared were abundantly apparent in later years when Ireland's little fighting force was locked in death-grips with the minions of the mighty British Empire.

Ardfert: A meeting for the purpose of strengthening the Irish Volunteer movement in the district was held beside the ruins of the old historic abbey, towards the end of September 1914. Armed Volunteers attended from Tralee, Lixnaw, and other surrounding districts. William O'Grady presided, and, amongst those on the platform were Michael Maguire, RDC, and William Lynch of the Ardfert corps. Eugene O'Sullivan of Killarney and Maurice P. Ryle of Tralee addressed the men.

Abbeyfeale: Over four hundred Volunteers were enrolled at the inaugural meeting held in the town towards the end of April 1914. A large number of subscriptions were immediately handed in, and officers for the branch appointed. Among those who attended were: Mr B.C. Collins, JP, MCC, chairman; Messrs William D. O'Connor, William O'Sullivan, R.C. Harnett, P. O'Connor, DC,

W. O'Connor, do., J.D. Riordan, do., J. Buckley, do., J.J. Harnett, T. Ryan, Seán Ó Cearbhaill, Gaelic League organiser; J.D. Harnett, M.L. Harnett, C.D. Riordan, E.C. Leahy, D. McEnery, D. O'Neill, D. Collins, P. Woulfe, T. Woulfe, J.M. Broderick, J. Broderick, D.D. Collins, D. Woulfe, J. Cahill, P.J. Harnett, J. Sweeney, W.P. Flynn, T. O'Keeffe, D.B. Harnett, P. Scannell, M. Loinasnic, D. Sullivan, M. Collins, J. Collins, P. Moloney, W. Collins, T.J. Keane, J. Moloney, M. Buckley, J.W. Flynn, J.J. Cahill, J. Wrenn, P. Brouder, J. Brouder, P. Collins, M. O'Connor, J. O'Donnell, J. Fitzgerald, P.D. Riordan, E.P. Moloney, M. Stack, J. O'Connell, P. Woulfe, J. McAuliffe, J. Corridan, P. Fitzgerald, J. Aherne, T. O'Connell, D. O'Connell, M. Roche, M. Collins, M. O'Connell, J. Mara, P.M. Scannell, J. Lane, P. O'Donnell, W. O'Connor, P. Lane and J.J. Collins. Activities faded out in the district following the Redmondite 'split', until the corps was reorganised by S. Wall and took its rightful place under the banner of the Irish Volunteers.

Abbeydorney: Sunday 21 November 1914 was a historic day in the village of Abbeydorney, when the local Volunteers were reorganised. A branch had been formed in the spring of 1914, but interest had fallen off, due to the Redmondite 'split', until the revival meeting which was announced in the village as 'Irish Volunteer Day'. From early morning Abbeydorney was full of activity, people having flocked from the surrounding districts to help the good work and to welcome the Volunteers from other districts. First to arrive was the Tralee contingent, fully armed and equipped, and headed by a piper playing the Irish war pipes. Eighty-six recruits were enrolled, after which the visiting corps drilled with the local men in a field kindly lent by Mr Kearney. An official welcome was extended to the Tralee Volunteers by Murty O'Connor, and Austin Stack suitably returned thanks. Murty O'Connor was appointed honorary treasurer to the corps, and Garrett Scollard the honorary secretary.

Ballyferriter: Corps of Volunteers was unanimous in repudiating Redmond and remaining true to the Irish Volunteers.

Ballylongford: Rev. Canon Hayes, PP, and David O'Sullivan were active in the formation of the corps which took place early in 1914. John Moran was the first chairman, and Roger Mulvihill was appointed honorary secretary in June 1914. In the beginning there were one hundred and twenty men on the roll, but the company was considerably weakened by the Redmondite 'split'. The Volunteers who supported MacNeill and the original Provisional Committee, continued active, and drills, parades and lectures took place regularly. Daniel Mulvihill, Main Street, and Thomas Carmody, Bridge Street, represented the corps when the Volunteers of the county were reviewed by Eoin MacNeill at Killarney on Whit Sunday, 23 May 1915.

Ballybunion: One hundred and fifty men from the parish lined up after eleven o'clock Mass at Doon, on 28 June 1914, and joined the local corps of Volunteers which had just been established. The men, who were first drilled by J. Summers of Lixnaw, later paraded through the village, headed by the Listowel Temperance Band. J. Boland, JP, MCC, presided over a meeting to explain the object of the Volunteers. Amongst those who spoke were Eugene O'Sullivan, Killarney; J. Leahy, New York; Thomas Keane, JP, MCC; Professor P. Breen, Saint Michael's College, Listowel, and William O'Sullivan, Ballybunion.

Brosna: The Very Rev. Canon Arthur Murphy, PP, was president of the Brosna corps of Volunteers, which was formed in May 1914. The committee included D.J. Moriarty, RDC, Cornelius Connell, J.M. O'Keeffe, RDC and P.M. Murphy. Captain Maurice Harnett was honorary treasurer, and James J. O'Connor, junior, honorary secretary. The corps paraded and drilled under the command of Instructors Cotter and Delea. Following the Redmondite 'split' D. Guiney exhorted the young men of the parish to remain faithful to the Irish Volunteers, in the organisation of which body he was assisted by D. Mahony, commander of the Castleisland corps, and by Austin Stack of Tralee. There were fifty Irish Volunteers in Brosna village in December 1914.

Ballymacelligott: Over fifty men joined when the corps was formed in the Hibernian Hall, Ballymacelligott, in April 1914. The meeting took place at night, and whilst it was in progress two members of the Royal Irish Constabulary patrolled outside the hall, under cover of darkness. On the following week the new force had its first drill under the direction of Instructor Slattery. The corps was unanimous in supporting the Irish Volunteers.

Cordal: Corps decided to remain true to the Irish Volunteers by sixty-eight votes to two votes cast in favour of the Redmondite Volunteers. The decision was taken in October 1914.

Castlegregory: Corps was unanimous in supporting the Irish Volunteers.

Craughdarrig: A branch of the Volunteers was founded at Craughdarrig Cross in July 1914, following a route march to the locality by the Ballylongford men. The company numbered close on three hundred men, with A. O'Callaghan, captain. Shortly after the formation of the corps, colours were presented by Mrs M. Mulvihill, and the following committee was elected: J. O'Callaghan, E. McElligott, James Collins, Patrick Deenihan, and Seán Coughlan, secretary. J. O'Callaghan was drill instructor.

Currans: A branch of the Irish Volunteers was formed in Currans on 1 May 1914, and in a short time there were one hundred and fifty men on the roll. The original committee comprised Ulick O'Sullivan, chairman; Jeremiah F. Cronin, Denis O'Sullivan, Patrick Cronin, James Grady, Michael Mahony, John Daly, Donal O'Sullivan, Francis Fitzgerald, and D.P. Cronin, honorary secretary.

Foylemore: Corps of Volunteers was formed 5 July 1914, when Messrs Jeremiah O'Connell, Micheál Breathnach and D.J. O'Connell, MCC, addressed the inaugural meeting. Jeremiah O'Connell was later dismissed from his post as a national schoolteacher because of his activities with the Irish Volunteers.

Glenbeigh: Volunteers came into being 25 July 1914, at a meeting presided over by the Rev. J. Lynch, CC. Fifty members were enrolled, and thirty additional members after Mass on the following Sunday. T.G. Evans, JP, MCC, was appointed honorary treasurer, and John Moriarty, honorary secretary. Drill instruction was given by J. O'Shea, Volunteer organiser, from Tralee.

Keel: T.G. Evans presided at the inaugural meeting of the Keel Volunteers, which took place on 8 June 1914. The objects of the movement were outlined by J.J. Kavanagh of the Dublin Volunteers, and the following committee was appointed: T.G. Evans, chairman; J. O'Shea, RDC, vice-chairman; Pat Murphy, Michael Myles, W.B. O'Brien, Tom Lawlor, RDC, David Griffin and M.J. Teahan, honorary secretary.

Knockanure: Corps was formed in the late spring of 1914. Rev. Fr O'Flaherty, CC, was chairman; J. Lynch, honorary secretary, and John Cronin, drill instructor.

Lixnaw: Corps of the Irish Volunteers was formed on 13 June 1914. Drill instructor was J. Sommers, auctioneer, of Irremore, who later became chief instructor for North Kerry. Sommers commanded a big force of North Kerry Volunteers who attended an enthusiastic rally in the village on 19 July 1914. Michael Mangan of Kilfeighney presided, and amongst those on the platform were: John Flaherty, RDC, Eugene Sugrue and Tim Reidy. Fr Dillon delivered an interesting and impressive lecture on the Volunteer movement. Eugene O'Sullivan of Killarney, Jeremiah O'Connell and Tom Lawlor also spoke. Large contingents from Ballyduff, Kilflynn and other outlying districts attended. The Ballyduff men were accompanied by two bands, a brass band, under the baton of James Hennessy, and a fife and drum band. Kiltomey (Lixnaw district) corps was formed shortly after that of Lixnaw, and the first drill instructors were John Scanlon and William Dineen.

Rathmore: company of Volunteers was formed in February 1914. The Redmondite 'split' scarcely affected the locality, as the support for the Irish Volunteers was overwhelming. The town and district companies were very active from the beginning, and careful attention was devoted to drill and other military exercises. There is a record of a big turn-out in the town in November 1915, on the occasion of the Manchester Martyrs' celebration, when over 1,000 Volunteers mobilised and marched to Nohoval cemetery. They were led by a torchlight party and by a detachment of horsemen under P. Moynihan and E. Buckley. The torch-bearers were L. Hickey, J.C. Hickey, F. Flavin, D.T. Dennehy, T.T. Murphy, D. Leary, M. Daly, D.P. Kelliher, M.J. Kelliher, D.M. Duggan, J.T. Daly, P.J. O'Leary and Dan O'Keeffe. Marshal of the procession was D.M. O'Connor, RDC. The Rathmore contingent was commanded by Captain P. Murphy; Ballydaly contingent by Captain D. Brien, and the Cullen contingent by Captain J. Dennehy. Fred Crowley, later TD for South Kerry, addressed the meeting at the cemetery. The Rathmore men worked hard to organise all districts within reach, and on Sunday, 5 December 1915, they marched to Rathduane in the parish of Millstreet, where over fifty recruits were enrolled and formed into a company. The objective for Sunday 12 December, was Knocknagree, where T. Collins addressed a large meeting and enrolled close on a hundred recruits. His speech was reported by a police note-taker.

Mastergeehy: Speaking in Mastergeehy in favour of the Irish Volunteer movement, in October 1914, Fr Tom Curtayne, now parish priest of Tarbert, said, 'We cannot afford to lose any men except the landlords, and the Recruiting Sergeants are welcome to them.'

Scartaglin: Branch of the Volunteers was founded on 7 June 1914, following a route march to the village by the Castleisland and Cordal companies.

Tarbert: Over one hundred Volunteers were enrolled when a branch of the movement was founded in the village. Chairman was Rev. Fr Martin, PP.

Ventry: Corps of Volunteers was formed the first week in May 1914. The inaugural meeting took place in the old schoolhouse, and was addressed by John Curran and Desmond Fitzgerald.

The officers elected included John Curran, president; Desmond Fitzgerald, honorary secretary; D. Courtney, honorary treasurer, and W. Rooney, instructor. The corps was unanimous in supporting the Irish Volunteers.

Waterville: Volunteer corps was formed towards the end of June 1914. About two hundred and fifty men paraded in the village, and the objects of the movement were explained to them by Instructors Kennedy, Walsh and O'Connell. Following the 'split' a local doctor, who worked hard on behalf of the Redmondites, advised the Volunteers in the valley of Finglass to boycott *The Kerryman* because of its support for the Irish Volunteer movement.

THE GERMAN EXPEDITION
TO TRALEE BAY

by JOHN McCANN

THE LEADERS OF the 1916 insurrection had expected arms and ammunition from America, through the agency of Clan na Gael. This course not being practicable, the executive of the latter organisation, headed by the veteran Fenian, John Devoy, decided to ask Germany to make the shipment. And ultimately through the German Embassy at Washington came the following reply:

> Between 20 and 23 April, in the evening, two or three steam trawlers could land 20,000 rifles and ten machine guns, with ammunition and explosives at Fenit Pier in Tralee Bay. Irish pilot boat to await the trawlers at dusk, north of the Island of Inishtooskert, at the entrance of Tralee Bay, and show two green lights close to each other at short intervals. Please wire whether the necessary arrangements in Ireland can be made secretly through Devoy. Success can only be assured by the most vigorous efforts.

The offer was accepted by the Irish Republican Brotherhood Military Council. Roger Casement, however, who had been in Germany since 1914, had negotiated for ten times the number of rifles and a German expeditionary force with submarines. He knew nothing of this final arrangement. John Devoy, with typical Fenian secrecy, had communicated very little to Casement regarding the latest

American moves. Casement's Irish Brigade, numbering fifty-two, which he had been permitted to organise from Irishmen among the British army internees in Germany, disappointingly small as it was, would, nevertheless, sail with such an expedition. Joseph Plunkett was in Berne, in Switzerland, in connection with the arms, and on 6 April he sent a message to Casement informing him that Easter Sunday was fixed for the Rising; that the arms should arrive in Tralee Bay not later than dawn of Easter Saturday; a German submarine would be needed in Dublin Bay; and what was imperative – German officers would be necessary for the Irish Volunteer Force. Casement despaired. He felt that he had been treated like an office boy in the whole business. He immediately wrote to Joseph Plunkett giving the details of what was actually being dispatched to Ireland – no German officers, no submarines. Besides, it had now been decided to send but one ship with the full cargo. That to Casement was utter madness. It would never run the British blockade. Nor could he see his way to ask the men of his brigade to go to what he considered certain death, in the altered circumstances. Incidentally, his message to Plunkett was never delivered.

In the meantime, the German Admiralty had all arrangements made for the gun-running. Captain Karl Spindler was selected to command the *Libau*, a 1,400-ton vessel, formerly the British prize ship *Castro*. Captain Spindler had been informed of his selection to take charge of a dangerous expedition and was asked to provide a crew of unmarried men, young and of good physique. Service was optional but Spindler had no difficulty in finding the requisite number. He himself was glad of an opportunity to do something big. 'I reckoned myself at that moment,' he said, 'the luckiest man on earth.' At the outset Captain Spindler was told nothing of the nature of the task he had been allotted. The crew were bound to secrecy concerning what had already taken place. The *Libau* put out from Hamburg with her commander, five petty officers, and sixteen ratings, flying the flag of the German Mercantile Marine at her stern. She sailed down the River Elbe through the Brunsbüttel canal by Cuxhaven to Neuwark, anchoring overnight before proceeding to Wilhelmshaven, where some cargo was taken aboard. While the *Libau* berthed at Wilhelmshaven, Captain Spindler was called to Berlin, where, for the first time, he was told of his mission and destination. The German navy would demonstrate off the east coast of England, in order to divert attention from the west coast of Ireland. Meanwhile, Casement had prevailed upon the German High Command to send a submarine in which he proposed to travel with Robert Monteith and Beverley, a member of the brigade, known as Bailey. Spindler's orders were to meet the submarine in Tralee Bay on Good Friday. The *Libau* sailed from Lübeck on 9 April, apparently carrying a cargo of timber. The crew donned Norwegian attire; daily journals of the same country were carelessly strewn around; the men carried letters and photographs of their girls in Norway; and all tinned food bore the origin stamp of that country. Additional equipment aboard would enable Captain Spindler to change his ship to German or British if desired. She did not carry wireless. In appearance she looked like any ordinary tramp, her sides daubed with red lead. The name *Libau* had also been effaced, after the rumour had been circulated in Lübeck that the vessel was bound for Libau in Latvia. The first night, in heavy seas, the name *Aud-Norge* was painted on the sides in yard and a half long letters. Fore and aft, huge Norwegian flags were hoisted, and *Aud Bergen* conspicuously painted on the deck. Next day, sailing along the Danish coast, Captain Spindler encountered a German destroyer. The warship drew alongside, and Spindler recognised its commander, to whom he had spoken but a few days gone in Kiel. Recognition was not mutual, and when the naval officer enquired in German what port he hailed from, he feigned ignorance of his native tongue. To the question, repeated in English, he answered 'Danzig'; and when asked where he was bound for, he said: 'Christiania'. Another officer at the commander's elbow, said in German: 'I'll be hanged if that fellow is on the square.' But the destroyer having circled the *Aud*, after intensive scrutiny, the commander shouted: 'All right, Captain!'

At Falsberbo, where Danish and German territorial waters meet, Captain Spindler ordered more speed to elude a Danish pilot boat – which had been insistent upon piloting – after he had shouted that he knew the waters well and did not need a pilot. Further on the *Aud* came up with a Danish schooner, which caused Spindler some concern, as the ship had been astern the *Libau* in Lübeck Harbour. It was possible that the Danes would recognise the *Aud* in her new garb. The pilot boat and schooner both headed for port, increasing the captain's fears, as Denmark was in full sympathy with the British to whom a message would probably be sent if suspicion had been aroused. Soon the lights of Copenhagen were left behind and on the horizon those of Helsingborg became faintly discernible. On through the racing currents of the Kattegat; and then, to port, the dim outline of a torpedo boat. The rays of its searchlight play on the *Aud* for what seems an eternity, while the Danish coastal watcher takes full stock of the name and the blue, white and red colours on the *Aud*'s side. 'A Norwegian tramp' is apparently the verdict, and no questions are asked. But real danger was now ahead, outside the three-mile limit, for in the Skaggerack and along the Norwegian coast the British navy was in force for the prosecution of the blockade. Previously, it had been ordered that neutral vessels should follow a course within a ten-mile limit of Scandinavia, to facilitate examination. Spindler decided to run the gauntlet by steering well outside the limit, hoping that the British fleet was concentrated around the coast. His calculations proved correct, and the *Aud* sailed on without incident.

Four days at sea and save for a few drifting mines the might of Britain had not been sighted. Seventy-five miles east of the Shetlands, a British warship was observed heading north-east, the same course, roughly, as the *Aud*. There was nothing to do but hope for the best. Escape was impossible, as the cruiser bore down upon them with great speed. Then of a sudden she changed course to eastward! The look-out had evidently not sighted the *Aud* after all. The engines were now giving slight trouble, so Captain Spindler sought the shelter of Bremanjerland on the Nordfjord, where repairs were done and the ship's lettering and flags repainted. At sea again, Spindler was resting in his bunk when through the voice pipe, from above, came the loudly shouted observation: 'waterspout to starboard, Captain'. Again the narrowest escape as the huge black column of water swept past at a safe distance away from the *Aud*'s course. The seventh day was Sunday, and as the arms ship sped on through heaving seas and a thick fog towards the North Atlantic, a 10,000-ton auxiliary cruiser was sighted. The *Aud*'s siren tooted, as if inviting inspection from the warship. The cruiser's deck was stripped and ready for action, guns pointing menacingly at the little tramp. Still providence was on the side of Spindler for no interference was offered. Now a great storm came up, rains lashing and winds buffeting as the breakers swept over the little ship's bows. Top-heavy from the manner in which her cargo was, of necessity, loaded, she rolled perilously, making but four knots. Changing course slightly to the south to avoid the blockade line west of the Hebrides, the *Aud* gallantly fights her way in the worst tempest that her captain has ever experienced. A huge sea strikes the little craft broadside, laying her on her beam ends. Everything on deck is swept overboard, the crew being hurled into the lee scuppers. Higher the waves rise, breaking in thunderous roars. Soon the treacherous Rockalls west of the Scottish coast are sighted. It will take superb seamanship to keep her away from certain disaster. For a few terrible minutes it seems that all is lost. Then she rights herself. Now, a furious hailstorm. The *Aud* stops, with a flooding to the bulwark rail, giving the impression that she is aground. But, even then, there is no commotion. Willing and expert hands, that refuse to admit defeat, work feverishly. And Captain Spindler brings her through, with barely one day left to keep that all-important appointment in Tralee Bay. Four British cruisers are passed in turn, letting the Norwegian tramp pass unchallenged.

Next a 6,000 ton vessel appears. More inquisitive than the others, the *Aud* is subjected to a critical scrutiny. The cruiser moves nearer; and as it does Captain Spindler thinks 'what a pity having got so far'. But, again, the incredible. The cruiser changes direction to search for more pretentious prey. A miserable 1,400 tonner – phsaw! 'Well, that puts the lid on it, captain,' grins a second officer, 'let's make all speed for Tralee and sail in with flying colours. If they don't have a triumphal archway ready to welcome us, they're not the men I take them for.'

Success, thought Spindler, was now assured. It remained only for the Irishmen to play their part. And full speed ahead it is through the night and well into the next day, Holy Thursday, 20 April. A few more hours and Tralee Bay will be reached. The crew are making ready the steam winches and unloading tackle. Hatches are uncovered; slings are put in position; case openers are at hand. If a landing is made, and the British are waiting, the crew will fight. If, at the last moment, the ship is attacked at sea, then the British will never get the *Aud*'s precious cargo, for explosives and incendiaries are already placed in position with significant purpose. The German naval ensign is lying handy. The crew change into the uniform of their country. Now Captain Spindler informs the majority of them, for the first time, of their real destination and detail. He tells them, also, that their uniforms may not save them from being shot out of hand in the event of failure. Welcome now is the sight of the rugged Kerry mountain outline. Slowly Spindler steers his good ship into the bay, nearer, nearer ... Where is the Irish pilot-boat? The Kerry Hills now seem to glower down upon them. No life apparent anywhere. Not a craft in sight. The two-hundred-foot masts of the British wireless station loom up in relief on the Head, guarded by guns pointing seaward, beside which stand the unmistakable figures of British Tommies ... Course is changed slightly north. Soon they come near the little, group of islands. Yes, that's Inishtooskert at the head of them. But where is the pilot-boat with the green flag and the green-jerseyed men in the bows? The exact spot is reached. Still no sign. Minutes are like hours … waiting … waiting … waiting …. Spindler ponders all the things that may have happened. Without wireless equipment he knows nothing of what has happened since he put to sea on 9 April. He does not know that the Volunteers are not expecting him until Easter Sunday, three days hence. How could he? Philomena Plunkett had not arrived in New York until 14 April with this message from the Irish leaders: 'Arms must not be landed before the night of Easter Sunday, the twenty-third. This is vital. Smuggling impossible.' John Devoy gave the message to Von Papen, who had it wirelessed to Berlin on 15 April. The *Aud* was then six days at sea. If only the *Aud* had wireless! The Irish leaders were also unaware of this lack of essential equipment, for, long before Spindler put into Tralee Bay, Joseph Plunkett was vainly endeavouring to make contact with the German ship, he having been experimenting for some time with a home constructed apparatus at Larkfield House, Kimmage. Nor did Captain Spindler know that on 18 April the United States Secret Service – in contravention of international law – had raided the office of the German Embassy in New York, discovered the message from Ireland, and had it communicated to the British.

Cautiously, at first, then brazenly open the agreed signals are given from the *Aud*. In vain. Nothing can be seen on the mainland, save the disturbing sight of a British soldier pacing his beat. The *Aud* cruises slowly between Fenit and Kerry Head. The German captain calls the crew together. They are of one mind with him. They will see this business through, whatever the result. Night comes, bringing hope. Perhaps the Irish are waiting for the cover of darkness. From the arms ship a little green light flashes at intervals – to land – to sea … No response. No damned response! Boldly Spindler steers to one hundred yards of the pier. The signal is again given. The result is the same. Close to the headland the *Aud* moves to the shelter of Inishtooskert and drops anchor. At daybreak the look-out shouts: 'Steamer on the starboard bow – the pilot steamer'. The crew's delight, however, is short-lived, for as the supposed pilot-boat approaches the ensign of the British navy is seen clearly. They are again dressed for the part ready even to the last to bluff their way through as Norwegians. His Majesty's warship, *Shatter II*, draws alongside. 'Where are you from?' shouts the ruddy-faced commanding officer. 'Hullo! Where are you from?' he bellows again, having received no answer from the *Aud*'s mate. Again he asks and again receiving no reply he explodes: 'God, damn you man! I asked you where are you from?' The *Aud*'s mate shouts, 'Good morning.'

'Hell and damnation!' blurts the Englishman, 'I don't want your civilities. I want to know where you came from.'

Without more ado, the captain and six men board the tramp, and after an inspection, are satisfied as to its Norwegian nationality. Being shown the ship's papers, the captain accepts a good cigar from Spindler, but refuses a cup of coffee. His ruddy face, however, did not lie, and he says 'yes' to a good glass of malt. And having said 'yes' many times, the *Shatter*'s commander becomes loquacious. It was but a couple of weeks gone that he had been sent from Aberdeen to intercept a German steamer bound for Tralee with a cargo of arms. 'The damned Germans want to join the Irish in bringing about a revolution. Look around,' he said half incoherently, 'the whole bay is bristling with guns. Nothing can get in.' And, wishing Spindler 'safe voyage', he leaves, albeit very unsteady on the legs.

Eagerly, Captain Spindler scans the newspapers that the Englishman had given him. He reads of the arrest of prominent Sinn Féiners. An Irish pilot had also been taken into custody. To Captain Spindler that explained everything. Still he did not give up hope, but waited for a sign from the shore; the men meanwhile overhauling the engines. Near noon a more up-to-date warship than the *Shatter II* was observed altering her course at a distance of about nine miles, and speeding towards the *Aud*. Captain Spindler decided to make a run for it. It looked as if the arms ship was now suspect, as signals flashed in all directions around the bay. The *Shatter II* again came into view. Spindler decided to ram her and go down together. Full speed ahead towards the *Shatter II*; and to his amazement the warship made way and signalled: 'Bon voyage.' The second warship continued to give chase and, coming up with the *Shatter II*, after a short exchange of words between the officers, the latter joined in. But the *Aud* making fifteen knots outdistanced them, and they turned for port, with Spindler well out into the Atlantic. The respite, however, was but short-lived. For now a warship making twenty knots came up, and having cursorily inspected, turned away. It was the beginning of the end, for soon smoking funnels could be seen on all sides. The *Aud* was trapped! At seven o'clock the British warship *Bluebell* signalled: 'Stop at once' … 'What ship is this?' … 'Where are you from?' … 'Where are you bound for?'

The *Aud* replied: 'Genoa and Naples.'

The *Bluebell* signalled: 'Proceed.'

And even as the *Aud* did so, the whole squadron set out in pursuit. The *Bluebell*, with guns trained, kept her distance. She fired across the bows, ordering: 'follow me to Queenstown'. Captain Spindler had no choice. He signalled a breakdown of engines in response to the *Bluebell*'s injunction: 'Faster'. The *Aud* still dictated the play, being only able to make five knots. Spindler inspected the explosives and incendiaries. The German naval ensign was ready. Captain Karl Spindler donned his uniform. Fifteen minutes now from Queenstown Harbour. He calls for four Volunteers to blow up the ship with him. The rest to lower the boats. An angry 'No' comes from the assembled company. All will remain to share the danger. 'All right,' commands the captain, 'lower the boats!'

'All ready,' came the answer from engine room and deck. 'Hard astarboard! Stop!' That was the signal. The German ensign was run up. A muffled explosion. The gallant *Aud* shudders from stem to stern. The crew take to the boats. Now they are rowing hard to get clear. The *Bluebell* fires once. A white flag is raised in the lifeboat.

The *Bluebell* does not fire again. The ammunition is exploding on the *Aud*, as she belches smoke and flames. Then with a last deafening farewell to her crew, the little tramp rises perpendicularly as if in salute, and plunges into the gurgling waters. And with the *Aud* went Ireland's hopes for a general Rising, for her cargo was to have been distributed in various centres.

KERRY'S PLACE IN THE GENERAL PLAN, 1916

by A. COTTON

Mr A. Cotton, author of this important contribution to the story of events in Kerry immediately prior to the Rising of 1916 and of the county's part in the general plan of campaign decided upon, became a member of the IRB when not quite out of his teens and was associated with Joseph Robinson and the Countess Markievicz in organising and training Na Fianna Éireann in Belfast. In 1912 he became a civil servant and, after a short time, in Dublin was transferred to Sligo, in May 1912. Before leaving Dublin he had been appointed organiser by the IRB. From May 1912, in addition to organising the IRB, he was active in establishing a branch of, the Gaelic League, the Freedom Club, and later the Sligo battalion of the Irish Volunteers, of which he was honorary secretary. He was transferred to Dublin early in 1914.

I FIRST ARRIVED in Kerry about the end of June 1914. I was then a civil servant employed in the Labour Exchange. I had been an organiser for the IRB and was also an active Volunteer. I was appointed captain of the Tralee Volunteer cycle corps, a position which enabled me to carry on my organising work. After my dismissal from, the civil service early in 1915 on account of my Volunteer activities, I became full-time Volunteer instructor and organiser for County Kerry, acting as vice-commandant of the Tralee battalion and brigade adjutant. Some time in the fall of 1915 I accompanied Austin Stack, who was then commandant of the Kerry Volunteers, to an interview with P.H. Pearse at St Enda's, Rathfarnham. Having impressed us with the necessity for absolute secrecy, Pearse informed us that a Rising had been planned for Easter, 1916. He then stated that arrangements had been made with Germany to send rifles, machine guns, ammunition and explosives to Tralee Bay. We would have to make the local arrangements for the reception and distribution of the armaments.

The plans decided upon for the Rising were not given to us in detail but merely a general outline of what was intended. In the first place a general mobilisation of all Volunteer companies and battalions throughout the country would be ordered. Instructions as regards positions to be occupied and objectives to be carried out would be given in each case. In a general way the position would be that the Cork Volunteers would move out to Macroom and link up with the Kerry brigade which would be in touch with the Volunteers from Clare, Limerick and Galway. They would ultimately hold positions on a line running roughly down the Shannon through Limerick and East Kerry to Macroom. The Volunteers from Ulster would move to positions on a line running from the Shannon along south Ulster. The actual Rising would begin with the Dublin Volunteers seizing and holding strategic positions in the city and the proclamation of the Republic. In the counties surrounding Dublin the Volunteers would take action against British forces as directed and some contingents would move on the city to relieve the pressure on the Dublin men. The arms and ammunition to be landed at Fenit would be distributed between the Cork, Kerry, Clare, Limerick and Galway Volunteers. We were to arrange to have a goods train ready to proceed to Fenit for the armaments. Part of the cargo would be detached at Tralee for the Cork and Kerry Volunteers and the remainder would be taken by goods train towards Limerick for distribution amongst the Volunteers in the west. It would also be necessary to arrange for a pilot to be ready and on the look-out for the arranged signals from the arms ship so as to meet her and bring her in to Fenit pier. Arrangements were also to be made to send a cable in code 'to our friends in the USA' informing them that the Rising had taken place and that the Irish Republic had been proclaimed.

Every effort was to be made to have all in readiness, but no hint of the plans or intentions were to be given to any other person. It was essential to preserve absolute secrecy up to the last minute – only the very minimum of information considered necessary was to be given to the men selected for any special work and these were to be carefully selected for their particular job. During the discussion the difficulties of running the British naval blockade, the risk of delay by storm or fog and the uncertainty of the ship arriving at Tralee Bay on time were mentioned. I suggested the possibility of the landing of smaller quantities of arms (say 500 to 1,000) at various points around the coast without much risk of any serious clash. Germany would not agree; the plans already made were final and we would have to make preparations accordingly in the hope that everything would work out as arranged.

In this connection it is interesting to note that Captain Monteith in his book, *Casement's Last Adventure*, mentions a conversation he had with the quartermaster on the submarine bringing him and Casement to Ireland. The quartermaster said to Monteith, 'Why don't you run arms to Ireland as we did to Senussi?'

Monteith inquired, 'In what manner do you mean?'

The quartermaster replied, 'We had special submarines for that purpose.'

Monteith then makes the comment: 'This was news in view of the fact that in Berlin I repeatedly asked that arms be shipped to Ireland in this way.'

Now it is clear that if Germany could land arms in North Africa for the Senussi revolt and invasion of Egypt in 1915 she could more easily have sent them to Ireland. A little organisation and co-operation would have enabled the Volunteers to take delivery of small quantities of arms at various points around the coast without much risk of any serious clash with the British forces during 1915. Every thousand rifles landed would have meant a fresh influx of recruits, especially in the country districts, and by the end of 1915 we might easily have had another 20,000 well-armed Volunteers. The effect on the national spirit would have been tremendous. Recruiting for the British forces would have been killed and the young men would have flocked into the Volunteers. Every week would have seen our strength increasing and by the spring of 1916 we would have been in such a strong position that the British might well have hesitated to attack such a well-armed force. Furthermore, America was still reluctant to depart from her traditional policy of not getting embroiled in European wars and any attempt by Britain to forcibly suppress the Volunteers and enforce conscription in Ireland would have caused repercussions in America which might well have had disastrous effects in so far as obtaining the American aid which she was so anxious to procure. The history of 1782 might well have been repeated and in any event if Britain had finally determined to attack, our position would have been incomparably stronger. Large forces of British troops – which she could ill afford to use – would have been necessary and, pressed as she was on the continent, any delay in American aid might well have given victory to the Central Powers. At any rate we would not have had to stake all on the single chance of the successful landing of one large quantity of arms and the success of a sudden revolt. It appears, however, that any such arrangements could not be made with Germany. The fateful decision to take the risk was made and so we had to make our plans accordingly. Stack and I returned to Tralee to carry out the necessary arrangements.

It is only right to state here that the mere outline of the general plan as given conveys little idea of what would eventually have to be arranged in detail in each area. In Kerry our immediate objective would be to ensure the safe landing and distribution of the arms and ammunition. Assuming that the ship would not arrive until after the Rising had started in Dublin and that the British forces had no suspicion of what was intended, our plans would be as follows: simultaneously with the Rising in Dublin the Volunteers mobilised in Tralee would seize the post office, so as to control telephone and telegraphic communications; they would seize and hold the railway station and have the goods train ready to proceed to Fenit. Members of the RIC on duty or outside their barracks would be captured. Those in the barracks would, if possible, be enticed outside and a party of Volunteers 'conveniently' passing would 'rush' the barracks, capture and disarm the police, and take possession of any arms and ammunition found in the barracks. If this action was impossible, or failed, Volunteers would take suitable positions covering all exits from the barracks and force the police to surrender, if necessary destroying the barracks either by fire or explosives. Similar action would be taken to deal with the small force of British troops in Ballymullen barracks. All roads leading from the town would be closed to prevent any British adherents carrying information to Cork or Limerick. Local Volunteers in each area throughout the county would, where necessary, take similar action to capture or destroy all RIC barracks, especially those in such places as Listowel, Castleisland, and Killarney. Posters announcing the proclamation of the Republic would be posted up throughout the area; citizens committees and special police would be formed in the towns to prevent disorder and to co-operate with the Volunteer authorities. Having thus established full control in the area the way would be clear for the reception and distribution of the arms.

In connection with these plans the element of surprise would be of the utmost importance not only for their immediate success – an important factor in itself – but also in the husbanding at the beginning of the fight of our small supplies of ammunition and without the shedding of much blood. Hence the necessity for the utmost secrecy, even up to the last hour, lest an idle word should start rumours and give warning to the British forces. As soon as the British authorities in Cork would hear of the Rising in Dublin they would naturally send warnings to all British forces in their area. On finding that they could not make contact with Kerry they would probably send out dispatch riders, and possibly small forces by road or train to Tralee. The Volunteers from South Kerry along with the Cork contingent would, therefore, prepare to intercept such forces by holding positions on the main roads from Cork and by destroying the railway line at some suitable point where an ambush could effectively be arranged. When the arms were safely landed and brought to Tralee some would be diverted for the Cork and Kerry Volunteers and the remainder would be taken towards Limerick under armed guard for the Limerick, Clare and Galway Volunteers. If the Ballymullen military barracks and the police barracks in Tralee had not already been captured, some of the high explosives brought by the arms ship could be used to reduce these places. The Tralee Volunteers would then be free to proceed to the assistance of those engaged with any British forces coming from Cork or Limerick. How the fighting would develop afterwards it is impossible to say, but it is probable that if it continued for any length of time it would have developed into guerrilla warfare.

In connection with the arrangements made for the reception of the arms I may here mention that I had previously held a few weekend camps for Volunteers at a spot on the shore near Banna Strand and convenient to Fenit. These camps were just weekend holiday camps attended by a few unemployed Volunteers who would go out on Friday or Saturday morning and members of the cycle corps going out from Tralee on Saturday evening or Sunday morning. The time was mainly spent in bathing, playing games and generally enjoying themselves. The Volunteers carried arms but there was little display of military activity. At first the RIC were curious as to what we were up to but after a visit or two they took no further notice of our activities. As these camps had ceased to interest the

RIC I intended that on Good Friday a small but effective armed force of Volunteers would be encamped there to deal with any emergency which might arise and to have men on the spot when the arms ship arrived. But unfortunately this intention was not carried out, for while on a visit to Belfast in March 1916, I was served with an order under the Defence of the Realm Act forbidding me to return to the counties of Cork and Kerry and confining me strictly to the city of Belfast. On the following morning I went to Dublin and reported to Seán McDermott, showed him the order and stated that I proposed to ignore it, slip off to Limerick and remain under cover in the Limerick and Clare district so as to be on hand when the arms ship reached Tralee. I mentioned the weekend camp and explained my plans.

McDermott discussed the position with me for some time and finally refused to agree to my proposals. He argued that such action on my part would immediately arouse the suspicions of the British authorities. Their attention would be directed to Kerry, a hue and cry would be raised and an intensive search to discover my whereabouts would ensue, every movement of the Volunteers in Kerry would be watched and the whole plan of operations might be endangered. He stated: 'I must return to Belfast, obey the order and sever all connection with Kerry until the Rising took place. I could then make every effort to reach Kerry and take my place with the Volunteers, but until then I was not to make any move.'

I could not get him to alter his decision and so I had to return to Belfast and obey the order as directed. It is only fair to state that after-events seemed to prove that McDermott had been correct in his judgment, for from the day of my return to Belfast I was kept under the closest surveillance by the CID. Detectives took up positions within a few yards of my home. When I moved out I was followed closely, often within arms reach. I had had previous experience of being shadowed but never so closely or so tenaciously. There seemed no way to elude their vigilance and so things remained until Easter.

I was unaware of what was happening in Kerry but I was confident that the Volunteers would be ready when the time came.

The history of the voyage of the *Aud* to Tralee Bay has been vividly described by Captain Spindler, and Captain Monteith has similarly dealt with the events, which followed his arrival with Casement on Banna Strand, but when I first heard of these happenings my feelings can better be imagined than described. I thought of what would have happened had a party of Volunteers been in camp close by when the ship arrived and if Casement and his comrades had found our men ready to give immediate assistance when they came ashore. However, there was no weekend camp and I remembered that McDermott did not like the idea of that camp. He seemed to think it would be dangerous. I was quite confident that it would not arouse any suspicions. I don't think he was satisfied and orders may have been given to cancel any such arrangement. This, of course, is only surmise on my part, for I did not know what action was taken in Kerry after my interview with McDermott.

A point arises as to why the ship had orders to arrive between Holy Thursday and Easter Sunday and why those orders were changed and directions given that she was not to arrive until Easter Sunday night. I think that the explanation is simple, for if my memory serves me right, there was at first an intention to fix the Rising for Good Friday and that later on it was decided not to act until Easter Sunday. The landing of such a large quantity of arms and their distribution could not take place without a clash with the British authorities. This would probably have put the British on the alert and consequently the surprise effect, with all its advantages, would have been lost. It was hoped to have all Volunteer forces occupying their allotted positions without raising any suspicions. Obviously then the landing of the arms must not take place before the Volunteers were ready to strike. The pity is that the ship had no wireless and that her captain was unaware of the change in his orders. On the other hand the Volunteers in Kerry were unable to make any move before the time fixed in view of their strict orders. This latter point was stressed by Mr Con Collins in an article published in *The Kerryman* some years ago.

I have been informed by Seán Fitzgibbon, who was a staff captain in Dublin at the time, that he was sent down from Dublin to see Commandants Colivet in Limerick, and Stack in Tralee, in connection with the final details as to the reception and distribution of the arms. He discussed the position in Limerick with Colivet and then proceeded to Tralee, where he saw Stack. About 1,000 British troops were in Limerick and it was arranged that the Limerick Volunteers would move out to North Kerry. The Clare men would cross the Shannon and join up with the Volunteers at Listowel. The combined force would take over that town, capture and disarm the police, take the police station and occupy the railway station. When the train with the arms and the Volunteer guard from Tralee arrived at Listowel the Clare men would join it and proceed north to contact the Limerick men. In this way it was hoped to be strong enough to fight off successfully any British forces which might attempt to seize the train and capture the arms. Having settled details with Stack, Fitzgibbon returned to Limerick on the Wednesday night to check up with Colivet and arrange some details at that end.

It is clear that the Kerry Volunteers carried out their part of the plans as instructed. The only blame, if any, due to them is that they, like good soldiers, obeyed their instructions to the letter. In the stress of the events which took place on Good Friday less disciplined men and weaker leaders could not have borne the strain and would have taken precipitate action. The pledge of secrecy and the strict instructions not to disclose the plans before the time to strike had arrived, along with the confusion which orders and counter orders gave rise to, placed the Kerry Volunteers in the terrible predicament which Monteith so ably describes in his account of the position which he found in Tralee. As I have already stated, the success of an effective and sustained Rising of the Volunteers throughout the country depended on the successful landing and distribution of the arms. Great credit is due to Captain Spindler and his gallant crew for their wonderful achievement in bringing their ship through all dangers to the appointed place at the time arranged. If only he had known of the changed plans in time there is no doubt but that his courage and initiative would have enabled him to complete his mission successfully and deliver the arms to the Volunteers.

Before ending this narrative I think it right to refer to the difference of opinion amongst the members of the Volunteer executive in regard to the Rising. Some of those who strenuously opposed the contemplated action were men who had given many years of unselfish service in the national cause. They had been most active in organising and arming the Volunteers. They were not averse to the use of armed force to obtain freedom – on the contrary, they had used every effort to prepare for such action. Their objections to the plans were based on military grounds alone. It was a question of strategy and tactics – the most effective way of using the forces at their disposal so as to attain their objective. They favoured the use of guerrilla tactics, rather than to stake all on the result of a stand-up fight or pitched battle between the small forces of badly-armed Volunteers and the well-armed, well-equipped and much superior forces which the British would be able to muster for a quick decision. They believed that action by the British to disarm and suppress the Volunteers would arouse resentment amongst the people. It would have been looked upon as a preliminary step towards conscription and resistance by the Volunteers would have had the sympathy and support of the whole nation. By adopting guerrilla tactics to meet this attack a long sustained resistance would be possible. Such action would entail the continued use of a large body of troops in Ireland by the British, a position which would strain all her resources. If Germany won the war we would gain our objective – an Irish Republic; but if Britain won our sustained revolt would have strengthened our position so much that we could hardly fail to get a hearing at the Peace Conference, and would obtain at least Dominion status for all Ireland. Such was the position amongst the members of the Volunteer executive, and it was this serious difference of opinion amongst men whose sincerity was unquestionable which caused the confusion. Each side strove to convince the other of the justice and merit of their viewpoint; the one as to the absolute necessity to strike without delay – to make the sacrifice, be it ever so great – and the other side striving to stay the blow which they honestly feared could only bring disaster. As for the rank and file of the Volunteers they were ready and willing to follow their leaders in whatever course was decided. They proved their courage in Easter Week and their tenacity, determination and resource were clearly demonstrated in the guerrilla fighting in the following years.

The leaders of Easter Week in spite of all opposition made their fateful decision. They sacrificed themselves willingly in the sincere belief that such a sacrifice was necessary to save the nation's life. Their sacrifice roused the national spirit, other men came forward to carry on their work. The IRA, adopting the guerrilla tactics, won a political and military victory, but we have not yet gained all our objective – the unity of the country and the restoration of the language have yet to be achieved. The battle for the language must be fought by the present generation. It is the most vital struggle and on its success depends the life of the Irish national success can only be achieved by waging the battle with all the vigour loyalty and grim determination which characterised the men of the IRA who by their efforts won for us the liberty we now enjoy. Will the present generation prove equal to the task or will it have to bear the shame and disgrace of being the first generation of Irish men and women who failed their country in its hour of need? God grant that it may not fail!

CASEMENT AND HIS COMING TO KERRY

by VOLUNTEER

WHILST THE *AUD* cruised off Inishtooskert on Holy Thursday night, awaiting the pilot boat that never came, she was sighted by the German submarine, U-19, bringing Sir Roger Casement, Captain Robert Monteith, commander of Casement's Irish Brigade, and Sergeant Beverley of the brigade, to Ireland. This important statement is made by Captain Monteith in his book, *Casement's Last Adventure*. Particular attention is directed to it because of the contradictory opinion expressed by the late Pádraig S. Ó Cathail in an article which follows. According to Monteith the captain of the U-boat decided that it would be unwise to contact the arms ship but cruised about for some hours waiting vainly for two green lights, the pilot boat signal to the arms ship agreed upon with the German government. Eventually, the German commander advised the Irishmen that he could not risk his submarine by remaining in that locality any longer and he accordingly headed for Tralee Bay at top speed on the surface. Casement and his comrades tried vainly to hide their disappointment, and Monteith suggests that it was then apparent that something had gone seriously amiss with the plans for landing the arms. Dawn was almost at hand when three exhausted men scrambled up the beach at Banna, having battled through stormy seas for an hour-and-a-half in a small row boat in which they put off the submarine. Huge breakers struck the boat and caused her to capsize near land, and all three having narrowly escaped drowning, were famished and exhausted when they crawled ashore. None of them had eaten much for several days, and all had been without sleep for twenty-four hours. They showed signs of physical and nervous strain, particularly Casement who had been in poor health for some years. He was barely conscious when land was reached, and until dragged to safety by Captain Monteith he lay below high water mark with the sea lapping his body from head to foot. Such was the home-coming of Casement, one of Ireland's most patriotic and unselfish sons.

Roger David Casement was born on 1 September 1864, at Doyle's Cottage, Sandycove, Dublin. His father, Roger Casement, a captain in the Antrim militia, came of an Ulster Protestant family, whilst his mother, Annie Jephson, was a Catholic until her marriage, after which she ceased to practise. Her four children were brought up as Protestants. Roger was educated in Ballymena, and was eighteen years of age when he took up his first post with a Liverpool shipping company. He spent two years in Liverpool before travelling to South Africa in one of his company's steamers.

Although Casement entered the British Consular Service rather by chance, and at a comparatively late age, he attained tremendous prestige and authority in British diplomacy. In 1902 he was appointed to undertake a thorough investigation of the Congo, and performed that highly dangerous task with such courage and ability that the British government issued his report as a White Paper. It became the principal evidence in the Great Powers' attack upon the Congo administration of King Leopold of Belgium. Eight years later, following a series of rapid promotions, Casement was deputed to conduct a still more difficult investigation in the swampy valley of the Putumayo river. Following this assignment, in which he was constantly exposed to the danger of death, he issued a ruthless report upon the conditions of the rubber industry in the Putumayo. This was published as an unanswerable document, and issued to all embassies to bring pressure to bear upon Peru. The constant strain of these two investigations, which obtained an immediate improvement in the treatment of natives, both on the Congo and on the Putumayo, reduced Roger Casement to a nervous wreck. At the age of forty-eight he retired from the Consular Service with a knighthood, an international reputation, and a small pension as his only means of livelihood for the few years he could still expect to live with his shattered constitution.

Within a few months of his return to Ireland Casement became one of the principal organisers of the Irish Volunteers which he helped to found. Like many other Ulster Protestants in Irish history, he had developed strong nationalist views early in life. As early as 1903 he had become intimately associated with a group of advanced nationalists, many of them Protestants like himself, in east Ulster. He was convinced that self-government would never be won for Ireland by constitutional means, and a little more than six months after the formation of the Irish Volunteers, in Dublin in December 1913, he set out for America to openly enlist the sympathies of Irishmen in the United States with the Irish Volunteer Movement in which he had taken such an active part. He left Ireland on 2 July 1914, and Glasgow on 4 July in the *Cassandra* as a second-class emigrant to Montreal. He chose that route in order to avoid publicity and possible interviews at New York, and the attention of British spies whose agents in Ireland had been following him since early 1914. Casement reached New York about 19 July and quickly made contact with the Fenian, John Devoy, and with Joe McGarrity, and others. He had spoken at two public meetings in the States when war broke out. A lucrative post was then his for the taking, provided that he was willing to return home to the British service and, incidentally, to assist in the Empire's assault upon the liberty of his country. Letters to this effect were to sent him from several quarters. Far from responding to the calls on his British 'patriotism' proffered with both hands, Sir

Roger Casement had already determined his stand on the outbreak of hostilities. To keep Ireland out of the war so far as it was possible for one man to do so, became for him the immediate call of duty. He accordingly wrote an open letter to Irishmen to remain neutral in answer to John Redmond's recruiting appeal that they should 'flock to the colours'. That letter appeared in the *Irish Independent* of 5 October 1914. At the same time Sir Roger determined to travel to Germany and look after Irish interests there, and to foster them. He thus became Ireland's first ambassador of modern times, and travelled with credentials from Bernstorff, the German ambassador at Washington.

Casement's immediate difficulty was to reach Germany from America. The British authorities had been accustomed for years to watch the movements of all prominent Irishmen at home in Ireland, and of all leading Irish-Americans in the United States. Casement had been the object of considerable espionage whilst in America and, accordingly, when he had taken his decision to travel to Germany, he was forced to adopt a disguise, and a false name and identity, in order to cross the ocean. These matters were speedily effected through the good offices of some leading Irish-Americans. He decided to go first to Norway, and as a double precaution, engaged as his servant a sailor named Adler Christensen, a Norwegian whom he had helped. They boarded the *Oscar II* at Hoboken, on Thursday, 15 October, and although the British navy had eight battleships or cruisers out looking for him, Casement arrived at Christiania on 29 October. British agents were close upon his heels, however, and the *Oscar II* had not docked many hours in Christiania before Adler Christensen was approached by an agent of the British Ambassador to Norway, Mr M. de C. Findlay, who offered him £5,000 and safe conduct, provided that Casement was delivered to the British authorities either dead or alive. This offer was later advanced to £10,000, but the Norwegian's loyalty to the man who had befriended him was not for sale.

On 30 October 1914, Casement left Christiania for Berlin, where he was soon received by German Under Secretary for State Zimmerman, and Count Wedel, to whom he outlined his mission to Germany. Germany accorded him all the courtesies of an ambassador, and he was constantly in touch with the German foreign office. He drafted an agreement on behalf of the Irish nation which was signed by Zimmerman on behalf of the Imperial German government, and which included in its provisions the recognition of a free Ireland and permission for the formation of an Irish Brigade from the Irish internees in Germany. The formation of the brigade was denounced in the allied press as 'black treachery', and received more space than did the defection of Red Russia. The men who joined the Irish Brigade in Germany received no pay from the Germans. They were asked by Sir Roger Casement to fight in Ireland and for Ireland only against her old enemy, England.

Casement's work in Germany created an immediate and lasting effect so far as Ireland was concerned. Up to the time of his reception by the German government, Ireland was looked upon as the natural provider of cannon-fodder and vital food supplies for England in time of war. Casement showed the world that Ireland was not a British province but a nation nationally conscious. To the military commanders of the Central Powers Ireland took on a new significance in the international scheme of things. The British commanders saw this too. Unfortunately, Casement's health, which had cracked under the rigours of his early life, broke down completely soon after his arrival in Germany. He was repeatedly laid up in bed for weeks and, consequently, unable to press forward his mission with all the energy he wished to employ.

Towards the end of November 1915, Casement brought a new organiser to the Irish Brigade. He was Robert Monteith, an Irishman who had served with the British army during the Boer War. Because of Volunteer activities the British had dismissed him from his employment in the Ordnance Department, Island Bridge, Dublin,

on 12 November 1914. Not content with that they also ordered him
to leave his home at 6, Palmerston Buildings, Broadstone, Dublin,
at thirty-six hours notice. The order served on him prevented him
from living in the vicinity of any defended port or prescribed area.
Having conferred with Thomas J. Clarke and James Connolly, as
to his course of action, Monteith moved to Limerick city, where
he organised the Volunteers until August 1915 when, following a
further meeting with Thomas J. Clarke, it was decided by Volunteer
headquarters to send him to Germany to assist Sir Roger Casement.
With the permission of the British, who considered that he had
probably had enough of Volunteer activity, Monteith first travelled
to America with his family. After a brief stay in the United States he
stowed away on a ship bound for Christiania, Norway. In order to
provide him with food during the voyage, Adler Christensen, who
had accompanied Casement from America about a year previously,
travelled with Monteith. Christensen had been back in America
for some time. Monteith reached Norway safely, despite the fact
that the ship in which he travelled was boarded by the British,
thoroughly searched and detained at Kirkwall in the Orkney Islands,
for five days. After further adventures whilst evading police and
customs officers in Norway, Sweden and Denmark, he arrived in
Germany and was soon in contact with Casement, who was at that
time recuperating from illness. Monteith immediately arranged to
have the men of the Casement brigade trained in machine gunnery,
knowing that a company of well-trained machine gunners would be
invaluable in the event of a landing in Ireland.

This work and other routine matters proceeded until one day in
March 1916, when Casement was ill in a Bavarian hospital, an urgent
message from the German general staff awaited Captain Monteith.
It requested him to proceed without delay to Berlin, where he was
informed that a dispatch had been received from Irish Revolutionary
Headquarters, relative to a proposed Rising in Ireland, and asking the
German government to help by sending munitions, field guns, gun

crews and officers; machine guns, rifles, &c. It was requested that the boat conveying the arms be accompanied by submarine escort, and that she should reach Fenit on Easter Sunday. It was also suggested that the German fleet should make a demonstration in the North Sea at the same time, and that a submarine should be detailed to Dublin Bay. Sir Roger Casement was requested to remain in Berlin as ambassador. Questioned by the Germans as to the number of rifles required, Monteith specified 100,000. Eventually, in spite of pressure by Casement and Monteith for more generous assistance, they agreed to send 20,000 rifles only, with ten machine guns and a quantity of explosives, but no field artillery, trained crews or officers. Monteith asked for English artillery, machine guns and rifles, but got none. The machine guns were of the Maxim type, bored to take German Mauser bullets. The rifles were of Russian manufacture. This entailed a dual ammunition supply which Monteith foresaw would inevitably lead to complications in action. Monteith did not ask for English arms because he thought they were in any way superior to German or other manufacture, but wanted them to ensure ammunition supply. He anticipated that before the ammunition sent by the Germans was exhausted the Irish Volunteers would have captured all they needed from the British garrisons in Ireland. Monteith also secured a million rounds of ammunition for the Howth rifles.

The ship selected to carry the arms to Ireland had been captured from the English at the outbreak of war, and the story of her voyage to Tralee Bay is told in another chapter. As the Germans would not agree to send a submarine escort with the arms ship Casement decided not to send his Irish Brigade. On the evening of 7 April, however, the German Admiralty advised Casement that it was decided to send himself, Monteith and Sergeant Beverley, to Ireland by submarine. They left Wilhelmshaven on the morning of 12 April, on the German submarine, U-20, which took them as far as Heligoland. At Heligoland they were transferred to U–19, and after a short delay set out for Ireland. The trip from Heligoland to Tralee Bay lasted five days, the submarine experiencing rough waters until she rounded the north of Ireland on the home run. On the evening of 20 April 1916, shortly after dark, the U–19 passed the mouth of the Shannon, about five miles off the coast. The Loop Head Light was barely visible on the port side. Eventually, the spot was reached where the commander judged the pilot boat to be waiting. He had said nothing of trying to find the arms ship, which Monteith declares had been sighted before dark about two miles starboard of the submarine, which, according to his statement, cruised about for several hours, trying vainly to locate the pilot boat until the commander decided to land the Irishmen near Tralee Bay.

Good Friday dawned to find Casement, Monteith and Beverley ashore at Banna, hungry and miserable in their wet clothing. Following a brief council of war it was decided to bury everything they had brought with them, with the exception of their overcoats. Two reasons dictated that course, of events. In the first place their overcoats were all their strength would permit them to carry, and, secondly, it would be unwise to be seen carrying heavy Mauser pistols, ammunition belts, field glasses and other such items as they had brought with them from Germany. They decided that it would be comparatively easy to return during the night and dig them up again. Having buried their kits the little party set out for some suitable place where Casement could lie concealed whilst Beverley and Monteith went into Tralee to procure a motor car to take him to Dublin. It was still dark as the men floundered along, wet to the skin, their teeth chattering. As the sun appeared they passed a farmhouse on the road, the gable of which was parallel with the road. Looking over the wall they saw a girl, her hair tousled and untidy, blinking at the sun and looking over the half-door. She saw them and stared in a manner that showed it was unusual for strangers to pass along the road so early in the morning. The girl's name was Mary Gorman, who afterwards was one of the principal witnesses against Casement. Of her it might be said that she knew not what she did. English propaganda and Irish politicians of the John Redmond and Tom O'Donnell persuasion, were to blame for the evidence which she gave at Casement's trial. About half a mile from the spot where Mary Gorman saw them they came to an old fort with thick-set hedges, which was thought to be the best available place of concealment for Casement. Here they took off their wet coats, sat down and rested for some time whilst they went over their plans. It was decided that in the event of one or two being captured he who should escape would send word to the Volunteers of what was coming in the arms ship, and that no consideration of the fate of his companions should turn him from that course. All three went through their coat pockets to destroy whatever papers they possessed, before Monteith and Beverley set out for Tralee. Monteith, thinking that by going into Tralee his danger of capture was greater than Casement's, gave Casement a code furnished by the German general staff before leaving Berlin. Later, when Sir Roger was arrested he contrived to throw away the code, unnoticed by the police. However, a small boy named Collins, observing his action, picked up the paper and handed it to his captors, so that it became an important link in the chain of evidence against him.

Casement's arrest came about like this. About half-an-hour after landing the boat was discovered by a farmer named John McCarthy, who called his small son and sent him off to one of the neighbours' houses to fetch Pat Driscoll, so that they might drag the boat onto the shore together. They failed to get the boat ashore, and decided to await the turn of the tide to reach it. Inside the boat they found a dagger, and close at hand, barely covered with earth and sand, they also found a tin box that was corded up. On the sand were clear traces of footprints made by the three men who landed from the boat during the night. It was apparent to McCarthy and Driscoll that whoever had arrived in the boat had got away. When McCarthy and Driscoll returned from the boat they found McCarthy's little daughter playing on the sand with three revolvers which she had picked up. Looking around further to discover anything else that might have been washed ashore, they found a bag. McCarthy took possession of all the items and sent Driscoll to Ardfert to inform the police.

Chief Constable Hearn went with another constable on bicycles to the strand, where a crowd was already gathered round the boat. McCarthy then handed over to the police the three revolvers and the dagger, and before long the police discovered three discarded life-belts, a brown handbag, and a large black bag. The tin box when opened was found to contain nine hundred rounds of revolver ammunition, and the bags contained maps and a flash lamp. The police then armed themselves with carbines and spent the morning searching for the missing men. It was after one o'clock when their search brought them to the old fort in which Casement was hidden. This was a circular stone ruin, surrounded by a deep trench. The police with their loaded carbines worked their way through and, eventually Constable Reilly caught sight of the head and shoulders of a bearded man peering over the undergrowth inside the fort. Reilly immediately covered him with his rifle, threatening to shoot him if he moved a foot. Casement gave his name as Richard Morton, and explained that he was an English artist who lived at Devon, in Buckinghamshire. The sergeant, however, noticed that the lower portion of Casement's pants was wet, and that there was sea sand on his boots. That had decided him to place the stranger under arrest, and Casement was marched on towards Ardfert until the sergeant found a boy driving a pony-trap whom he ordered to take the constable and the stranger to Mary Gorman's house where she gave evidence that he was one of the men she had seen early in the morning.

The only incriminating evidence discovered by the police was in the bags, which contained flags, rifles, ammunition, and a number of maps. The most serious evidence was the German code which the small boy Collins had seen Casement drop from behind his back as he walked from the fort with the two policemen. This when discovered left no doubt as to where Casement had come from, and he was accordingly brought to Tralee barracks, to remain there in custody. On Easter Saturday he was conveyed to Dublin by train under heavy escort. He was told of the Ballykissane drownings whilst on the train for Dublin, on arrival in which city he was immediately rushed to Dún Laoghaire and put aboard the mail boat for England. He arrived at Euston Station, London, on Easter Sunday morning, 23 April, and was there handed over to District Inspector Sandicock of Scotland Yard.

Some time prior to the Casement landing at Banna two Scotland Yard men are believed to have been sent to Kerry to arrange for the capture of those who landed. This action was taken as a result of information supplied to the British government by the American secret service who, in violation of international law, raided the office of the German minister. It will be remembered that Germany and America were not at war at that time. Amongst the documents captured in the course of the raid were some detailing the plans of the German aid to Ireland, and these were duly passed along to the British government. The British Admiralty did not make the information public but issued orders that patrol boats should be specially alert. A graphic, if rather fanciful account of how the British authorities succeeded in learning of the departure of Casement from Germany is told in Mr Hugh Cleland Hoy's book of reminiscences entitled *40, O.B.*, or *How The War Was Won* (First World War), publication of which was delayed four months by the British Admiralty. As Hoy's references to Casement and the Irish Brigade are very largely incorrect too much trust cannot be placed in his story of how the British learned of Casement's departure from Germany. According to Hoy it was not until January 1916, that the British received their first report of the formation of the brigade, whereas in fact the British press had made a great deal of capital of the story very shortly after Casement had commenced recruiting. Hoy, who was on the secretariat of the director of naval intelligence during the First World War, describes 40, O.B. as one of the best kept secrets of the war. It was a room bearing the innocent-looking number '40' on its door in a quiet wing of the old building of the Admiralty, and in it 'some of the most secret of all war work' took place in tracking enemy movements and intercepting cryptograms. According to Hoy, these reached the remarkable total of about 2,000 a day when the department was working to capacity, and none of them completely defeated the code experts. Of this mysterious department even cabinet ministers are stated to have known next to nothing. It is Hoy's belief that 'those whose work brought them into contact with the hidden activities of this essentially confidential office', were of opinion that 40, O.B. won the war. Hoy reveals that on the choice of two such simple words such as 'oats' or 'hay' flashed through the ether as the keyword of a signal, depended the tragic faith of Sir Roger Casement:

> The German wireless had been silent about Casement. Then, suddenly, 40, O.B. received a message which showed that his departure from Berlin was imminent. This was the code signal for the hour of his sailing, and was intended for John Devoy in America. The signal 'oats' was to be given the moment the submarine left with Casement on board; but if there was any hitch or delay 'hay' would be the code. Our excitement at the Admiralty may be imagined, every day – indeed, every hour – we expected to get from 40, O.B. the deciphered message containing one or other of the significant words. It came during one afternoon; it was the 12 April. In the usual batch of wireless intercepts sent on from the East Coast and decoded in 40, O.B. was one containing the word 'oats'. Casement had set out on the journey that was to end on the scaffold. In the wild, blustery dawn of Good Friday, 1916, the submarine in which he had cruised the seas nosed her way slowly inshore, to the West Coast of Ireland near Tralee Bay. Into the tiny canvas boat that was lowered from her side tumbled three men, Casement and two officers of the Irish Brigade.

'Ireland is treated today among the nations of the world as if she were a convicted criminal,' said Casement in his speech from the dock after he had been sentenced to death. 'If it be treason to fight against such an unnatural fate as this, then I am proud to be a rebel, and I shall cling to my rebellion with the last drop of my blood.' Casement knew that he would be execrated in England as a 'traitor'. He did not anticipate, however, that the British would stoop so low as to attempt to vilify his moral character. In the weeks that the appeal against his death sentence was being heard before the Court of Criminal Appeal, a deliberate campaign to discredit him on moral grounds was undertaken by Scotland Yard. At the time a strong movement was on foot to secure his reprieve, and a petition to that end had been prepared and signed by many influential persons. Furthermore, public opinion in America was very strongly against a continuation of the executions which followed the Rising, It seemed that Casement might yet cheat the gallows. The British cabinet was then greatly influenced by Ulster Carsonites who hated Casement with an all-consuming hatred that would stop at nothing to bring about his death. The attorney-general was Sir F.E. Smith, a leading member of the government, who, two years previously, had been 'galloper' to General Richardson in the Ulster Volunteers' campaign against Home Rule. His reckless speeches, both to his own constituents in Liverpool, and on the platforms of the Ulster Covenanters in Ireland, had brought him into the front rank of the younger English unionists. Smith boasted afterwards that he made his continuation in office conditional upon Casement's execution when the cabinet sat down to discuss the matter of his reprieve.

In the course of his speech from the dock, Casement declared:

> … If English authority be omnipotent – a power as Mr Gladstone phrased it, that reaches to the very ends of the earth – Irish hope exceeds the dimensions of that power, excels its authority, and renews with each generation the claims of the last. The cause that begets this indomitable persistency, the faculty of persevering through the centuries of misery the remembrance of lost liberty: this, surely, is the

noblest cause men ever strove for, ever lived or, ever died for. If this be the cause I stand here today indicted for and convicted of sustaining, then I stand in a goodly company and right noble succession.

While in prison Casement became a convert to the Catholic faith. The following letter, written to a close friend of Casement's by the priest who attended him during the minutes before his execution, tells how Casement died:

I know you will be glad to learn that your friend, Roger Casement was reconciled to the Church and made his First Confession on last Wednesday evening. He died with all the faith and piety of an Irish peasant woman, and had so far as I can judge, all the dispositions, faith, hope, charity, contrition and resignation to God's will to meet his Creator. He marched to the scaffold with the dignity of a prince and towered straight as an arrow over all of us. He feared not death and he prayed to the last.

KERRY IN HOLY WEEK 1916 AND AFTER

by OLD SOLDIER

WHEN CAPTAIN MONTEITH and Sergeant Beverley parted company with Casement at McKenna's Fort, near Banna, they set out for Tralee and reached the town about seven o'clock on the morning of Good Friday. There were few people on the streets at that hour, and all the shops were still closed. Neither man knew anybody in the town, not even the name of the commander of the local Volunteers. Their only hope was to meet someone wearing the tri-colour, or to find some shop displaying revolutionary emblems. Eventually, they saw posters advertising *The Irish Volunteer* and *The Workers' Republic* outside a hairdresser's saloon. The proprietor's name turned out to be George Spicer, and he informed them that he worked both newsagent's and hairdresser's shops. Ascertaining that they needed a shave he told them that his son would be down in a minute to shave them. Whilst awaiting Mr Spicer's son they stood at the shop counter, looking over the various papers displayed on it. Taking up *The Irish Volunteer* and *Honesty*, Monteith remarked, 'You sell the right sort of papers.' Mr Spicer looked inquiringly and replied, 'Oh yes, sir, I sell all sorts.' It was evident that Monteith had made him suspicious by his remark, and further attempts to open up conversation failed. Time was flying, so Monteith decided to hazard all on a chance. 'Look here, I am in a hole,' he declared, 'and have to trust you as an Irishman to help me out. I must see the commander of the local Volunteer corps at once: can you give me his name and address?'

George Spicer seemed puzzled, and his manner showed that he did not trust Monteith. That was only to be expected, as the police were so unscrupulous in their dealings with the people and so greedy in their efforts to entrap the Volunteer leaders that every stranger was regarded with suspicion, especially if he asked questions. George Spicer wanted to know why they should have come to him for information. Before Monteith could answer, Mr Spicer's daughter, Hanna, now Mrs William Allister, who had, although unseen, been listening to the conversation, came into the shop. She regarded Monteith sharply, and then said to her father, 'Don't give these people any information, father.'

By way of explanation Monteith said to her: 'I don't blame you for doubting me, madam, but please let me explain. I have a message for the commander of the Tralee Volunteers; this message is so urgent that we had to swim to get here.' Drawing to her attention his wet clothes, Monteith went on: 'You need not give me the commander's name or address: I merely want word conveyed to him that a man named Murray has arrived with a very urgent message, a message which must be acted upon at once.'

Miss Spicer considered a moment, and then sent her brother to Austin Stack, commander of the Volunteers. Stack, who had never heard of a man named Murray connected with the revolutionary movement, sent back word that he would be down in an hour. Monteith declared that his message was too urgent for such delay, and again sent young Spicer to stress the immediate nature of his business. To the second message a reply was sent that Stack would be to hand in half-an-hour. Whilst awaiting Stack, George Spicer's son accompanied Monteith and Beverley to a place nearby where the lady of the house served them with tea and delicious bread, butter and eggs, the first food they had tasted for over twenty-four hours, and their first square meal since leaving Germany. The pleasant fare would have tasted much better had they not thought of poor Casement away out in McKenna's Fort, wet, cold and hungry, waiting for the car that was to take him to Dublin. When they had finished their meal Monteith and Beverley at once returned to Spicer's shop, to find that Austin Stack had not yet arrived. There was nothing to do but wait. Miss Hanna Spicer invited the men into her sitting-room, and did everything in her power to make them comfortable. She brought them two complete sets of underclothing and a pair of trousers for Monteith. She provided Beverley with a suit of clothes, in addition to a cap which fitted him splendidly. Someone also gave Beverley a mackintosh, and the clothes appeared to make a new man of him. The men changed and warmed themselves before a glowing fire. Monteith fell asleep in his chair and George Spicer then took him upstairs and made him comfortable on a sofa. He was unable to walk owing to an injury to his foot, sustained when attempting to scuttle the small boat in which they had landed at Banna. The foot had become so swollen that he could not get it into his boot. His right hand was also badly injured.

Whilst Monteith rested on the sofa some men came in whom he did not know, but for whom Miss Hanna Spicer vouched. They chatted until the arrival of Stack. Stack was accompanied by Con Collins who recognised Monteith at once. Everybody left the room whilst Monteith explained matters to Stack and Collins; told them that Casement doubted the intentions of the German government in the matter of aiding the Volunteers, and that being ignorant of existing conditions in Ireland he wished to go to Dublin to meet the Provisional Committee of the Volunteers. Stack immediately sent a man to procure a motor car in order to go to Casement's assistance. Whilst awaiting the arrival of the motor car Monteith told of the nature of the munitions which the German government had sent, viz. 20,000 rifles with bayonets and ammunition; ten machine guns, ammunition for the Howth rifles together with a supply of explosives and incendiary bombs. He also informed them that field guns or crews were not coming, nor were the officers asked for in the dispatch to Berlin, and that the arms had no escort. Monteith, in his book, *Casement's Last Adventure*, states that he then asked Stack about the non-appearance of the pilot boat, and that Stack replied that as far as his instructions went the ship was not due until Sunday night. Word came that the car was ready and Monteith directed Beverley to go with Stack and Collins as a guide to Casement's hiding place. Miss Hanna Spicer accompanied them in order to give the appearance of a pleasure trip. That was the last that Monteith ever saw of Stack, Collins and Beverley. That night he heard of the arrest of Stack and Collins, and of Beverley's escape. The same evening he learned of the arrest of Casement in one of the Tralee evening newspapers. With Casement in the hands of the enemy, it became Monteith's immediate duty to send a message through to Volunteer headquarters to advise on the extent of the German assistance. Through the medium of a Dominican Friar, Fr Ryan, OP, Tralee, a message had also come through from Casement in the police barracks to local Volunteer headquarters, to get word to Dublin detailing the inadequacy of the German aid. The report was put in writing against Monteith's judgment, and copies handed to William Mullins of Moyderwell, brigade quartermaster, and to William T. Partridge, of the Citizen Army. Monteith addressed them to Eoin MacNeill, but on the instructions of the Tralee Volunteer leaders they were not delivered to him. They were, instead, taken to James Connolly at Liberty Hall. Monteith was not aware that during his absence from the country Eoin MacNeill and Bulmer Hobson had become mere figureheads, and the Tralee men did not advise him of that development.

Austin Stack with Collins and Beverley having set out for Banna to attempt to locate Casement and get him safely away to Dublin, had not travelled very far when they found themselves beset by groups of police at every turn. The British were very much on the alert and the little party was forced to return to Tralee after many escapades. There they separated to avoid suspicion and Stack proceeded to the Rink. Collins was quickly spotted by a detective and taken in custody by the Royal Irish Constabulary. A fake message was later sent to Stack stating that his comrade, Collins, desired to see him urgently in a certain house. The police were waiting at the address quoted knowing that Stack would never turn a deaf ear to a comrade's request. Thus was the arrest of the Kerry leader accomplished.

When news of the arrest of Casement, Stack and Collins reached the Rink many of the officers urged that an immediate attack should be made on the police barracks to effect rescue. Vice-Commandant P.J. Cahill had the greatest difficulty in holding the men in check, in accordance with orders issued from the revolutionary headquarters in Dublin which had impressed upon the Kerry leaders that on no account was there a shot to be fired or any action taken which might lead to a flare-up before the hour appointed by Dublin.

On Good Friday night Monteith slept in an upstairs room in the Ancient Order of Hibernians Hall. Whilst he slept the Volunteers had stationed an armed sentry to guard him. Next day he learned that the town was swarming with police, and that they were still coming in on all sorts of conveyances, motor cars, jaunting cars, traps, bicycles, and on foot. Two train-loads of troops had arrived in Tralee during the night and details patrolled the town regularly. About ten o'clock on Saturday night three Volunteers came in, and having provided a disguise for Monteith, went with him to the Rink, the headquarters of the Volunteers. There he found that a group of twelve or fourteen armed men had been placed on guard, and there also he met the vice-commandant of the Volunteers, P.J. Cahill. According to Monteith, whilst talking over matters with the vice-commandant, he remarked: 'Now that Stack has been arrested you will take command to-morrow.'

'No, you will take command,' replied the vice-commandant, adding that he was not qualified to do so, having acted only as secretary to the battalion with no military experience whatever.

Monteith pointed out that he would be at great disadvantage as commander of the Tralee men whom he did not know, and because he knew none of the plans of the leaders and had no topographical knowledge of Tralee and its surroundings. Following some deliberation and further discussion Monteith declared that he considered it best to take command and make what arrangements he could, especially as the vice-commandant insisted and said that he had orders to that effect Monteith's first action as commander was to meet the other officers and talk matters over. 'They were splendid fellows,' he recollected later in his book *Casement's Last Adventure*, 'spoiling for a fight, but they had not much training.'

Monteith began to map out a general plan of operations for Sunday, and having enquired what plans had already been made for the fight was told that Stack had made them all but that none of his subordinates knew anything about them. They had a general idea of taking military barracks, police stations, telegraph offices and railway stations. This completed they were to run a special train to Fenit and unload the arms ship, after which they were to dispatch arms and ammunition to Killarney, Limerick and Galway. His officers estimated that Monteith would have about three hundred men under his command, of whom about two hundred would have firearms. As there were five hundred military in the barracks at that stage, and about two hundred fully-armed police in and about the town, all on the alert, it was obvious that a full day's work lay ahead. Having obtained this information Monteith asked for a pilot boat to be sent to the arms ship, and that all the men be ordered to stand ready for instant action. It soon transpired that these things could not be done as all boatmen were watched and no boats could get out beyond the British patrols. Furthermore, it was declared impossible to get the men together that night. Monteith asked for a map of Tralee and district but none of the officers had one. Eventually, a map was found but it was out of date and, consequently, useless. The military situation was desperate, as untrained and half-armed boys had little hope of success against regular infantry greatly superior in numbers and in armaments. However, the day had come and all were determined to make the best fight.

Meanwhile Sergeant Beverley, who had landed from the submarine with Casement and Monteith, was arrested in Tralee, on Saturday evening. Within half-an-hour he had told the whole story of the landing to the police, and betrayed his companions in return for a promise that he should go unpunished. At the subsequent trials in London his name was given as Bailey.

At seven o'clock on Easter Sunday morning Monteith dispatched scouts to Fenit to report on the arms ship; to Ardfert, and to patrol the town of Tralee. One, who had a motor car, was dispatched to Killarney with orders to get in touch with the commander of the Volunteers there, and to find out what his plan of operations was. Owing to subsequent events Monteith had no reply to that message, and never saw the messenger again. Soon afterwards Brigade Quartermaster William Mullins of Moyderwell arrived with a reply to Monteith's dispatch to Dublin. The reply came from James Connolly, and its nature was to go ahead as everything was all right. Monteith derived some comfort from the fact that Volunteer headquarters in Dublin knew exactly how they stood with regard to the German aid. About that time he also learned of the tragic happening at Ballykissane Pier, dealt with elsewhere in this volume. About 8.30 a.m. two scouts arrived from Dingle, reporting that the Dingle contingent was on the march and would arrive probably about 11 a.m. Monteith then gave orders that if there was any money in the funds it should be spent at once to provide a good meal for the Dingle men. About the same time the women of the Cumann na mBan arrived at the Rink and bustled about providing breakfasts. The Dingle men came in on schedule; they were over one hundred strong, foot-sore, weary and hungry, having marched all the way with the expectation of a hard fight at the end of their journey. They were immediately attended to by the women, and after a meal most of them stretched themselves on benches or on the hard floor, and were soon asleep. Whilst the Dingle men were eating, the Ballymacelligott company, numbering forty men, arrived. Smaller parties came from other districts until, eventually, Monteith had about three hundred and twenty men under his command. Roughly estimated, two hundred had rifles, Lee Enfields, Martini Enfield Carbines, Mauser rifles, double barrel fowling pieces and single barrel shotguns. Some had revolvers, and a few rifle men were also equipped with bayonets. Eighty per cent of the men were young and athletic, splendid material; the remaining twenty per cent, were boys and elderly men. The most wonderful part of the whole business was to see boys of fourteen and seventeen years of age marching in without as much as a walking stick to defend themselves, but all in the sure and certain hope of beating the hateful English.

Rain had been falling steadily since eleven o'clock, and the downpour increased in volume towards noon. Soon after this a man was admitted to the Rink, whom Monteith recognised as Lieutenant Patrick Whelan, of the Limerick City Regiment. Whelan stated that he had been sent to carry orders to the commander of the Tralee men that all operations for Easter Sunday had been cancelled. Lieutenant Whelan quoted as his authority, The O'Rahilly, who had that morning motored from Dublin and stopped in Limerick city on his way to Cork with the countermand. Whelan was in turn dispatched by the Limerick commander with this information to Tralee. The Volunteers gave expression to their natural feelings of disappointment, on learning this latest development, but like good soldiers they faithfully carried out Monteith's orders to exercise caution and patience lest there should be an incident with the police which might lead to a general engagement. Monteith then handed back command of the Volunteers to Vice-Commandant P.J. Cahill, and determined to get out of town as quickly as possible. The police had been searching for him since Friday, and by that time quite a number of people knew that he was the odd man of the three who had landed from the submarine. If captured by the British nothing could save him from the gallows.

It was decided that in order to show reason for the mobilisation of the Volunteers an effort should be made to carry out some military exercises. Accordingly the men drilled in a nearby field, and at five o'clock in the afternoon they returned to the Rink again. There they were made comfortable and provided with food by the Cumann na mBan. After dark Monteith marched out of town with the Ballymacelligott corps, who provided him with an overcoat, uniform cap, bandolier, and an old hammerless double-barrel shotgun which had been used for drilling purposes. Unnoticed, Monteith fell into the ranks of the Ballymacelligott men, only two of whom, in addition to the commander, were aware of his presence and identity. These two men were placed one on either side of him. As they marched out of the Rink, opposite which a bright gas lamp burned, the men were subjected to the scrutiny of police on each side, but owing to their rapid pace and blinding rain, Monteith passed unnoticed. As the Ballymacelligott men marched through the town they were accompanied by the Strand Street Band and a company of Tralee Volunteers which Vice-Commandant P.J. Cahill dispatched with them as an extra safeguard in case of Monteith's detection and attempted arrest. In one quarter of the town they encountered 'separationist' women who booed them derisively and followed them for at least a quarter of a mile. On arrival at Ballymacelligott the corps started to break up and go to their homes. Every few hundred yards one or more dropped out of the ranks, until Monteith was left with three companions, the captain, Lieutenant John Byrnes, and Volunteer Tom McEllistrim. Lieutenant Byrnes was awaited by his wife and sister although they did not expect him back that night. As Monteith wrote subsequently in his book *Casement's Last Adventure*, 'Women the world over have a fashion of waiting the return of the men to the household, even when they have a foreboding that they might not return.' Mrs Byrnes served a splendid supper, and later

Monteith was taken to Tommy McEllistrim's house, whilst a safer location was sought.

On Tuesday at mid-day Monteith heard the first news of the Rising. Tommy McEllistrim had been into town and returned with news that a meeting would be held to decide on the advisability, of Tralee going out. He also said the vice-commandant told him that if they went out Monteith would have to take command. On receipt of this information Monteith said that he would rather not take command, but that he would march with the Ballymacelligott corps, and give all the assistance in his power. He stated that he could command the Ballymacelligott men and assist the Tralee vice-commandant by making a flank or rear attack on whatever party he might engage, or carry out such other action as the vice-commandant might order. There was a considerable quantity of cartridges in Tommy McEllistrim's house, partially filled, that is capped and charged with powder but not filled with shot. These cartridges were suitable for rifles of the Ballymacelligott corps which was armed with single-loader shotguns. Tommy McEllistrim had the necessary wads and shot as well as a machine for filling them. He informed Monteith that there were an additional five hundred cartridges in a shop in a nearby village, for the purpose of being filled. Monteith instructed him to go at once to get the other five hundred and distribute them to his company, and then find out the decision of the Tralee Volunteer council. Tommy McEllistrim returned dejectedly that night as he brought neither cartridges nor orders to turn out.

Following enquiries next day about a stranger in Ballymacelligott, the captain of the company and Lieutenant Byrnes brought Monteith further on, to the house of the late Arthur Lenihan. Here Monteith remained until the following Saturday when news came that Lenihan's house was in danger of being searched. That afternoon Monteith moved to the house of Seán Tadhg Óg Lenihan, an old recluse, who lived in Glenaneenta, where next day Arthur Lenihan came to him with news of the surrender in Dublin.

Some time afterwards Fr O'Flaherty of Brosna was approached and asked to help in getting Monteith away. Fr O'Flaherty consented and motored to Glenaneenta taking with him a clerical suit in which Monteith dressed. They had many exciting adventures on their way to Limerick, including an encounter with Royal Irish Constabulary searching motor cars at Headley's Bridge and the evading of a county inspector. The Jesuits harboured Monteith for some time. He left County Limerick in the middle of November for Cork city where he got on a boat for Liverpool from whence he subsequently worked his passage as a fireman on a ship for the USA. Monteith sent Seán Tadhg Óg many gifts, the last one, £100, arriving two days after the old man's funeral.

Austin Stack and Con Collins who had been arrested and taken to the Tralee police barracks on Good Friday afternoon were removed to Spike Island, which they reached late on Easter Saturday night. They were immediately taken to one of the dungeons, and by lantern light, stripped to the skin and thoroughly searched by soldiers. Then they were left in complete darkness and without their clothes. During the days which followed they were subjected to similar cruelties and indignities; at no time were they permitted light, ventilation or intercourse. After some days the men made contact and determined to fight for better treatment. Con Collins opened the campaign by demanding the attention of the prison doctor. The demand was not acceded to, and was repeated for several days to an officer who made entries in a notebook but spoke not a word. Eventually, the exasperated Collins backed up his demand by plastering his breakfast, which consisted of cocoa and other slops, about the face of the officer. The doctor turned up immediately after this incident, and ten days later the prisoners were transferred to the Richmond barracks, Dublin, where they were tried by court martial and sentenced to penal servitude for life.

Shortly after the suppression of the Rising, British forces comprising cavalry, infantry and police, turned out in Kerry for wholesale arrests of prominent members of the Irish Volunteer organisation. Detachments halted opposite each house in which arrests were to be effected, and amongst those taken into custody were: J. O'Donnell, MCC; P.J. Cahill, merchant's secretary; Thomas Slattery, RDC; P.J. Hogan, RDC; T.J. McCarthy, engineer and surveyor; E. Barry, CWS employee; Michael Doyle, carriage carpenter; Daniel Healy, time-keeper; Dan Finn, Urban Council employee; William Farmer, labourer; J.P. O'Donnell, publican; William Mullins, clerk; Tim O'Sullivan, labourer; Joseph O'Brien, plumber; Florence Walsh, clerk; Joseph Vale, clerk; William Drummy, insurance agent; Maurice Griffin, *The Kerryman* Ltd., all of Tralee. The following Tralee men had already been held in custody: Thomas McMahon, Patrick Landers, mechanical engineer; Servelus Jones, tailor; Austin Stack, A.W. Cotton, J. Melinn, John Dunne, Michael J. O'Connor, M.J. Moriarty, T. Moriarty. Jack O'Reilly, Tralee, Technical School Instructor, was arrested in Ballinasloe.

The following arrests were made throughout the county: Daniel O'Mahony, commander, Castleisland Volunteers; David J. Griffin, adjutant; Michael Reidy, Castleisland; William McSweeney, Castleisland; Thomas Fitzgerald, publican, Castleisland; John Byrne, creamery manager, Ballymacelligott; Thomas McEllistrim, farmer's son, Ballymacelligott; Thomas O'Connor, farmer's son, Ballymacelligott; Brian O'Connor, RDC, Gortglass; T.T. O'Connor, Cordal; Brian O'Connor, Scartaglin; Henry Spring, RDC, Firies; Michael Moriarty, teacher, and his brother, James Moriarty, carpenter, Dingle; Michael O'Connor, fisherman, Dingle; James Counihan, Annascaul; Tadhg Brosnan, Castlegregory; Frank Goodwin, pilot, Maharees, Castlegregory; Michael Duhig, Castlegregory; Abel Mahony, Castlegregory; Michael McKenna, Castlegregory; James Kennedy, Castlegregory; Daniel O'Shea, Castlegregory; J. Goodwin, pilot, Castlegregory; Timothy Ring, Caherciveen; John F. O'Shea, Portmagee; Tom O'Donoghue, Renard; Maurice O'Connor, Farrandoctor, Currans; Mortimer O'Connor, Abbeydorney; James

Sugrue, draper's assistant, Listowel; Dick Fitzgerald, Killarney; T. Spillane, Killarney; J. Sullivan, Killarney.

The Tralee prisoners were warned by the officer in command that if there was any attempt at rescue, his men had instructions to shoot to kill. This warning was hardly necessary, as the entire town was held by the military. Nineteen Kerry prisoners removed to Dublin were lodged in Richmond barracks for four or five days. Whilst there, they were well supplied with food, in marked contrast to the poor diet supplied whilst they were held in Tralee jail. After six days, on 23 May, they were marched from Richmond barracks, through the city, to the North Wall under a strong military escort. They were cheered by some people on the way to the boat, particularly at O'Connell Bridge. At the North Wall they were all huddled together in the part of the steamship *Slieve Bloom*, usually reserved for the transport of cattle. The night was rough and the journey to Holyhead was anything but enjoyable. The men reached Wakefield prison about 8.30 on the following morning, and were then allocated to different portions of the detention prison, then one of the largest in England. Few of them could have realised previously what solitary confinement really meant. They were all practically confined to their cells for twenty-three hours each day. At first they had nothing to read, smoking was strictly prohibited, and they were not allowed speak during the hour for exercise. No shaving was allowed, and the men developed long beards and matted hair. After some days the prisoners were allowed to speak at exercise, and smoking was also permitted. They were not allowed the use of a knife and fork, and had to gobble their food as best they could.

THERE WAS NO BLUNDER IN KERRY

by P.J. CAHILL

P.J. Cahill, lifelong friend of Austin Stack, was vice-commandant of the Volunteers in Tralee at the time of the Rising and gun-running. On the arrest of Stack on Good Friday he assumed command but later handed over to Captain Monteith. The article reprinted hereunder is published through the courtesy of The Kerry Champion *of which concern he was managing director until his death.*

IN AN ARTICLE *The Coming of Casement*, Captain Robert Monteith wrote:

> For the proposed Rising of Easter Week, 1916, the German Government had been asked by the Irish Republican Brotherhood to help by sending a shipload of ammunition together with officers, gun crews, machine guns, rifles and field guns. It was also recommended that Sir Roger Casement be sent to Ireland at once in a submarine, with a detailed plan for the landing of the arms.

As far as I am aware, the coming of Casement was unexpected by the leaders in Dublin. It is stated in an article written by Austin Stack:

> Monteith told me what purported to be the view of Casement with regard to the Rising itself, and this was that the attempt would be pure madness at that moment; that he had determined to come to Ireland to put his view before the leaders at home, and that if he

failed to persuade them he would do his duty as an Irish Volunteer and go out and fight with the others.

That was always my own impression, and it was also the view expressed to me by the priest who attended Casement in Tralee police barracks. In response to an inquiry, Mr George Gavan Duffy wrote me as follows:

> Your quotation from Austin is a correct statement of Roger's mind. As to the leaders in Dublin – what they were concerned about was the landing of the arms. Plunkett had seen Roger in Germany some time before, and I suppose the leaders knew he might come, but did not know his object in coming. He did try to convey to them a message that the Germans would 'let them down', and felt that he must come himself because he doubted if they had got his message or, having got it, if they really appreciated it. He believed they relied on German help much more than they actually did.

In response to a similar inquiry, Fr Joe Breen, who was Volunteer chaplain in 1916, wrote:

> In regard to the information you seek, I can say definitely that no intimation of any kind, either from official or any other source, was conveyed to Tralee about the intended landing of Casement. Had they known of it in Dublin they would surely have issued instructions to Austin to make arrangements for Casement's safety. Austin knew nothing of Casement's landing until told of it by Monteith in Tralee. I know that from my conversation with Austin in Tralee police barracks, on Easter Saturday morning, and from my subsequent conversations.

I think that the foregoing makes it quite clear that Sir Roger Casement was not expected – at least not in Kerry. With regard to the failure of the Kerry Volunteers to have the green lights (the signals agreed upon) shown, and to have the pilot at hand, there seems to have been some blunder; but that blunder was not made in Kerry, According to Monteith's article, and from the book published by the German commander of the *Aud*, there appears to be little doubt that the Germans expected the pilot boat to be waiting from Holy Thursday evening. I am quite convinced, however, that Pearse and the other leaders in Dublin believed that the boat would not arrive in Fenit until well after 6 p.m. on Easter Sunday night. It is possible that the original arrangements with Germany were as stated by the commander of the German boat. After the Rising had taken place, I heard that the leaders had contacted Germany through America, altering their original arrangements and asking that the arms boat arrive in Fenit on Sunday night. I heard also that a message was sent from Germany stating that the *Aud* had left, but that the messenger could not get in touch with the leaders in Dublin. I have never been able to verify these facts.

In regard to a messenger whom Casement was supposed to have sent to the leaders in Dublin, advising them of his impending departure from Germany, Mrs Úna Barry, Cushendun, County Antrim, a sister of Sir Roger Casement, writes:

> I do not think that Roger had any opportunity to communicate the date of his landing to the leaders of the Volunteers. I know he tried to send a message. He told me of having sent a man ahead, one Joe McGoey; and he asked me if the man ever got to Ireland. So far I have never traced McGoey, or heard of anyone who saw him or who received any message from Roger through him. That someone was sent I feel sure, but I do not expect he ever got to Ireland. Carl Spindler, the German Captain of the *Aud* told me that his instructions were to come to Tralee Bay and there await the signal in answer to certain signals he sent out. His signals received no answer and, as you know, he was sighted and captured. As I subsequently only saw Roger alone once (there were warders present every other time) it was impossible to find out much. We tried to learn about the mysterious McGoey who was sent ahead to warn the Volunteers, but with no success.

It will be clear from letters which I quote hereunder, that all of us in Kerry who knew of the coming of the arms ship, were told that it would arrive during the night of Easter Sunday, or early on Easter Monday morning. It will be understood how vital it was for Pearse and the others to have the boat landed within a number of hours after the mobilisation and the start of the Rising which was timed all over the country for 6.30 p.m. on Easter Sunday. If the German boat was expected between Holy Thursday and Easter Sunday, it would mean that the Volunteers should remain mobilised for at least three days, and that, consequently, the British would most likely, take the initiative. This, I think, was the reason why word was sent to Germany altering the arrival date, and it will also explain why the instruction to Austin Stack as to the time of the arrival of the German boat was so definite, and why the pilot boat was not at hand on Holy Thursday night.

In a further letter to me, Fr Joe Breen wrote:

> The landing of the arms at Fenit was to take place very early on Monday morning, which was the time the *Aud* was expected. I am absolutely certain of that because I discussed all the arrangements for the actual landing and distribution of the guns with Pádraig Pearse and Austin in my own room, on the occasion of Pearse's last visit to Tralee before Easter Week. The boat therefore could not be, and was not, expected before Sunday.

For my own part I, too, was told that the boat would come in on the night of Easter Sunday, and it was only about four weeks before the Rising that I was informed. Previously Austin Stack, Fr Joe Breen and A.W. Cotton, a Volunteer instructor now resident in Dublin, had been informed of the Rising by Pearse. It was at Austin's request, I think, that Pearse gave him permission to tell me. Austin sent me to Dublin about three weeks before Easter Sunday, and there I got two boat lamps from Seán McDermott for use in the pilot boat that was to meet the *Aud*. The lamps had green glass on the outside. They were kept in the Volunteer Hall at the Rink, and were to be taken on Saturday afternoon, or early on Monday morning, to the

Maharees, Castlegregory, where the pilot resided. Two green lights close together were to be shown from the pilot boat.

Mr Pat O'Shea, NT, Castlegregory, writes:

> It was, I think, some two or three weeks before Easter, 1916, that I received a message from Austin, to call upon him the first day I happened to be in town. I met him in the office of the late Dr O'Connell, a few days after that. He told me of the Rising that had been planned, and that one small vessel would shortly leave a German port, laden with arms and ammunition for the Irish Volunteers. Austin asked me to make the necessary arrangements for procuring a pilot. He stated quite definitely that the gun-runners would be off Inishtooskert on the night of Easter Sunday, or the morning of Easter Monday – but not before. As the ship was to arrive in the night, or at dawn, we were to look for a green light on her bridge. The answering signal was to be two green lights on the pilot boat. It was our intention to board the vessel, accompanied by Mort O'Leary and Maurice Flynn, both of Maharees. On Easter Saturday morning I went to Tralee to make final arrangements with Austin, and to bring out the lamps which were to be used for signalling. I learned of the arrest of Austin, and of those other events which are now a matter of history. I can repeat that the time of the arrival of the *Aud* was given to me quite definitely by Austin; it was the night of Easter Sunday or the morning of Easter Monday, when Fenit Pier and the Great Southern Railways were to be seized and the arms landed and distributed.

The pilot, Mort O'Leary, who was to meet the *Aud* and pilot her to Fenit, states:

> The only information which I got about the Casement landing was from Tadhg Brosnan, captain of the Castlegregory Volunteers, and that was very little. On Holy Thursday he told me that a small steamer coming with arms was due on Sunday night, and that I was to go up to him on Saturday afternoon when he would give me all particulars. That evening when I went home I saw a two-masted boat about a mile north-east of Inishtooskert, but having no information and not expecting any boat until Sunday night, I took no notice of her. I found out afterwards that it was the *Aud*. By what Tadhg Brosnan told me I did not expect such a big ship. I was up on Friday morning at dawn, and she was then steaming slowly west from Kerry Head. I

took her to be a British decoy boat as there were many such around at the time.

The notes from Pat O'Shea, Fr Breen and the pilot show that the arrival of the German boat was not expected until late on Sunday night at the very earliest. James Connolly had sent down William Partridge, one of his ablest organisers, to arrange for the local transport workers to help in discharging the boat on its arrival in Fenit. The Tralee engine drivers and firemen were to meet Austin Stack on Sunday morning and receive definite instructions about trains from Tralee to take arms to Cork and Limerick. Denis Daly, of Caherciveen, was sent from Dublin on Good Friday, in charge of a party, to dismantle the wireless installation at Caherciveen. Austin was to receive this at Ballygamboon Cross, about nine miles outside Tralee, on Good Friday night, and the wireless was then to be installed in J.P. O'Donnell's, Ballyard, Tralee, to attempt to contact the German boat.

I am, of course, only interested in the Casement landing from the Kerry point of view, and particularly how it affects the memory of Austin Stack. I will quote from the report signed by Éamon de Valera, then chief of staff, and issued by the IRA leaders in Dublin in March 1918, dealing with Munster generally during Easter Week 1916, this report states: 'Against Kerry no charge has been made'. That, I think, needs no comment from me.

In conclusion I quote a letter from Con Collins who was arrested with Austin Stack on Good Friday, 1916:

> You may rest assured that Casement was entirely unexpected by the leaders in Dublin. Joe Plunkett was then quite recently with him in Germany. At four-thirty p.m. on Wednesday, April 19th, I left Seán McDermott and Joe Plunkett together, having received my orders from him for Limerick and Tralee regarding the wireless installation at Ballyard. As you are already aware, that was my mission. Seán and Joe were the last people I met in Dublin, and having fixed the details of my own particular business in the transfer of the wireless

station, their instructions to the leaders in Limerick and Tralee were, 'All going well and according to previously arranged plan.' That plan was for the landing of the arms not earlier than midnight on Easter Sunday. Any alteration of that, if there were such, was unknown to both of these men at four-thirty p.m. on Wednesday evening, April nineteenth, 1916.

THE O'RAHILLY GRAVE

There is a grave in Erin's Isle,
Lying lonely and forlorn;
No monument is raised above,
Nor yet a marble stone.
On it the sunbeams brightly shine,
There wild birds sing their best;
Where one of Pearse's noble line
For ever lies at rest.

He fought with de Valera
'Neath the Green Flag flying free;
Seven times he charged the British lines
Though wounded sore was he.
They laid him down; his dying wish
To rest near Liffey's wave;
And shamrocks now are blooming green
Above The O'Rahilly Grave.

A hawthorn bush on guard above,
In May it blossoms sweet;
A mournful stream flows gently down
Where vale and mountain meet.
'Tis there the children come to pay
A tribute to the brave;
And night winds sigh their mournful cry

Above The O'Rahilly Grave.
Dear land, we faced grim death for thee;
Dear land of courage high;
Though some have fought in far-off fields
Beneath an alien sky,
The Lord have mercy on their souls
At home or o'er the wave;
These men who loved the rebel flag
Above The O'Rahilly Grave.

KERRY WAS PREPARED AND READY

by WILLIAM MULLINS

A further account of events in Tralee during Holy Week 1916, is given hereunder by William Mullins, of Moyderwell, Tralee, who was brigade quartermaster at the time.

WHEN DEALING WITH the Casement landing on Banna Strand, County Kerry, on Good Friday, 1916, the majority of writers have erred in their handling of the most important facts. The object of this article is to correct these early mistakes and to make available additional unpublished facts leading up to that tragic chapter in the history of the 1916 rebellion. In the months preceding the Rising, Kerry was thoroughly organised, and the Volunteer officers devoted a great deal of their time to the drilling and development of their units. Whilst the Rising was a close secret, the men instinctively knew that their intensive training must ultimately lead to something big. At the same time, throughout those early months of foot-slogging and heartbreaking ground work, the Kerry Volunteer executive was warned by the general headquarters in Dublin that at all costs they were to prevent any incident which might arouse the suspicions of the British authorities or precipitate an action. Here in Kerry our knowledge of the general plan of campaign was limited to the single instruction that not a shot was to be fired in the county until headquarters gave the order.

Some months prior to the Rising of 1916 I was partially taken into the confidence of the late P.J. Cahill, who, whilst he did not tell me outright of what was coming, implied that big things were afoot and that the near future held promise of another glorious chapter in our history. This, in fact, was then sensed by every Volunteer, and with further intensification of the work of organisation and training, matters were working rapidly towards a climax. One of the secrets confided in me by Paddy Cahill was the news that a cargo of arms was on its way to Ireland and that it would put in at Fenit; that a general mobilisation of the Kerry Volunteers had been planned to take place on Easter Sunday at Tralee whence detachments would proceed to Fenit, discharge the ship's cargo and distribute the arms between the counties of Cork, Kerry and Limerick. The mobilisation took place as arranged but during the preceding days the general plan for the landing of the arms went completely amiss, mainly because of the premature arrival of the German arms ship in Fenit harbour, its subsequent location by British warships, and the arrest of Austin Stack. We had all been ready and waiting, and events appeared to be moving along with clock-like precision. The first intimation that all was not going according to plan came with the news of the Ballykissane tragedy.

The story of the drowning at Ballykissane pier, near Killorglin, of three of the occupants of an ill-fated car dispatched from Volunteer headquarters in Dublin, is told by another writer in *Kerry's Fighting Story*. One of the drowned men, Charlie Monahan, was an expert wireless operator and the whole party was proceeding to Tralee under orders to erect a transmitter in the late J.P. O'Donnell's house in Ballyard. This portable wireless transmitter was to form the connecting link between the Volunteers ashore and the conveyors of the arms cargo bound for Fenit. Whilst on his way to Tralee, the driver of the car took a wrong road during his night drive and the unfortunate expedition ended in the Ballykissane tragedy which also severed the link planned to make contact between the Volunteers and the arms ship the *Aud*. The Volunteer executive was unaware that the *Aud* carried no wireless.

On Holy Thursday wild rumours circulated about Tralee to the effect that a foreign ship was observed off the Kerry coast near Fenit. The news was so persistent that I was detailed to go personally to Fenit and test its accuracy. In Fenit, I found that the rumours were without foundation. On Good Friday morning I left my house at Moyderwell to carry out some Volunteer business in Quille Street just outside the town. On my return I was advised that Austin Stack had called and that he had gone to Ardfert with Con Collins. Later in the day I learned that Roger Casement was in the Tralee police barracks. Con Collins was arrested subsequently and when Stack was taken soon afterwards, tragedy mounted upon tragedy. Then, too, news of the landing on lonely Banna Strand began to leak out when Monteith, who had accompanied Casement and escaped the vigilance of the Royal Irish Constabulary, made his way to Tralee. Meanwhile, Roger Casement, who was held in the Tralee police barracks, having sent for a clergyman, was attended by Fr Ryan, OP, Tralee, to whom he entrusted a message to deliver to Paddy Cahill for transmission to general headquarters in Dublin. Cahill had taken over command of the Volunteers when Austin Stack was arrested. He sent for me about 6.30 p.m. on Friday and having told me of the message for headquarters ordered me to board the seven o'clock train out of Tralee for the capital. William Partridge who was then doing intensive Volunteer organisation in Kerry, was also given a copy of the order and he left Tralee on the 7.30 train that evening. The idea was that if one of us was arrested the other might get through. Partridge joined my train at Limerick Junction, but from there we travelled to Dublin as though complete strangers. Having arrived in the city at 4.30 a.m., I went directly to Liberty Hall and delivered my message to James Connolly. Connolly sent out couriers immediately summoning a meeting at headquarters for 9.30 a.m. This meeting was attended by all the signatories to the Proclamation of the

Republic with the exception of Seán MacDiarmada. The conference had been in session for forty-five minutes when Partridge and I were both summoned before it and I was handed a letter with instructions to return to Tralee immediately.

When the train drew up at Tralee platform there was a concentrated rush towards the carriage which I occupied by a number of the Royal Irish Constabulary. I was saved from arrest, however, by the intervention of the local Volunteers, planned by Paddy Cahill. The police halted their rush towards my carriage because of some commotion at the end of the platform, from where there emerged fifty Volunteers led by the late Joe Harrington. The police were brushed aside and I was safely escorted from the platform. We marched to the Rink which was then the headquarters of the Volunteers, and there I gave my verbal message from general headquarters to my O/C, Captain Monteith.

On Easter Sunday morning Kerry mobilised as arranged, fully prepared to play its part in the fight. Volunteers were present even from the out-lying parts of the county, having left their homes prepared for action. There was tension in the atmosphere of Tralee which imparted itself even to townspeople who had no connection with the movement. Everybody sensed that the big moment was at hand and Volunteers on their way to mobilisation that Sunday morning were stopped by civilians who enquired if it was going to be a fight at last. When told by the Volunteers that such was their belief many civilians turned up at the Rink, shouldered a rifle and awaited orders. Patriotism and nationalism were the real brand in Kerry then. Confusion and some disillusionment followed the countermanding order, and the tragedy was that there should have been such an order. Kerry was prepared and ready to contribute its full share to the general Rising planned to take place throughout the country on that fateful morning.

THE FIRST CASUALTIES OF 1916

by MICHEÁL Ó DONNCHADHA

GOOD FRIDAY NIGHT, 1916! A dark, cheerless night, and more than unusually calm. There was nothing to disturb the wonted equanimity of the unsuspecting populace, no suspicion of impending calamity; not even the slightest hint of anything unusual in the quiet, peaceful atmosphere that pervaded the Irish countryside. It was the calm before the storm!

Killorglin's streets were all but deserted for it was approaching bedtime. A few belated groups stood here and there to have a final chat before turning in for the night. To such a group on the bridge at the entrance to the town, the driver of a motor car, which had approached from the east, addressed himself and enquired the way to Caherciveen. There was nothing unusual in this, for cars hourly passed this way and the absence of signposts in those days necessitated frequent enquiries. On receiving the instructions, 'Turn to the right and follow the main road', the driver proceeded and soon disappeared from the view of the unsuspecting group.

In less than five minutes after, three of the occupants of that ill-fated car had gone to their eternity, and the fourth, the driver, was struggling for his life in the treacherous waters of the River Laune at Ballykissane pier.

Instead of following the main road as instructed, the driver, at the junction a few hundred yards further on, kept straight on along the road which led to the pier and never realised his mistake until it was too late. Even when actually on the pier he still kept thinking he was passing over a bridge and that the wide river immediately in front of him was an unfenced field. It was only when the car began to bump and jolt over the rough paving stones of the pierhead and the water suddenly appeared before him that he swiftly jammed on the brakes and brought the car to a standstill on the very edge of the pier with the front wheels already over.

Instantly realising his position the driver roared a warning to his companions and jumped clear of the poised car into the water below. His companions quickly tried to follow his example, but were less fortunate for, in their forward movement they unbalanced the car and it fell heavily in, taking with it its human cargo to death and eternity.

There is a house at Ballykissane pier occupied by Mr Timothy O'Sullivan. The family had just recited the Rosary preparatory to retiring when the sound of a passing motor car attracted their attention. Knowing well the danger of the unprotected pier from past experience – for it was not the first tragic occurrence at this spot – Mr O'Sullivan hastened to the roadway to ascertain what was afoot. Seeing no trace of the mysterious car or its occupants he at once concluded that the worst had happened, and quickly returned to procure a light. Hurrying onto the pier with a piece of Christmas candle that had remained over from the festive season, he held the light aloft, shading it with his hand. Almost immediately a cry for help came from the dark waters of the river. Shouting words of encouragement to the struggling man in the water, he at the same time called aloud for the other members of the family and bade them call for help. Neighbours were summoned with the minimum of delay, and in a short time men, women and children, some coatless and bootless, were rushing to the scene of the accident, carrying with them ropes and lanterns to help in the work of rescue. Meanwhile, the driver, guided by the kindly light from the shore, had reached the strand to the west of the pier, in an exhausted condition, and was helped into Mr O'Sullivan's house. The feat which he had accomplished was truly remarkable and goes to show the extraordinary endurance of the human body and the terrible odds which a man can overcome when fighting for his life.

With the handicap of a heavy overcoat, in addition to his other clothes and boots, he had succeeded in covering at least two hundred yards, for not knowing that he could have made land within twenty yards of the spot where he had jumped in, on the pier side of the river, his first thought was of swimming to the lights on the other side, which although seeming very near, were quite half a mile away. It was only the timely appearance of Mr O'Sullivan with the light that saved him from certain death by drowning. At Mr O'Sullivan's house he changed his water-soaked clothes for a dry suit provided him. Before divesting himself of his overcoat he drew from one of his pockets a six-chamber revolver fully loaded which he placed on a súgan chair beside the fire.

By this time a big crowd had gathered outside and some neighbours were already within. Among these were Mr Patrick Begley and his son Michael. The latter, who was then home on holiday, was one of the very few in Killorglin at the time, who had any knowledge of the expected Rising at Easter. Immediately he had heard of the occurrence at the river he guessed that the strange travellers were in some way connected with the coming event. Communicating his suspicions to his father they both hastened to the scene. Arrived at O'Sullivan's they called the driver aside and questioned him as to his and his fellow travellers mission. At the same time they assured him of their support and assistance if any new danger threatened from the authorities. Their conversation was not yet over when two burly members of the Royal Irish Constabulary appeared at the door.

In the general excitement the loaded revolver still lay on the chair completely forgotten, but the elder Mr Begley, now noticing it for the first time, instantly took in the situation and realising the awkward position in which the driver would be placed, thought quickly and acted more quickly still. Walking coolly to the chair and at the same time cutting off the policemen's line of vision, he calmly sat on the chair, nor would he on any account be induced to leave this position until the representatives of the law had departed to make further inquiries. I believe the revolver remained a long time in Mr Begley's possession until it was finally returned to the driver, Tommy McInerney.

While the incidents just related were taking place at Mr O'Sullivan's house, hundreds had gathered without and lined the pier and riverside. The tide was still almost full and rendered futile all attempts at recovering the bodies (for the missing men were now long presumed dead). There was nothing to be done therefore but watch and wait until the ebbing tide should disclose its grim secret and perhaps reveal the identity of its victims, whom all were anxious to know, but none yet knew. The driver, Tommy McInerney, denied all knowledge of his passengers who, he said, had engaged him for the journey. He had no knowledge of their business but carried out their instructions under compulsion and at the point of the revolver.

This information spreading among the watchers, whetted their curiosity all the more. The very mention of arms gave rise to wild and vague rumours of bank robberies, train-wrecking and other such conjectures, but only very few were acquainted with the real facts, and these were wise enough to hold their peace. So the long watch began and continued throughout the weary night until the grey dawn threw back the curtains of night and the tidal waters rolled slowly home to the depths of the mighty deep. And now, at the first glimmer of the morning sun the retreating tide bared the hood of the car. Preparations were made at once to have it hauled to land for it was supposed that the bodies were still inside or penned beneath. Boats were brought up, ropes were fastened to the car and all at length being ready, the order was given to haul. But all efforts were unavailing. Men strained at the ropes but the embedded car obstinately refused to budge. The teams were reinforced, but now the ropes were unable to stand the strain, and snapping suddenly, threw the haulers violently to the ground in a confused heap.

Other attempts were made and in turn failed. It was not until Mr Begley (already mentioned), who was taking a prominent part in the work, bethought him of an eighty-foot chain which was at his house and which was fetched immediately and so employed that the obdurate car at last was forced to yield. But disappointment again followed – no bodies were within the car.

A further delay ensued. Nets were provided and dragging operations begun. After about an hour's strenuous search the first body was located – not as was expected, near the position occupied by the car, but a good way off to seaward. It was brought to shore – the body of an unknown man. The mystery deepened.

The search was resumed but yielded nought – until close on mid-day the second body was recovered and immediately recognised as the body of Con Keating of Caherciveen. This was the first clue to the great riddle. To those who knew the inner working of the Sinn Féin movement, it opened a whole book of information; for others it only gave rise to further wild conjecture and rumours of foreign invasion, of Zeppelins and submarines and all the varied paraphernalia of war. But this was only for the time – a few days more and all would be revealed.

Again the search was resumed, but though it was continued throughout the day and maintained intermittently for several days after, the third body was not recovered. It was thought – and it was whispered convincingly in local circles – that the third Volunteer, for it was now established without doubt that Volunteers they all were, had succeeded in swimming across the river to Callinafercy where, concealed by the people of that place for some days, he made his way back to Dublin and took an active part in the Rising. It is this belief at the time which no doubt has given rise to the error into which nearly every writer on the subject has fallen, viz., that only two lives were lost in the tragedy. The belief was, however, without foundation, and the assumption is incorrect. The third body was recovered later, and was interred with that of his companions in Dromavalla cemetery. A beautiful granite cross marks the spot where they lie at rest, having done their part in their country's cause. The body of Con Keating was conveyed to Caherciveen and interred in the family burial ground at Killovarnogue.

With the excitement and shock of the terrible tragedy still upon them, the people of Killorglin were given further food for reflection when the news came of the capture of Casement at Banna Strand and the failure of the *Aud* expedition. Things were moving rapidly and the suddenness of the Easter Rising with its train of startling events took people's minds off the local tragedy for the time being at any rate. It was only in the light of subsequent happenings that the full story of the tragedy of Ballykissane came to be known; it was only when the conflagration that dazzled the country from Mizen Head to Cape Clear had subsided, when the horror of cruel murders and merciless executions had passed that the purpose and importance of this mission to Kerry on that eventful Good Friday of 1916 came to be fully understood and realised. It was only when the fight was over and lost and defeat, once again, our portion that we began to look back and ask what might have happened if that mission had but succeeded; if only that wrong turning had not been taken; if only the chain which now spans the entrance to that treacherous pier had been there on that fateful night. But what a lot of *ifs* and such big, very big *ifs*.

I quote from an appeal for funds issued by the committee set up in Killorglin to undertake the erection of a memorial at Ballykissane to the victims of the tragedy:

> On Good Friday, 1916, three men – Charles Monahan (Belfast), Donal Sheehan (Newcastle West), and Con Keating (Caherciveen) – left Dublin for Valentia Island, County Kerry. They were the first to take up duty in that soul-stirring struggle of Easter Week which,

though resulting in temporary defeat and in death and execution for many brave soldiers of Ireland, nevertheless succeeded in saving the very life and soul of our Nation and in paving the way for ultimate victory and the establishing of an Irish Republic as a living practical fact.

Their mission was to seize wireless apparatus and send out messages to British warships to decoy them from the Kerry coast, and so clear the way for the landing of arms from the *Aud*.

What of it if their mission was a failure? It would, even had they lived, been a failure just as well. They did not know that the *Aud*, owing to a misunderstanding, had already reached the Kerry coast a few vital days before it was expected, thus adding another pathetic chapter to the history of Easter Week.

They never reached their destination, nor lived to learn the result of that glorious fight in which they on Irish soil were the first under orders to take an active part.

The facts set out in this quotation have been thoroughly substantiated. That the occupants of the car were in possession of the closely guarded secret Admiralty code, shows the marvellous power and scope of the organisation of which they were members, and the daring coup they were about to undertake is a remarkable instance of the brains and resource that were behind the whole movement. But fate dogged their every step and that many of their well-considered and carefully laid plans miscarried, was not by any means the fault of the organisers or of those who were entrusted with putting them into execution. A good deal of criticism was and has since been levelled at the leaders of the Sinn Féin movement in Kerry by some who are ignorant of the main factors that led to the failure of the *Aud* expedition and to the capture and subsequent execution of Casement. The premature arrival of the arms ship mentioned in the third paragraph of the appeal quoted above, explains much and completely exonerates the Kerry Volunteers from all blame for this failure.

But let us now turn to these brave men, the first to answer the nation's call to arms, who so tragically lost their lives in this gallant bid to burst for ever the yoke and shackles that so long had bound their country and free her from thrall and tyranny.

KERRY HEROES OF THE RISING

by SCEILG

These hurried sketches are drawn in the main from notes on the Kerry martyrs of 1916 which I made over thirty years ago when the military censor's hand fell ruthlessly on current records of Irish patriotism. Though not pretending to anything like the fullness to be desired, they will help to show the rising generation that Kerry courage took high place in the records of that glorious effort for national liberty, and that all sections of the historic 'Kingdom' were nobly presented on the martyr roll.

CORNELIUS KEATING, born at Reenard, Caherciveen, was Kerry's first martyr in the Uprising of 1916. He came of a militant nationalist stock that treasured and transmitted all the literary and social traditions of the Gael. When England, in 1860, sent public addresses, money and men to help Victor Emmanuel and Garibaldi in their designs on Rome, Con's uncle, Geoffrey Keating, was one of the Iveragh Volunteers who went out to fight in defence of Pope Pius IX; and within that historic decade his relatives were prominent among the 'stout-hearted Fenians of Caherciveen'. Though trained at Glasnevin Model Farm for an agricultural career, he abandoned it for wireless telegraphy, and while yet in his teens had been practically round the world. His political convictions obliging him to sever his connection with the wireless service, he returned to Dublin, where he soon became recognised as one of the most earnest and trusted members of the Volunteer organisation. Sent on an urgent, highly important and very confidential mission to Kerry on the eve of the Rising, the motor car by which he travelled plunged over Ballykissane pier in a fog, and he and his comrades were drowned. The tragic news, followed by tidings of the arrest of Roger Casement, cast a gloom over all the circles in which Con had moved from Dublin to Valentia, particularly as he was known to be a man of fine athletic mould and capable of swimming up to ten miles. The Volunteers of Iveragh marched in his imposing funeral procession to Caherciveen in the beginning of Easter Week, oblivious in great part of the eventful happenings in Dublin.

Accompanying him on his fateful mission was Donal Sheehan, born at Ballintubrid, Monegay, County Limerick, birthplace also, I think, of Con Collins, arrested with Austin Stack after the capture of Casement. Both Con Keating and Donal Sheehan paid me a visit as they were about to set out for Iveragh, little mindful of the tragic fate so soon to befall them. Accompanying them as driver was Charles Monahan, of Belfast, hurler, Gaelic Leaguer, machine man in the wood trade, armourer in the 2nd battalion, Dublin brigade, worthy comrade of indomitable men.

PATRICK O'CONNOR, a native of Rathmore, entered the civil Service at the age of eighteen, having obtained first place in the United Kingdom in open competitive examination for which he presented himself direct from the local national school. Thus in 1900 he became attached to the post office in London. After a few years there he got transferred to Dublin, and at once became active in Gaelic Athletic and Irish-Ireland circles. On the fateful Good Friday before the Rising, he attended the funeral of his brother Denis, who had also been in the civil service in London. When leaving for Dublin on Easter Saturday, in response to an urgent message, he said significantly to a friend: 'I don't think I'll ever again see MY OLD

GREY HOME IN THE WEST.' On Monday night, with a number of comrades, he found his way to the General Post Office, where P.H. Pearse, holding a lighted candle, received him. Later, they crossed the street to Clery's. Tuesday was spent largely in boring lines of communication, and on Wednesday they assisted the brigade in putting out fires in Tyler's, Clery's stables and adjoining buildings. The raging fires threatening their line of retreat on Thursday, they crossed Earl Street and thence to Cathedral Place. Reconnoitring towards dawn on Friday morning, O'Connor made his way along Thomas Lane, and never returned. Soon afterwards his comrades were taken into custody.

MICHAEL MULVIHILL, born at Ardoughter, Ballyduff, Lixnaw, in 1880, received his early education at Ballincrossig school, where his father, John Mulvihill, was principal teacher. Second son of a family of nine children, he left home at the age of eighteen, and after two years in a London college, obtained an appointment in the General Post Office there. From an early age he took a deep and active interest in the concerns of his native land. He became a fluent Irish speaker and was an earnest member of the London corps of Irish Volunteers. During his fifteen years' residence in London he never neglected his annual visit to Ireland to see his parents and family, to whom he was devotedly attached. With other friends he decided to spend the Easter of 1916 in Dublin, and arrived there on Easter Sunday morning. On being informed of the seizure of the post office, he immediately volunteered his services and was posted on the roof of the building. He was at his post up to the time of the evacuation, but notwithstanding the most exhaustive inquiries, could not be traced or heard of subsequently.

THE O'RAHILLY, representative of the distinguished Kerry clan that gave the illustrious Aodhgán to our patriotic literature, is credited with having been the first to conceive the idea of founding the Irish

Volunteers. Certain it is that he was the first in our time to awaken the young men of Ireland to the humiliation of permitting isolated little groups of the Royal Irish Constabulary to hold rural Ireland for England. A native of Ballylongford, it was, I think, while studying medicine in Dublin that he decided to go to the United States, where in due course, he was happily married to the gifted daughter of Robert Browne, of Philadelphia, and of Fifth Avenue, New York. After some time he returned to Ireland, and travelled extensively on the continent. Instinctively he became an ardent worker in the Irish language movement, and was long an active member of the governing body of the Gaelic League. He devoted special attention to the elucidation of Irish place-names, based on O'Donovan's lists for the Ordnance Survey, and he also wrote learnedly on the family arms of Irish clans. Not only was he a most versatile writer, but he had a rare grasp of every phase of the Irish question. When national feeling became intensified largely through the teaching of the Gaelic League, he accompanied the late Señor Bulfin on a patriotic mission to the United States. Possessed of considerable private means, he devoted himself strenuously from the very outset to the interests of the Irish Volunteers.

Like his comrades in the organisation, he was a man of exemplary private life, and was prominent among the hosts of prominent Gaels who at that time constituted the new Irish-speaking sodality at Gardiner Street, Dublin. Discussing the national situation with a western priest after the unfortunate split in the Volunteers, he said: 'I suppose, Father, I'll be accounted a fool from the worldly point of view. I am giving this movement all my time, all my thoughts day and night, my money as far as I can. I do not suppose I'll ever have a fortune to leave my children; but one thing I will try to leave – the memory of a father of whom they need not feel ashamed. That will be their heritage, Father; with that they can face the world.' On the eve of the Rising, after the capture of Roger Casement, he left a sick bed and motored to Limerick to countermand the manoeuvres there; but finding his comrades in arms on his return he joined them in the General Post Office. When that centre became untenable, he led a charge on the barricade near the Rotunda, and was fatally wounded in Moore Lane, where he slowly bled to death.

PATRICK SHORTIS, born in 1893, was the eldest son of the late William Shortis, of Ballybunion. He passed from the local schools to Saint Brendan's Seminary, Killarney, winning a first-class scholarship at his entrance examination. After four years in Killarney, he was sent to continue his ecclesiastical studies at All Hallows College, Dublin; but, feeling that he was not blessed with a vocation for the priesthood, he left there after two years, having meanwhile obtained his BA degree in the National University. Subsequently he attended the Wireless College, Caherciveen, with a view to becoming a wireless operator; but, though he successfully passed his examination in London, he was denied his certificate owing to his views on Irish affairs. He remained in London for some years, and was active in Volunteer circles there. Returning to Dublin in January 1916, he at once became attached to the 2nd battalion, Fairview. A young man of the highest character and intellect and an athlete of promise, he fell by the side of The O'Rahilly in heroically charging the barricade at the Rotunda end of Moore Street on the Friday evening of Easter Week. By the side of The O'Rahilly fell also Francis Macken of Dublin.

JACK O'REILLY, truly one of the most versatile sons of the Kingdom of Kerry, was born in Tralee, where his father was a highly respected builder and contractor. At an early age, Jack became technical instructor under the county councils of Monaghan and Kerry, and was soon recognised as an amateur entertainer of rare ability and promise. A beautiful singer and inimitable story-teller, always bubbling over with fun and humour and innocent drollery, his talents and time, and even his money, were ever at the service of the national cause, particularly of the language and industrial movements. When his prospects and popularity were at their highest, he walked up to the Tralee station one evening and, to the astonishment of his friends, set out on the long journey to New Zealand. Having obtained his degree of civil engineer in New Zealand, and travelled much in Australasia, he eventually reached the Friendly Islands, spending two years on Tonga, the capital, as principal of the technical schools. In Tonga his attainments soon attracted the attention of royalty, with the result that he became a popular figure at the royal palace there.

'I myself,' wrote a friend, 'possess a Christmas greeting from his Dusky Majesty, the King of Tonga, to his beloved brother, O'Reilly, with a wish that he may live forever.' Deciding in time to return to Ireland, he was fairly lionised by Kerry friends from San Francisco to New York, and arrived in Dublin for one of these thrilling football matches in which Kerry helped to win national renown for the Gaelic Athletic Association. The comrades of other days who foregathered on that occasion are not likely to forget the infectious joy that radiated from the genial Jack O'Reilly. Within a few weeks he was appointed technical instructor for County Galway and principal of the Ballinasloe technical school. After the Rising, he was there arrested and conveyed to Richmond barracks, Dublin. On removal to Wandsworth under a strong escort, he roused his comrades as they left the North Wall in a cattle boat by his spirited singing of 'Galway Bay'. He was subsequently transferred to Frongoch, where he was affectionately known as Major O'Reilly, and placed in charge of a fumigator for the disinfection of articles of clothing. On his release in ruined health, though previously 'a man of volcanic energy', he had tales to tell of the cruelties suffered since his arrest. In a few weeks symptoms of a fatal disease manifested themselves and, in spite of the best medical care, he died of pernicious anaemia. His funeral cortège was said to be one of the most imposing ever witnessed in Tralee; the coffin was draped with the national flag; the Dead March played by the Tralee Pipers, and the Last Post sounded before his remains were laid in the family burial place at Rath.

THOMAS ASHE, born at Kinard, near Dingle, was in his thirty-third year at the time of his martyrdom. He was brought up amid Ireland's most historic surroundings – Cathair Chonroi, Cnoc an Áir, Ventry, Gallarus, Kilmalkedar, Cnoc Bhreandain, Smerwick, Ferriter's Castle, Castlemaine, then constituted the theme of the fireside stories that thrilled the unspoilt houses of Kerry. And the Ashe fireside was typical, the father of the family an accomplished *seanchaidhe*, versed in the choice lore of the land, an excellent singer, with a rare repertoire of traditional songs. In this atmosphere Thomas Ashe grew to budding manhood. The school of his boyhood was worthy of his house and the general environs, for Lispole school earned fame as the first in Ireland to win the coveted cup offered by William O'Brien to the teacher successfully presenting the highest number of pupils for examination in the Irish language. In this school, Tom taught as monitor for five years, winning the Reid prize in competition with the best talent of Kerry at the end of his third year, and repeating his victory at the end of the fifth. About this time he wrote an Irish drama, which, later, was produced in the open in the park at Tralee. The production took place at night by the light of torches, the result being a fairy scene which impressed itself indelibly on the memory. Those that had the good fortune to be present that night, under the shadow of one of the great outposts of the Desmonds, will not forget the boyish author, supported by an equally boyish caste, and accompanied by his comely sister who, just then, had been attracting notice for exquisite stories of great promise, over the pen-name of Caitlin.

After a two years' course of training at De La Salle Training College, Waterford, the brilliant monitor of Lispole obtained a school at Corduff, County Dublin. There he soon founded the Black Raven Pipers' Band, interesting himself collaterally in the Gaelic League, the Gaelic Athletic Association and, in due time, in the Volunteer movement, and incidentally encountering not a little opposition on the way. But his beautiful traditional singing and kindred gifts made his presence always welcome at social entertainments, while the charm of manner which remained with him to the last, combined with his attractive personality, to win him hosts of sympathisers everywhere. Recognition of his services to the national language soon came in his election to the governing body of the Gaelic League, and in the spring of 1914 he was chosen, with Diarmuid Lynch, to seek in the United States much-needed financial aid for the organisation. On the outbreak of the World War in the ensuing autumn they hastened back to Ireland. Easter Monday, 1916, found him in command of a detachment of Volunteers at Finglas. Thence by stages they moved towards Ashbourne where, on Friday, what was, perhaps, the most notable engagement of the whole Rising was fought. With a comparatively small number of followers, he found himself pitted against an overwhelming force of police, well officered, and fully equipped, the upshot being that the police suffered serious casualties and utter defeat. On Low Sunday, however, after the general surrender, the Ashbourne victors were rounded up and their leader court martialled and sentenced to death, but the sentence was commuted to penal servitude. While undergoing sentence in successive English prisons, he wrote a number of charming songs and set them all to popular airs. One of the pieces, 'Let Me Carry Your Cross for Ireland, Lord', has since attained a deservedly wide vogue, and reflects the chaste and unconquerable spirit that undying love of faith and fatherland which has left the Gael invincible on his own sacred soil.

Released on the eve of the Clare election, urgent national work, which embraced a memorable address at the Casement anniversary celebrations, so occupied his time that he was able to spend but two days with his people before his re-arrest for a speech at Ballinalee, County Longford. On the evidence of two policemen's recollection of that speech he was sentenced to two years' imprisonment. Not a few among his friends regarded his arrest and conviction in the circumstances as portending his doom. Determined to join in a sacred fast for liberty after being deprived, without cause, of bed, bedding and boots for fifty hours, and left thus to lie in a dismal cell, he died shortly after removal to the Mater Hospital – of forcible feeding brutally administered. The chair used for the purpose is still there, and I since sat in the ill-starred contrivance for a dental examination.

The tragic death of Tom Ashe moved the whole country to the deepest resentment and soon made more adherents to the republican cause than did all the executions following the Rising. His remains, while lying-in-state for four days in the Mater Hospital and the City Hall, were visited by an unending procession of mourners, and his funeral to Glasnevin – though the provinces were practically precluded from participation in it – proved the greatest and most impressive manifestation of national sympathy ever witnessed in Ireland. The cruel circumstances of his death resulted in an inquest destined to become historic. 'They have added another blood-spot to the Irish Calvary,' said the late T.M. Healy in addressing the Coroner's jury; 'they have added bloody foot-prints on the road on which Irish martyrs have trodden. Have they gained by it? No. Other nations – not merely our own – will read with horror and will set to the account to which properly it should belong, this terrible story of the death of Thomas Ashe. Other nations will read of it; and when they read it in time long yet to come, they will be enheartened, and perhaps in their distress consoled, by the story of the uncomplaining martyrdom of this humble schoolmaster. Schoolmaster! He has given us all a liberal education in how to endure discomfort, suffering, sleeplessness, pain and sorrow, and to endure them uncomplainingly and without a murmur.

'Even those who inflicted the torture on him must admit he made no reproach. But you, whose function it is to appraise the blame, as to how this man met his untimely end – it is for you to frame your verdict in accordance with the facts, in accordance with truth, in accordance with the light of equity, that the race and nation and people to whom you belong may know that this man was no suicide, that this man was the victim of injustice and illegality.' And the jury did frame their verdict accordingly.

'Let me carry Your Cross for Ireland, Lord!' enshrined the innermost thoughts of Tom Ashe in his prison cell at Lewes where he was among the leading members of the prisoners' choir. 'Pray to Bishop O'Dwyer and the Dead who died for Ireland,' he whispered to his comrades in Mountjoy prison on the Sunday before his death, 'that we may have strength to see this trial through.' To the lord mayor of Dublin he said about the same time: 'If I die, I die in a good cause,' and to the Capuchin Fathers who visited him as he breathed his last, 'Well, we have put up a great fight anyway.'

AUSTIN STACK, born at the close of 1879, had scarcely left the cradle before his harassed Fenian father, William Moore Stack, was re-arrested, borne off to Limerick, and thence to Dublin, where he was held as a 'suspect' for a further twelve months. Austin's aunt, Miss O'Neill, who came then from Dublin to keep his mother company, threw herself wholeheartedly into the Ladies' Land League, and with Miss Hogan, his godmother, and Mrs Hanlon of Tralee, was sentenced by Clifford Lloyd to six months' imprisonment for attending meetings in Castleisland, and answering 'No Surrender' to the charge preferred against them.

Moore Stack, whose health had been ruined beyond repair, died after a few days illness in 1899, while yet under sixty. His wife having predeceased him, Austin before he had reached the age of twenty, had to shoulder the main responsibility for the maintenance of a helpless family. Despite this responsibility and the management of a law office, he threw himself with eagerness into the work of the Gaelic Athletic Association, and not only on the field of play but on the Councils of the organisation. He was also a practical supporter of the Gaelic League, and, though not what might be regarded as a clubman, he was a serious member of the Liberal Club in Tralee. This club once had a picture of the late King Edward. Entering the reading room one day, Austin found the picture prominently displayed, and it goes almost without saying that he pulled it down and consigned it to the flames.

Meeting him in Dublin one night soon after, he and I called on a mutual friend. As we passed 'the Bank' at College Green on our way home, Austin lisped something about the invincible army of England! Forward towards the railings at that very moment strutted a red-coated sentry in a ponderous busby. Austin stepped lightly onto the stone steps and swung himself lithely against the metal bars that separated him from the sentry. What words passed between them were not quite audible, but Austin's suddenly raised arm came down on the crown of the busby with a thud, and sent the pompous headgear literally spluttering down over the soldier's shoulders, so blinding him for the moment that he might easily have been disarmed. 'The invincible army of England!' he repeated, as he joined us, and walked leisurely away.

The advent of the Irish Volunteers found Austin a natural military leader ready to hand in Kerry. I have a vivid mental picture of him at the parade in connection with the Oireachtas in Killarney, 1914. Volunteer detachments came from various southern centres, the most formidable and efficient coming from Tralee and Limerick. As I emerged from the Killarney post office that brilliant afternoon, the Tralee contingent, largely armed with rifles and fixed bayonets, swung round the corner at the Town Hall, led by Austin Stack and one of Kerry's most popular young priests, both fully armed like the resolute men who followed them. Austin looked every inch the military leader that day.

It is not necessary to detail his unceasing activities in the interval which followed before the landing of Roger Casement at

Banna Strand, or the familiar incidents which led to the arrest of Con Collins and himself on Good Friday and their removal next evening by special train with the blinds drawn, to Mallow, thence to Spike Island, and later to Richmond barracks, Dublin. I managed to be present at their court martial there, and I can still recall with admiration their manly bearing, holding their heads high in face of armed despotism, and regarding their accusers with unwincing defiance. A year passed and more, and I had a handshake over the barrier with Austin Stack when, with his fellow-prisoners he was brought in handcuffs to the historic inquest on Thomas Ashe. The following year he found himself a prisoner in Dundalk, whence he was transferred to Belfast, where he led a revolt which cost the alien government £7,000 and took three hundred armed military and police to quell.

From Belfast he was sent to Strangeways prison, Manchester, and escaped therefrom, October 1919.

On returning to Ireland he undertook the duties of minister of home affairs. Forthwith he set himself to have the alien courts and alien police superseded by republican courts and republican police with a success to which even political opponents bore unstinted testimony. After the tragic split which resulted from the Articles of Agreement for the Treaty, he and I were sent to the United States. Singularly, when we were in mid-Atlantic an ex-Black and Tan in another portion of the ship, finding Austin's name on the passenger list, sought an interview through the chief steward. Austin complied with his wonted urbanity. The Black and Tan simply came to inform him that he had been stationed three months in Tralee. 'On arrival there we thought we dominated the situation,' he said. 'After a fortnight, the position seemed difficult to understand. After a month things had got badly on our nerves. At the end of six weeks the tables seemed turned on us completely. In two months we were nervous wrecks. Within a couple of weeks more we were all in open revolt, and the very stoutest amongst us wished himself

3,000 miles away from Tralee. I take off my hat to your home town and its indomitable people.' We were back from the United States in time to enable Austin to act as secretary to the re-assembled Pact Convention.

I was in Melbourne the following year when the newspapers there offensively announced that Austin Stack had been found dazed in a ditch at Clonmel, and that his doom was sealed. That night, at a public meeting in the Town Hall, paraphrasing Mitchel's prophecy that 'the star of Thomas Francis Meagher was never kindled to set on a Clonmel hurdle', I ventured to predict that the star of Austin Stack was never destined to set in a Clonmel ditch. I was myself a prisoner at Botany Bay when I heard that Austin was again a prisoner in Mountjoy; but when in time I got back to the United States I was grieved to learn that he was among the vast host of prisoners fasting for freedom in Ireland, a fast he heroically maintained for upwards of forty days. Release came in time; but it was only temporary. Protesting against his recent arrest, a short time before his final illness, he said at the last meeting he addressed in Dublin: 'The Free State authorities say they arrest no one but criminals and those suspected of complicity in underground crime. Why have they arrested me? I have been secretary of Sinn Féin since 1917, and I mean to remain so as long as I am considered of service. I have recruited for the IRA since its inception, and I am recruiting still, and I'll continue to do so when I find myself unable to do anything better.'

Appropriately his last public appearance was at a commemoration in Caherciveen, Easter Sunday, 1929. May Day he called at headquarters on returning to Dublin, to seek release from a public meeting which he was announced to address that evening. That evening week his comrades conveyed his remains from the mortuary in the Mater Hospital to St Joseph's church, where previously lay the remains of Cathal Brugha. When I joined a stream of mourners to take a last look at his remains before the coffin was closed down I was followed by a son of toil long past middle age. As he looked at the dead face – as firm-looking in death as in action – he exclaimed with a tremor, heedless of everybody and everything: 'Austin Stack! truly one of Ireland's bravest and best.'

LET ME CARRY YOUR CROSS FOR IRELAND, LORD!

(Written in Lewes jail, England, in 1916, by Thomas Ashe the leader of the IRA at the Battle of Ashbourne. He carried the cross a little over a year later when the English killed him during a hunger strike in Mountjoy jail, Dublin.)

Let me carry your Cross for Ireland, Lord!
The hour of her trial draws near,
And the pangs and the pains of the sacrifice
May be borne by comrades dear.
But, Lord, take me from the offering throng,
There are many far less prepared,
Though anxious and all as they are to die
That Ireland may be spared.

Let me carry your Cross for Ireland, Lord!
My cares in this world are few,
And few are the tears will fall for me
When I go on my way to You.
Spare oh! spare to their loved ones dear
The brother and son and sire,
That the cause we love may never die
In the land of our heart's desire!

Let me carry your Cross for Ireland, Lord!
Let me suffer the pain and shame,
I bow my head to their rage and hate,
And I take on myself the blame.
Let them do with my body whate'er they will,

My spirit I offer to You,
That the faithful few who heard her call
May be spared to Roísín Dubh.

Let me carry your Cross for Ireland, Lord!
For Ireland weak with tears,
For the aged man of the clouded brow,
And the child of tender years;
For the empty homes of her golden plains;
For the hopes of her future, too!
Let me carry your Cross for Ireland, Lord!
For the cause of Roísín Dubh.

IN MEMORY OF THOMAS ASHE

by 'BENMORE'

Alone at eve, near the Sanctuary place,
When lights were turning grey,
And the sinking sun was setting low
At the close of a glorious day.
The solemn steps of a footfall tread
Came sounding down the aisle;
A soul with a message for God on High
For a soldier of Éire's Isle.

The peace that's sweet to angels near,
Peace streaming from Realms on High,
In the lonely silence 'twas truly there
The gift of the great who die.
There the wanderer bowed in reverence lone,
Where the tapers flickered with flame,
Pleading for light, God's heavenly light
To illume the martyr's name.

'Let me carry your Cross for Ireland, Lord!'
Flashed bright on the wanderer's mind,
As he prayed to God in that silent church,
For the noblest of his kind.

Here let me breathe a prayer, O Lord
For the man so true of soul;
Here let me pray with Thee, O Lord
That he may reach Thy goal.

And he bore Your Cross for Ireland, Lord,
And for glorious Mary's name,
He struggled with a daring soul
To enrich his country's fame.
And the glory of that Cross was his
When triumphant, dead he lay
With the men of Ireland round his bier
And the stranger's strength at bay.

O take from me this offering, Lord,
These tapers, but a few,
That Eternal Light may shine for aye
On the soul of one so true.
Loved mother of thy suffering son
To thee one prayer I send
That He may guard in darkest hour
Tom Ashe's every friend.

Here let me light these candles, Lord,
To burn with radiant glow.
Here let me pray, O Lord, for one
All brave and good men know.
Make bright the path that heavenward leads
For one who like to Thee
Bore well that Cross for Your dear sake,
For friends and Ireland free.

A HOUSE OF MEMORIES

by ÓGLACH

THERE IS A modest little house in Mountjoy Street in Dublin – just near the Broadstone railway station – which, if walls and doors could talk, could probably tell more about the whole pre-Truce campaign from the foundation of the Volunteers to the signing of the Treaty, than any other house in Ireland.

No. 44 Mountjoy Street – also known as Grianan na nGaedheal and the Munster Private Hotel – is owned by Miss Myra T. McCarthy, a native of Waterville, County Kerry, and has been conducted for upwards of fifty years as a very popular 'digs' where students and young business and professional men lodged. In the late years of the last century and in the beginning of this it was a favourite resort for members of the Gaelic League, and in fact it might be said to have been the headquarters of Cork and Kerry Gaelic Leaguers whenever they were in Dublin. Fionán MacColuim, then chief organiser of the Gaelic League, 'An Seabhac', Peadar Ó Annrachán of Cork, Cormac Ó Cadhlaigh, now professor of Modern Irish in University College, Dublin, the late Fr John Lynch (brother of His Honour Judge Fionán Lynch) are amongst the Irish language pioneers that I can remember as staying regularly at '44' whenever private business or the interests of the language movement brought them to the capital. And there were hosts of others. One can imagine how saturated with Irish ideals the atmosphere of '44' became with such a gathering of ardent and selfless enthusiasts for the language revival.

It was not until April 1912, however, that the hectic career of 44 Mountjoy Street might be said to have really commenced for it was in that month that Fionán Lynch and Gearóid O'Sullivan (subsequently adjutant general of the pre-Truce IRA) came to Dublin to take up teaching appointments, and made their abode in '44'. They had become fast friends during their college course in St Patrick's, Drumcondra, were already keen language enthusiasts and immediately threw themselves wholeheartedly into the language and Sinn Féin movements. They very soon became prominent members of the Keating Branch of the Gaelic League – the Munstermen's Branch in Dublin – and they were in close association with men who soon became prominent in the extreme national movement. Cathal Brugha was then president of the Keating Branch, and amongst the members were Piaras Béaslaí, subsequently TD for East Kerry; Seán McDermott executed after the Rising and Con Collins arrested in Tralee in connection with the Casement landing in Easter, 1916. Of all the branches of the Gaelic League there was none in those days containing so many men holding extreme national views as the Keating Branch did – and the lady members were as keenly national as the men. As an offshoot of the Keating Branch, Piaras Béaslaí, who was already a distinguished playwright, with the help of Fionán Lynch, Gearóid O'Sullivan, Máire Ní Chonaill, BA (a native of Mastergeehy near Waterville and now a nun in the Presentation Convent, Killarney); Treasa Ní Mhuirthuile (now wife of Professor John Nolan, University College, Dublin), Con Collins and others, founded Na hAisteoirí – an Irish Drama League for the purpose of producing plays in Irish – and for a few years before the Rising these Gaelic players were seen at each Oireachtas producing several plays during Oireachtas week.

Naturally the associations of the Keating Branch had their reflection on life in '44'. Piaras Béaslaí lived across the street from '44', and was a frequent visitor, as were Seán McDermott and Con Collins who were then in 'digs' in the North Circular Road.

With the founding of the Volunteers at the end of 1913, things began to stir in '44'. Fionán and Gearóid joined the movement on the night in which the Volunteers were founded, and when companies were being formed shortly afterwards they were attached as members of 'F' company, 1st battalion. The first election of officers for the Dublin companies took place in the spring or early summer of 1914 and Piaras Béaslaí became Captain of 'F' company with Fionán Lynch as one of the Lieutenants. When the Dublin brigade shortly afterwards became organised into battalions Piaras Béaslaí became vice-commandant of the 1st battalion, and Fionán Lynch was appointed captain of 'F' company.

The friendship between Seán McDermott and Con Collins on the one hand and Fionán Lynch and Gearóid O'Sullivan on the other became more closely cemented from the founding of the Volunteers and poor Seán and Con were frequent visitors for a game of bridge at '44'. Seán was then running the extremist paper *Irish Freedom*, the organ of the Irish Republican Brotherhood, to which Piaras Béaslaí regularly contributed articles, as did P.S. O'Hegarty, formerly secretary of the department of posts and telegraphs – and Fionán, Gearóid and Con Collins helped in turning out and circulating each issue. Bundles of the issue were frequently brought to '44' when raids under the Defence of the Realm Act were expected at the printers or at the *Freedom* office.

In 1914, the Irish Parliamentary Party, seeing the growing strength of the Volunteers, looked with jealous eyes on them and started to manoeuvre towards getting control. After certain negotiations it was decided by a majority of the old executive to allow in a number of Mr Redmond's nominees, though a big number of the Volunteers were bitterly opposed to this – and especially the members of the Fenian organisation, the Irish Republican Brotherhood, including Fionán Lynch and Gearóid O'Sullivan. The union did not last long, however, because it soon became obvious, even to those who voted for allowing Mr Redmond's nominees into the executive, that Mr Redmond's aim was to line up the Volunteers behind the Parliamentary Party and to prevent them embarking on a revolutionary outbreak against England. Redmond's nominees were thrown off the executive and the Volunteers split into two parts – the original Irish Volunteers and Redmond's Volunteers. Every company suffered to some extent by the split, and 'F' company did not entirely escape, though it was one of those that suffered least, as the rank and file followed their officers (Captain Fionán Lynch and Lieutenants Seán Shouldice and Diarmuid O'Hegarty) all of whom stood firm with the old executive.

During the year 1915, two men came to 44 Mountjoy Street to stay – Mortimer O'Connell of Ballinskelligs (now assistant clerk of the Dáil) and Floss O'Doherty of Killorglin, and both immediately joined 'F' company, so that '44' had now quite an armed garrison, and it became the rendezvous of prominent Volunteers who came up on Volunteer business from various parts of the country and from England.

Early in 1916 there was another recruit brought to '44' for special work – Con Keating, from Renard, near Caherciveen, one of the few in those days who was a trained wireless expert. Poor Con was sent down on a special mission in connection with the Rising to Caherciveen, and everybody knows of the tragic ending of that mission when the car in which he with his comrades were travelling, ran over the quay at Ballykissane, Killorglin. Denis Daly, former TD for Kerry, was in the second car on that job, and he succeeded in getting back to Dublin to take part in the Rising. The prominence of Fionán Lynch in the Irish Volunteers was brought to the notice of the National Education Board early in 1916 and he was summarily notified through the manager of his school that he must resign from the Volunteers or lose his job. It is a coincidence that the first three national teachers to be 'warned-off' the Volunteers prior to the Rising by the National Education Board, were all Kerrymen – Diarmuid O'Connell, of Caherciveen, then principal teacher of

Filemore National School; Thomas Ashe and Fionán Lynch, who were teaching in Dublin. He immediately reported to Volunteer headquarters, and Thomas McDonagh and Seán McDermott, explaining the difficulties that headquarters were already confronted with in 'maintaining a big number of Irish Volunteers who had come over from England, ordered him to lie low for the present'.

The writer was a member of 'F' company, and I shall ever remember the night that Fionán explained to the company what had happened, and the cheer that arose when he told his men: 'Boys, when there is anything doing, I'll be back to lead you'; nor can I ever forget the even more memorable night – Holy Thursday 1916 – when Fionán came back to take over command again. Certainly no company in Dublin had a straighter tip than 'F' company that there was something immediately going to happen, for Fionán's words which are indelibly impressed on my mind even now, over thirty years after, were: 'Boys, you remember what I told you when, on the advice of headquarters, I gave up the command of 'F' company some weeks ago. You remember that I said that when there is anything doing that I would be back to lead you.' And then, after a pause, he said, 'Well, boys, I am back to lead you.' I'll never forget the deafening roar with which his words were greeted, and the wild excitement that prevailed amongst us of the rank and file as the meaning of his words sank into our minds.

Everything by now was moving at lightning speed and one can imagine what '44' was like in those days. During the week before the Rising it was feared that some of the leaders might be arrested, so they went to stay in various houses through the city, with armed Volunteers to protect them. Seán McDermott came to '44' and stayed there until Easter Sunday – the day on which the Rising was originally to take place. On Easter Saturday morning – between 4 and 5 a.m. – '44' was alarmed with a heavy rat-tat-tat at the hall door, and the Volunteers inside sprang from their beds and handled their guns, for everyone thought it was a raid by the British. A window upstairs was opened and the early visitor was identified as Seán Connolly, who was subsequently killed during the first half hour of the fighting while he and his men were attempting to capture Dublin Castle. Seán Connolly was the bearer of an important dispatch to Seán McDermott with reference to the arrest of Sir Roger Casement in Kerry, and messages were sent to various leaders at once to come to Liberty Hall for a conference. Fionán Lynch and Gearóid O'Sullivan went in a taxi to St Enda's college, Rathfarnham, to bring in Pádraig Pearse to that conference, while Tom Clarke, James Connolly, Thomas McDonagh and other leaders were notified by others.

That conference lasted throughout the greater part of Saturday and it was decided in spite of the bad news from Kerry, to go on with the Rising as arranged. There were certain important members of the executive, however, who were not summoned to that conference. These included Professor MacNeill, the chairman. This was, in the light of later events, unfortunate, for on Easter Sunday morning the Sunday papers contained a notice over MacNeill's signature cancelling the 'manoeuvres' arranged for that day. This notice created consternation amongst the more extreme members of the executive, and Sunday was again a day of many conferences. The final one of these was held in the rooms of the Keating Branch of the Gaelic League and finished about midnight with the decision to go on with the Rising on Easter Monday.

On Easter Sunday evening there was a stir when some members of the Dublin Metropolitan Police called to '44'. They came to enquire about 'a man named Con Keating', and it was then for the first time that his comrades in '44' heard of the tragic occurrence at Ballykissane. In view of the authorities having connected poor Con with '44' it was decided that it would not be the safest place in which to stay the night before the Rising, so Seán McDermott and Gearóid O'Sullivan went to stay at Fleming's Hotel. Fionán Lynch went with Diarmuid O'Hegarty to his 'digs' in St Peter's Road and Floss

O'Doherty went with Mick Collins (who, a few months before, had arrived in Dublin from London) to Mick's 'digs' in Rathdown Road. Mort O'Connell alone remained in '44' that night and as nothing had happened, he had the dump of rifles and ammunition taken from the roof when his comrades arrived in the morning to get into their uniforms and collect their weapons for the great adventure.

One can imagine Miss McCarthy's feelings during that week, with the roar of guns and the rattle of machine guns and rifles filling the air. Con Keating was already dead and would she see alive again any of 'her boys', as she fondly called them. The incidents of the Rising itself need no recounting here. Gearóid O'Sullivan fought in the General Post Office, having been commissioned immediately prior to the Rising and attached to Seán McDermott's staff. 'F' company held a line along Church Street, from North King Street to May Lane, adjoining the Four Courts, and from the Wednesday of Easter Week up to the surrender, were under constant fire. Mort O'Connell and Floss O'Doherty were fighting in that area and so of course was the captain of the company, Fionán Lynch. Floss O'Doherty escaped following the surrender, and after some very exciting adventures, made his way back to '44', and resumed his ordinary avocation as a teacher, as if nothing had happened. Of the other '44' lodgers, Gearóid O'Sullivan and Mort O'Connell were deported and subsequently interned in Frongoch, while Fionán Lynch was sentenced to death, but the sentence was commuted to ten years penal servitude.

The history of '44' after the Rising and up to the Truce, is largely the history of Mick Collins, for when 'the boys' were released from Frongoch, Mick went to stay at '44' with Gearóid O'Sullivan, and it was there that they continued to live up to the Truce. Or perhaps it would be more correct to say that they kept their quarters and their clothes there, because from the end of 1919 they were badly wanted men and rarely slept two consecutive nights in the same bed. But their absence did not save '44' from the attentions of the

British authorities. There was not a week during the Black and Tan regime when the place was not raided several times. And through all that period Mick paid flying visits there for change of clothing, and even to meet persons who came up from the country on Volunteer business. But his visits were purposely irregular, so that much as the place was watched he was never caught.

And what of '44' today? To all appearances it is the same old '44' as ever, but to one who knew it of old, what a change! Miss McCarthy died a few years ago at the age of eighty-five, but in that house of memories there is still living one of 'her boys', Floss O'Doherty, the only unmarried survivor of the batch of young '44' residents who helped to make modern Irish history. Poor Mick's gay laugh is stilled forever; Gearóid became a barrister and was a TD for County Dublin, now Special Commissioner for Income Tax; Fionán, now His Honour Judge Lynch, was TD for Kerry for over a quarter of a century, never losing an election; and Mort O'Connell, reinstated in the civil service after the Treaty, is now assistant clerk of Dáil Éireann.

CONSCRIPTION AND THE GENERAL ELECTION OF 1918

by VOLUNTEER

THE TWO YEARS which immediately followed the Rising of 1916 were marked by the amazing spread of the Sinn Féin movement and by intensive training and re-organisation of the Irish Volunteers. Actually the Volunteers were not officially connected with either Sinn Féin or the secret, oath-bound Irish Republican Brotherhood. Sinn Féin proper, as evolved by Arthur Griffith, might be termed the right wing of the independence movement; the Irish Republican Brotherhood, the left. The recognition of a republic had become the declared aim of Sinn Féin, although, that once achieved, the people were to be permitted to determine whatever form of government they preferred. With the Volunteers daily adding to their numbers, and the Sinn Féin organisation gathering force, the British government resorted to all of their old and tried methods in a frantic effort to cope with the situation. The tri-colour was banned, meetings were proclaimed and republican publications were suppressed. Even the *camán* was proscribed as a lethal weapon. The people answered the coercion code by defiantly flying the republican flag everywhere. From all sorts of strange places it waved, it being not an uncommon occurrence for the Royal Irish Constabulary to find the Orange, White and Green flying from their barracks at daybreak, as happened in Killarney. Banned meetings were held at

places other than the advertised venues, and Volunteer leaders openly
addressed them. Organisation and drilling of the Volunteers went on
apace, and Irish language classes were attended by ever increasing
numbers. Arrests were numerous; but the British courts were held
up to ridicule, prisoners refusing to answer and boldly proclaiming
their non-recognition of the foreign judicature. Kerrymen amongst
those arrested included Thomas Ashe, Kinard, Lispole; Austin
Stack, Tralee; Fionán Lynch, Caherciveen; J.J. O'Kelly ('Sceilg'),
Caherciveen; Tadhg Brosnan, Castlegregory; Michael Moriarty,
James Moriarty and John Rael, Dingle; William Mullins, Joe Melinn
and Michael J. O'Connor, Tralee. Having been held in jail about four
months the men were released and accorded a tumultuous reception
on their return home on Wednesday, 20 June 1917. The North
Kerry, West Kerry and Tralee ex-prisoners were met at Killarney
railway station by Dr Michael Lawlor, Jack Lawlor, P.J. Quinlan and
others, who brought them by motor car to Tralee. At Ballycarthy
Cross there was a great muster of the Volunteers and of the general
public, to welcome them home. Jack McKenna, Listowel, chairman
of the County Council, and Morty O'Sullivan, Abbeydorney, led the
North Kerry contingent, whilst the Castleisland men were in charge
of W.H. O'Connor and Con Browne.

Volunteers of the cyclist corps led the huge procession into
Tralee, where bonfires blazed a welcome and republican flags were
flown from most buildings. In many private houses there was a
display of lighted candles in the upstairs front windows. The event
provided one of the most extraordinary and spectacular scenes ever
witnessed in Tralee. On arrival at the outskirts of the town the
prisoners were taken from the motor cars of their friends and amidst
wild cheering were borne shoulder high, first through the streets and
then to their homes. With the Kerry prisoners was Frank Fahy, now
ceann comhairle, Dáil Éireann. The home-coming of the prisoners
was filmed and shown to enthusiastic audiences at the Old County
Hall, a few weeks later. Fionán Lynch was accompanied on his

triumphal return to Caherciveen by his brother, Rev. Fr Lynch, then curate in Glenbeigh, and by Miss McColum and Floss O'Doherty. At Killorglin, Glenbeigh, Mountain Stage, Kells and other stations along the line, enthusiastic crowds were assembled to welcome him home. At Kells he was greeted by Mrs Pearse, mother of Pádraig and Willie Pearse, who were executed after the Rising. Biggest welcome awaited him in his native Caherciveen, thronged by Volunteers, Cumann na mBan and general public, eager to do him honour. First to shake his hand were Miss Kathleen O'Sullivan, D.J. O'Connell, MCC, James J. O'Shea and Eugene Ring. Jerome Riordan had charge of a party of two hundred horsemen; the Volunteers on foot were commanded by Denis Daly and Mort O'Connell, whilst the Cumann na mBan were led by Mrs Jeremiah O'Connell. When Mrs Pearse and Captain Lynch addressed the cheering multitude from a window of J. Riordan's house, both were received with indescribable enthusiasm, and it was evident that Mrs Pearse was greatly moved as she wished God's blessing on the people. At Lispole, Kinard and Dingle, bonfires blazed and huge crowds assembled to welcome home Thomas Ashe, and the other West Kerry prisoners who were accompanied by Austin Stack of Tralee.

Back on their native heath the released Kerry leaders, immediately resumed activities. A meeting of the Kerry organising committee of Sinn Féin, held in the sportsfield on 8 August, was addressed by Austin Stack, Thomas Ashe and Frank Fahy. J.D. O'Connell, solicitor, presided. Three days later Kerry's greatest ever republican hosting assembled at Casement's Fort, Banna, on the occasion of the anniversary of the execution of Sir Roger Casement. Under scorching sunshine more than 12,000 people listened to the words of Thomas Ashe, Austin Stack, Fionán Lynch and Frank Fahy. Volunteer contingents with their bands, Cumann na mBan and general public were there from every town and village in the county. Mid-August brought further intensification of the British coercive measures, and fresh arrests. Amongst prominent Kerrymen who again found themselves behind prison bars were Thomas Ashe, Austin Stack, Fionán Lynch, and Ned Barry of Tralee. Thomas Ashe was arrested in Dublin, on Monday 3 September. Having been found guilty by court martial of attempting to create disaffection by a speech in Longford, he was sentenced to twelve months' imprisonment with hard labour. Committed to Mountjoy jail where he was lodged in the civil prison with common criminals, Ashe and the other republican prisoners there immediately demanded treatment as prisoners of war. The demand ignored, a regular battle ensued between the men and their gaolers, as a result of which Ashe was deprived of bed and bedding, and more of the prisoners were left naked in their cells. All went on hunger strike.

Meetings were held everywhere in support of their demands, and De Valera addressed a monster rally in Dublin where a resolution was passed 'calling the attention of the European Powers and the United States to the fact that Irishmen are being arrested and tried by English courts for declaring, in the words of President Wilson's message – "that no people shall be forced to live in a sovereignty in which it does not desire to live".' The prison authorities then resorted to forcible feeding. Prisoners who resisted were overpowered, tied down, and feeding apparatus forced up their nostrils. After forcible feeding many prisoners were carried, bleeding profusely, back to their cells, where they were left without bedding or covering. Whilst being thus fed on the fourth day of his hunger strike, Thomas Ashe collapsed, was immediately released, and died five hours later in the Mater Misericordiae Nursing Home. The coroner's jury brought in a verdict against the prison authorities, and added that forcible feeding was inhuman and dangerous. The jury censured the prisons' board for their refusal to give evidence, and for their failure to hand over relevant documents for which they had been asked. Dressed in the uniform of the Irish Volunteers the body of Thomas Ashe lay in state in the City Hall, where Volunteers formed a guard of honour. Kerry was strongly represented amongst 30,000 people who marched in the funeral procession. At the grave the Last Post was sounded, and the firing party paid final honours to the dead soldier.

De Valera, the only commandant to survive the Rising and the inspiration of the country, was unanimously elected president of Sinn Féin on 25 October 1917. During the same week he was chosen president of the Irish Volunteers. Michael Collins, then about twenty-seven, was made director of organisation, and infused new vitality into the Irish Republican Brotherhood, from the inside of which he intensively developed the military resurgence.

By that time it was becoming more obvious every day that the country was through with the Parliamentary Party, whose hat-in-hand policy of seeking ameliorative legislation for Ireland at Westminster had lost caste with the people. While Irish prisoners were still confined in British jails, Count Plunkett and Joe McGuinness, himself a prisoner, won by-elections for Sinn Féin. De Valera, released in 1917, won East Clare, and Cosgrave did likewise in Kilkenny. It was the first triumph for republican Ireland, for the Sinn Féin MPs were pledged never to take their seats in the British parliament. The Parliamentary Party managed to win by-elections in South Armagh, Waterford and East Tyrone.

All the while Kerry had been intensively active, perfecting the organisation of the Volunteers and spreading the gospel of the Sinn Féin movement. Every week the Volunteers paraded, drilled and manoeuvred openly, whilst lectures and concerts were regularly given under the auspices of Sinn Féin. Ned Barry of Tralee, who had been, on hunger strike in Mountjoy at the time of the death of Thomas Ashe, was given a tremendous reception when he appeared on the stage to sing at a Sinn Féin concert in the Theatre Royal, Tralee, on 14 November 1917. Other artistes in the same concert included Criss Stokes, Mona McMahon, Dodo Kepple, C. Foley, N. Foley and Mrs K. Burke; Dr Michael Quinlan, Dan Hobbs (Cork), George Reid, Joe Melinn, William Horgan, Seán Neeson (Cork), George Ralph, George McLeish and Jackie Fleming. Relating his experiences of forcible feeding whilst on hunger strike in Mountjoy jail, Ned Barry told the audience that:

> On Saturday the twenty-second of September warders came to my cell and took me to the room used for forcible feeding. Warning the doctor about my health, I told him that he would be held responsible if anything should happen to me, and that the warders who were Irishmen would convey my warning to the public. Referring to his experiment with forcible feeding I told him that he would get enough of fighting before he had finished, as he was not now dealing with conscientious objectors. When I refused to drink liquid voluntarily he ordered the warders to strap me to the chair. This done a tube was rammed up my nostrils, through which food was pumped. I was greatly shocked and became unconscious, after which I have been told that I was conveyed to my cell by four warders. At all events, when I recovered consciousness I was lying in my cell with nothing to sit upon except an old tin can. In order to get some sleep I lay on the floor, using a bible for a pillow. The only thing which comforted me was to hear the voices of the boys in their cells, singing patriotic songs, about two o'clock in the morning. I knew that they were all in the same desperate position as myself, and finding them in such spirits I joined in the singing.

On Tuesday 29 November, British forces made a swoop in Tralee and arrested William Mullins, Moyderwell; Tom Foley and John Foley, Rock Street; John McGaley, Daniel Healy, Spa Road, and P.J. Cahill, Strand Street. Tadhg Brosnan of Castlegregory had been arrested earlier in the month. The Tralee prisoners were all removed to Cork barracks, where they were tried by court martial on 10 December. The charge against Thomas Foley was that he had participated in movements of a military nature and worn a uniform of a military character whilst in charge of an advance party of eighteen which formed part of a parade of six hundred and forty men. He was sentenced to eighteen months without hard labour, one year of which was remitted. John McGaley, charged with being in charge of twelve cyclists who made up the rearguard of the parade, was sentenced to eighteen months without hard labour, one year of which was remitted. Paddy Cahill, charged with marching at the head of the parade of six hundred and forty men, and with wearing a Volunteer uniform, was sentenced to two years' imprisonment without hard labour, one year of which was remitted. Daniel Healy, charged with marching beside Paddy Cahill at the head of the parade, and with wearing a Volunteer uniform, received eighteen months' imprisonment without hard labour, one year of which was remitted. William Mullins was charged with being in charge of the cycle corps in the parade, and with wearing a military uniform. He was sentenced to eighteen months without hard labour, one year of which was remitted. On the same date Tadhg Brosnan, charged with practising military movements in Castlegregory on 20 October, was sentenced to eighteen months without hard labour, one year of which was remitted. All prisoners refused to recognise the court. Evidence was given against the Tralee prisoners by Detective Sergeant McKenna and Constables George Kneazer, O'Rourke and Quinlan of Tralee. Sergeant James Regan and Constable Michael Brophy gave evidence against Brosnan. When sentence was pronounced Paddy Cahill and Thomas Foley were sent to Cork jail, and the others to Dundalk. All went on hunger strike from the time of their arrival in these prisons from which they were released shortly afterwards.

Volunteers and Sinn Féin continued their open defiance of British rule and institutions, and the government replied with an ever intensifying campaign of raids and arrests. Early in 1918 Ned Horan of Tralee was arrested at Listowel, and Tom Foley and John Foley, of Rock Street, Tralee, were re-arrested. All three went on hunger strike, and were released soon afterwards. In March a young Dingle man, Tom Russell, died as a result of bayonet wounds which he received when the military dispersed a gathering at Carrigaholt, County Clare. The alienation from England was soon to receive further and more urgent impetus.

In April 1918, Lloyd George proposed the extension of the Conscription Act to Ireland, under the same conditions as in

England. The result was the formation of the most solid front which had yet faced the British in this country. Sinn Féin and Parliamentary leaders addressed protest meetings from joint platforms, but it was Sinn Féin which really developed and expanded under the grave menace. The Lord Mayor of Dublin, Lawrence O'Neill, availed of the situation to bring the different parties together in the face of the national danger, and on 18 April 1918, he convened the famous Mansion House Conference. The representatives who attended were Éamon de Valera and Arthur Griffith, Sinn Féin; John Dillon and Joseph Devlin, Parliamentary Party; William O'Brien, Tom Johnson and Michael Egan, Labour; Tim Healy, Independent; and William O'Brien, Cork, All for Ireland League. The result of the conference was the issuing of an anti-conscription pledge which read: Denying the right of the British government to enforce compulsory conscription in this country, we pledge ourselves solemnly to one another to resist conscription by the most effective means at our disposal.

The conference also passed the following declaration unanimously: Taking our stand on Ireland's separate and distinct nationhood and affirming the principle of liberty that the governments of nations derive their just powers from the consent of the governed, we deny the right of the British government or any external authority to impose compulsory military service on Ireland against the clearly expressed will of the Irish people. The passing of the Conscription Bill by the British House of Commons must be regarded as a declaration of war on the Irish nation. The alternative to accepting it as such is to surrender our liberty and to acknowledge ourselves slaves. It is in direct violation of the rights of small nationalities to self-determination, which even the prime minister of England – now preparing to employ naked militarism and force his Act upon Ireland – himself officially announced as an essential condition for peace at the Peace Congress. The attempt to enforce it will be an unwarrantable aggression, which we call upon all Irishmen to resist by the most effective means at their disposal. Both pledge and declaration were drafted by Éamon de Valera.

On the same evening the Catholic bishops in annual session at Maynooth issued the following manifesto: An attempt is being made to force conscription on Ireland against the will of the Irish nation and in defiance of the protests of its leaders. In view especially of the historic relations between the two countries from the very beginning up to this moment, we consider that conscription forced in this way upon Ireland is an oppressive and inhuman law, which the Irish people have a right to resist by every means that are consonant with the law of God. We wish to remind our people that there is a higher power which controls the affairs of men. They have in their hands the means of conciliating that power by strict adherence to the divine law, and by more earnest attention to their religious duties, and by fervent and persevering prayer. In order to secure the aid of the Holy Mother of God who shielded our people in the days of their greatest trials, we have already sanctioned a national novena in honour of Our Lady of Lourdes, commencing on 3 May, to secure general and domestic peace. We also exhort the heads of families to have the Rosary recited every evening with the intention, of protecting the spiritual and temporal welfare of our beloved country and bringing us safe through this crisis of unparalleled gravity – *Signed, Michael, Cardinal Logue, chairman; Robert Browne, Bishop of Cloyne, secretary; Patrick Foley, Bishop of Kildare and Leighlin, secretary pro tem.*

Thus, by April 1918, was the country face to face with the unlovely fact that her manhood was about to be conscripted to fight for England. It did not matter a button that England had no moral right to force the issue. The 'democratic' tyrants of that punitive land of freedom had evidently made up their minds to enforce military service on the Irish, which they had just as much right to do as the Germans would have in the case of Belgium. In each case at that time the weaker country was occupied by the soldiers of the stronger. Just as in the days of her power Imperial Rome had no claim founded on justice to hold France or Germany or Judea, in bondage; so the top dogs of 1918 could only justify keeping another people in subjection either by the consent of that people or by strength. After seven hundred years of regularly recurring defeats Ireland had not forsworn her right to nationhood; neither had Belgium after nearly four years' subjection. England was just as little justified in compelling Ireland to fight for her as Germany would have been in the case of Belgium.

The members of the then British cabinet, which included the famous Arthur James Balfour, had worked overtime occasionally in telling touching homilies of the rights of 'small nationalities'. The elegant dialecticians, Balfour in particular, had expended quite a considerable amount of verbiage which touched the justice of a nation's demand for what he termed self-determination. Ireland did not stand in at all so far as that policy was concerned. But the conscription of a whole country, unitedly and resolutely opposed to the measure, constituted a proposition which proved too much even for the intellect with which the Lloyd George cabinet was furnished.

Whilst a sincere, even fervent desire, to subject Ireland to military service, was no doubt in existence, a long distance and a rugged road separated the desire from its fruition. Kerry took a leading part in the fight against the measure, and protest meetings were held throughout the towns and villages of the county. The Sinn Féin Clubs became to a greater degree than ever the rallying centres for the people. It was only natural that the sections which had previously kept aloof from the movement should have turned to it when the fabric of the Irish Parliamentary Party, upon which they had built their hopes, had been destroyed by the breath of an English politician. The British replied by reorganising the Dublin Castle executive, and the service was purged of all personnel suspected of Irish leanings. The viceroy, Lord Wimbourne, was replaced by Lord French, who, on the day on which he took up office, declared that he would soon name the date before which recruits must offer themselves in the various districts.

'If they do not come,' said Lord French, 'we will fetch them.' General Shaw was appointed to the military command in place of General Sir Bryan Mahon. But these changes, far from having the desired effect, served only to awaken British public opinion, a large section of which, though not in favour of the anti-conscription idea, became, nevertheless, alarmed by this new turn of events in Ireland. It was then that the scheming, fertile brain of Lloyd George 'discovered' a new 'German plot'; a new and urgent reason to again hustle off to British jails de Valera, Arthur Griffith, Austin Stack, and most of the leaders. Outside the barbed wire, however, there remained the energetic, dominant Collins, scheming, drilling and reorganising with greater intensity than ever.

The object of the bogus plot was to deal a vital blow at Sinn Féin by the imprisonment of the leaders, and by attempting to justify such action in the eyes of the world, especially of America, by proving the existence of a fresh alliance with the German enemy. The elimination of Sinn Féin would remove the biggest obstacle to conscription. By the summer of 1918, however, the 'German plot' was completely debunked, and it had become increasingly apparent that the application of conscription to Ireland was off. Britain's army council wanted to go ahead with the measure, but the government funked putting it to issue. Lord French, who had made conscription a condition of office, resigned the vice-royalty. There was great rejoicing in Ireland, although the government had initiated a campaign of rough treatment for the people, which took the form of an intensive campaign of raids, arrests and ill-treatment of prisoners. The outcome of it all was revealed by the general election of 1918, when Sinn Féin, fighting on an abstentionist and republican ticket, won every seat but one throughout three parts of Ireland.

Those who at the time held that it was a wise policy on the part of Ireland's Parliamentary representatives to attend the British House of Commons found much food for thought in the attitude of the British press on the policy of abstention. The Irish Parliamentary representatives left the House of Commons in a body and remained away for some months following Lloyd George's attempt to extend the Conscription Act to Ireland in April 1919. During that period the English Liberal papers repeatedly appealed to them to go back, and the English Tories agitated for the introduction of a bill to make it compulsory on candidates for parliamentary vacancies to take the oath of allegiance to the English king. This policy was formulated to exclude Sinn Féin candidates whom the Tories knew were certain to be returned in the general election which all felt to be near at hand. If the contention that the presence of the Irish Party in the House of Commons was a source of embarrassment to the government, why was there such feverish anxiety to arrange their return to that august assemblage? The English *Daily Chronicle* gave the answer in its issue of the 22 August 1918. Here is a quotation from its political correspondent:

> Two practical reasons against a premature general election in the midst of the war are summarised in a couple of words – an ineffective register and Ireland. The prospect of a clean sweep of the constitutional nationalists (Irish Party) by the irreconcilables (Sinn Féiners) must be faced sooner or later, but why precipitate it now? A House of Commons without any representative of Ireland – for Sir Edward Carson and his friends are but the wing of the British Tory Party – would be a world scandal, and that is what the inevitable Sinn Féin victory at the present time would mean. British relations with Ireland are still at least transactable; they would be untransactable if there were no Irish spokesmen in the Imperial Parliament.

The last sentence put the case in a nutshell. As long as British relations with Ireland were transactable – on English terms – so long was Ireland to be laughed at as a fool and kicked as a slave. Interest as well as honour demanded that Ireland's leaders should have no further negotiations with England's statesmen. 'It is a mistake,' said Parnell, 'to negotiate with an Englishman; he knows the business better than you do.'

When it was obvious that a general election was approaching, the British decided to make the best possible job of it and action against the Sinn Féiners was greatly intensified. There were many arrests throughout the country, and Kerry did not escape, Dan McCarthy, chief organiser for the movement, was arrested in September at Milltown, where he had been on the run for some weeks. By such methods it was hoped to reduce the effectiveness of the Sinn Féin electoral machine. Austin Stack, Fionán Lynch and James Crowley, three of the Sinn Féin candidates nominated for Kerry, were in jail at the time of their nomination, whilst the fourth, Piaras Béaslaí, was on the run. Austin Stack was also selected by the South Tipperary Sinn Féin Executive to be their parliamentary candidate for the constituency. Police entered the room where the executive meeting was in progress and demanded to know what business was being transacted. As they refused to leave, the Sinn Féiners withdrew and resumed their meeting in a wood about half-a-mile outside Cahir, where they chose Austin Stack. The West Kerry Sinn Féin executive, whilst expressing their appreciation of the compliment paid to Austin by the South Tipperary men, pointed out that they could not part with him as he was urgently needed at home. J.D. O'Connell, solicitor, presided over the West Kerry Sinn Féin executive meeting which nominated Austin Stack. Other members who attended were Diarmuid Crean, J.P. O'Donnell, RDC, Tom Slattery and Tom Dennehy, Tralee; Tadhg Brosnan, Castlegregory; J.E. O'Shea, Milltown; Dr McDonnell and 'An Seabhac', Dingle; M.E. Mangan and J. Conroy, Tralee, secretary.

Following some preliminary skirmishing, all four sitting Kerry MPs withdrew from the contest, when it was obvious that they stood no chance of re-election. They were T.D. O'Sullivan, East Kerry; M.J. Flavin, North Kerry; T. O'Donnell, West Kerry; J. Boland, South Kerry. Tom O'Donnell gave his swan song to a representative meeting of his supporters in Tralee, on 27 November 1918. Said he:

I offered myself for re-election in order to give the people an opportunity to express their views in one of the most momentous crises that has ever occurred in our country. I think the Sinn Féin policy, devoid of reason and sanity, has ruined and will further ruin my country. It has embittered and united opposition to our claims for freedom, both in Ireland and abroad. It advocates a policy in which no honest or sane man believes, and it pushes its programme by methods which are the very antithesis of liberty. My friends, in spite of noisy shouting there are yet thousands of sane decent Irishmen who will save our country in the near future. It has been agreed that in view of the state of the register, packed with boys and girls, we will not engage in the contest at present, and with that decision I most heartily agree. A whirlwind of political insanity is passing over the country; promises are made which can never be realised, and there are appeals to prejudice to embitter feelings and distort men's vision. The storm will pass, leaving the stable, honest Irishman untouched after it had scattered the froth and the chaff. With confidence I await that time, and most earnestly appeal to my friends throughout West Kerry to bear themselves as men in what is only a temporary and very short-lived period of Confusion.

As a result, of the withdrawal of the representatives of the Parliamentary Party, there were no elections in Kerry, and the four Sinn Féin nominees were returned unopposed, as follows: Austin Stack, West Kerry; James Crowley, North Kerry; Piaras Béaslaí, East Kerry; Fionán Lynch, South Kerry.

When the announcements of the bloodless victories were received there were scenes of the greatest enthusiasm in the principal centres such as Tralee, Killarney, Listowel, Dingle, Caherciveen and Castleisland; while, when the glad tidings spread to outlying districts, the same spirit of jubilation was in evidence. Many regretted that there were no contests; that the Party nominees did not elect to stand to their guns. But, all matters considered, it was better that they decided to hoist the white flag. Thus, the good old 'Kingdom' acquitted itself magnificently, and made a clean sweep of the 'Party's' representatives. As the county returned the first Home Rule candidate in Ireland, almost fifty years previously, it took a leading and early part in strengthening the Sinn Féin movement. Just imagine – the 'Constitutional' Home Rule game was roughly fifty years old at the time of the 1918 general election, and it was quite as ineffective then as it was during any part of its career. For over fifty years Irish MPs were humbugged and laughed at by successive British governments – except for the all too brief period when Parnell was in power. The Sinn Féin movement was led by men who could neither be fooled nor bribed. At that time when the world's statesmen were about to engage, in attempting to right the wrongs of small nationalities, it was mighty awkward that Ireland, the oldest of small nationalities, should start in to claim in most unequivocal style, her right to self-determination. England strove with might and main to deny her that right, though Ireland's case and Ireland's claims were placed before the world. When Ireland's demands were later backed by action even Lloyd George, craftiest and most intolerant of statesmen, found that he could not ignore a united nation. By the unopposed return of the four Sinn Féin representatives, Kerry proved her worth in the 1918 election; in a quiet way it is true, but it proved it anyway. The 'vested interests' of the parliamentary aggregation funked putting the issue to a test. In the words of *The Kerryman*:

> Glory be to our own Kerry – north, south, east and west! – a clean sheet! A complete walk-over for Sinn Féin. Kerry will give a great impetus to the Sinn Féin movement in other parts of Ireland where there are to be electoral contests. Bravo Kerry! Up The Kingdom!

The names of the assentors and nominees of the Kerry Sinn Féin candidates are worthy of record. Forty names were handed in on behalf of Piaras Béaslaí, the East Kerry candidate. In the principal paper he was proposed by the Rev. Fr D.J. Finucane, CC, Killarney, and seconded by Patrick Spillane, Killarney. The assentors were Maurice Horgan, New Street, Killarney; Michael J. O'Sullivan, Ardshanavooly; Richard Fitzgerald, College Street, Killarney; Pádraig Dubháin, Kenmare Place, Killarney; John O'Leary, Old Market Lane,

Killarney; Timothy Horgan, Moyaghtra; William Bland, Moyaghtra; Patrick O'Shea, Walsh's Lane, Killarney. One of the nominations was filled and signed in Irish but was rejected by the Returning Officer. Fr Finucane was accompanied by Patrick Spillane, T. O'Shea, solicitor, election agent; Fathers O'Herlihy, Supple, Brosnan and Harris; R. Fitzgerald, Seán Ó Cathasaigh; Jeremiah O'Leary, Seán Kerins, P. Dubháin. In the other nominations the proposers and seconders, respectively, were: Jeremiah O'Sullivan, Saint Anne's Road, Killarney; Denis Lyne, Mangerton View, Killarney; John Casey, High Street, Killarney; William Ahern, High Street, Killarney, Bridget Gleeson, Henn Street, Killarney; Sheelagh O'Shea, New Street, Killarney; Lawrence Buckley, Radranagh; Timothy O'Sullivan, Knocknanane; Rev. D.J. O'Herlihy and Rev. Fr Brosnan, St Brendan's Seminary. Thomas M. Fleming, Inchicorrigane; Daniel Cooper, Knockmanagh; John Prendergast, Scartaglin; James O'Sullivan, Scartaglin; John J. O'Connor, Tooreenamult; John J. Cronin, Tooreenamult; Michael D. Scannell, Shronebeg; Patrick J. Cahill, Stagmount; Daniel Mahony, Cloonacurrig; Thomas P. Griffin, Castleisland; Jeremiah Nolan, junior, Castleisland; William H. O'Connor, Castleisland. John McCarthy, Brehig; Timothy T. Connor, Cordal; Batt Murphy, Knocknagoshel; James J. Hickey, Ballyduff; Rev. T. Kelliher, Killeentierna; T.P. Brosnan, RDC; Jeremiah Long, Knocknagoshel; Daniel O'Connor, Knocknagoshel; Rev. W.J. Behan, Rathmore; Rev. C.J. Fitzgerald, Rathmore. Assentors: Rev. Donal O'Sullivan, Rev. Thomas Supple, Rev. Timothy Harris, Rev. Bro. J.K. O'Connor, Rev. Bro. Timothy J. Cahill, Rev. Bro. Cornelius Shine, Rev. Bro. Eugene O'Sullivan, Rev. Fr Hartigan, Firies; H. Spring, RDC, P.J. Moynihan, MCC, J.P. Slattery, RDC, D. Long, RDC, P.T. Kearney, RDC, J.J. Courtney, RDC, M.D. Scannell, RDC, G. Griffin, RDC, J. Brosnan, RDC, Timothy O'Connor, Cordal.

At four o'clock on the afternoon of the election, David Roche, solicitor, declared Piaras Béaslaí returned as parliamentary representative for East Kerry. There was great enthusiasm by the large gathering at the courthouse, and a procession, headed by two bands, marched through the town to the Market Cross, where a meeting was addressed by Tim O'Shea, solicitor, election agent; Dick Fitzgerald and Henry Spring. Rev. Fr Finucane was in the chair.

There was a tremendous crowd at the Tralee courthouse where it was found that Austin Stack was the only candidate nominated, and he was duly declared elected representative for West Kerry, amid scenes of great jubilation. The vote of thanks to the deputy Returning Officer was proposed by J.D O'Connell, solicitor, election agent, and seconded by Joe Melinn. In the principal paper Austin Stack was proposed by Gregory Ashe, Kinard, Lispole, and seconded by Patrick Casey, Trades Council, Rock Street, Tralee. The assenting electors were: Rev. J. Casey, CC, Rev. C. Hillee, CC, Rev. William Behan, CC, Messrs J.P. O'Donnell, T. Dennehy, D. O'Sullivan, Mrs Ellen Hickey and Mrs Mary Moynihan. Other nomination papers were: proposed by Patrick Power, Rock Street, Tralee; seconded by Thomas Slattery, Rock Street, Tralee. Proposed by John O'Donnell, Glendene, Camp; seconded by Michael Fitzgerald, Camp. Proposed by John O'Connell, Castlegregory; seconded by Maurice Flynn. Proposed by Thomas Walsh, Cloghane; seconded by John Flaherty, Cappagh. Proposed by John Moriarty, Ballinagall; seconded by Patrick Callahan. Proposed by Rev. J. McGrath, Ballyferriter; seconded by Michael Granville. Proposed by John Curran, Dingle; seconded by J.J. O'Connor, Dingle. Proposed by John Ashe, Kinard; seconded by Jeremiah Kavanagh, Kinard. Proposed by John O'Donnell, Inch; seconded by Daniel Foley, Inch. Proposed by Patrick Murphy, Keel; seconded by Eugene Deane, Keel. Proposed by Rev. Denis Linehan, Milltown; seconded by Dr D. Sheehan, Milltown. Proposed by William O'Brien, Killorglin; seconded by Thomas Foley, Killorglin. Proposed by Patrick Prendeville, Rathass; seconded by John Talbot, Rathass. Proposed by Thomas Healy, Listellick; seconded by Edward McMahon, Listellick. Proposed by Michael Fitzgerald, Ballyroe; seconded by James Kenny, Ballyroe.

Proposed by Jeremiah D. Brosnan, Chapeltown; seconded by John Moriarty, Chapeltown. Proposed by Michael McKenna, Curraheen; seconded by Francis O'Donnell, Curraheen. Proposed by D. Crean; seconded by P.J. Walsh. At four o'clock, the sub-sheriff (Mr Roche) as deputy Returning Officer, appeared on the Courthouse steps and declared Austin Stack elected MP for West Kerry. There was great applause.

Dan Browne, solicitor, Tralee, handed in fifty nomination papers at the Listowel courthouse, on behalf of James Crowley, VS, Sinn Féin candidate for the constituency. In the principal paper James Crowley was proposed by Dr Michael O'Connor, The Square, Listowel, and seconded by the Rev. Charles O'Sullivan, CC, Listowel. The assentors were: Messrs. T.D. O'Sullivan, Thomas J. Walsh, chairman, UDC, Jeremiah Keane, chairman, RDC, James Lynch, UDC, D.J. Flavin, UDC, D. Browne, merchant, Church Street, John Moran, solicitor, D.H. Leane, LPSI. Amongst other nomination papers the following were the proposers and seconders: Very Rev. P. Canon Hayes, PP, VF, Ballylongford, and Rev. James Beasley, PP, Duagh; Rev. J. Breen, Listowel, and Rev. William Fitzgerald, Duagh; Rev. John Finucane, Duagh, and Rev. J. O'Brien, Duagh; Rev. Michael Dillon, Kilmorna, and Dr Conor Martin, Ballylongford; James O'Hanlon, RDC, and Daniel Wren, Tarbert; John Walsh, RDC, and James Cremmins, Ballydonoghue; James Clarke and William O'Carroll, Ballybunion; John J. Sheehy, RDC, Duagh; Michael C. Mulvihill, RDC; Patrick Broderick and P.D. Kennelly, Newtownsandes; E. McElligott, RDC, Asdee; David Walsh and J. Collins (junior), Ballylongford; John Barrett, RDC, and Richard O'Callaghan, Ballyduff; John Mulquin and Michael P. O'Connor, Ballyheigue; P. Carmody and John Slattery, Ardfert; Mortimer Galvin and Patrick Lyons, Lixnaw; Edward Slattery and Michael O'Sullivan, Kilflynn; Timothy Donovan and Mortimer O'Connor, Abbeydorney; John Rice and Eyre Stack, Ballyconry; Jeremiah McMahon and James M. Walsh, Ballyoneen; Edward Mulvihill and J.M. Hanrahan,

2,000 volunteers from Tralee and district paraded before Captain Maurice Talbot Crosbie, in the Market, Tralee, on 14 June 1914.

A Tralee Irish Volunteer group photographed in Tralee Sportsfield (now the Austin Stack Park) in 1915. FRONT ROW *(left to right): Danny Healy, Austin Stack, Alfred Cotton;* MIDDLE ROW: *Michael Doyle, Frank Roche, Danny Mullins, Eddie Barry;* BACK ROW: *Joe Melinn, Ned Lynch, Mick Fleming.*

A Killarney Irish Volunteer group, photographed on 3 November 1915.
FRONT ROW *(left to right):* M. Connor, Jim Galvin (Tralee); Michael
Donoghue; BACK ROW: *Pat O' Shea, Gerry Sullivan, M. Spillane,*
M.J. O'Sullivan, Maurice Horgan.

Austin Stack – 'Truly one of Ireland's bravest and best.'

Some hefty specimens of the RIC photographed in the garden attached to the Tralee Barracks.
FRONT ROW *(left to right)*: *M. Hennessy, Sergeant R. O'Donnell, T. Henry.*
BACK ROW: *J. Sullivan, James Clancy, J. Murphy, A. O'Connell, G. Barins, W.J. Wright.*

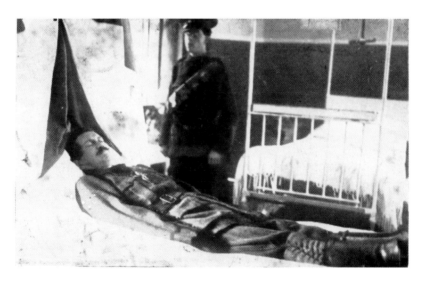

Lying-in-State of Thomas Ashe, hero of the Battle of Ashbourne.

Remains of Austin Stack, surrounded by guard of honour and banked with flowers, prior to interment in Glasnevin.

His Honour, Judge Fionán Lynch, photographed when Captain of 'F' Company, Dublin Volunteers, 1916.

Tralee IRA Officers – left to right (standing): D. Barry, T. Lynch, T. Foley,
M. Fleming, J. Horan, J. McGaley, E. Hogan, C. Counihan, D. Jeffers;
(seated): N. Stack, E. Barry, P.J. Cahill, M. Doyle, W. Farmer, P. Barry;
(in front): M. Switzer, J. Fleming.

Tralee Military Barracks: British military cycle unit on parade at Ballymullen
Barracks Square, Tralee, before leaving to assist in attempts to round up IRA
active service men. Some of the building shown here was destroyed before the
republicans evacuated it in August 1922.

Killarney Volunteer Pipe Band
STANDING *(left to right)*: P. Gardner, J. Coffey, W. O'Brien, M. Sullivan,
C. Mahoney, W. Horgan.
SEATED *(left to right)*: P. MacCarthy, M. McCarthy, T. McGillycuddy,
R. Clifford, C. O'Leary.

*The notorious pair, 'Big Paddy' (Culleton) and 'The Jewman' (de la Roy) whose
names are inseparably linked to the 1920–1921 days in Tralee.*

Jackie Fleming, Tralee, and Charlie Daly, Knockane, Firies, both of whom are mentioned for their activities against the British crown forces, later made the supreme sacrifice for the Republic, when captured by Free State troops during the Civil War.

George Nagle, of Ballygamboon, Castlemaine, who gave his life for the Republic during the Civil War in which he fought on the republican side. He had been a member of the pre-Truce IRA, during which time he was employed by James Baily, of Castle Street, Tralee.

Commandant Liam Scully, of Glencar, killed in action during the successful attack by the IRA on Kilmallock RIC Barracks, in June 1920. He taught for some time at Strand Street National School, Tralee.

'A' (Boherbee) Company 1st (Tralee) Battalion Kerry No. 1 Brigade, IRA

The above picture was taken at the Sportsfield. Its capture by the crown forces, who used it for identification purposes, seriously impaired the fighting powers of a unit from which great things were expected. Amongst those in the picture are:

FRONT ROW: *T. Barrett, T. Moriarty, H. Carrick, D. O'Donoghue, J. Griffin (mascot), J. Drummond, M. Dowling, P. O'Donoghue, T. Moriarty.*

SECOND ROW: *J. Mason, P. Colgan, T. Vale, J. Wall, J. Fleming, T. Hannafin, R. Fitzgerald, J. Dowling (Captain), J. Mullins, M. Moroney, J. O'Keeffe, T. Leahy, J. O'Connor.*

THIRD ROW: *E. Kerins, P.J. O'Connell, T. Devane, T. Fitzgerald, F. Morris, J. Colgan, T. Moriarty, J. Moriarty, T. O'Connor, J. Hannafin, J. Myles,*

P. Conway, M. Sheehy, J. Pendy, M. Teahan, T. Hawley, J. Finnerty, L. Dowd, P.J. Hogan, M. Murphy.

FOURTH ROW: J. Taylor, P. Brosnan, T. Foley, M. Higgins, J. Brosnan, J. Geary, T. O'Sullivan, J. Ryan, T. Roche, M. Hanafin, E. Looney, J. Riordan, T. Daly, D. McMahon, T. Flynn, P. Griffin, M. Maher, T. Cremins, P. Enright, W.J. Fitzgerald, T. Gilligan, J. O'Sullivan, D. Brosnan, J. Dunne, J. Foley, P. Comerford, T. Morris, R. Enright, J. Curtin.

FIFTH ROW: J.J. Sheehy, J. Dee, J. Doyle, T. O'Connell, J. Weir.

BACK ROW: J. Falvey, W. Fitzgerald, D. Fitzgerald, M. O'Connor, M. Bower, T. Duggan, M. Hogan, W. Sweeney, S. Horgan, W. Finnerty.

Ruins of the Old County Hall, Tralee, burned down by crown forces on November Eve, 1920.

Major McKinnon: 'Always the alert leader of the pack, out for the kill.'

Cornelius Healy, Tralee, who played a prominent part in the fight for freedom. A British ex-soldier, he was an excellent marksman.

Commandant Daniel J. Allman, East Kerry brigade column, IRA, killed in action at Headford, 21 March 1921. Aged 30 years.

The remains of an officer, sergeant and other ranks of the First Royal Fusiliers, killed at Headford ambush, received military honours at Killarney railway station when their coffins were entrained for England.

The remains of the district inspector and Black and Tans killed at Castlemaine ambush, entrained for England at Tralee railway station.

A North Kerry flying column
FRONT ROW *(left to right)*: *Patrick J. McElligott, O/C 5th battalion 1921; Denis Quille, column commandant 6th battalion flying column 1921; James Sugrue, O/C 6th battalion 1920–22; Brian Grady, company captain, Ballylongford.*
SECOND ROW: *Volunteers Martin Quille, Christy Broder, Con Brosnan, Timothy O'Sullivan.*
BACK ROW: *Volunteer Dan Grady, Miss Mai Ahern (Cumann na mBan), Seán Coughlan, company captain, Asdee.*

Celtic cross in the republican plot, Rath cemetery, Tralee, erected in memory of republican dead. Names inscribed on the base of the cross are (buried in the republican plot): Thomas Hawley, Cornelius Healy, John Moriarty, William Myles, Michael Flynn, James O'Connor, Michael Sinnott, John O'Connor, John Fleming, John Drummond, Jeremiah O'Sullivan, Patrick Reidy; (buried elsewhere): Frank Hoffman, Patrick Hanafin, Thomas Flynn, John O'Sullivan, Michael Ryle, Thomas Drummond, William Harrington, John Clifford, Eugene Fitzgerald, Daniel Foley, John Conway, James Walsh, George Nagle, Daniel Daly, Austin Stack.

Daniel O'Mahony, commander of the Castleisland Volunteers.

IRA maintenance party at Farranfore Barracks.
Included in the group are T. McEllistrim, TD, T. Woods, Johnny Connor and
Maurice Galvin. Some of them participated in the engagement against the British
warship in Kenmare Bay.

Scene in Denny Street, Tralee, when Madame Maud Gonne MacBride laid
the foundation stone of the Tralee 'Ninety-eight Memorial, on 21 September
1902. The memorial was smashed by Auxiliaries in April 1921 and replaced by
the present memorial in 1939, when the unveiling ceremony was performed by
Madame MacBride.

Thomas Ashe.

*The firing party at the graveside of Thomas Ashe, Glasnevin cemetery,
24 September 1917.*

Commandant Michael Robert McElligott.

Seán O'Leary of Killarney, member of a Tipperary active service unit, who was killed in action against British crown forces early in 1921. He was son of Jerome O'Leary and Mrs O'Leary of Park View House, Killarney, and brother of Dave O'Leary, chemist, Dublin.

Percy Hanafin of Tralee, a prominent member of Fianna Éireann, who died of wounds received in an engagement with Black and Tans in Edward Street, Tralee, January 1922.

Willie McCarthy, Adjutant 3rd (Lixnaw) battalion IRA, arrested by Black and Tans on Easter Saturday, 1921. His mangled, bullet-ridden body was found next morning in The Green, now the Tralee town park.

RDC, Newtownsandes. A nomination paper was also handed in on behalf of the Listowel Irish Volunteers and Cumann na mBan. Mr H.J. Marshall, solicitor, deputy Returning Officer, duly declared Mr Crowley elected to the North Kerry constituency. In the evening the Listowel Volunteers, headed by a brass band, paraded the town and addresses were delivered from the window of the election headquarters, then popularly known as 'Liberty Hall'. The Sinn Féiners of the constituency were congratulated on their notable victory by D.J. Browne, solicitor, election agent, Thomas Fitzgerald, Tarbert, Charles Troy, MA, NUI, and Dr O'Connor.

Thirty-five nomination papers were handed in at the Caherciveen courthouse by Mr Rosney, solicitor, on behalf of Fionán Lynch. The principal paper was proposed by Patrick J. O'Shea and seconded by Denis J. O'Connell, both of Caherciveen. There were exciting scenes in the town at four o'clock in the afternoon when the candidate was declared elected for South Kerry.

Amongst the Kerrymen arrested at the time of the 'German plot' affair, and for Sinn Féin and Volunteer activities about the same period were: Austin Stack, Tralee; Fionán Lynch, Caherciveen; James Crowley and Jack McKenna, Listowel; Tadhg Brosnan, Castlegregory; Michael Fleming, Tralee; Patrick Sugrue ('An Seabhac'), Dingle; Michael Spillane, Killarney; Tom Walsh and Patrick Kennedy, Annascaul; Dan Jeffers and Ned Horan, Tralee; Daniel Mahony, Clooneasig, Castleisland; John Francis O'Shea and James O'Shea, Portmagee; Timothy Matt O'Connor, Doolaig; Daniel McCarthy, Knockeen; Timothy Leahy, Meenas; William Sweeney, Castleisland; Patrick Riordan, Longfield; John Brosnan, Dromore; Cornelius Morley, Rathbeg; John Sharry, Rathmore; John M. Fleming, Kilcummin; Jeremiah Downey, Garrett Barry, Frank T. O'Keeffe, Francis J. O'Keeffe, Terence O'Connor and James Stack, Brosna; James J. Joy, Patrick Moloney and Jeremiah Keane, Duagh; John P. Sheehy, Kilcara; Thomas Kelly, Ballygarrett; E. Barry, D. Fealy, D. Flaherty and J. Kirby, Mountcoal; Jim Morgan,

Moybella, Ballybunion; Michael Moroney and John Moroney, Ballylongford; Garrett Heaphy, John Nolan, Daniel Leahy and Daniel Murphy, Ballyline, Ballylongford; Patrick Costelloe, John Dunne, Philip Stackpoole, John Holly, Maurice Hayes, Glin; John T. Fitzgerald, Tarbert; Paul Scully and Joe Taylor, Glenbeigh; Michael Dennehy, John Hegarty, Denis Hegarty, Thomas Beckett, Michael Murphy and Martin Hackett, Kilgarvan; Alexander O'Shea, Glin Inchequinn, Tuosist; Maurice F. Beasley and Jeremiah Breen, Ballybunion; Thomas O'Grady and J. McCabe, Listowel; Patrick O'Neill and John Walsh, Cappa, Clahane; D. Brennan, T. Brennan, C. Brennan, T. Kelliher, W. Sheehan and F. Daly, Farranfore; John Regan, Kilmore; William Dineen, Ardoughter; Dominick Spillane, Dromdarlough; Humphrey O'Sullivan, Knocknaroor, Headford; A.J. Moynihan, Shronderagh; John Conroy, Tralee; Thomas O'Connor, Daniel Keane, Cornelius Corcoran, Knockreigh; Denis Quirke, Lyre; Patrick Flynn, Rathpook; T. O'Sullivan, Killarney; J. Foley and T. Foley, Tralee; John Deane, Ballyknockea, Camp; Daniel Scannell, Ballyarnett, Camp; Patrick O'Shea, Camp; J. O'Donnell, Rathmore.

Following his arrest in April 1918, Austin Stack was sent to Belfast jail where he automatically became commandant, and so successfully organised his fellow prisoners that they were able to wring from their bigoted gaolers the status of political prisoners. These hard-won rights, however, were gradually withdrawn until, in December, Austin headed a veritable revolution which broke out behind prison walls. The affair had been carefully planned in advance, and for a considerable time previously food and drink were conserved. Then, one day the prisoners cut loose, and having demolished the staircase they barricaded themselves in an inaccessible position close to the roof in one wing of the building. They were besieged by some three hundred military and police, reinforced by a bitterly hostile populace. The damage was estimated at £7,000. From Belfast jail Austin Stack was later transferred to

Strangeways prison, Manchester, from which he escaped in broad daylight with a number of fellow prisoners in October 1919.

IRISH REPUBLIC ESTABLISHED

THE VICTORS OF the general election of 1918 immediately proceeded to carry out their programme. They abstained from the British parliament and refused to recognise British authority in Ireland. In all seventy-three Sinn Féin candidates had been returned out of a possible total of one hundred and five. Of these twenty-six met at the Mansion House, Dublin, for the purpose of convening Dáil Éireann; the remaining forty-seven were in jail. The first Dáil Éireann assembled on 21 January 1919, and with President de Valera and Arthur Griffith still in jail, Cathal Brugha presided, on the proposition of Count Plunkett. On that day Dáil Éireann issued to the nations of the world, in Irish, English and French, a declaration of Irish Independence. It established the Irish Republic, constituted itself the legislature, appointed an executive, and proceeded to carry out plans for the peaceful supplanting of the British government in Ireland by a *de facto* Sinn Féin government. On democratic principles the representative quality of Dáil Éireann was undeniable, its claim to the active support of the overwhelming majority of the Irish people was indisputable. In a short time, however, it became apparent that mere voting at the polls, and other pacific means of ventilating grievances were going to accomplish nothing. At a meeting of Volunteer headquarters staff, Cathal Brugha, acting chief, pointed out to the Volunteers that they had become the army of a lawfully constituted government elected by the people, and that they were entitled, morally and legally, when in the execution of their duties, to slay the officials and agents of the foreign invader who was making war upon the native government. Ireland, accordingly, changed her methods, and in two years her results were changed.

By December 1919, sixteen policemen had been killed, including a number of prominent members of the 'G' Detective Division of the Dublin Metropolitan Police. In fact, the 'G' Division had been, rendered largely impotent because, in addition to the members killed, others had been scared into inactivity, whilst many had been induced to lend secret help to the IRA. During the same month Lord French, the lord lieutenant, was ambushed, and was lucky to escape unhurt.

The year 1920 brought an intensification of the struggle, and in January, Carrigtwohill barracks, County Cork, became the first Royal Irish Constabulary bastion to be captured by serious fighting, when it surrendered after a few hours' siege. Attacks on police barracks, and on police patrols, became so common and successful that by the summer the Royal Irish Constabulary had given up all pretence of carrying out their civil duties, and had been withdrawn into the larger towns. The evacuated barracks were invariably burned down by the IRA, and in one night 315 such buildings were given to the flames. For these reasons, and also because of competition by the civil and criminal courts of the Republic, the British law courts became deserted and practically no business was done. Meanwhile, Dáil Éireann had become the real government of the country, and departments of finance, defence, trade and commerce, agriculture, home affairs, local government, labour and propaganda had been established. Sinn Féin secured overwhelming victories at the local elections in January and June 1920. De Valera raised $6,000,000 in America, and Collins £380,000 in Ireland, on interest bearing bonds to provide finance for the Dáil. Amongst new institutions set up were a land bank; a land commission; courts of arbitration to settle land disputes; a commission to develop Ireland's natural resources; a set of civil and criminal courts, and a new force of republican police. By July 1920, there were few places outside of Dublin and North-East Ulster where the King's Writ continued to run. Meanwhile, operations of the Irish Republican Army in the field had become more frequent and were attended by ever mounting success; so much so that by the summer of 1920 the Royal Irish Constabulary, which had been regarded as the spearhead, of the British forces of occupation, was reduced to a pathetic wreck.

About that time there appeared in certain English Sunday papers an advertisement directed to British ex-servicemen, calling for recruits 'at ten shillings a day and all found', for the Royal Irish Constabulary. Later an Auxiliary division of 15,000 alleged ex-officers was recruited by similar methods, though the wages for this force was £1 a day instead of 10s. In a short while the 'police' force in Ireland numbered upwards of 15,000 men, of whom nearly 1,500 were Auxiliaries. The proportion of Irishmen remaining in the force at that time was small. When the first of the English recruits for the Royal Irish Constabulary arrived in Ireland they were dressed in khaki with black belts and caps, due to the shortage of the standard uniforms. The first company was immediately nicknamed 'Black and Tans', after the famous Limerick pack of hounds. The name stuck. The Auxiliaries wore dark blue uniforms and black Glengarry caps.

During the summer of 1920 coroners' inquests were replaced by military courts of inquiry, and there was an intensive drive against Sinn Féin courts which resulted in many of them being broken, up or driven underground, together with the republican police and other Sinn Féin machinery of government. Martial law was applied to eight counties within which there was also introduced a policy of 'authorised' or official reprisals. By that time nearly the whole of the south was solidly behind the IRA, but because of the small quantity of arms and ammunition available, and of the difficulties of financing wholesale release from civil occupation, only about 3,000 men could be used for active service out of tens of thousands who presented themselves. This little force of 3,000 inexperienced IRA men, always inadequately armed and equipped, was opposed by over 60,000 British troops and 15,000 British police. If IRA men were captured after a fight, or even found with arms in the martial law area, their lives were forfeit, and their fate the hangman's noose or the firing squad. Yet the IRA invariably spared their prisoners, and having no prisons usually released them. Michael Collins summed up the Irish methods as follows:

> England embarked on an underground war of assassination, and I replied with the same weapon. England's shock troops were assassinators; mine were ambushers, but at times we, too, assassinated. We had no jails and we had, therefore, to kill all spies and 'double-crossers'.

The close of 1920 brought the perfection of the Irish Republican Army system of flying columns in the country districts, and in the capital an astounding series of ambushes were carried out by the Dublin brigade. The British fought with no respect for the rules of the Hague Convention; they carried hostages, terrorised the civil population by murder and pillage, and destroyed the property of civilians when there was no military necessity to do so. It was war to the death. For instance, on Sunday morning, 21 November, 1920, fourteen British officers and ex-officers, living in Dublin, and undoubtedly engaged in intelligence work with the British enemy, were shot in their beds or as they were dressing. As Collins declared to General Crozier some time afterwards: 'We learned that some of your fellows were out to get some of our chaps, and we got there first.' On the afternoon of the shooting Black and Tans fired on a large crowd gathered at Croke Park for a football match between Dublin and Tipperary. Twelve people were killed, including Seán Hogan, a Tipperary player; eleven were dangerously wounded, and fifty-four injured. That night Dick McKee, Peadar Clancy and Conor Clune were hacked to pieces by Black and Tans in Dublin Castle, and subsequently shot. The shooting at Croke Park and the subsequent murders of the republican officers in Dublin Castle were part of a general British policy of 'unauthorised reprisals' – or allowing the police to have a free hand. That policy was distinct from the authorised reprisals carried out inside the martial law area. The peculiar barbarity of the British policy explicitly condoned and implicitly pointed the way to arson, pillage, assault and massacre. A party of Black and Tans having captured six unarmed Volunteers at Kerry Pike, near Cork, cut out the tongue of one; the nose of another; the heart of another and battered in the skull of a fourth. In a single week the British shot up and sacked Balbriggan, Miltown Malbay, Lahinch, Ennistymon, Trim and Mallow. In a month they did likewise with twenty-four other towns, murdering as they went. They burned property in Cork city, to the value of £3,000,000. By April 1921, they had burned down sixty-one co-operative creameries. At Abbeydorney, County Kerry, the actual incendiaries who burned the local creamery re-appeared later to hold an inquiry into the burning. They robbed shops, post offices and banks, and, according to General Crozier, one member of the Auxiliary Division opened a depot in the north of England for the sale of goods stolen in the execution of his duty. They flogged, beat up and murdered as fancy moved them. A seventeen-year-old boy whom they tied on a triangle, was flogged daily over a period, to make him talk. They tortured for information, according to the limit permitted by individual commanders, and murdered a long list of non-belligerents. Most of the outrages were the work of Black and Tans and Auxiliaries, although the military were not always blameless. Referring to the men who went through the terror, General Crozier declared that 'most British military officers tried their best to hand them out a fair deal, but the police played a dirty game throughout.'

The very nature of the British policy, coupled with the incessant activities of the IRA, and life amidst a hostile population, completely undermined the morale of the British forces, both military and police.

At Ballinalee twenty Volunteers, under Seán McKeon, ambushed and routed with heavy loss over one hundred Auxiliaries, bent on a reprisal expedition. Some time later, with twelve IRA men,

McKeon fought eighteen Auxiliaries; killed three of them, mortally wounded two, and compelled the others to surrender. Twenty-four soldiers were killed in a fight with a Kerry flying column at Headford Junction, and shortly afterwards a Black and Tan patrol was wiped out near Castlemaine. Earlier in the campaign, military, Black and Tans and Auxiliaries had been dealt overwhelming blows at Kilmichael, Crossbarry and Roscarbery, in County Cork.* These are but a few examples of the successful campaign conducted by the IRA, whose biggest operation was the burning of the Custom House, Dublin, on the 25 May 1921. The destruction of the Custom House reduced the most important branches of what was left of the British civil government in Ireland, to virtual impotence. Six weeks later England was forced to call a Truce. Shortly beforehand General Macready stated in a memorandum to the British cabinet:

> Unless I am entirely mistaken, the present state of affairs in Ireland must be brought to a conclusion by October, or steps must be taken to relieve practically the whole of the troops together with the great majority of the commanders and their staff.

Whilst negotiations with the British were in progress, General Macready further declared that 150,000 troops would be needed to ensure victory in the event of a resumption of hostilities. To such extent had the Irish Republican Army gathered force since 1919. Kerry's part in the fierce guerrilla war fought during these stirring years is told in the chapters which follow.

See Rebel Cork's Fighting Story.

GORTATLEA FIRST BARRACK ATTACK AND CASUALTIES

by VOLUNTEER

THE FIRST ATTACK on a police barracks in Ireland took place at Gortatlea, County Kerry, on Saturday night, 13 April 1918, and caused a tremendous sensation. The capture of the police arms was the object of the raid, which was unsuccessful, and in the course of which two Volunteers, John Browne and Richard Laide, lost their lives. Both were farmers' sons and lived in the neighbourhood of Gortatlea. Browne was shot through the head and died shortly afterwards, whilst Laide who received bullet wounds in the stomach, lingered for some time in Tralee County Infirmary, and died of peritonitis on Sunday evening.

The Gortatlea police hut, which had been a couple of years erected at the time of the attack, was a substantial building, garrisoned by a sergeant and three constables. On the night of the attack, Sergeant Boyle and Constable Fallon were out on patrol duty. Both were armed, Fallon with a carbine and the sergeant with a revolver. One of the two remaining constables opened the door of the building, following a knock. A party of armed and masked men immediately forced their way in, and having presented shotguns and revolvers to the two astonished constables, demanded surrender of their arms. The police, startled out of their usual routine, were at first uncertain of the seriousness of the situation, and were inclined to resist, until menaced by the arms of the raiders. Meanwhile, Sergeant Boyle and Constable Fallon, who had been patrolling the railway crossing, noticed the attackers on their way to the hut. At the time the police patrol were not aware that an attack on their barracks was contemplated, but nevertheless, they decided to follow the men. Approaching the barracks, they heard appeals from Constables Denning and Considine not to shoot, and guessed that a raid was in progress. The sergeant and constable then took up positions at one end of the hut which commanded a view of the kitchen window through which they fired. Browne was seen to fall and was carried away by his comrades. Later he and Laide were found by the police in a position about twenty yards from the hut. In the course of the inquiry which followed the Gortatlea shooting, evidence was given that the attackers had the two constables in the hut at their mercy, and could have killed them easily have they wished to do so. It was also shown that the sergeant and constable who had returned from patrol duty deliberately picked off two of the attackers by shooting them through the kitchen window.

Browne and Laide are buried in the same grave in Rath, Tralee. About 6,000 people attended their funeral which was the largest ever seen in the town. Richard Laide was son of John Laide, farmer, Gortatlea, and nephew of Jeremiah McSweeney, auctioneer, Tralee. Sergeant Boyle and Constable Fallon, who fired the shots which killed John Browne and Richard Laide during the raid for arms at Gortatlea police hut, were fired upon on the streets of Tralee about two o'clock on Friday 14 June. The policemen were on their way to the Tralee barracks from the courthouse, where they had given evidence in a case arising from the Gortatlea incident. As they were about to enter the square, two young men with guns suddenly appeared in the street, took deliberate aim at the constable and sergeant, and fired, both shots going off simultaneously. Fallon was shot through the shoulder and removed to the Infirmary. He was only slightly wounded, and later lodged a claim for £1,000 compensation,

According to newspaper records, Boyle, who was uninjured, ran pell-mell to the barracks. At the vital moment somebody in the street shouted 'Look out!' and Sergeant Fallon turned round, an action which probably saved his life, as he would otherwise have most likely been shot through the heart. Scenes of wildest excitement followed, and crowds congregated in excited groups in the streets to discuss the occurrence. Armed police searched the town and district for the attackers. Later, Maurice Carmody of Clogher and Robert Browne of Feale's Bridge were arrested and charged with the attempted murder of the police. Three dints were made on the wall of Michael McDonnell's premises, near The Square, by the bullets which missed the policemen. At the trial of Carmody of Clogher, on 29 June 1918, it was stated that a military officer visited J.D. O'Connell, solicitor for Carmody, and both by promises of reward and threats, attempted to induce O'Connell to betray the trust imposed upon him by Carmody.

Sergeant Boyle was promoted to head constable some months later, and Constable Fallon was promoted sergeant. Constables Denning and Considine, the other two men in Gortatlea barracks on the night of the raid, were given first-class records, with £20 and £10 bonus, respectively. All got the constabulary medal.

POLICE ATTACKED AND DISARMED AT CAMP

ONE OF THE earliest official actions against crown forces in Kerry took place when Sergeant Bernard Oates and Constable J.J. O'Connell, of Camp police station, were attacked and disarmed at Meenascarthy, near Camp, Castlegregory, on Tuesday night, 24 June 1919. The police were returning on bicycles from patrol duty in Aughacasla. The constable had a loaded rifle attached to his bicycle and a quantity of ammunition in his pouch. The sergeant was unarmed. As the police approached Fitzgerald's house at Meenascarthy, a number of armed men rushed them from behind a gateway, and carried off the constable's rifle and ammunition. The police endeavoured to grapple with their assailants, and a thrilling life and death struggle followed. The police were at the mercy of the attackers, who could easily have shot both of them dead. Instead they grappled with them, and in a few moments all the fight was knocked out of the sergeant and constable. The attackers smashed their bicycles, and keeping them covered for some time with revolvers, they eventually retreated in the direction of Aughacasla.

Arising out of the attack, Michael Spillane, Timothy Spillane, John Butler, Michael Flynn, Michael Maunsell, Martin Griffin, John Farrell, Tom Crean, Denis Sugrue and Michael Griffin were arrested and brought to Tralee police barracks. Sergeant Oates identified Michael Spillane, Timothy Spillane and Flynn as having been in the attacking party, and Constable O'Connell identified Maunsell and Griffin. At the Cork Assizes in December 1919, Timothy Spillane was sentenced to three years' penal servitude for his part in the attack;

Michael Spillane and Michael Flynn got eighteen months with hard labour; Michael Maunsell was sentenced to fifteen months with hard labour, and Michael Griffin got nine months with hard labour.

A LISTOWEL SENSATION
OF 1918

by N.K.M.

THE KERRY SENSATION of the week ending 4 May 1918, was an order for 'attachment' for contempt of court, issued from the Dublin High Courts against fourteen well known Listowel men. Towards the end of February, acting as the Sinn Féin Food Committee, they had been concerned in some interdicted ploughing operations in what was known as Lord Listowel's front and back lawn, for which activities they were adjudged worthy of a month's hospitality each on the part of the government. Had such a happening taken place in earlier times it would have created a profound impression; but the people then lived in such a stirring period that the occurrence was only looked upon as part of the day's work.

On Monday, 25 February 1918, contingents of Volunteers from Moyvane, Knockanure, Finuge, Rathea, Ballyconry and Ballylongford, marched into the town of Listowel. All were armed with hurleys and headed by bands, while ploughs and horses brought up the rear. They were enthusiastically welcomed by the Listowel company of Irish Volunteers with their brass band, and the combined Volunteers, led by Commandant James Sugrue and Patrick Landers, marched to Lord Listowel's estate office in Feale View, where they waited on M. Hill, his lordship's chief clerk. Some time previously successful negotiations had taken place between the promoters of the Sinn Féin movement in Listowel and the graziers of Lord Listowel's lands at Gurtenard, whereby the graziers relinquished the fields in favour of the townspeople who required them for tillage purposes. Despite the arrangement with the graziers, however, Hill refused to give up to the people's representatives the keys of the gates leading to the fields in question, on the grounds that he had received no orders to do so from Lord Listowel. Whilst discussions between the people's representatives and Hill were taking place, the Volunteers and large crowds of sympathisers waited outside. When the discussions had ended, Jack McKenna, who led the people's delegation explained that Hill had evinced the same lack of interest in the town of Listowel as he always had done, and that his excuse for the refusal to give up the keys was the absence of Lord Listowel's authority to do so. 'As everybody knows that Hill is Lord Listowel,' declared Jack McKenna, 'keys or no keys, we are determined to enter the fields and plough them up, whatever the cost.' The Volunteers then broke open one of the gates leading into the back lawn near the national school house, and also the main gate at Danaher's Lodge leading into the front lawn, and made a triumphant entry, ploughs, horses and men going into operation immediately, while others worked similarly on the front lawn. There was tremendous activity during which a large force of police under County Inspector Heard and District Inspector Molloy, who had got a company of British military over from Tralee, had placed three machine guns in strategic positions covering the entrances to the lands. D.J. Flavin with some other members of the committee went down to interview the inspector in charge, taking with them the graziers to whom the lands had been let, viz. John Keane and James Kenny, both of Church Street, who had surrendered their rights to the Sinn Féin Food Committee legally through a solicitor. Having shown the transfer documents to the officer-in-charge, he said: 'As far as I can see this is a dispute between Lord Listowel and these two gentlemen who hold the land as graziers and I don't see that the military have any right to interfere as he has his remedy in the courts.' The officer thereupon withdrew his men again and returned to Tralee.

Having successfully completed their day's tillage, the ploughmen and Volunteers returned to town, and marched to Upper William Street where Jack McKenna addressed them from the balcony of the Temperance Hall. He declared that the people of Listowel could never be too thankful to the Volunteers and ploughmen for the great victory which had been achieved that day. They were assembled as the defenders of the people of Listowel, for whom they had procured land and tilled it to provide them with food. As long as they lived they would hold that land for the people. E.J. Gleeson advised the people to show by their demeanour as Irishmen that they were soldiers as well trained as any that the British government had available. They had done a noble day's work for the people of Listowel by assuring them, of a plentiful supply of food, none of which would ever find its way into the corn stores of England. P. Landers thanked the outside contingents in the name of the citizens of Listowel, and of the Listowel Volunteers, for answering the people's call. The Volunteers were then dismissed, and the great operation terminated in a highly satisfactory manner, the different corps leaving the town early, in a most orderly and disciplined manner. Notwithstanding the big number of Volunteers who were assembled in the town, there was not a single case of drunkenness or misconduct of any kind, a fact which spoke volumes for the self-respect of the different Volunteer companies and of the people generally.

Early in May 1918, an application was made in the Chancery Division, Dublin, on behalf of the Earl of Listowel, for an order 'attaching' fourteen Listowel men for contempt of court in disobeying an injunction from trespassing on the lands at Gurtenard and ploughing them up. The injunction had been posted on the gates of the lands and copies had been served upon the defendants and other persons found trespassing. Notwithstanding this the locks of the gates were smashed and the people entered the lands. On 23 May a big force of police was drafted into Listowel to execute the 'attachment' order. There was tremendous excitement in the town, and all shops were closed during the day in sympathy with the arrested men who were conveyed to Cork to serve a month's imprisonment. They were: Dr Michael O'Connor, UDC; Thomas Walsh, chairman, UDC; D.J. Flavin, UDC; T.D. O'Sullivan, chairman, Board of Guardians; R.M. Danaher, auctioneer; James Lynch, UDC; Thomas Murphy, Michael Mulally, Patrick Sharry, Edward Murphy, William Lawlor, E.J. Gleeson and Morgan Sheehy. The name of Jack McKenna was also included in the list, but he was already in Cork jail (later transferred to Belfast) serving twelve months for concealing arms contrary to the Defence of the Realm Act. Known as Convict 242 in Belfast jail, he dedicated the following 'doggerel' to his thirteen fellow townsmen then serving their month in Cork:

SKILLY AND MILK

A Jail Ballad by J. McK.

In the days that are gone, grabbers were shot,
In the days that are now, grabbers are not:
They are housed, fed and cared in a fine big hotel;
Where his majesty's servants attend on them well.
Being men of distinction, they must have attention,
So their meals – à la carte – deserve serious mention;
In the morning at eight to their bedside is brought
The skilly and milk, served fine and hot,
Lest their appetites fail them, they later are seen
Industriously trudging the walk round the green,
Preparing their tummies for mid-day reception
Of soup that is Epsom, but good for digestion.
Their evening siesta is seen to as well
For nothing's neglected in that fine hotel.

Then off to the wood-yard with pipe and tobacco
Preparing the way for the dry bread and cocoa,
Locked up for the night, they sing them to sleep,
To dream of the Hill, and the cattle and sheep,
That made of them guests in a furnished cell
From the Kingdom of Kerry in a kingly hotel.

The 23 June brought another day of excitement to Listowel town, when the thirteen townsmen who had served their month's imprisonment in Cork jail arrived home following their release. For hours prior to the arrival of the train in which they travelled, the outer approaches to the station were occupied by a large number of armed police under the command of District Inspector Molloy. The townspeople turned out in great numbers, and as the train steamed in they cheered enthusiastically and rushed towards the carriages containing the ex-prisoners who were borne shoulder-high to a waggonette on which were hoisted two republican flags. They were driven in triumph through the streets, headed by the Listowel Brass Band, and followed by a huge procession carrying banners. They first proceeded to the square, then turned up Church Street and Forge Lane; then down Charles Street, deafening cheers being maintained all the while. A stop was made opposite the Temperance Hall, where T.J. Walsh, as chairman of the Urban Council, addressed the gathering. There were cheers for Jack McKenna, still in Belfast jail, following which the people dispersed to their homes. Whilst they were in Cork jail, Mr Hill sold the lawns to Mr Armstrong, proprietor of the North Kerry Creamery and of the N.K.M. Sweet Factory. Later the Sinn Féin committee bought the lands from Mr Armstrong for £1,400, the price which he had paid for it. The front lawn was divided amongst twenty people, each of whom have the right to graze one cow in perpetuity; and the back lawn was divided amongst twenty-eight poor people for tillage purposes. That is the position today.

ATTACKS ON GORTATLEA, SCARTAGLIN AND BROSNA BARRACKS

by VOLUNTEER

THE CAPTURE OF a fortified police barracks by direct attack was out of the question, owing to IRA lack of military resources. Only such places were chosen, therefore, as presented some feature that enabled the attackers to come close up under cover to the hut or barrack, and set it alight. Five Royal Irish Constabulary men and a sergeant occupied the double police hut at Gortatlea, when it was decided on 25 March 1920, that its existence should end. A party of IRA entered the stationmaster's house which overtopped the police hut by a storey, and was separated from it by a space six feet wide. Having removed an invalid girl, the attackers broke through the roof of the stationmaster's house and opened fire on the corrugated iron roof of the police hut at the same time throwing bottles of blazing petrol on it. Within twenty minutes the hut was well on fire, and was half destroyed before the defenders surrendered shortly after midnight. Two of them were wounded. The attackers captured four rifles and three revolvers. More would have fallen into their hands had not explosives stored in the hut started to explode compelling everyone to keep clear.

The party which participated in the attack on Gortatlea police barracks included: Moss Galvin, Johnny Duggan and Johnny Connor,

Farmer's Bridge; T. McEllistrim, John Cronin, Eddie McCarthy, Pa Connor, Din Prendeville, Charlie Daly, and Tom Daly in charge of the section.

The following month an attack on Scartaglin barracks failed. Unlike Gortatlea, the barrack in Scartaglin stood isolated and on rising ground. The attack took place in April 1920, and was directed by Thomas McEllistrim. In those eventful days, the barracks was a redoubtable fortress, setting the attackers a tough problem, the cracking of which could easily prove costly to them, as the police were heavily armed and were provisioned to withstand a siege of several days. The building, which was of the standard hut type, had its outer walls protected by shell boxes filled with gravel and sand. The steel shutters with which the windows were provided were slotted to make loop-holes. The roof was the only vulnerable part of the barracks, and it was on this that the IRA commander decided to concentrate his efforts. The village of Scartaglin is built on rising ground, and a row of houses on its east side were occupied by members of the IRA column. A fence which ran along the east of the hall, and which still stands, was also manned. One section of the attacking party was detailed to approach the barracks as closely as possible, with the object of throwing bottles of petrol and other inflammable material on the roof and against the shell boxes which protected the walls. This operation having been carried out successfully, the building was soon in flames. The garrison of Royal Irish Constabulary replied with heavy rifle fire, and sent up Verey lights to attract assistance. It was then about 12.30 a.m., and the air was filled with the sound of gun-fire and exploding hand grenades.

Thus far the attack was working out according to plan. The barracks was aflame and subject to concentrated, harassing fire which made the position almost untenable. It was then that fate took a hand and came to the assistance of the besieged. Had the attackers permitted the fire to run its course, there is no doubt but that the police would have been compelled to surrender; but, impatient of delay, and anxious to hasten the end, the IRA hurled a home-made landmine at the building, with the object of dislodging the protective shell boxes. On one corner of the barrack roof was a water storage tank and the explosion of the mine burst the galvanised container which discharged a strong stream of water onto the roof. This acted as an ideal fire extinguisher, and proved of far greater assistance to the besieged than did their rifles, hand grenades and Verey lights.

Whilst this was taking place, the Volunteers on the village side of the building maintained incessant, raking fire. Another attempt on the roof with incendiaries was unsuccessful, and the attackers were further discomfited when one of their number, Eddie McCarthy, of Castleisland, was seriously wounded. His comrades succeeded in bringing him from the line of fire with great difficulty. All efforts to restart the fire on the barrack roof had to be abandoned when supplies of petrol gave out. By that time also British reinforcements had reached the village, and the attack was abandoned about 4.30 a.m. Amongst those who participated in the engagement were: Thomas McEllistrim, O/C, Ballymacelligott; Johnny Duggan, Mossie Galvin, Johnny Connor, Farmer's Bridge; Michael Cronin, Christy Cronin, 'Bowler' Mac, Moss Carmody, Ballymacelligott; Humphrey Murphy, Jeremiah Leary, 'Pa' Connor, Eddie McCarthy, and David McCarthy, Castleisland; Mick Leary and Den Prendeville, Cordal.

Originally the attack on Scartaglin barracks was planned to take place exactly a month before it actually did and on the first occasion the attackers were about to take up positions when the project was abandoned as the result of the skilful and clever reconnoitring by Thomas McEllistrim, now TD for Kerry. McEllistrim's work saved a group of men from being cut to pieces, and later on it indirectly led to the unmasking of a British agent who had wormed his way into the confidence of the IRA.

On the occasion on which the attack was originally planned to take place a small detail of IRA comprising about twelve men assembled in a field at the rear of Scartaglin police barracks. Amongst the group was one who represented himself as Peadar Clancy, of headquarters staff, Dublin, and in appearance he closely resembled the great republican leader. Information at the disposal of the attacking IRA men was to the effect that the barrack windows would not be protected as their steel shutters would still be open at the hour scheduled for the commencement of the attack. Accordingly, it was planned that each of the twelve attackers would hurl grenades through the windows. In charge of the operation was Tom McEllistrim, and Patrick Connor, captain of the local company, was amongst the attacking party. Uneasy about the information regarding the barrack windows, McEllistrim decided that he would personally approach the building as closely as possible and observe the position. He could not understand how the Royal Irish Constabulary could be so lax in their precautions as to permit their barrack windows to remain unprotected in the midst of an extremely hostile area.

Having been absent on his scouting mission about twenty minutes, he returned with information that the windows were competently guarded by bomb-proof steel shutters fitted inside and already in position. During the urgent conference which followed this discovery 'Peadar Clancy' argued strongly in favour of proceeding with the attack as planned, but Tommy Mac having decided that it would be foolish to do so in the circumstances, the operation was called off and the party disbanded. 'Clancy' accompanied some of the men to Ballymacelligott and later left for the Cordal area. Here he billeted with others of the IRA in a farmhouse owned by the Castleisland merchant, W.H. O'Connor. One day whilst some of the IRA were seated in the kitchen, an IRA man named Dave McCarthy noticed that one of 'Clancy's' arms was tattooed in a manner much in vogue amongst members of the British forces. His suspicions aroused, McCarthy kept a close eye on 'Clancy' who was later questioned and who answered most unsatisfactorily. He was placed under arrest and brigade headquarters having been notified, he was transferred to East

Limerick and some time afterwards court martialled, found guilty and executed. It turned out that Crowley was 'Clancy's' real name, and Dave McCarthy, who succeeded in unmasking him, now lives at Breahig, Portmarnock, County Dublin, where he runs a dairy farm.

Amongst those who participated in the attack on Scartaglin barracks were: T. McEllistrim, O/C, Mossie Galvin, Johnny Duggan, Johnny Connor, John Cronin, T. Bowler, C. Cronin, Humphrey Murphy, J. O'Leary, subsequently killed in the Civil War; P. Burke, Jack Herlihy, Paddy Reidy, Pat Connor, David O'Connor, David McCarthy and Eddie McCarthy.

In June 1920, anxious to emulate the successful attack on Kilmallock police barracks by the combined East and West Limerick columns, the East Kerry IRA, under Dan O'Mahony, enlisted the aid of the men of West Limerick. Owing to its remoteness, and being in the midst of bogs and hills which offered favourable possibilities for its capture, Brosna barracks was selected for the attack. Once previously arrangements had been made to take this barracks, but the police were informed of the intended attack. Under cover of night, a surprise party of military from Castleisland captured a large body of the IRA on their way to Brosna village.

The second attempt took place on 5 June 1920, and on this occasion the attacking party met in a large field across the river from Brosna. T.M. O'Connor and Dan McCarthy were in charge of the Kerry column, and Mossie Hartnett of Tournafulla had under his command sixteen West Limerick men armed with police carbines and rifles. These men included Paddy Buckley, who subsequently lost his life at Ballyseedy; James Roche, Tommy Leahy, Con and Ned Cregan, Paddy Mulcahy, Jack Ahern, Paddy Aherne, J. Kiely and T. Bourchier. The men were divided into sections and marched to various positions round the barracks.

Fire was opened from the barracks before all the men were in position, as the police were warned of things to come by the noise caused as some of the IRA got into vantage points prematurely. Soon the village resounded to the continuous discharge of rifle fire from and against the barracks, which occupied an isolated position at the south-eastern corner of the square beside the local cemetery. Some of the West Limerick men were placed in front of the barracks near the church, and the remainder in an old house at the back. Humphrey Murphy directed the attack on the barracks himself, in person, and made every effort to break in the roof and gable with grenades and bombs. The attack lasted all night and continued into early morning. The sound of shouting and firing, re-echoing back from the hills and valleys around, was deafening. Verey lights were sent up by the police at intervals, rendering the scene more weird and terrifying. Inside the barracks the police and Tans could be heard distinctly playing a melodeon and shouting 'Come on the Rainbow Chasers'. Counter slogans were lustily slung back by the besiegers. The morning was advancing and considerations of inadequate equipment suggested the advisability of raising the siege. Necessity demanded this as an engagement with the superior numbers of the reinforcing military surely on their way to the relief of the beleaguered garrison was to be avoided. It was decided to withdraw and as a preliminary the attack was intensified while the different sections were withdrawing. There were many hairs-breadth escapes at this stage. Later, over a soldiers' breakfast of bread and cheese incidents of the night were jokingly interchanged.

That morning the West Limerick column narrowly escaped being wiped out. They were saved by the courage of some IRA members of the Abbeyfeale company under James Collins. On the night of the Brosna attack some seven or eight of these men were assigned positions at Glenesrone Wood to keep an eye on any supporting movement of the Abbeyfeale Royal Irish Constabulary, and if possible to frustrate it. In the early morning the 'look-out' at the Abbeyfeale barracks reported to his sergeant the appearance of Verey lights over Brosna. As a result nine of the Royal Irish Constabulary were dispatched by the nearest route for Brosna. This happened to be by the old road at the rear of the barracks, known as Betty's

Road. This cut across the line of retreat from Brosna of the West Limerick section engaged there. It was vital to intercept the police and prevent them cutting off the retreat of those returning from Brosna, and the men entrusted with the responsibility succeeded in accomplishing this at Glenesrone Wood. The brunt of this fight was borne by Jerry Sullivan of Springmount and the late Jim O'Connor of Mountmahon. They were armed only with double-barrelled shotguns. At close range they opened fire on the advancing police, seriously wounding Constable Martin, and slightly injuring some others. The police halted when challenged and returning rapid rifle fire, they retreated to the barracks, firing as they went. Reaching the barracks, they maintained an intense fire in the direction of the hill. None of the IRA suffered casualties either at Abbeyfeale or Brosna.

The attack on Brosna barracks was carried out on the orders of Dan O'Mahony, then O/C of Kerry No. 2 brigade. The battalion staff in charge of the attack were T.M. O'Connor, O/C; Dan McCarthy, Vice-O/C; David Griffin, adjutant; Maurice O'Sullivan, quartermaster; and Captains Jim Mahony, Davie McCarthy, David McAuliffe and Jack Carmody. Amongst the others who took part in the attack were Humphrey Murphy, Charlie Daly, Jerry Leary, Ned Mahony, Jack Mahony, Michael Connell, Denny McCarthy, Jim Lacey, Paddy Fitzgerald, Pat Connor, Davie Connor, David Horan, Jim McAuliffe, Jack Prendeville, Jim Prendeville, Mick Leary, Denny Prendeville, J. Prendeville, Mick Burke, Jerry Connor, J. Brosnan, Martin McCarthy, J. Brosnan, Tim Connor, Philip Hartnett, Dick Rearden and Berty Mahony.

SEIZURES OF ARMS AT TRALEE AND GLENBEIGH

ONE OF THE greatest difficulties with which the IRA had to contend was the scarcity of arms and the shortage of ammunition. For every rifle there were a hundred men. Various ruses were employed by the IRA to augment their precious stores of war materials. Here are typical actions by Kerry columns with those objectives in view.

A guard of British soldiers occupying two railway carriages drawn up at the old North Kerry platform, Tralee Station, were protecting military coal supplies in July 1920. Their movements were carefully observed for three days by scouts of Fianna Éireann who noted that the soldiers were engaged at their mid-day meal when the train from Fenit passed. On 10 July members of 'D' (Rock Street) company left their employment at noon and proceeded to the Spa where they boarded the train. Two IRA men rode on the engine. At Mounthawk the train was halted while more IRA men boarded it. Opposite the carriages used as a guardhouse the Fenit train was pulled up and from it dashed young men who rushed across the intervening platform at the feeding Englishmen and took their rifles. Meanwhile, a sentry at the 'North Kerry' cabin was disarmed by two men who had whiled away the time reading a newspaper until the right moment. The whole 'job' was neatly planned and despite pursuit the eleven rifles of the guard were successfully removed to become the back-bone of 'D' company's armoury.

Due either to a friendly word or incautious remark or again to the luck of the game, it happened an odd time that an ambitious IRA plan came to nought owing to behaviour out of the ordinary by the enemy.

A half-hour's march through an April night of 1921 brought a Kerry column to halt before O'Mahony's house in Aughills. A short wait and they were being rowed across the bay to Cromane Point. It was 3 a.m. and pitch dark when they tramped across the gravel strand towards Glenbeigh. At Dooks station they entered the railway line, and were within half a mile of Glenbeigh station when scouts reported that a body of men were moving towards them. Friend or foe? The column took up a position across the path of the advancing men and waited developments in the dim light before dawn. They were friends – men of the local battalion coming up to help the column. At Glenbeigh positions were occupied in and around the station. It was expected that a party of military would leave the barracks five hundred yards away to board the train at 8 a.m. for Killorglin.

Four Volunteers occupied the station master's office. The telephone bell rang. Two of them went to find the station master to answer the call. As they walked out of the office door they barged right into a party of soldiers who had entered the platform. It would be difficult to say whether it was the British soldiers or the Irish Volunteers were the more taken aback. The consternation was promptly ended when the Volunteers on the opposite side of the station opened fire. Taken completely by surprise, the soldiers dropped twelve rifles and a Lewis gun, and dashed back to their barracks. As the Volunteers withdrew with their precious booty the train which the soldiers intended to board passed. The passengers waved handkerchiefs and shouted encouraging words. Back across the bay again went the column. Next day they were amused to read the British official report ascribe the coup to a column from Cork.

CAUSED MUTINY IN LISTOWEL SHOT IN CORK

by LEE-SIDER

IN JUNE AND July 1920, the initiative in the struggle between the Irish and British for dominance in this country was passing to the Irish. British institutions in all departments of national and local government were repudiated and the alternative machinery set up by Dáil Éireann was everywhere being recognised and resorted to by the people. Public bodies declared their allegiance to the government elected by the Irish people; British courts were boycotted, and whatever little business came before them was transacted behind barbed wire entanglements, guarded by military and police; the Sinn Féin Courts openly dispensed justice and penalised wrongdoers at the instance of the Volunteer police. While the Irish civil population were freely making use of the new Irish institutions and cheerfully obeying their edicts the IRA were daily attacking the British crown forces and restricting their movements. Resignations of justices of the peace and police were numerous. In six weeks at this period one hundred and seventy-seven resigned. The British judge at the Kerry summer assizes told the Grand Jury that in Kerry twenty-five police barracks, three courthouses and four coastguard stations had been burned and six police patrols attacked. It was always the same as far as the police were concerned, he said; they were unable to obtain a clue and they got no assistance from the people. Railway employees refused to man trains with armed military and police as passengers and were dismissed.

British military and police could only move out from their strongly held barracks in numbers and were everywhere the objects of hostility and resentment, if not of actual attack. Whether they realised it or not, they were fighting a native army backed by a united people. The highly efficient Royal Irish Constabulary, on which the British had been wont to rely in every emergency in Ireland for information and loyal co-operation, were proving unequal to the strain. They were in a most unenviable position. Drawn from the homes of the people against whom they were expected to enforce repressive measures, many of them had brothers in the IRA, and many of them, too, had long service and were not prepared to forego generous pensions. If they resigned they lost their pensions and went out among the people who might distrust their motives and they left behind an organisation from which they could expect hostility and accusations of cowardice.

The infusion of British recruits into the Royal Irish Constabulary was begun and the quartering of British troops in the same barracks with the Constabulary did not make for harmony within the force or good relations. The Royal Irish Constabulary man found himself no longer a peace officer. In the rural districts especially he lived behind steel shutters, ostracised by the people from whom he sprung, nightly expecting attack by brother Irishmen. It was a galling situation for spirited men. They had either to lend themselves completely to the designs of their authorities or sullenly wait the outcome of events with no stomach for the work on hands. The British were not content to let the initiative pass from them without a fight. They decided to turn every Royal Irish Constabulary barracks in the country into a fortress from which military would sally forth, guided by the Royal Irish Constabulary with local knowledge, to harass the people night and day, carry out wholesale arrests and kill off the IRA, whom they affected to believe were terrorising the civilian population. This further militarisation of the Royal Irish Constabulary was entrusted to army officers with Great War service who could utilise their knowledge of defensive raiding tactics to the full.

Colonel Gerald Bryce Ferguson Smyth was appointed divisional commissioner for Munster on 3 June 1920. He had entered the British army in 1905, served in the Great War, in which he lost an arm and was mentioned four times in dispatches. He had commanded a battalion of the King's Own Scottish Borderers and was thirty-five years of age.

On the 17 June 1920, the Royal Irish Constabulary in Listowel were ordered to hand over their barracks to the British military and to transfer themselves, with the exception of three who were to remain in Listowel to act as guides for the soldiers, to different stations in the district. The Royal Irish Constabulary men held a meeting and decided not to obey the order. Next morning County Inspector Poer O'Shee visited Listowel and tried to induce the men to obey. Fourteen of them tendered to him their resignations which were not accepted. On the morning of 19 June two motor cars arrived in Listowel conveying Colonel Smyth, General Tudor, County Inspector Poer O'Shee and other military and police officers. The constables were assembled in the barrack day room, where they were addressed by Colonel Smyth, the divisional commissioner. The only report of this speech is that supplied subsequently for publication by the fourteen policemen, from which the following is an extract:

> Sinn Féin has had all the sport up to the present, and we are going to have sport now. The police are only strong enough to hold their barracks. As long as we remain on the defensive, Sinn Féin will have the whip hand. We must take the offensive and beat Sinn Féin at its own tactics. Martial law is to come into force immediately, and a scheme of amalgamation will be complete on the twenty-first of June. I am promised as many troops from England as I require. Thousands are coming daily. I am getting 7,000 police from England.

Colonel Smyth then explained why it was necessary to quarter military in towns like Listowel. He is reported to have, said:

> Police and military will patrol the country at least five nights a week. They are not to confine themselves to the main roads, but to take across country, lie in ambush, and when civilians approach shout 'Hands Up!' Should the order not be immediately obeyed, shoot and shoot with effect. If persons approaching carry their hands in their pockets, or are suspicious looking, shoot them down. You may make mistakes occasionally, and innocent persons may be shot, but that cannot be helped. No policeman will get into trouble for shooting any man. Hunger strikers will be allowed to die in jail. Some have died, and it is a damned bad job all of them were not allowed to die. That is nearly all I have to say to you. We want your assistance to wipe out Sinn Féin. Any man not prepared to do so had better leave the job at once.

Colonel Smyth then asked the first man in the file if he were prepared to serve. This constable referred the divisional commissioner to the men's leader or spokesman, who said: 'By your accent I take it you are an Englishman. You forget you are addressing Irishmen.' The spokesman then took off his cap, belt and bayonet, and laying them on the table, said: 'These, too, are English. Take them as a present from me, and to hell with you, you murderer.'

Colonel Smyth immediately ordered the arrest of the spokesman, but owing to the threatening attitude of the other policemen he left the barracks, which remained in the hands of the mutineers. Five of the men concerned subsequently resigned. Because of the number involved, the fact that the men concerned were the first to give publicity in a signed statement to Colonel Smyth's speech, and the raising of the matter in the British House of Commons, the Listowel barrack incident became famous. But there were others, though not in the same dramatic setting.

On a Sunday evening in June 1920, Colonel Smyth, a tall man of impressive appearance, wearing full military uniform and staff cap, his breast ablaze with medal ribbons, arrived at the Milltown

(County Kerry) barracks of the Royal Irish Constabulary, and summoned the sergeant and six men to the dayroom. Having taken an automatic from his pocket and placed it on the table, he directed the men to sit down. He prefaced his remarks by stating that he was responsible to no man in Ireland; that he was directly responsible to the prime minister. The Royal Irish Constabulary, he said, had been on the defensive too long and were now going to take the offensive. Block-houses would be erected and barracks fortified. The houses of leading Sinn Féiners would be taken over. The police were to go out and not hesitate to shoot and if mistakes were made, he would break no man for doing so. Rubber shoes would be provided for patrols so that they could move along the roads noiselessly. He outlined a scheme under which Royal Irish Constabulary men dressed in khaki would accompany military raiding parties to identify Sinn Féiners. British recruits for the Royal Irish Constabulary and military reinforcements would be brought over from England. He said that the scheme which he had outlined would be issued as an order in the course of a week or ten days. The Royal Irish Constabulary men, three of whom were middle-aged, did not quickly realise what Colonel Smyth was about, and were inclined to look on his visit as one of the 'comings and goings' of highly placed officers. The barrack orderly, one of the younger men, said that when he joined the force he did not anticipate having to shoot anybody. Colonel Smyth said that times had changed and tactics had to be changed with them, and from that out things would be different. He made little of the arguments advanced by the young policeman, and suggested that cowardice was at the bottom of them. Dominion Home Rule, he said, was coming, and after a few years Royal Irish Constabulary men who continued to serve would be awarded big pensions. After a stay of about an hour in the barracks, Colonel Smyth departed.

In a few days the barrack orderly received notification to go to Rathmore. He refused to accept the transfer. On 29 June County Inspector Poer O'Shee came to Milltown accompanied by two lorries of Royal Irish Constabulary men armed with rifles and bombs. He spoke to the young policeman in a fatherly way and asked him why he would not take his transfer. 'Well, if you want to know,' came the reply, 'I did not join the police to lead around Black and Tans and the scum of England which have been brought into the force.' The officer tried to soften his subordinate and drew a picture of his bright prospects in the force, at the same time pointing out that such an attitude as he (the policeman) was taking up would create disaffection among the other men. Seeing that the young man was adamant, the county inspector, after an interview lasting two hours, declared he would have to suspend him. 'Take that and that,' said the policeman, throwing his revolver, belt and jacket on the table in front of the county inspector. After spending a few days around Milltown the suspended constable went to Killarney, where he was well known, having previously served in Beaufort. There the district inspector reasoned with him and pointed out that he was going out into a hostile people who would treat him as a spy. 'I understand well what I am doing and I'll take what is coming,' was the spirited reply.

In the British House of Commons on Wednesday, 14 July 1920, Mr T.P. O'Connor asked for information regarding the incidents in the Listowel police barracks and the speech delivered there by Divisional Commissioner Smyth. Sir Hamar Greenwood, chief secretary for Ireland, replied: The recent events presumably refer to the resignation of five constables in Listowel, County Kerry. On 19 June last the divisional commissioner, Colonel Smyth, made a speech to the members of the force, eighteen in number, stationed at Listowel. I have seen the report in the press, which, on the face of it, appears to have been supplied by the five constables already mentioned. I have myself seen Colonel Smyth, who repudiates the accuracy of the statements contained in that report. He informed me that the instructions given by him to the police in Listowel and throughout the division were those mentioned in a debate in this

House on 22 June last by the attorney-general for Ireland, and he did not exceed these instructions. The reason for the resignation of the five constables was their refusal to take up duty in barracks in certain disturbed parts of Kerry. They had taken up this attitude before the visit of the divisional commissioner. I am satisfied that the newspaper report is a distortion and a wholly misleading account of what took place. Subsequently, Mr T.P. O'Connor asked and was refused leave to move the adjournment of the House to discuss the incident and the remarks attributed to Divisional Commissioner Smyth as calculated to produce serious bloodshed in Ireland.

The scene shifts to Cork city, where in July 1920, the Volunteer organisation was already reaching a high state of efficiency and the development of its intelligence department was receiving special attention. The County Club, resort of the landed families, and high military officers, had a staff as loyal as its frequenters who enjoyed its first-class club and residential amenities. All efforts of the IRA intelligence department to penetrate into the staff were frustrated until contact was made with a young waiter. Thereafter the names of British officers, military and police who stayed at or visited the club, were known to the IRA. Colonel Smyth was staying there during the first fortnight of July. This information was conveyed to the IRA. It was decided to shoot him on Friday evening, 16 July. That day he packed his bags and announced his intention of going away for the weekend, so that arrangements for shooting him fell through. He returned unexpectedly the following evening, and the receipt of this information caused the IRA to mobilise hastily a squad of six armed men. They entered the County Club at 10 p.m., held up the waiter, who was expecting them, and passed down the passage to the lounge, where Colonel Smyth was seated with County Inspector Craig, of the Royal Irish Constabulary. Advancing into the lounge the leader of the armed party confronted Smyth, saying: 'Were not your orders to shoot at sight? Well, you are in sight now, so prepare.' Fire was opened. Smyth jumped to his feet and ran towards the door. Despite two bullets in the head, one through the heart, and two through the chest, he succeeded in gaining the passage, where he dropped dead.

THE SACK OF TRALEE

IRELAND AND THE world had watched the long drawn out agony of Terence MacSwiney in Brixton prison; eighteen-year-old Kevin Barry awaited in Mountjoy jail with a dignity beyond his years the hangman's noose. In Kerry, ambushes had been carried out, coastguard stations from Ballyheigue to Ventry been burned and barracks attacked; MacSwiney had drawn his last breath and November 1920, was being ushered in.

That date saw in Tralee a fierce outburst of savagery and ruthlessness on the part of invading forces which threatened to outrival the burning of Cork city. From Sunday, 31 October, to Wednesday, 10 November, Tralee was in a state of siege; armed military went through the town firing volleys as they sped by, public and private buildings were razed to the ground, civilians were shot dead on the streets. The outside world could only guess from wild rumours what was happening in the besieged capital of Kerry.

On Sunday 31 October, two policemen were captured by Volunteers in Strand Street area, and a policeman named McCarthy was fired on and wounded in the leg, and a naval wireless operator was also wounded in Tralee on the same day, and reprisals were not long delayed. Police, Tans and Auxiliaries swept through the town in motor lorries, firing volleys indiscriminately in the streets and into houses. Most of the inhabitants of the town were then unaware of the attacks which had taken place on policemen on the same day when one was wounded at Abbeydorney, one shot dead in Ballyduff, two wounded at Causeway, two shot dead in Killorglin, and four wounded in Dingle.

Tralee people had no sleep that night. The Volunteers had

ambushed the military pickets in the town on November Eve and the reign of terror commenced shortly afterwards.

First to receive the wrath of the maddened crown forces was the Old County Hall which housed all the public offices. Lorry loads of military and Auxiliaries swept through the town from Ballymullen barracks to Staughton's Row and petrol tins were quickly in action. In the building at the time were the late Tommy Lynch and Assistant Town Clerk Jack Conroy. They had a thrilling escape through the roof and over high walls to adjoining back streets. Following this the stationery premises in Upper Castle Street, known as the '1916 Shop', was also destroyed by fire.

The following day was Monday 1 November, All Saints' Day. On their way to Mass the people of Tralee were cognisant of the grim events of the night before from the charred buildings, and armed military lining the streets poked guns at the Mass-going people and fired shots at random. A regular fusillade of shots greeted the congregation leaving last Mass. All day long this firing was kept up, and by nightfall three civilians were casualties. John Conway, painter, aged fifty-seven, the father of six children, was shot through the brain at Upper Rock Street when returning from devotions, and was found dead two hundred yards from his own door. An old woman named O'Leary was shot through the ankle, and an ex-soldier named Simon O'Connor was shot through the groin. Uniformed men smashed the windows of Messrs Murtagh, tobacconist, and Dennehy, publican, and the arrival of military prevented further orgies in this direction.

Still smarting at the kidnapping of the two policemen, the British posted the following notice in prominent places in the town on Monday night as a climax to their first day of terror: 'Take notice of the warning that unless the two Tralee policemen in Sinn Féin custody are returned before 10 a.m. on the second instant, reprisals of a nature not yet heard of in Ireland will take place in Tralee and surroundings.'

This warning was ignored as far as the return of the captured policemen was concerned, but shops were kept closed and all business suspended on Tuesday 2 November. The indiscriminate firing from lorries continued throughout the day, and an ex-soldier named Tommy Wall was standing at Blackpool corner when he got the 'Hands Up' order from a number of uniformed men. He received a blow of a rifle-butt on the head, and was told to run, and while running he was fired at and shot through the stomach and died next morning at the county infirmary.

The burning of houses reached its height on Wednesday, 3 November. The closing embargo on business premises remained in force while the people suffered from want of bread and other necessaries. During the night the grocery and spirit business premises of Thomas Slattery, Rock Street, his adjoining flour and meal establishment and adjoining premises of Mrs Brosnan, publican, were destroyed by fire. An attempt to burn the licensed premises of Thomas Dennehy, also in Rock Street, failed. Simultaneously with this arson, uniformed men were similarly engaged in Upper Castle Street and Boherbee. In the former area, the grocery and licensed premises of Mrs Dunne and the adjoining premises of Mrs O'Connor were demolished. Éamonn O'Connor's stationery shop in Ashe Street suffered a similar fate. An attempt to fire the licensed premises of Mrs O'Rourke, Boherbee, was only partially successful.

During all this time, it must be remembered that the civilian population was without food and fuel and was in a pitiable state. Added to this, Brigadier Willis published an order prohibiting the holding of fairs and markets, as well as public assemblies within three miles of the post office. On Thursday 4 November, following the burnings and terrorism of the previous night, the military took charge of the town and remained on duty until dawn. Business was still suspended, and a deputation, representative of the principal merchants, waited on the officer commanding the troops in Tralee, pointing out the hardships being forced on the people through lack of food, especially bread, the supply of which was exhausted, as the bakeries, like all other establishments, had been closed. The officer told the deputation the place was not under martial law, and that he could not usurp civil power.

On Thursday evening, four or five young men who were removing furniture as a precaution against further outbreaks, had some terrible experiences, and one a miraculous escape. While they were in Kelliher's store at Basin View, a number of uniformed men entered and gave the order to a man named Sullivan to put up his hands. The order was complied with, and on a blow being made at his head with a rifle, he took to his heels and narrowly escaped being hit. The others were in turn held up, and on being asked what was the idea in removing the furniture, produced the military notice threatening reprisals. The householder himself arrived, and was also ordered to put up his hands. He stated that he was the father of a family, and invited his tormentors to shoot him.

In the morning the situation remained unchanged. Tralee was still a beleaguered town on Friday 5 November. The people were still without food, and a pitiable sight was the women and children taking away the charred timber of the burned houses for fuel. In the alleys and laneways starvation was at hand.

Saturday is Tralee's market and busiest day, but on 6 November 1920, no country people came into town. Motor lorries of military had the streets to themselves, as they patrolled up and down, firing rifle shots when and where the whim seized them. The merchants of the town wired to General Macready, Sir Hamar Greenwood and the lord lieutenant, as the plight of the people was nearing desperation. The merchants received no reply from any of these, and then appealed to T.P. O'Connor and the leading English newspapers.

Harrowing tales were told that day in Tralee of happenings in Ardfert, where a young man named Maguire was arrested in the village and taken in a motor-lorry to Causeway where he was subsequently found dead on the fair green. A labourer named

Archer, who was working in a field, and who ran in terror when he saw lorries coming along the road, was shot dead.

An attempt was made in the evening to set fire to the technical schools and Carnegie Library in Tralee, but the flames were extinguished before much damage was done.

The reign of terror continued on the next day, Sunday 7 November. The privations, particularly in the case of the poorer classes, were appalling, and starvation had by now entered many homes. The bread-winners were in many cases left without wages on Saturday, and some only received partial wages. It is impossible now for anyone to visualise the wretched condition of a prosperous town in that week. The Sabbath brought no traditional peace either, for the fiendish work of destruction went on apace at the hands of the desecrators of the Lord's Day. Threatened earlier in the day to remove his name written in Irish on the fascia board, Mr Talbot saw his grocery and spirit premises in Ashe Street wrecked by a bomb.

A little relief came on Monday 8 November, for the well-nigh starving people of the town, when the bakeries were permitted to open and supply bread. On the next day calm prevailed, and about 8 p.m. the following notices were posted up in the town:

> Business may be resumed in Tralee on tomorrow (Wednesday) in view of the hardships imposed on loyal subjects. Other means will be resorted to for the recovery of the two police in Sinn Féin custody. Public houses will remain open until the usual hour.

Owing to the fact that it was not safe to stir out after nightfall, these notices were not seen until late on Wednesday, with the result that business places were closed until a very late hour, and even when the shops were opened, shutters were kept on throughout the day.

News came that evening of the shooting of Frank Hoffman, a twenty-one-year-old farmer, of Farmer's Bridge, and IRA active Volunteer. He was held up three miles from the town by a convoy of police and, on answering his name, he was told, 'You are the man we want.' He was then placed against a fence and shot dead. At the subsequent inquest and field court martial, quite a different story was told by his slayers and a police constable who was charged with his death was found not guilty.

Fairly normal conditions prevailed in Tralee after 10 November. The siege was lifted and the naked terrorism of an armed oppressor against a defenceless civilian population was eased. The reign of terror cost human lives, the loss of property and brought starvation to its most innocent victims, the women and children.

AMERICAN EXILES' GENEROSITY

THE IRISH EXILED kith and kin of Tralee folk quickly rallied to protest against the outrages committed in the name of law and order in the town. Mr de Valera, at a convention at Worcester, Massachusetts, of 1,000 delegates from Massachusetts, New Hampshire, Rhode Island and Connecticut, spoke of the new American Association for the recognition of the Irish Republic. The convention, in compliance with the request of Mr A. Griffith, recommended each state to 'adopt' one of the devastated towns. The state of Massachusetts at once adopted Tralee and decided to aid in relieving distress there.

THE MOCK BATTLE
OF TRALEE

AN EVENT WHICH at first caused amusement and subsequently fierce anger when the true motives behind the story were revealed, took place in November, 1920. Tralee people were amazed at that time to read a detailed and impressive account of an ambush at Ballydwyer on the Tralee-Castleisland road. An official pronouncement from Dublin Castle stated that a party of English pressmen under police escort were ambushed between Castleisland and Tralee. Two of the attackers were reported to have been killed and wounded in what was described as the biggest and fiercest engagement of any fight between crown forces and the Volunteers. The English newsagency the Press Association subsequently supplied the following fanciful account of the alleged ambush: 'Further details are forthcoming regarding the ambushing of the motor car containing a press representative and some photographers near Tralee when several of the assailants were captured and two believed killed and several wounded. The outstanding facts are that the attack took place at four o'clock in the afternoon on the very spot where another party of military and police had been ambushed in the morning some time before noon and that the engagement was the fiercest and probably on the largest scale of any fight between the crown forces and the Volunteers. According to the official message reporting the morning ambush this party of military and police were engaged in a search for wanted men when they were attacked, returning the fire. They claimed to have shot dead two of their assailants and wounded two others who were stated to have run away and refused to halt. This ambush was alleged to have taken place at Ballymacelligott where a trench was cut across the road. The men left to hold the trench opened fire on the military and the crown forces replied, inflicting the casualties stated.'

Dealing with the alleged second ambush in the afternoon, the Press Association became more lyrical and stated: 'Now, as to this ambush in which the press men had their thrilling experience, they were travelling in a motor car escorted by police in another car. The officer in charge of the party says the attackers opened fire from the brow of a hill and 'the convoy halted', this valiant officer's account continues, 'the escort and all available hands got into action, extending into open order and advanced opening fire as they did so. The enemy fled, scattering and hiding among hedges and ditches. Six prisoners were captured and some of the wounded got away. Two are believed to have been killed and there were no casualties to us. While we were collecting the prisoners a second attack developed and heavy rifle fire broke out from the surrounding higher slopes and from a farmhouse. Flanking parties of the attackers pressed forward along the road. Seeing these we fell back on our cars which had turned round and while covering fire was maintained we collected on the site of the ambush where there was a Ford car with a doctor, who was attending a Sinn Féiner who had been shot in the morning ambush. The enemy going along the road failed to close with us, but maintained a sporadic fusillade until we were clear of the scene of the ambush. The battle lasted about half-an-hour and owing to the large number of the attackers on the hillside and the road and a general doubt as to the safety of the road before us, which was reported blocked, and the fact that our ammunition was running out, I deemed it best to retreat to Castleisland with the prisoners already secured.'

Amongst this so-called press party was a cinema operator, who, it was stated, calmly produced his camera amid the strife and took an excellent film depicting the fighting. Another account to which publicity was given stated that on the approach of several lorries containing uniformed men, farmers and others assembled at a creamery and corn mills between Tralee and Castleisland for the purpose of doing business, took to the fields for safety. The occupants of the lorry pursued the fleeing men and opening fire, shot dead J. Herlihy, creamery sub-manager, and a farmer named McMahon. Tim Walsh, the engine-driver at the creamery and two workers named McElligott and McEllistrim were severely wounded. This account was getting nearer to the truth of the events and the incredulous amazement of the townspeople at the story of the attack on the press party was giving way to a gradual realisation of the foulness of the deed committed by the uniformed assassins.

Further confusion though was added before the facts became really known. In pursuance of the official policy of laying a smoke-screen over the acts of its tools, Dublin Castle issued another statement stating that a party of police and military had made a search of farmers in the Ballydwyer area and that some arms had been found, and apparently, it stated, the approach of cars bearing police and pressmen was unexpected from the direction in which they came and consequently the attackers were placed at a disadvantage. The doctor who was attending to one of the republican wounded in the morning fight had been released with his servant and car. One of the attackers, who was badly wounded, was left at the creamery, the other prisoners being handed over at Castleisland. One of the attackers, wearing Volunteer uniform, was believed to have been amongst those killed. In the two engagements the attackers were stated to have lost four killed and six wounded.

What was the object of all this official lying which went so far as to invent a large-scale action between the invaders and the Irish Volunteers? Enquiries about the personnel of the press party revealed that it included Mr G. Jones, one of Sir Hamar Greenwood's personal secretaries; Captain H.P. Pollard, RIC; a number of press photographers and one journalist, Mr Clifford Hutchinson of the *Yorkshire Post*. The *Belfast Telegraph* said that the tour would appear to have been arranged on a request from English cinemas for permission for a party of their men to visit the disturbed areas to get pictures of the daily life of the RIC. But Tralee people recalled that on Armistice day, young men were forced to march on the streets of Dungarvan with Union Jacks pinned to their clothes while a cinematograph operator and a photographer were with the armed men in lorries. Cynically Tralee wondered what Roman holiday had been provided for this bunch of English publicists and were not long in learning. The real happening, which the authorities did so much to cloak with their brazen hypocrisy and lying by inventing a mock battle, was that six or seven lorries of uniformed men arrived at Ballydwyer Creamery at noon and opened fire on the creamery from the road. Two young men named McEllistrim and O'Mahony who were convenient to the creamery ran towards the back of the building for shelter and O'Mahony was shot dead. Herlihy, Walsh and McAlister were wounded. While Herlihy was on the ground wounded further shots were fired at him and he was killed. The creamery was burned after the uniformed men had threatened to shoot the manager, John Byrnes. The haysheds of Jeremiah Hayes and of two farmers adjoining named Doolin were also destroyed by fire as well as the farmhouses of Hayes and Dunne.

Towards evening a crowd collected at the creamery to make arrangements for the removal of the remains and to have the wounded dressed. Dr Michael Shanahan, Tralee, was present and his car, which was on the road, was commandeered by a number of armed men who again arrived in four lorries from Castleisland and fired further shots at the creamery. Rev. M. McDonnell, CC, asked the man who appeared to be in charge to control the men, but he replied that he had no control over them. Dr Shanahan was driven in his own car to Castleisland. When the bodies were being removed shots were fired over the heads of the mourners; but when the 'valiant' uniformed assassins found their fire being returned, they decamped. Arrested on, the occasion were Thomas Connor, William Dowling, William Herlihy (brother of the murdered man), James Carmody and R. McAlister.

Miss Dowling, of Queen Alexandra's Imperial Nursing Service Reserve, who attempted to render aid to the wounded at Ballydwyer, told a press representative subsequently that she had nursed in Egypt and England during the war and was mentioned in dispatches for bravery. She was home on leave, and on the day of the attack on Ballydwyer creamery was in her brother's house when Fr McDonnell requested her to attend a wounded man named Walsh who had been shot near the creamery. 'I was attending to the wounded,' she said, 'when the police told me they would shoot me. After that they went to the house of my brother, Jack Dowling, and searched my trunk, from which I subsequently missed several articles of value. They must have known I was a nurse, because on top of my trunk was a nursing certificate and a card from the War Office stating I was mentioned in dispatches. They took my active service ribbons and my reserve badge from me. While they were taking my things more of them kept the women in the kitchen with their hands up.' As to the alleged ambush and pitched battle, Miss Dowling said that nothing had happened beyond the shooting at the creamery. To maintain the bluff the British authorities apparently thought that the inspired newspaper stories were not sufficient and had the hardihood to show in cinemas a *Pathe Gazette* feature stated to have been taken under fire at the 'battle near Tralee'. The film showed wounded Sinn Féiners being led away as prisoners by Auxiliaries and RIC, and an Irish girl pleading uselessly with the British troops to allow her brother go free. The film was as authentic as the newspaper stories or Sir Hamar Greenwood's perjury.

The *Irish Independent* subsequently showed in pictures how this film was faked. The locale of the film was identified by them as being in Dalkey, from a lamp-post which the fakers overlooked. It was subsequently proved that a British armoured car and soldiers were used in the faking of the picture. This must have been interesting news for Mr Bonar Law, who a few weeks earlier in the British House of Commons, when shown pictures of the destruction in Cork, replied: 'There are such things as faked pictures.'

A CHIVALROUS ENGLISH JOURNALIST

THOUGH THE ENEMY with lies and calumnies tried to distort the true happenings in Tralee during November week, 1920, the truth emerged to the world, and strangely enough through the medium of British newspapers and British journalists. One English newspaper correspondent who made himself thoroughly unpopular with crown forces during the Black and Tan terror in Ireland was Hugh Martin of the London *Daily News*. Mr Martin believed in telling the truth no matter who resented it, or no matter how awkward it might make things for those who were supposed to be 'protecting' the people while condoning murder and arson. The experiences of Mr Martin while in Tralee in November 1920, make interesting reading. In a message to the *Daily News* he said: 'Our motoring party, consisting of special correspondents of the Associated Press of America, *The Journal*, Paris, *The Times*, the *Manchester Guardian*, besides myself, was joined by the correspondent of the *London Evening News*. At 9.30 Mr McGregor, *Evening News*, said that as it would be necessary for him to send an early dispatch on the following morning, he was prepared to take a walk through the town to see the extent of the damage and ascertain if all was quiet. Would anybody go with him? I volunteered for the reconnaissance. Upon leaving the Grand Hotel we noticed a party of from twenty to twenty-five men standing on the opposite side of the road. Retreat and mere evasion were equally out of the question. McGregor and I therefore crossed the road in the direction of the figures. We then saw that they were armed with rifles and all wearing full uniform. We greeted them and said we were journalists. One of them said, "What have you come for; to spy on us I suppose." He then asked what newspapers we represented. I decided to lie boldly and mentioned the name of the coalition journal, which both by silence and occasional comment favoured the government's Irish policy. I also gave my name, when it was demanded, as that of an English journalist associated with the coalition. "Is there a Hugh Martin among you?" was the next question, "Because if there is we mean to do for him and it's him we want and we are going to get him." I was informed it was Hugh Martin who had been at Listowel and informed the men that the last time I had seen him myself was at the funeral of the lord mayor of Cork. It struck me as a fact worth noting that these men were roaming the streets without an officer – a fact brought home to me later, when, as I lay in bed, now so common of nights in Ireland, of plate-glass windows being smashed in the principal shopping street. At eleven o'clock this (Tuesday) morning word was brought to me that in spite of all precautions the fact of my presence in Tralee had leaked out and was being eagerly discussed by the townspeople. I decided to leave before it came to the ears of the police, and at a quarter to twelve set out for the place where I now am. For more than a month past hints have been reaching me from various quarters that it would be well for me either to cease telling the truth in print or to take special precautions for my own safety.'

M. de Marsillac, London correspondent of *The Journal*, Paris, who was with Hugh Martin in Tralee, gave a vivid story of the scenes in Tralee during that fateful November week, 1920. 'I do not remember,' he wrote, 'even during the war, having seen people so profoundly terrified as those of this little town, Tralee. The violence of the reprisals undertaken by representatives of authority, so to speak, everywhere, has made everybody beside himself, even before facts justified such a state of mind. The thing is understandable. Imagine that the civil authorities are powerless, that there is literally nobody in the world to whom one can appeal and from whom one can demand protection. You who read these lines in a country where life is normal, can only picture to yourselves with difficulty by this narrative the fear in the hearts of this unhappy population. All the afternoon, except for soldiers, the town was as deserted and doleful as if the Angel of Death had passed through it. Not a living soul in the streets. All the shops shut and the bolts hastily fastened. All work suspended, even the local newspapers.'

Thus two independent journalists lifted the veil of silence drawn discreetly over Tralee and Sir Hamar Greenwood had the lies he told in the British House of Commons thrown back in his teeth. Replying to Mr Joe Devlin in the British parliament, Hamar Greenwood admitted that 'a woman with a child in her arms had been killed by a shot fired as lorries conveying armed servants of the crown were passing the house,' and added that it might perhaps have been fired in fear of an ambush. The English *Daily News* commented on this: 'The mere transcription of that answer is tenfold more eloquent than any comment on it that could be made. That is Ireland today, or rather it is one example among hundreds of what Ireland is today. To questions on such crimes as those committed in Tralee, Sir H. Greenwood habitually opines that he is having enquiry made. On Friday the results of two such enquiries were forthcoming. In regard to the authenticated case of threats to murder Mr Martin, Sir H. Greenwood informs the House that the county inspector was not present at the encounter and knows nothing of the facts. Rarely has ignorance been more opportune. In the case of John Conway, said Sir H. Greenwood, the court, after enquiry, found that death had been due to natural causes. The special correspondent of *The Times* at Tralee made a statement in Thursday's issue to the effect that he went to the house in Rock Street of John Conway and saw him lying on his bed with a bullet wound in the temple. The vital fact in the tragedy is that while the chief secretary is repeating his stereotyped assurances that things are getting better, it is patent to the readers of newspapers the world over that they are getting daily worse. At the moment the supreme need is to withdraw the troops. If the police cannot remain unprotected, let them go too. Ireland could not be worse off without than with them. There is every reason to believe that her state would be incomparably better.'

TWO BLACK AND TANS SHOT AT BALLYBRACK

TURNER AND WOODS were two of the most notorious blackguards amongst the Black and Tans stationed in Kerry during 'The Trouble'. On the morning of 9 November 1920, they were observed boarding a train at the Tralee platform en route for Killarney. Word was immediately sent to Ballymacelligott, and Volunteers proceeded to Ballybrack where it was decided to attack the Black and Tans. The IRA men moved up the station, carefully scanning each carriage until they came to the compartment in which the two Black and Tans were seated facing each other. Fire was opened immediately. One Tan was killed outright and the second was fatally wounded.

BRAVE TOMMY HAWLEY

(Tommy Hawley, aged twenty-two years, was fatally wounded at Lispole ambush, on 21 March 1921. He died on the following day.)

When the boys of the hills get together,
And speak of that day at Lispole;
They will think of you, brave Tommy Hawley,
And fervently pray for your soul.
They'll tell of your deels [*sic*] on the mountain
From Tralee to the high hills of Keel;
And the tears will flow like a fountain
As our heroes express what they feel.

CHORUS

Then, here's to you, brave Tommy Hawley,
Who battled so valiant and true;
You fought 'neath the Green Flag of Érin
And conquered the Red, White and Blue.

They'll tell how you fought like a Trojan
In defence of the cause you loved well,
Of your hair-breadth escapes and encounters
With the Black and Tan devils from hell.
And though hunted through streets and through by-ways,
With a ban and a price on your head,
Never once did you cringe or falter
But met them with merciless lead.

CHORUS

Then here's to you, etc.

They'll tell how you came by your death-wound
In the way you would wish it to be,
With Black and Tans fleeing before you
And your comrades shouting with glee.
That day in the wild mountain valley
The Tans ran like rats to a hole
From a handful of young Irish soldiers,
Sweet vengeance that day at Lispole.

'Tis a death all brave men will envy,
And the boys who are left to condole
Will tell of the price paid for you
By the Saxon that day at Lispole.

Then, here's to you brave Tommy Hawley
May your memory be never forgot,
While brave men are left to remember
And women to weep o'er the spot.

And many a young Irish hero
Gave his life as you did at Lispole
For the glory and freedom of Ireland,
Tommy Hawley, may God rest your soul.

THE LISPOLE AMBUSH

by VOLUNTEER

AMBUSHES DID NOT always develop as anticipated. Here is an instance of where an IRA column lying in ambush had a counter-trap set for it. On the morning of 25 March 1921 the column were in position at Lispole where it was decided to ambush a lorry of Black and Tans, who were in the habit of patrolling the road from Dingle to Annascaul at least once a week. This was their third morning waiting, and they had already spent two days in their positions, retiring at night to the houses in the villages of Minard, Kinard and Bawnogue where the people did everything that could possibly be done for the comfort of the column. At 9.30 the scouts reported that a lorry of Tans had come from Dingle, and were halted at Ballinsteenig where a trench had been cut on the road. It was assumed that they were getting out planks to place across the trench and would be along any moment. The main body of the column was placed inside a ditch on the left-hand side of the road leading into Lispole village and an old schoolhouse on that side of the road was occupied. Across the road from the school a house standing by itself was also occupied and another batch of Volunteers were on the railway bridge below the road. A punt gun had been fixed in position to the right of the old school.

Everything was in readiness, but still the lorry of Tans made no move to advance towards the waiting column and it looked as if the

Tans were not coming any farther that day. The meaning of this delay was soon made plain. Whilst the scouts were busy keeping the party in the lorry under observation, a mixed body of troops, composed of Marines, Auxiliaries and Black and Tans, to the number of three hundred, were moving to surround the ambush position. Dressed in civilian attire, they were almost on top of the column before they were recognised. Immediately a party of men were dispatched to try and delay the oncoming foe, while the remainder made quick preparations to face the new situation which had arisen.

Before the column's plans for coping with the new turn in affairs were complete the British began an attack from all points. Rifle and machine-gun fire were raking the column's positions. The men posted on the railway bridge were in a very exposed position and could do nothing but lie under the parapet. The bullets came so fast and thick that it was impossible to return the fire. The Volunteers began to crawl along the ground towards a ditch which would afford them shelter and at the same time put them at the rear of the British. Before reaching the ditch, however, they had to cross a gap which the British had covered with a Lewis gun. As the Lewis-gunner stopped to refill his pans, which was only a matter of seconds, a man jumped across reaching the other side just before the gun started to fire again In this way the whole party who had been posted on the bridge succeeded in crossing safely and reaching a position where they could open fire on the enemy.

The Volunteers in the school and the house opposite in the meantime were subjected to a heavy fire. As there was a danger of the house being surrounded, it was decided to evacuate. To do this it was necessary to cross the road under a steady stream of bullets. It was a stirring sight to watch the men crossing the road one by one with a complete absence of panic. Each man behaved as if he were on the parade ground. Their bravery met its just reward. The whole party crossed the road without a casualty. The position of those who were trying to hold the enemy back from advancing down the mountain was now a desperate one. They had very little cover and were exposed to a merciless hail of bullets. The British repeatedly tried to close in on them, but the Volunteers' fire succeeded in holding them in check.

In one of these advances a few of the scouts who were unarmed were captured by a party of the British. The Volunteer officer in charge, the late Paddy Cahill of Tralee, succeeded with a few men in creeping up to the party of Britishers who had captured the scouts and by shouting 'surround on the right; surround on the left; surround in the centre' gave the British the impression that they were being attacked by a very large number. As darkness began to fall the British retired. It is not known what casualties they suffered, but judging from the fact that the Volunteers captured ten rifles and a quantity of ammunition, it is estimated that they must have been heavy. The Volunteers' casualty list was three killed and one wounded, which was not a heavy one when one considers that they were completely outnumbered. It is surprising that they did not sustain more losses. The punt gun was captured by the British.

THE FATAL CHALLENGE OF MAJOR McKINNON

by FIANNA

IN THE AUTUMN of 1920, Ireland, represented by the Irish Republican Army, and England, represented by crown forces comprising the British army, the Black and Tans and the Royal Irish Constabulary, were locked in death-grips when the Auxiliary division arrived to administer the *coup de grâce*. They were admirably equipped and selected for the task. Every one of them had seen service during the Great War as officers in the British army. Most of them sported medal ribbons that testified to their personal valour on the field. Each one of them was capable of acting on his own in an emergency. Together they were the most perfect instrument that could be devised for the task allotted to them. Skilled in the use of arms, inured to war, brave, self-reliant and arrogant, they had come to cow the civilian population into submission, and to seek out and smash the IRA, who were, to them, terrorists, gunmen, murderers, or, in milder terms, just 'Shinners'.

The company detailed to operate from Tralee was commanded by a remarkable figure of a man. Major McKinnon was tall, broad in proportion, handsome, with hawk-like eyes. With his Glengarry cap perched at a rakish angle, his holster swinging loosely at the thigh, the gun always at the ready; the huge bearskin gloves that he affected, his air of ruthlessness and military efficiency stamped him for what he was, a modern son of Mars. When the humour took him he could be suave and jocose, most often with a purpose. Always he was the alert leader of the pack out for the kill. He was not content to direct: he led. Quickly his personality manifested itself, and in town and country 'The Major' was well known and feared. With him the 'round-up' was a favourite procedure. Suddenly the western end of the town would be cordoned by crown forces, a house to house visitation would follow, during which all men and boys would be herded into Denny Street. There they were detained for hours while they were searched, questioned and scrutinised individually.

Another day he would take the eastern side and have all the males gathered into the sportsfield. The market would serve for the men of the north side some other time. In the country districts he adopted similar tactics. He would select a central part and have all the men of that district driven to it. A batch of prisoners usually resulted. Some were kept over-night, others a day or two, and a few found themselves in jail or internment camps. These 'round-ups' frequently took place in the middle of the night, light being provided by a concentration of Crossley tender and motor car lamps. It was then a fearsome business. In all these goings-on 'The Major' dominated. He would have to see everybody and be seen by them. He was not above delivering a harangue in which he expressed contempt for the IRA, and their methods, and challenged them to get him, for he was not afraid of them. He had a most disconcerting trick of turning up at places where he was the last man expected. He was not afraid to travel alone.

At night time in a country district he would emerge from behind a fence on a lonely road and hold up a passerby, or startle a group at a crossroads by his sudden descent upon them. He would enter a remote house in the dead of night, apparently on his own, though it was often suspected an escort was near at hand. He would drive through Tralee in an open car, daring his enemies to do their damnedest. He knew the psychological effect of these acts. He developed an early hatred of Ballymacelligott, where there were IRA men on whom he would dearly like to lay his hands. He traced every act hostile to the crown forces to Ballymacelligott until its very name obsessed him. He raided the district in season and out of season, giving no quarter and saying he expected none. On Christmas night, 1920, when one might have expected a lull in hostilities, he threw that countryside into mourning by shooting to death two young IRA men – Leen and Reidy – into whom he walked unexpectedly while they were enjoying the hospitality of a much raided neighbour's house. Thereafter McKinnon's name was loathed. The perpetration of such a deed at that season of the year brought home to the people the type of man they had in arms against them.

McKinnon continued on his arrogant way. From his headquarters at the technical school he and his men sallied forth on forays through town and country. Now to Ballymacelligott, tomorrow to Ardfert, he led them to rounds-up by day and by night, harrying the people in their homes, at the creameries, on the roads, in the streets, anywhere. The IRA determined that McKinnon must be shot. Many a time hands closed over revolver butts as he passed through the streets of Tralee, but the risk to other lives, and the necessity for a 'clean job', meaning that he was to be killed or not at all, prevented fire being opened.

In the early days of March 1921, Friday the third to be exact, a party lay in ambush for him at Ballyroe bridge, awaiting his return from the Ardfert district. The accidental discharge of a rifle when all were in position led to the abandonment of the attack on him. Rumour spread like wild fire that 'The Major' had been shot. The following day boy scouts sent to a dump in Ballybeggan for the arms for another attempt were discussing the rumour when who walked towards them from the direction of the old castle but 'The Major'. He was living up to his reputation for turning up unexpectedly. He questioned the boys closely, for he was by this time very suspicious, but accepted their tale of a bird-nesting expedition.

Few will deny that McKinnon was fearless. Through a hostile population he moved with a careless swagger, knowing from his six months' experience of the country that practically every man's hand was against him. His evening visits to the golf links were noted. Scouts were detailed to shadow him. Their reports were favourable, so an ambush was laid for him at the third green. On the following evening he turned up, but with ladies in his company, so there could be no shooting. When the ambush party dispersed, two of them jumped over a fence and proceeded across the links towards the town. Suddenly 'The Major' halted them. The ambushers, thinking that their game was spotted, steeled themselves for what they expected would follow. In a pleasant voice he told them keep to the left as he was playing to the right. They kept to the left until they were out of his sight.

Every day for a fortnight an ambush party was in position near the third green at 3 p.m. Why was he not showing up? Had he sensed something? Was he playing cat and mouse with them? Was he angling to take them red-handed? It was a nerve-racking ordeal for the four men in a position surrounded by roads, and they were becoming restless.

On Friday 15 April, the four ambushers, armed with a rifle and three shotguns, were at their posts. A scout up an ash tree had a good view of the surrounding country. He could see the other scouts at Clash cross, Oakpark cross, the race-course gates and the railway gates. The latter two had instructions to lock the railway gates to delay lorries of soldiers, Tans or Auxiliaries who might attempt to encircle the ambush position. For an hour or more the usual watch dragged on. Would another day close leaving that which was determined on unaccomplished? In another half an hour the links would be cleared and the ambush party would be going home to meet again on the morrow. The scout on the ash tree gives a signal. He has observed a party of five beginning to play from the first green. Three detach themselves and play ahead. They are quickly recognised as McKinnon's escort in civilian attire. McKinnon and his aide-de-camp, Valentine, are following after. They have played from the first and second, and are approaching the third green. Another signal and the ambush party file out of Kenny's Fort and line the fence twenty yards from that fateful third green. With a hearty laugh 'The Major' approaches it and takes up his stance. He is enjoying himself. Suddenly, the sharp crack of a rifle shatters the evening's peace. 'The Major' starts and reels. Rifle and shotguns speak together and he falls to the ground writhing. The deed is done. Valentine and the escort throw themselves on the ground. Two women who are approaching are frightened off with a round from one of the shotguns. The get-away is going to be easy, as the bodyguards do not show any inclination to engage the attackers, who are now moving off, their retreat covered by the rifleman who stayed until they were clear away. At Clash the arms are dumped, and then the attackers seek refuge in the hills for the night.

The scouts, with typical coolness, went home playing a mouth-organ. Meanwhile the bodyguard pulled themselves together and dashed down the bohereen at the back of the sportsfield, the shortest route to their headquarters at the technical school. A schoolboy on his way home was tossed from his bicycle and a badly scared 'Auxie' pedalled furiously through Boherbee and Moyderwell to report the shooting. Soon lorryloads of excited Auxiliaries dashed through the town at terrific speed. Edward Street was 'up' for repairs so the longer route by Ashe Street had to be taken, to the accompaniment of the usual language and discharging of shots. Ten minutes later they returned with the lifeless body of their commanding officer, from whose head brain matter oozed. Rumours flew in all directions. People said that he was heard to moan as he was carried through the town, and that with his dying breath he told his men to wreak their vengeance on Ballymacelligott. It is scarcely credible that a man, no matter how full of vitality, could live more than a few minutes with two rifle bullets fired at close range in his brain.

A curfew notice ordering all to be indoors at 9 p.m. was posted in Tralee that night. With or without McKinnon's direction, enraged Auxiliaries and Tans wreaked vengeance on Ballymacelligott. They brutally murdered one man, maltreated several, and gave seven houses to the flames.

THE SHOOTING OF MAJOR McKINNON

Attend again, brave comrades
While I retell the tale,
In few and simple verses
Of a despot's bloody trail;
From cursed England's reeking shores
He came to mow us down,
And laughed to scorn a voice that warned
'Don't go to Tralee Town.'

Now this grim British Major
Had planned to crush Sinn Féin,
To shoot and loot and play once more
The good old Empire game;
But rebels of The Kingdom swore
Our dear old land to free,
And shot the tyrant Major
In the Golf Links at Tralee.

His murderous comrades heard the news
And rushed like beasts around,
While the sorely wounded Major
Lay writhing on the ground;
They cried aloud 'We will revenge'
Forgot that Christmastide
When, in the bloom of manhood,
Poor Leen and Reidy died.

Of these two Irish soldiers
We need not here relate
But remember 'twas the Major
Who sealed their bitter fate.
He caught them unexpected
As Christmas night came on,
And stood behind a woman
As he shot them one by one.

As England's pawn he swore to nip
The flowering of Sinn Féin,
To shoot down Irish leaders
And win a glorious name;
His thirst for blood was quickly quenched
By Kerry's noble sons. You see,
No more he'll swing his clubs
On the Golf Links of Tralee.

MILITARY AMBUSHED AT HEADFORD JUNCTION

by FIANNA

ON SAINT PATRICK's Day 1921, the Kerry No. 2 brigade column, one of the most active units of the Republican Army during the Black and Tan war, lay in ambush at Dysert, Castleisland. Farranfore police barracks had just been attacked and the men of the flying column hoped to intercept the British party which they expected would be sent to reinforce the Royal Irish Constabulary in the district. No reinforcements passed the ambush position which the column abandoned about 3 a.m. It moved off towards Scartaglin and Ballydesmond and thence to Kilquane, Barraduff, where friends of the IRA observed a suspicious-looking 'prowler' in the locality. The column having been apprised, the man was arrested about six miles from Killarney town, and it is believed that he was on his way there to give information of the IRA movements to the British. On Sunday night the column crossed the railway line under Two Paps Mountain, about six miles from Headford. Next morning the men were given orders to 'stand-to' and prepare for an engagement with enemy forces. Equipment was examined and everything made ready for what has now passed into recent local history as 'Headford Ambush', certainly the biggest engagement in Kerry during the Anglo-Irish War. About one o'clock on Monday the column moved into positions at Headford, one section occupying the east side of the railway station, whilst Dan Allman, O/C of operations, Tom McEllistrim, second-in-command, Jack Cronin, Moss Carmody and Dave Healy entered the station itself, to inspect the place. Their plan was to attack the British ration party which travelled by rail to Killarney each week and which always stopped at Headford Junction. The time factor, which had been carefully worked out beforehand, showed that at least five or six minutes were still available to the attackers to complete their dispositions. However, Allman and his comrades had no sooner arrived on the platform than the ration train was seen approaching, ahead of schedule. There was immediate confusion amongst the column, men rushing in all directions to take up points of cover. As the train steamed into the platform Johnny O'Connor of Farmer's Bridge held the rifles of Dan Allman and of another Volunteer in addition to his own weapons. He rushed to the platform, threw the rifles to the two Volunteers and then dashed to the rear of the signal cabin. The train was then at a standstill and because of its unexpectedly early arrival the Volunteers were as yet without definite orders. Dan Allman and Dave Healy slipped into the lavatory which was immediately visited by one of the soldiers from the train. The soldier dashed out again but before he could reach the train Allman shot him with his .45. This precipitated matters and the fight at Headford had begun. Even prior to the opening incident related the British appeared to sense that something was afoot and an IRA man, having observed one of the soldiers take up his rifle, fired on him. Immediately the whole column opened up a fusillade. The captain of the enemy forces, who was standing at a carriage door, was struck three times and killed instantly. His sergeant took over control and the entire detachment dashed towards the Rathmore side of the platform. Civilians, mostly cattle and pig buyers returning from Kenmare Fair, were scattered about the station and directly in line of fire. One woman with two young children ran the length of bullet-swept Headford Junction and all three escaped unscathed.

Meanwhile, the attackers advanced to within twenty yards range of the military, with whom they exchanged volley for volley, but with more deadly effect. The British were getting the worse of matters; their dead lay about and firing became intermittent as the main body of the enemy was practically wiped out. The sole remaining pocket of resistance came from a position between the train and the embankment, which was occupied by a party of soldiers early in the fight. Captain Allman dashed across to Johnny O'Connor's position and remarked, 'I think we have them now; there are only a few alive under the train.' Jim Coffey, an ex-British soldier with the column, joined Allman and O'Connor and it was decided to make a dash towards the rear of the guard's van with the object of wiping out the last enemy position. The new advance point was readily reached and Coffey, who was in front, knelt down to take better aim. Portion of his arm was exposed, and this provided sufficient target for a British soldier who inflicted a flesh wound on it. Dan Allman next dropped on one knee, took aim, but was shot through the lungs before he could fire. He stood up and blood trickled between his lips before he fell. 'Water,' he muttered faintly as he lay dying in a comrade's arms, and Johnny O'Connor was about to get this when Allman weakly indicated a bottle of Holy Water in the top pocket of his coat. This was sprinkled over him and such of his comrades who had attempted to drag him under cover. All were immediately caught in close range enemy fire, and were compelled to take cover momentarily. Captain Allman wore a green and gold rosette on the lapel of his coat that day, and as he lay dying at Headford Junction his broken-hearted comrades watched his life-blood slowly supersede the green and gold he loved so well. When Allman was dead the rosette on his breast was crimson red.

When the O/C was hit Jim Coffey immediately dashed across the platform to the stationmaster's office, where Tom McEllistrim, second-in-command, had taken up position. He immediately assumed charge of operations. Meanwhile, Johnny O'Connor and his group continued to engage the enemy from their side of the station. Eventually Johnny lobbed a Mills bomb amongst the soldiery under the embankment and there was a tremendous explosion. Before the end the column suffered another casualty when Jim Baily was shot through the head and killed instantly. He and Tommy McEllistrim had been great friends, and as Tommy looked for the last time on the face of his dead comrade, he was heard to murmur sadly, 'Ireland, what we've given you.'

At this stage there had been no firing for some minutes although the surviving members of the British continued to hold out. The end appeared close at hand when Johnny O'Connor, who had lifted his rifle to fire upon a soldier who had exposed himself, was squeezed on the arm by Tom McEllistrim, who directed his attention to a trainload of British troops entering the platform from the other side. With such superior enemy forces on the scene there was no alternative but to retreat as quickly as possible. Peter Browne, ex-commandant in Tralee, Jackie Brosnan, Tommy McEllistrim, and Johnny O'Connor managed to get into a little bohereen about sixty or seventy yards long and running west towards Killarney. At the end of this the way to safety lay across open country, mostly cut-away bog, and no sooner had the little party appeared on this terrain than the British opened fire on them with a tremendous fusillade. The four Volunteers found meagre shelter behind a fence, during which time Johnny O'Connor fired upon the enemy, thus slowing up pursuit at a vital juncture. The party then decided to split into two groups and Tommy McEllistrim and Johnny O'Connor having paired off, succeeded in crossing the bridge over the Flesk, which was covered by British machine guns. Soon afterwards they were picked up by local Volunteers, a few miles from Headford, and later that night the whole column reassembled. It was then confirmed that the column had suffered two men killed, Captain Dan Allman and Volunteer James Baily. Twenty-four soldiers were killed in the engagement and four wounded. Two civilians were killed and several others wounded. The original plan was to attack the guards at the end of the platform and capture their arms. Later the British GHQ communique stated:

> As a train containing one officer and twenty-nine other ranks, First Royal Fusiliers, and a number of civilian passengers was nearing Headford Junction, it was heavily fired into from both sides of the cutting. The troops detrained and engaged the attackers, sustaining heavy casualties while doing so. The survivors held off the ambushers for fifty minutes, when they were reinforced by the arrival of another train, which contained a party of the First Royal Fusiliers, and the combined parties drove the rebels off. No arms or equipment were lost by the troops. The casualties were one officer and six other ranks killed; twelve other ranks wounded; one civilian passenger killed, and two civilian passengers wounded. It is believed a number of casualties were inflicted on the ambushers, and the dead body of one of them was found by the troops.

Amongst those who participated in the Headford ambush were: Dan Allman, O/C, who was killed; T. McEllistrim, TD, John Cronin, Jack Herlihy, Paddy Burke, Moss Carmody, John Connor, Moss Galvin, Jimmy Baily, also killed; all of Ballymacelligott company. The others included: Jack Shanahan, Dan Healy, Jack Brosnan, Peter Browne, Neilus McCarthy, Patrick Cronin, D.B. Cronin, Tom Connor, John Flynn, John Herlihy, Dave McCarthy, Tim O'Meara, Pat Shea, Dan P. O'Sullivan, Jim Coffey, Denis Sullivan, Peter Sullivan, Tim Donoghue.

HOW ALLMAN FELL

(By kind permission of the author, Mr Paddy Breen, Beaufort)
(Air: 'The Felons of Our Land')

I'm dying, said a warrior bold, for my dear native land,
I'm dying, gallant comrade, let me grasp your hero-hand,
This day at Headford Junction, you've proved yourself to be
A model of that faithful band, who fight for liberty.

Chorus:
A flask of Holy Water, in my pocket you will find,
The only thing I brought from home, when I left all behind,
Sprinkle o'er my body, then my spirit shall be free,
And tell them all how Allman fell, in the fight for liberty.

The long sought hour has come at last, I dreamt of o'er and o'er,
I knew that fate ordained that I should share my country's gore,
Your rights, Dark Rosaleen, I loved, your wrongs I vowed they'd rue,
I face the Throne of Mercy now, my duty's done to you.

Across that fence Jim Baily lies, but 'ere the twilight's fall,
At Heaven's gate we both shall wait, the dread Tribunal's call,
'That greater love that no man hath', shall be the angel's plea,
They stood to save their fellow-man, they died their land to free.

And still the din of battle rings, my column lads are true,
I leave their fate and guiding now, to Tommy Mac and you,
I bid you ne'er to mourn the fate, or pause at Allman's name,
'Till you have helped to raise the cry, A Nation Once Again.

POLICE PATROL ANNIHILATED AT CASTLEMAINE

by FIANNA

ON THE MORNING of 1 June 1921, it was reported to an IRA column that a cycling party of Black and Tans in extended order had passed through Castlemaine on their way from Killorglin to Tralee, and that they would return by the same route and in the same order that evening. It was decided to lie in ambush for them on the Milltown side of the Castlemaine railway bridge. The column was placed in extended order inside a ditch on the left of the Castlemaine–Milltown road, from Flynn's house to a cottage half a mile beyond it. By this arrangement it was hoped that the head of the cycling party, having been allowed to ride the full length of the ambush position, all the Black and Tans would be brought into the attackers' field of fire.

Events did not turn out as anticipated. The Tans, having regaled themselves in a public house in Castlemaine on their way back to Killorglin, re-mounted their bicycles simultaneously, and rode into the ambush position more or less bunched together and not by any means in the extended order that was expected. This threw the column order of attack out of gear, and decisive action was necessary to adjust matters. The four Volunteers, stationed twenty yards apart at the end of the ambush position, were ordered to close up and open fire on the Tans when they reached them. The feelings of the four Volunteers, upon whom the success of the operation depended, can be better imagined than described, as they saw the Tans cycle unsuspectingly towards them. It was only a matter of seconds from the time the Tans came into view until they reached the firing line, but it seemed like hours to the waiting four.

A volley rang out. The fight was on. Instinctively the four Volunteers must have trained their rifles on the district inspector leading the Tans, for he was found dead subsequently with four bullets in his body. The two sergeants, who rode with the district inspector, passed through, but a Mills bomb brought them down. The remainder of the Tans hastily dismounted, and began to run back towards Castlemaine, taking what cover offered on the way. They ran into the jaws of death. The other members of the column came into action against the fleeing Tans, and for half an hour firing was hot and heavy. The road was littered with the bodies of dead and dying Tans. Two Tans managed to escape along the railway line to Killorglin, glad to leave their rifles behind them. It is estimated that seven Tans were killed and three wounded.

As the scene of action moved towards Castlemaine, keeping pace with the fleeing Tans, a section of the IRA, going out on the road to collect arms, found that the district inspector, whose revolver was strapped to his wrist, had discharged one round. He had apparently managed to do so after four rifle bullets had entered his body. Crossing a field during the course of the fighting, a member of the IRA heard behind his back an English accented shout: 'I have got you.' Wheeling sharply, and dropping on one knee, the IRA man found himself face to face with a Tan lying against a ditch. As the Irishman brought his rifle to the firing position, the Englishman pulled the trigger. The bullet entered the Volunteer's left shoulder and travelled down his back where it made its exit. Falling downward and coughing blood, the Volunteer must have fainted. When he came to, he was unable to lift his hand, and had the Tan advanced over the ditch he would have found a helpless Irishman at his mercy. Thinking the IRA man dead, the Tan moved off, and, shortly afterwards, ran into two of the column who shot him dead. The wounded member of the ambush party was removed by horse and car, with a kitchen door for a stretcher, to the River Laune, near Beaufort. Taken across the river by boat, he was carried into a house, from where, after two hours, he had again to be removed as military were raiding all over the countryside for the column. He eventually found a resting place in Glencar, where he stayed until he recovered. By then the Truce had come.

Amongst the Tralee men who took part in the Castlemaine ambush were: Jerry O'Connor, Donnacadh Donoghue, Joseph Sugrue, Dan Sullivan, Johnny Sullivan, now in USA; Paddy Paul Fitzgerald, John L. Sullivan, Michael McMahon, Miko Leary, Billy Myles, killed in action October 1923 at Curraheen; Jerry Myles, who was wounded; Eugene Hogan and Dan Jeffers. Tadhg Brosnan, of Castlegregory, now in the USA, was in charge of the operation. Milltown and Castlemaine areas were represented by Tom Connor, Dan Mulvihill, Jack Flynn, ex-TD, and Jerry Cronin.

DARING COUP FRUSTRATED AT CASTLEISLAND

SOON AFTER TRALEE'S night of terror, November Eve 1920, the IRA planned an operation for Castleisland, which, had it succeeded, would have ranked among the most daring episodes of the Black and Tan War. As events turned out, the merest accident came between it and success at the vital moment. At the time it was customary for the British military in Castleisland to parade daily to the post office for the collection of mails. As a rule the party comprised fifteen men who moved in extended formation. The coup was arranged for a Fair day when the street was certain to be thronged by a huge number of farmers and buyers. It was planned by Tom McEllistrim and thirty IRA men were mobilised to participate in it. The plan of action decided that the IRA men would work in pairs and that only one of each pair would be armed with a revolver. The men were instructed to move through the crowd at the fair, and each pair was ordered to cover one member of the British patrol. A whistle blown by Tom McEllistrim was to be the signal for the IRA to close in on the soldiers and disarm them. Everything seemed to be moving according to plan and Tom McEllistrim was about to set the operation in motion when he observed a strong and heavily armed contingent of military move up Castleisland's main street. Immediately he beckoned to his men to slip away quietly but all did not succeed in doing so before the British sensed trouble. The troops became very uneasy and fired several rounds into the air. Indescribable confusion followed as farmers, buyers and animals bolted in all directions. During this uproar the IRA men quietly melted away, their scheme upset by the unexpected and, as it transpired, accidental arrival of superior enemy forces.

THE CAMPAIGN IN NORTH KERRY

by W.N.F.

THE NARROW MEANDERING Galey twists and turns on its winding way through that countryside which holds many of North Kerry's most delightful beauty spots. Especially picturesque is the view from the river bridge close by the O'Connor farmhouse, a few miles from Listowel. It is difficult to imagine this lovely, peaceful countryside sullied by violence, blood and sudden death. Yet, all three were present there in March 1920, when a sergeant and two constables of the Royal Irish Constabulary were ambushed. Midway between the O'Connor farmhouse and a tree plantation about two hundred yards distant in the Listowel direction are two gates which face each other on opposite sides of the road. It was at this point that Sergeant McKenna and two constables, who were returning from Listowel to Ballylongford, were engaged by officers and men of the Ballydonoghue company, IRA. The fight developed into a bloody hand-to-hand struggle in which Sergeant McKenna was killed and both of the constables were badly wounded.

BALLYDUFF AMBUSH AND ITS SEQUEL

ON THE NIGHT of 31 October 1920, it was arranged that picked men of the Lixnaw and Ballyduff companies of the IRA with others would ambush a patrol of the Royal Irish Constabulary at Ballyduff; so positions were taken up at that village. In the subsequent fight one constable was killed and others were wounded. The attackers got safely away. After the engagement James and Willie Houlihan, both of whom were in the fight, thought it wiser to get away from the village that night, fearing reprisals. Their brother, Seán, against their advice, thought it best for him to stay at home.

When the news of the ambush reached Listowel, crown forces rushed at once to Ballyduff and with their entry to the village the sinister rattle of rifle shots was heard and the bursts of machine-gun fire swept the streets, striking terror into a defenceless people. The first lorry halted outside Houlihan's and the house was at once surrounded. It was then impossible for Seán to escape. The enemy forced their way into his home, reached his bedroom and, with drunken cheers, dragged him forth, kicking him downstairs ahead of them. But still they had not finished in their devilish conduct; they knew what torture was and how to carry it out. Seizing his poor mother, who was already fearful of the pending tragedy, they made her gaze on the ghastly butchery taking place on the roadside. They had dragged Seán to the fence opposite his house, only a few yards from his mother. There they riddled his body with bullets and as his poor pain-racked body writhed on the ground, one of the Tans, filled with blood lust, dashed in and drove his bayonet through the heart of the dying soldier. Sobbing and delirious the broken-hearted mother rushed to her dying son, his hot blood gushing forth on the roadway. Incoherently but passionately she prayed that the Good God, comforter of all Irish mothers, might receive her bullet-riddled boy to His Sacred Heart, and called for Irish vengeance on his slayers.

Over their cups the drunken Tans had boasted in Ballyduff that there was an IRA Officer in Listowel whom they had next to 'send aloft', as they called it. True to their word they made a raid on his home at Listowel, but, fortunately, information had reached him of their coming and he had gone to a friend's house, thus escaping the terrible fate of Seán Houlihan.

Men from Derry (Newtown) company of the IRA attached to the North Kerry flying column entered Listowel on Thursday, 19 January 1921, and shot dead District Inspector O'Sullivan, one of the officers of the Royal Irish Constabulary who had been operating in the district for some time. The point where the shooting occurred was within fifty yards distance of the Royal Irish Constabulary barracks, and three hundred yards from the barracks of the Auxiliaries and military.

ATTEMPTED ENEMY ROUND-UP AND THE MURDER OF BOB BROWNE

TOWARDS THE END of January 1921, unusual activity on the part of the crown forces was observed in Listowel. Several lorries and armoured cars carrying Auxiliaries, Black and Tans and military, had moved into the town, and, as many officers of the 'Murder Gang' were noticed amongst the enemy, it was obvious that an offensive was planned. In charge of the British was the notorious Auxiliary commander, Major McKinnon, who had been implicated in many shootings and who later paid the penalty for his crimes on the Tralee golf links. Our battalion O/C at that time was the late Bob McElligott, a most resourceful officer to whose alertness we owed our lives that night. Bob received early information that the purpose of the enemy concentration was to wipe out the North Kerry column, then billeted at Derk, some miles from Duagh. He immediately gave orders to a capable dispatch rider to take us news of the attempted round-up. This was a most difficult task; yet, in spite of the fact that all roads round Listowel were closely watched, the scout succeeded in getting through and ultimately reaching Duagh the same night, which was wild, wet and stormy. There he contacted the captain of the Duagh company, and a column officer who had just crossed the River Feale with ammunition. All hurried onto Derk, where a consultation was held by the various column leaders.

We knew the enemy, no matter in what strength, would not travel until some time before dawn, fearing ambushes. This night was one of the worst we had ever experienced, with rain, sleet and storm. All of our men and our local scouts were drenched to the skin, but, of necessity, we had to keep on the alert; our lives depended on it. Unfortunately, at the time we did not have enough arms to justify waiting for a fight with such an overwhelming force as we knew was coming out, so in accordance with guerrilla tactics we decided to move. Making our journey towards Rathea we left some hours before the dawn. Not long after we had gone Duagh was first invaded by McKinnon and his forces, and in a short time after Derk was surrounded. Had we been caught within the circle, there would have been a holocaust such as happened afterwards at Clonmult, because with McKinnon and his 'Murder Gang' there would have been no quarter. Of course, it would have been a fight to a finish. We were poorly equipped and, though hand-to-hand fighting would have suited us and we would have inflicted several casualties, there could only have been one end, as we were heavily outnumbered.

Infuriated by our escape the Tans and Auxiliaries savagely beat up all the young men of the district, stabbing them with bayonets in the body, pulling their hair out with pincers. But their attempt to strike terror into the people failed, their vicious savagery and wanton cruelty only serving to inflame the district into a more wonderful spirit of patriotism and, no matter what torture was inflicted at that or any other time, no information was given against us. The thanks of the column men are due to all persons who ever helped us or who suffered on our account. In one district the only son of a poor old woman was savagely beaten and knocked insensible before her eyes. She herself was then threatened with murder, but still she would not let the enemy know even the direction in which our column had gone. Pluckily she sneaked across country that night, herself, eluding the military scouts, to inform us of the raid. We could never have lost at this period, with such heroism, steadfastness and indifference to persecution exhibited by our people.

When we reached Rathea we were exhausted, hungry, cold and drenched, but some good friends there put us right. About twelve o'clock on the following day we heard that two lorries of Black and Tans, some of the search party, were scouring round the district. This was our chance. We took up positions adjacent to Rathea chapel. By using shotguns, desperate weapons at close quarters, surprising and striking terror into our foes with the first volley, we should be able to capture the lorries with the arms and ammunition. All was ready and while we were waiting tensely there, hoping for success and listening intently for the purr of the motors, a girl scout cycled up with the information that an armoured car was also travelling with the lorries. Thus we were foiled again and had to decamp, as we had no equipment to engage the enemy's armour. Rathea was combed for us on the following day in the same savage manner as was Duagh, but we had gone to Stack's Mountain and thus the game continued.

Late the following night while we were at Stack's Mountain our scouts informed us that seeing lights on the edge of a bog they investigated the matter and discovered that a large number of Auxiliaries and other forces had collected and that they feared an attempt would be made by them to comb the district. We got ready at once and travelled to a place which would be more advantageous for a fight if we were cornered. The 'Auxies', however, fearful because of their lack of knowledge of the district and the lateness of the night, never ventured down, but departed to Tralee. On the following day we slipped down towards Lixnaw and outwitted our pursuers by crossing the river there, a trick we used with much success during subsequent activities.

During the search for us at Rathea and Stack's Mountain at the beginning of February, the crown forces covered a wide district. Unfortunately, they captured Bob Browne of Feales Bridge who was on the run at Knockalougha. Though he was unarmed, they beat him savagely, afterwards taking him down a by-road into a bog where they murdered him, thus adding another tragic chapter to the story of a glorious Irish family who had already suffered enough. This was the history England left behind her in our country; of ruined homes, torture, imprisonment and murder. A fleeting, seeming victory gained by such methods could never survive when dealing with a proud people who had such a wonderful tradition of fighting and resistance to oppression.

COMMANDANT MICHAEL ROBERT McELLIGOTT

OF SURPRISING COOLNESS and wonderful resourcefulness, Commandant Michael Robert McElligott was one of those who, very unassumingly, did much excellent work with the IRA. In police records, the confusion of his name with that of his inseparable friend, the late Captain Michael McElligott, of Charles Street, Listowel, permitted him to move about his battalion area more freely following the arrest of the latter. For this fact all who served with the North Kerry flying column can be thankful, for it was Bob McElligott who sent the warning dispatch from Listowel to Duagh in January 1921, giving information of the movements and intentions of the crown forces, thus saving the column from being hacked to pieces by McKinnon and the 'Murder Gang'.

Commandant McElligott was an officer in whose proud heart were instilled the will to do and the nerve to dare. Undefeated, undeterred by terrorism, he had lived his glorious life. His recklessness in the face of danger was afterwards his undoing and, to the deadly rattle of British musketry, he died on 19 February 1921, killed in action against forces of the British crown, at Derrymore, near Tralee. As a friend he had no equal; one who was always interested in the comfort and welfare of his brother officers and men. His straightforwardness made him the idol of the 6th battalion. Because of his timely help some of us lived to carry on the good work for which he died.

BLACK AND TANS ENGAGED
AT BALLYLONGFORD

ON 22 FEBRUARY 1921, acting on reports and information received about movements of the enemy, column officers decided that attacks should be made that night on patrols of British Crown forces at Ballylongford and Ballybunion. The O/C of the 3rd battalion went with a body of men to Ballybunion, whilst another party accompanied by a column officer of the 6th battalion set out for Ballylongford. The Ballylongford party reached its objective without mishap, and members of the column quickly and silently took up positions in the town, some near the barracks and at other points of vantage. Volunteers were detailed to cover the roads leading to Ballylongford, in order to prevent a possible surprise attack by enemy forces from Listowel or Tarbert. Five men with an officer occupied an advantageous position under cover of gate piers by the side of the road leading to the barracks, on the route usually travelled by the expected patrol of seven or eight Black and Tans.

Dusk had set in, and the silence of the winter's night was shattered momentarily by the hysterical screams of a frightened woman. Tension gripped the waiting men who had been in their positions almost half-an-hour when a Volunteer of the Ballylongford company warned them of the approach of two Black and Tans, evidently returning to their barracks, following patrol duty. The Volunteer was ordered to make a quick get-away as the Black and Tans drew nearer the ambush position. On they came, almost noiselessly, their whispered conversation being the only sound to reach the waiting IRA men. Then came a sudden spurt of flame and a rifle shot shattered the quietness of the night. Quick as lightning both Black and Tans turned and opened fire point blank on their attackers. Shotguns, those deadly weapons at close quarters, were brought into action in support of the rifles, and there was an end to the flashing spurt from the service revolvers of the Black and Tans, both of whom lay sprawled upon the road. One appeared to have been killed outright, but the other was still able to move, and the three IRA men who vaulted the gate kept their guns clenched in their hands, as it was an old trick of the enemy to sham death until given further opportunity to use his weapons.

The officer in charge strode towards the constable still living, despite a warning by one of his men who shouted 'Mind yourself, that Tan has a gun in his hand.' The officer replied, 'It's all right, he can't use it,' and the Tan yelled in fear, 'My God! Can't you see I can't use it?' at the same time holding out a Webley in his open palm. As a matter of fact all his bullets had been fired. He was evidently mortally wounded, but medical attention was procured for him afterwards at the barracks, from which place fire had already been opened. Verey lights were being sent up as signals for help, and, amidst the bursting of grenades from the Royal Irish Constabulary, and the answering rifle fire of our men, one could hear the maddened nervous yelling of the enemy inside. As there was not much use in wasting rifle ammunition firing at Ballylongford barracks, we decamped to our billets on the hills, and as we marched away signals for help were still being sent up, and the mad insensate rifle fire continued.

On the following morning, Tans, several lorry loads of them, as a reprisal entered and sacked Ballylongford; beat up the inhabitants, burned down several houses, and looted the whole district, causing enormous damage.

At the present time it is interesting to read the report of the

British military transmitted from their HQ at Cork, relative to the destruction of Ballylongford. The report, given hereunder, is typical of the British propaganda methods employed against us.

> I beg to report that on the night of 22/2/21 Constable —— was shot dead and —— (naval rating) dangerously wounded at Ballylongford; police on early morning of 23/2/21 visited the scene to investigate the matter. When entering the village an intense rifle, shotgun and revolver fire was concentrated on them from the houses. The rebels occupied the village in strength and it has just transpired that some of them wore police and soldiers' uniforms. The rebels knew the police occupying the barracks would be expecting reinforcements and they expected to gain admission to the barracks without difficulty disguised as police and soldiers. These men disguised as police and soldiers caused the civilian population to evacuate the village early in the night and from police enquiries those who declined to leave were subjected to rough handling and their property was not spared. When the police entered the village after dislodging the rebels, not a human being of any sort was to be seen.

The detachment which set out for Ballybunion, under the O/C of the 3rd battalion reached there without much trouble. Members of the Ballybunion company reported that three Black and Tans, all wanted men, were in a public house in the village, and an attempt to capture them was immediately decided upon. Plans were quickly made, and men occupied suitable positions with a view to rushing the police in the public house when all was in readiness. Luck was not with the attackers that night, for their intentions were frustrated by a police constable near the barracks who perceived that something was amiss and managed to raise the alarm although pursued and eventually fired upon by a Volunteer. Intense machine-gun and rifle fire from the barracks opened at once on those under cover near the public house. The IRA men in turn replied with rifle and shotgun. Searchlights lit up the streets and pandemonium reigned as other sections joined in the attack on the barracks which then developed. The defending Royal Irish Constabulary men, having been thus forewarned of the attack on their position, the O/C of the IRA realised that their barracks could not be captured and ordered his men to break off the engagement to avoid useless waste of ammunition. Reluctantly the column left for Larha where, on the following morning, they had a narrow escape from capture by reinforcements of crown forces, on their way to sack Ballylongford, as a reprisal for the attack on the Black and Tans there on the previous night. Luck was then with the little column. The Black and Tans burned down the hall at Ballybunion on 23 February 1921, and maltreated several people.

MURDER OF JAMES KENNELLY OF MOYBELLA

AT THE END of February 1921, the column were billeted at Guhard when information reached us that British military were at Coolkeragh filling in a trench. As many of us as were ready rushed at once across country, but unfortunately the military had only paid a flying visit and were gone. Tired and disappointed we got back to Guhard and had just reached there when Thomas Kennelly, O/C 3rd battalion cycled on with the information that a patrol of the Royal Irish Constabulary from Ballybunion had raided for him at the home of his uncle, James Kennelly, of Moybella and that he believed they had intended to raid Ballyegan afterwards. About twenty of us or so 'doubled' from Guhard and just reached Lisselton as police boarded the train from Ballybunion. We fired at them maintaining a running fight and wounding some. In the returning fire Captain Patrick Dalton, who was afterwards murdered at Gortaglanna, had a narrow escape, a bullet cutting through his coat along the side.

As a reprisal Black and Tans came out again from Ballybunion on 10 March and murdered James Kennelly, uncle of Thomas Kennelly, a great, friend of ours and a sterling nationalist. It was the British method of waging war in those days, to take revenge on the parents and relatives of those soldiers of the republic who were conducting guerrilla warfare in the different areas. These methods failed in their purpose and only served to inflame the Irish people to a higher spirit of patriotism.

ATTEMPTED ATTACK ON LIXNAW STATION

IN MARCH 1921, it was reported to the O/C of the North Kerry column that British military were in the habit of using the 9.30 a.m. train from Listowel to Tralee. It was decided to ambush them at Lixnaw railway station, and the senior column officer with his men set out for that village where it was intended to contact the Lixnaw company captain and the Volunteers of the area. Another officer was dispatched to Listowel with orders that, on the following morning, he should telephone Lixnaw post office which would then have been taken over by our men. His duty was to report whether soldiers travelled on the train, their number and the positions they occupied in the carriages. In the event of military definitely travelling on the train some ruse was to be applied in Listowel and district in order to keep the British forces there engaged, and so give our men at Lixnaw an opportunity to bring off their expected capture. Following considerable difficulty the Volunteer officer reached Listowel where a capable man from the local company was given instructions that night to go to the Listowel station in the morning and report on any military travelling. All the while the column officer remained in an office near the telephone exchange. In the morning the local Volunteer reported that no military had travelled on the 9.30 a.m. train, and the column officer immediately tried to telephone Lixnaw, to pass on the information to the column. Luck was out, as the line to Lixnaw was down, and the telephone operator in the Listowel exchange was unable to give any assistance Meanwhile, men of the column and the Lixnaw company took possession of Lixnaw railway station, and occupied positions in preparation for the expected engagement. Although it was noticed that there were no military aboard as the train drew into the platform, our men nevertheless searched the carriages for enemy officers in 'mufti', but none was discovered. The mails were taken off and examined. The members of the local company were then dispersed and the column moved off, all disconsolate that no ambush had taken place, as at the time we were sorely in need of the rifles we had hoped to capture. There was an added thrill when engaging the British with their own weapons. The column officer who had gone to Listowel returned safely, following an eventful journey, and with a comrade reached a secluded farmhouse on the hillside where both slept the tired sleep of men who had been travelling far and fast. On the road below armed men did their turn of guard duty on a cold and frosty night.

THE MURDER OF ADJUTANT WILLIE McCARTHY

A YOUNG IRA officer who had given us much information and who had been a wonderful help in several matters was the late Adjutant Willie McCarthy of Lixnaw. He had been a brilliant ecclesiastical student and a promising athlete, and ultimately he became intelligence officer to the 3rd battalion. In 1921 he was working as secretary to the Kerry Farmers' Union and his knowledge of people and places gained in this occupation was of much assistance to us. Crown forces had been following him for some time, but he managed to evade them until that fateful Easter Saturday, 1921. On that day he visited Tralee with dispatches. When these had been safely delivered he went to Confession, afterwards going to the Railway Hotel. There he was arrested, having been 'spotted' by some of the enemy forces. He was then taken to the barracks of the Royal

Irish Constabulary at High Street, Tralee, where he was practically beaten to death, both of his hands having been broken, in a terrible attempt to extract information from him as to the various activities and ambushes. Those who have been through such torture and who have been lucky enough to survive it, can understand the dreadful agonies he went through. At such a time a prisoner would pray to God that unconsciousness or death would come quickly to deliver him from his tormentors.

Infuriated by their failure to extract information from their prisoner, who was then almost dead, the 'Murder Gang' took him that night to the Green (now the Town Park) in Tralee, and his mangled, bullet-riddled body was found there on the following morning, Easter Sunday, 1921. Unconquered, he had died, going to the God of Mercy who would relieve his pain, agony and torture.

TARBERT BARRACKS ATTACK

TARGETS FOR ATTACK on Wednesday night, 6 April 1921, were the police barracks at Tarbert and Ballyduff. One section, accompanied by our column O/C, set out for Tarbert where, in addition to attacking the barracks, it was thought they might also come to grips with a police patrol on the same night. Despite the assistance of scouts from the Tarbert company, the advance to the village of Tarbert was slow going, through wet, heavy fields and barbed wire fences. The O/C and another member of the column, both of whom had worked ahead of the others, reached a street just in time to fire upon two Black and Tans who were running towards their barracks. The Black and Tans were wounded in the exchange of shots, but managed to reach the safety of their barracks from which fire was opened immediately. The attackers responded wholeheartedly and in a short time there was joined to the sharp crack of rifle fire, the rat-tat-tat of the machine guns from Marines on their way up the

Island road to the assistance of the police. With the intensive rifle
fire and the bursting of grenades from the barracks, the answering
shooting of the attackers, the enthusiastic cheering of the column
and the yells of the Black and Tans in the barracks, bedlam seemed
let loose in Tarbert.

Much though we would have liked to continue the engagement,
we could not cope with the weight of the Marines, as we were without
a machine gun, had not many rifles nor enough ammunition for a long
scrap. But for the intervention of the Marines, Tarbert police barracks
would have been an easy capture for us. As we marched out of Tarbert
we could still hear the ominous rat-tat-tat of the machine guns as the
Marines entered the village on the side opposite to us, to find the
mystery men – hundreds of them, as they thought – gone, as usual.
What a terrible disadvantage we were at, during this period, through
lack of ammunition! As a matter of fact practically all the rifles and
revolvers in use by the column had been captured in hand-to-hand
skirmishes, so that invariably we were fighting against an enemy with
his own weapons. Our best assets were the sudden surprise and terror
inspired by shock. Knowing that the Marines would not follow us
into the country, as we would have the advantage there, even with
smaller arms, we marched quietly to our billets at Gortdromasillahy.
We arrived there about three or four in the morning with a gnawing
hunger and thoroughly exhausted. Meantime the others had gone on
towards Ballyduff, where they were informed that it would be useless
to try on any attack, so they returned.

FIGHT WITH THE MILITARY AT KILMORNA

Lieutenant Michael Galvin and some others of the column,
having returned from the abandoned attack on Ballyduff barracks,
and acting upon information received from a Volunteer of the

Knockanure company, decided to attack a party of British military who had gone to Kilmorna House, the residence of Sir Arthur Vickers, and who were expected to return to their barracks in Listowel later in the day. Including the Volunteer from the Knockanure company, the attacking force numbered eight, and was heavily outnumbered by the British military who were better equipped with service rifles and ammunition. Following careful consideration it was decided to wait in ambush for the military and to attack them from positions between two bends on the winding Kilmorna road.

Where the ambush took place the road was sheltered on one side by thick woods and heavy fencing; on the other side were open fields with fairly high hedges. The little column took up positions on the fields' side of the road, in order to cover off portion of the main road lying between the two bends. One of the column, Michael Galvin, was posted behind a gate pier, some little distance in advance of the main body. Patiently the IRA men waited until finally they were informed of the approach of the British military. All were tense as the advance party, comprising two soldiers, cycled round the bend of the road. They were immediately fired upon and both fell badly wounded. One of the IRA men jumped the fence and retrieved a service rifle before the main body of British military came into view. Our men were soon engaged by the soldiers, but without effect. Shooting was going hard and the military officer in charge, although slightly wounded, lay on the road with the other soldiers and all continued to send a hail of bullets against our positions. Their continuous fire prevented the column getting onto the road, although Michael Galvin and others made several attempts.

Eventually, the inevitable happened when shortage of ammunition compelled us to retreat. During the attack, however, we had captured one service rifle and wounded several soldiers, including their officer. Unfortunately the column, too, was not without casualties, and Lieutenant Michael Galvin was shot dead as the engagement was being broken off. An outstanding officer, he was a great loss to the column.

Other members of the North Kerry flying column who had participated in the Tarbert attack on the night previous to the Kilmorna engagement were billeted at Gortdromasillahy, Newtown. Late in the afternoon of 7 April the O/C was informed that rifles had been found by sympathisers of ours in Tea Lane, Listowel. It was later ascertained that some person had found a couple of rusty, useless shotguns, but this information was not available when the O/C and one of the men, having decided to inquire into the matter, set out for Mrs Larkin's, Carrueragh. Both men were armed with Webley forty-fives. At Gortdromagowna they met another member of the column who had been recuperating from an illness, and he informed them of the section which had gone to Kilmorna, and its purpose. All three decided to set out at once, in an attempt to get through in time for the fighting. Halting at Carrueragh to give a dispatch to Miss Larkin for transmission, they subsequently moved off rapidly to the road from Barretts and Sheahans, towards Mrs Stack's, and then over the fields to Kilmorna. Having travelled about five hundred yards they heard much shooting which seemed nearer as they advanced. As a matter of fact the three men had almost run into a large party of British military and Black and Tans who had advanced to the relief of their ambushed comrades. Retreating towards Larkin's our men travelled down by the fields in the direction of Coilbwee Bog, and at the corner of one of the fields they lay flat on the ground covered by furze bushes. Two minutes later machine-gun and rifle fire was directed on them by the huge forces of military and Black and Tans who occupied the hill above. Without even a rifle to reply to the fire our men retreated rapidly, utilising as cover the protection of the high fence, whilst bullets hissed and ploughed into the earth all round them.

Running zig-zag fashion through fields and streams, utilising every bit of cover afforded by hedges and turf banks, and all the time pursued by the crown forces who made every endeavour to cut them off, all escaped to Cuss, to the farmhouse of Michael Carmody, whose son had been murdered by the Royal Irish Constabulary, at Ballylongford, in 1920. One of our men, who had injured his ankle during the raid, was compelled to remain at the farmhouse whilst the other two, guided by a reliable Volunteer from Clounprohus, eventually rejoined their unit. Then was revealed to them the whole fateful story of Kilmorna where one of our best men, Lieutenant Michael Galvin, had fallen. The military and Black and Tans conveyed his remains to Listowel barracks where the dead body was insulted by deeds of barbaric and revolting ferocity. No wonder our hearts are embittered by dark and unforgettable memories.

VOLUNTEER OFFICERS MURDERED AT GORTAGLANNA

OWING TO THE serious illness of some members of our column, about the beginning of May 1921, on the advice of our medical officer, we were ordered to disperse to different districts, in groups of four or five. Our column O/C went to Mrs Walsh's of Tullamore, where he was visited on Monday evening, 9 May, by Captains Patrick Dalton and Cornelius Dee, who asked permission to attend a retreat given by the Redemptorist Fathers in Athea, a village some miles away towards the Kerry-Limerick border. Permission, which was granted, was accompanied by a warning to travel only along the by-roads and through the fields. With Captains Patrick Dalton and Cornelius Dee went Captain P. Walsh, all three of whom planned to rejoin the column on the following Wednesday night or, at the latest, on Thursday. On the following Wednesday evening a council meeting of the 6th battalion was held at Coolard, and at this meeting there were present, amongst others, Captains Jerry Lyons and Christy Broder (Duagh), who had that evening returned from a convention at Tralee. The two latter left the following morning (Thursday) about six o'clock to get home to Duagh, via Knockanure and Kilmorna. When near Knockanure Christy Broder left to visit friends of his a short distance away at Gortdromagowna, while Jerry Lyons travelled on and waited for him at Tim Carroll's (company captain, Knockanure). After some time Jerry proceeded alone, leaving word for Christy to follow him. Luckily the latter delayed and thus escaped the awful fate of the others. At Gortaglanna, Jerry met Con Dee, Paddy Walsh and Pat Dalton. Having much of interest to talk about they remained chatting. What occurred subsequently is best described in the statement of Con Dee, which was sworn at Tarbert, in June 1921. Here it is:

> About 9.30 a.m. on Thursday, 12 May 1921, I, Cornelius Dee, accompanied by Patrick Dalton and Patrick Walsh, left Athea, unarmed, where we had been attending a Mission given by the Redemptorist Fathers. We were walking along the road leading to Listowel when at Gortaglanna Bridge we met Jerry Lyons; he was cycling. He dismounted and began talking about various happenings. After a few minutes Paddy Walsh suggested that we should go into a field as it would be safer than the roadside. We moved and were just inside the fence when we heard the noise of a lorry. 'Take cover, lads,' I advised, and we tried to conceal ourselves as best we could. Jerry Lyons, Paddy Dalton and I took cover immediately. Paddy Walsh ran to the end of a field and lay down. Very soon we were surrounded by men in the uniforms of the Royal Irish Constabulary. 'We are done, Connie,' said Paddy Dalton. 'Come out, lads,' I said, 'with our hands up.' Jerry Lyons, Paddy Dalton and myself stood with our hands over our heads. Paddy Walsh ran towards us. We were met with a torrent of abuse and foul language. I remember such expressions as 'Ye murderers,' 'Ye b——.' 'We have got the real root,' 'We have got the flying column.' We were asked our names and gave them correctly; we were searched and found unarmed, having nothing but a copy of the *Irish Independent*. We were then compelled to undress and while we were fastening our clothes again we were beaten with rifles, struck with revolvers and thrown on the ground and kicked in trying to save ourselves. Then we were separated some distance from each other; four or five men came round each of us and my captors continued to beat me with their rifles and hit me with their fists. After about 20 minutes we were marched towards the road and then to the lorries.

Paddy Walsh and Paddy Dalton were put in the first lorry. I was put in the second, and Jerry Lyons in the third. The lorries were then driven for about a half a mile towards Athea. They were then stopped and turned round. Paddy Walsh and Paddy Dalton were changed to the lorry in which I was. Jerry Lyons was not changed out of the last lorry, which was now leading. The lorries were then driven the same road for about a mile. We were then ordered out of them. I looked at my companions; I saw blood on Jerry Lyons face and on Paddy Walsh's mouth. Paddy Dalton was bleeding from the nose. We were then asked to run but we refused. We were again beaten with the rifles and ordered into a field by the roadside. We refused but were forced into the field. We asked for a trial but the Black and Tans laughed and jeered and called us murderers. We were put standing in line facing a fence about forty yards from the road. I was placed first on the right, Jerry Lyons was next, Paddy Dalton next, and Paddy Walsh on the left. Then a Black and Tan with a rifle resting on the fence was put in front of each of us, about five yards distant. There were about ten more Black and Tans standing behind them. I looked straight into the face of the man in front of me. He delayed about twenty seconds as if he would like one of his companions to fire first. The second Black-and-Tan fired. Jerry Lyons flung up his arms, moaned and fell backwards. I glanced at him and noticed blood coming on his waistcoat; I turned round and ran. I was gone about twelve yards when I got wounded in the right thigh. My leg bent under me, but I held on running although I had to limp. I felt that I was being chased and I heard the bullets whizzing past me.

One of the lorries was driven along the road on my front and fire was maintained from it. After I had run for about a mile and a half I threw away my coat, collar, tie and puttees. The Tans continued to follow me for fully three miles. When too exhausted to run further, I flung myself into a drain in an oats garden. I was there about forty-five minutes when two men came along. They assisted me to walk for about forty yards. I was limping so much that one of them sent for a car and I was taken to a house.

I recognised Head Constable Smith [*sic*], Listowel, along with the Black and Tans present at the massacre; also Constable Raymond, and there was one in the uniform of a District Inspector of the Royal Irish Constabulary.

Maddened by the escape of Con Dee, the infuriated Black and Tans butchered his comrades, whose remains were a ghastly sight when handed over to relatives some days afterwards. Luckily Con Dee was found in an oats garden by a friendly farmer, and one of our men had him removed to a place of safety before hurrying to Tullamore where he reported the terrible tragedy to the column O/C. Immediate arrangements were made for Dee's removal to a different district, as, of course, it was realised that the enemy would comb out the whole place in order to destroy the evidence of their ghastly crime. As events turned out there was no time to spare, the whole district being raided that night and the following day. As was customary with their lying propaganda, the British reported there had been an ambush at Gortaglanna but everybody knew that no ambush had taken place there, and that those captured were unarmed. Dee was removed to safety. Naturally, for some time following his terrible experience he was nervy and jumpy; yet he did much good work subsequently. Despite the threats of the Black and Tans, Auxiliaries and military, huge crowds of people thronged to the funerals of the murdered officers at Gale, Duagh and Athea, where their Column comrades paid the last proud tributes. In their fury the Tans again attempted to capture the firing parties at these places, but luckily all escaped.

LIEUTENANT JACK SHEAHAN KILLED
AT COILBWEE

ON WEDNESDAY, 25 May 1921, Lieutenant Jack Sheahan and some men from the North Kerry column, together with the company captain and Volunteers of the Finuge company, planned an attack on Black and Tans. All assembled at Dromerrin, and were about to set out for their objective when three or four lorries of crown forces suddenly appeared upon the scene. The British opened fire on the little party which retreated as best it could, all the while returning fire upon the enemy. It was only with the greatest difficulty that the IRA men ultimately escaped, and the original project having been abandoned, Jack Sheahan and his men later rejoined their unit at Asdee.

That night we travelled from Asdee to Ballylongford, where we expected to fall in with a Black and Tan patrol. Having waited for a couple of hours none came along and as the night was pretty far advanced and no hope of a patrol, we decided to have a little bit of shooting at Ballylongford barracks. Scarcely had we fired the first shot when we heard the usual yells from inside, and immediately rifle and machine-gun fire was opened on us, while Verey lights were being rapidly sent up, wildly signalling for help. We were pretty safe in our positions and did not have to fire many volleys to get those inside going hard. These attacks had a very bad effect on the morale of the enemy forces. They had an exaggerated idea of our strength and numbers which was pretty lucky for us indeed! After some time we broke off the engagement to the accompanying farewell of hails of bullets. On the following day, Thursday, 26 May 1921, our column was billeted at farmhouses at Coil. As Jack Sheahan's mother and father lived only a comparatively short distance cross country, he received permission to go home that day. He reached home safely, and after some time there, went out with his brother Denis. They were chatting a little while when they heard the noise of approaching lorries. Denis then made back towards his own house, while Jack made for an old farm house at the edge of Coilagurteen, opposite his own home. Denis was not observed, and had Jack stayed in the old house he probably would not have been noticed either.

Unfortunately, he doubled across the bog to Knockanure, where the military sighted him – three lorries of them. They opened fire on him with machine guns and rifles, but he still continued to run zig-zag across the bog. His brother Denis, unseen by the military, was watching the whole tragedy. When the military officer saw that his men were failing he ordered the firing to cease, picked out about fifteen of the crack shots of the party and ordered them to fire as he called out the numbers. Jack Sheahan was then about five hundred yards into the bog. Numbers one, two, three, four, five, six, seven, eight, nine all fired and failed, but when the tenth man had fired Jack Sheahan was seen to stumble and topple over. Although still clutching his revolver in his hand he was too weak to fire on the military when they came up to him. Then died a gallant soldier, one who never knew wrong, as lovable a character as we have ever known. On the roadside outside his house at Coilbwee is raised a memorial to remind those who pass by of one who kept the faith.

ATTEMPTED AMBUSH AT KNOCKPOGUE, BALLYDUFF

INFORMATION HAVING REACHED the 3rd battalion column that a patrol of Black and Tans and Royal Irish Constabulary was occasionally travelling between Ballyduff barracks and the Cashen, it was decided to attack it at a bend of the road near Knockpogue. On the night of 6 June 1921, men of the column crossed the River Cashen and billeted in the houses of sympathisers. Next morning the column, with men from the local company, occupied positions, all keyed up in anticipation of a gripping fight. Always insufficiently armed we had to depend a great deal on the success of our first volley, especially from shotguns, and the extent of the initial disorganisation of the enemy often determined the course of an engagement. On this occasion we were more than hopeful, and the men were speaking confidently of the Webleys and Mausers they would soon possess. Time moved on, however, but the expected patrol of Black and Tans never left their barracks, much to the chagrin of the waiting men. It was learned afterwards that a little incident aroused the suspicions of the British, and caused them to decide against setting out on their usual journey. Next morning the entire area was combed by military, Black and Tans and Auxiliaries, but no capture was effected.

LATE CAPTAIN MICHAEL McELLIGOTT
OF LISTOWEL

ONE OF THE most daring officers of the 1st Kerry brigade, Captain Michael McElligott's recklessness and pluck were of the kind that surprisingly bring success. Born of proud Fenian stock, he was working with the Volunteers at an age younger than usual and his brilliance and daring were at once recognised. He was an enthusiastic Gaelic Leaguer and his obvious sincerity brought him friends all over the country. He was one of those who believe that where matters of principle are concerned there are no other tactics but one straight course to be followed to the bitter end. During his varied career he had been in many thrilling fights and the stories of the adventures of himself and his comrades in Kerry and Donegal and his escapades in prison prove that truth is often stranger than fiction. Having been a marked man he was, unfortunately for us, arrested in Listowel by Black and Tans in October 1920, and plans for an ambush were discovered on him.

He was court martialled and imprisoned for a stiff term, most of which he spent in an English jail. Into his young life had been crowded much active service and imprisonment as a result of which suffering his health completely broke down, and he died on 27 August 1927, beloved by all and especially by the uncompromising soldiers of the Republic. By his death we suffered incalculable loss.

WITH THE 2ND BATTALION
KERRY NO. 1 BRIGADE

THE 2ND BATTALION of Kerry No. 1 brigade, embracing companies in Ardfert, Ballyheigue, Kerry Head, Causeway, Abbeydorney, Kilmoyley, Kilflynn and Churchill, was well to the fore in the resistance to the Tan terror, and had in all thirty-three engagements with British forces.

The battalion was re-organised during that great preparatory period 1917–18, when all over the country companies, battalions, brigades and divisions were being reformed. The officers in the No. 2 battalion area were: battalion O/C, Thomas Clifford; vice-O/C, Patrick McKenna; active service column O/C, Michael Pierce; vice column O/C, William Leen: battalion adjutant, James Carmody; quartermasters, Michael McEgan, James O'Connor; intelligence, Francis Barnett; signal and communications, John Pierce; engineer, William O'Leary; medical officer, Dr Michael Lawlor.

Company Officers – (Ardfert company) – O/C, Patrick Sheehan, later John Kearney; first lieutenant, Mce O'Carroll; second lieutenant, Ml. Stack. Ballyheigue company – O/C, Michael Pierce; second lieutenant, Patrick Casey. Kerry Head company – O/C, Wm Leen; first lieutenant, David Lawlor; second lieutenant, Ml. Leen. Causeway company – O/C, Patrick O'Connor; first lieutenant, Edward O'Connor; second lieutenant, Maurice Leane. Kilmoyley company – O/C, James Griffin, later Thomas O'Connor; first lieutenant, Cors. Griffin; second lieutenant, Patrick McGrath. Kilflynn company – O/C, George O'Shea; first lieutenant, Stephen Fuller. Abbeydorney company – O/C, Maurice Nolan; first lieutenant, Thomas O'Leary.

CAPTURE OF BALLYHEIGUE COASTGUARD STATION

BRITISH FORCES WERE stationed in Ballyheigue, Causeway and Abbeydorney, and it was only natural that in those sectors Volunteer activity should be at its highest tempo. In February 1920, Volunteers from the Ballyheigue area carried out one of the first ambushes on the RIC in the south of Ireland, when they attacked and disarmed a party of RIC at Ballyronan. Then in April 1920, another party of RIC, returning to Causeway from Ballyheigue, were ambushed at Buncurrig. After a sharp exchange of shots, the police surrendered.

One of their number was seriously wounded. As two Volunteer officers approached to disarm the RIC, one policeman shot his hand into his haversack, grabbed a grenade and attempted to throw it. The IRA again demanded surrender, and the policeman dropped the bomb. Rifles, short-arms, and two dozen bombs were taken from the RIC.

One of the biggest engagements was the capture of Ballyheigue Coastguard and Marine Station in May 1920. This was a strong fortress, three storeys high, with port-holes at every angle, and a steel roof with cut stone parapet, steel doors and steel shuttered windows. An indoor passage led to the tower from the married quarters at each side and, in addition, a gunboat was on regular patrol from Fenit to Ballyheigue to Loop Head. The taking of this stronghold by rifle fire was deemed impossible, and the Volunteers planned to rush the sentry in the watch-room in front of the tower and count on the element of surprise. Failure meant exposure to enemy fire and many casualties. At two o'clock on the morning of 22 May, while the gunboat was on its way to Loop Head, the watch-room was rushed, the sentry overpowered. Dazed police were caught in their beds, and after a short struggle surrendered. The following equipment was captured: arms, ammunition, rocket gun, rockets, pistols, searchlight lamps, telescope and field glasses. Police were taken from the barrack which was set on fire. In the meantime, the gunboat on its return noticed the blazing building and landed a fire-fighting party. The Volunteers had foreseen this eventuality and had removed the water from the barrack tank, replacing it with petrol and oil. Hoses when connected to the tank sprayed petrol and oil on the already blazing building, completing the task of gutting. The barrack was completely destroyed.

FENIT BARRACKS ATTACKED

THIS ATTACK WHICH ended in the complete destruction of the barracks was carried out by a unit of the 1st battalion aided by members of the 2nd. The remainder of the 2nd battalion surrounded the radio station at Ballymacquin which was occupied by British troops. These the Volunteers prevented from going to the aid of the RIC at Fenit.

CAUSEWAY AND ABBEYDORNEY AMBUSHES

CROWN FORCES WERE ambushed at Abbeydorney and Causeway on Sunday, 30 October 1920.

The flying column with units from each company lay in ambush at Beenreigh, Abbeydorney, awaiting lorries of Black and Tans that had passed through that route on the two previous Sundays. All day the Volunteers awaited but the lorries did not come. It was then decided to split into two sections, one to proceed to Causeway and the other to Abbeydorney. Causeway village was surrounded and Black and Tans and RIC, surprised on the street, were fired on and many were wounded. In Abbeydorney a Black and Tan and a member of the RIC were shot dead. Several houses in the district were burned by the Tans as a reprisal.

At four o'clock on the morning of 5 November 1920, an IRA column took up position in houses adjacent to the RIC barracks in Causeway. This was a strong stone building, two storeys high, standing on its own ground, fortified with steel sheets, barbed wire and sand-bags. It was equipped with a radio transmitter and had a complement of forty-two men. Sometime in the morning between eight and nine o'clock, the garrison got word that they were surrounded, and a message was sent to Tralee and Listowel. IRA scouts came post-haste reporting that crown forces were closing in on Causeway from every direction. It was decided to withdraw and take up new positions to the rear of the village. The crown forces made contact and there was a fierce exchange of shots. A British machine gunner was shot in the fight that followed. The battle lasted up to four o'clock on the following evening. One IRA man was shot dead, another was seriously wounded and a few prisoners were taken. These were brutally beaten by the Tans who had suffered many casualties.

In a subsequent attack on Causeway in January 1921, one Tan was shot dead and another seriously wounded. On 4 March 1921, the Volunteers again attacked Causeway barracks. At 1 a.m. they fired a fusillade of shots at the building, pumping petrol and oil on the roof which was an inferno of flame. Again the unit had to retreat due to the arrival of strong reinforcements from Tralee. That night a spy was executed by the IRA in Causeway. A few days after this attack the British carried out a round-up which was supposed to be one of the biggest ever in the south of Ireland. A cordon of crown forces, which included military, Black and Tans, Auxiliaries and RIC was placed from Carrighan Strand to Kilflynn and from Kilflynn to the mouth of the Cashen. They advanced onto Ballyheigue, searched every house, farmyard and haggard on their way, and took all male persons they found, between the ages of about seventeen and fifty, as prisoners to Ballyheigue Castle. Though the IRA column was inside the ring, it succeeded in getting out the second night, with the exception of one member who was captured, and he, with the aid of Cumann na mBan, escaped from Ballyheigue Castle, where over six hundred people were held for a week. The Auxiliaries posted up notices in the area stating tersely that if they caught Thomas Clifford and Michael Pierce they would put them to death by burning them in oil.

Members of Cumann na mBan in Ballyheigue and Kilmoyley deserve the highest meed of praise for the work they did in getting the column outside the military cordon.

Again on 15 May 1921, the IRA attacked parties of Tans and RIC in Causeway. The column entered the village at 9 p.m. and took up positions. After about an hour RIC and Black and Tans left the barrack and proceeded to a public house. The IRA, who were about fifteen yards from the barrack, opened fire on them, and immediately fire was opened on the IRA from the barrack. When the Black and Tans and RIC who were on the street tried to retreat back to the barracks, some of their members were wounded. The IRA could not collect the arms as they were under direct fire from the barrack, and they had to retreat.

AMBUSH AT SHANNOW BRIDGE*

SHANNOW BRIDGE IS about half a mile from Abbeydorney Village and spans the river at the road junction between Abbeydorney, Lixnaw and Kilflynn. The IRA made two attempts to blow up this bridge before they finally succeeded. On the first two occasions a patrol of Black and Tans and RIC from Abbeydorney came to the bridge to inspect the damage which had been done. When the bridge was eventually blown up, the IRA column with units from Kilflynn and Abbeydorney lay in ambush in the vicinity in anticipation that the RIC and Black and Tans would come as before. Instead three lorries and an armoured car of crown forces arrived. The IRA got no warning of their approach as the district along the river was covered with a thick fog, and the signals failed to operate. They knew that the lorries and armoured car could not cross the river, so they opened fire on the crown forces, who returned it with rifles and machine gun. After about ten minutes, a party led by an Auxiliary officer attempted to cross the river. The officer was shot dead and the party retreated. After a short while the whole party of crown forces decided to withdraw, leaving a dead officer and wounded behind. Two Volunteers were wounded.

---

*   *Series Editor's note*: Mistakenly called Shannonbridge in the original edition.

THE CAMPAIGN IN EAST KERRY

In the days preceding Easter Week, the Rathmore company of Volunteers were actively preparing for the coming clash. On Saturday, 22 April 1916, trusted dispatch riders were sent out with important dispatches; but keen disappointment resulted when no orders came on Sunday. A member of the neighbouring Millstreet battalion – Sheamus Hickey – cycled to Cork, forty miles away, to try to get into communication with headquarters.

The members of the Rathmore company were not daunted by the events of Easter Week, though naturally all regretted the holocaust of Ireland's best and bravest sons in that sad but glorious epoch. They kept on drilling and enrolling new members; they felt in their hearts that Easter Week was not the end, that another day would dawn with brighter prospects of freedom for the old land. They continued the good work of preparing for the struggle, that all foresaw was at hand, up to the arrival of the Black and Tans in the village. This event took place in 1920. These were at first objects of curiosity only, then of terror which ultimately changed into intense hatred. For the first few months they did not show themselves in their true colours. At this time the strength of the native Royal Irish Constabulary in Rathmore was one sergeant and four constables.

RATHMORE BARRACKS ATTACKED

The local Volunteers soon saw that the presence of the Black and Tans constituted a challenge to them. They accepted it as such, and plans were made to teach the invaders a lesson. Several of these had to be postponed through various causes, until July 1920, when, under cover of darkness, the 5th battalion, Kerry No. 2 brigade, mobilised. By this time Rathmore barracks had been fitted with loop-holed steel shutters and doors and was considered impregnable to all except cannon fire. The Volunteers did try to use an obsolete cannon taken from Ross Castle which they placed on a railway truck to get it into position.

Sandbags were filled by the brigade and silently placed on the railway bridge. A party of snipers then took up positions behind these. The attack opened with rifles, shotguns and bombs; it continued throughout the night, and awakened the countryside for miles around. At dawn a bomb hurled through one of the upper barrack windows killed a Black and Tan; a sergeant and constable were also severely wounded. The attackers withdrew as the daylight got stronger, and silence settled once more on the countryside. As the day advanced strong parties of police, military and Black and Tans arrived from Killarney. Arrests and raids on houses followed and the crown forces made themselves as obnoxious as possible to the local inhabitants.

MINOR ATTACKS, RAIDS AND REPRISALS

SOME TIME AFTER the attack on Rathmore barracks, a strong convoy of British military was intercepted on the road between Rathmore and Barraduff. A soldier was shot dead. At the end of 1920, the early morning train to Killarney was held up at Freemount, some three miles from Rathmore.

Some days later a party of Black and Tans from Killarney searched Freemount, and then swept onto the village of Gneeveguilla two miles distant. The village was completely surrounded, and a respectable, well-to-do farmer was arrested and taken away in a lorry. On the following morning his bullet-riddled body was found on the roadside near Tralee. The unfortunate man's body showed that he had been the victim of a most brutal murder.

EXECUTION OF CON MURPHY

TOWARDS THE END of 1920 nine members of the Millstreet battalion whose names were on the 'murder list' of the Tans, formed a flying squad or small flying column. The late Jeremiah Crowley was in charge of this body of men, and under his direction training in military operations was carried out. The squad was reinforced considerably later on, and an effective column of close on forty men was formed. On the night of 3 January 1921, the squad which then consisted of nine men all told, arrived in Rathmore. The late Con Murphy having arranged billets, went home to his father's house in Ballydaly – a quarter of a mile from the nearest house where the squad was in billets. At about nine o'clock on the morning of 4 January, the scouts protecting the squad, reported the presence of a considerable force of military and Royal Irish Constabulary raiding in Ballydaly. The little squad immediately got into a position of defence. Retreat was out of the question as the only way out was occupied by the enemy. There was another line of escape if circumstances were favourable, by crossing the river Blackwater. On this day it was flooded, so that the only alternative in case of attack was to fight to a finish. With this end in view positions were taken up in the old rath. There was not, however, any raid or attack at Rathduane. After a few hours scouts brought the information that the raiders had departed in the Millstreet direction, taking Con Murphy, his father, Denis Murphy, and his two brothers, Tim and Denis, with them as prisoners. Con was later tried by court martial and found guilty of having a revolver in his possession. He was executed at Cork Military Barracks, and was the first man in the campaign to suffer the death penalty for carrying arms.

SUCCESSFUL TRAIN AMBUSH

IN JANUARY 1921, it was noticed that small parties of armed military travelled occasionally by train between Mallow and Tralee. The Dooneen and Coolinarna companies made preparations to ambush one of these parties. The first plan was to get the Volunteers to take up positions adjacent to Millstreet station with the view to rush either the seven o'clock train from Mallow or the 8 p.m. train from Tralee, if any of the parties of military were aboard. The danger to this plan soon revealed itself. It was next arranged to bring off an ambush on the nine o'clock train, at a 'cutting' in the line at Drishanebeg, about a mile to the east of the station. The plan was to get the engine boarded by two armed men and to compel the driver to stop at the ambush position, where elaborate preparations had been made. It was, however, found after about a week that the chances of any party travelling on the 8 p.m. train were getting remote. It was also observed that they occasionally travelled on the 7 p.m. train from Mallow. Early in February the battalion column took on the task. Plans were laid. Dooneen, Coolecross and Rathcoole companies under Commandant C.J. Meaney, co-operated with the column which was in charge of Adjutant J. Crowley.

On the night of 2 February, the column which at that time had only eight rifles (the remainder having shotguns filled with cartridges of home-made slugs) took up their position at 6.30 p.m. at the appointed place. In the meantime other important details were receiving attention elsewhere. At Rathcoole and Millstreet stations two Volunteers awaited their respective trains – ready to board the engine should either train carry armed military. At Banteer station, four miles on the Mallow side of Rathcoole, a Volunteer awaited the arrival of the Tralee bound train. His duty was to inspect the trains thoroughly for armed military, then board as an ordinary passenger and report to his comrade at Rathcoole. At this time the train from Mallow to Tralee used to stop fairly long at Banteer. It would not stop at Rathcoole unless it carried a passenger for that place, or unless signalled to do so by the station-master; hence the necessity of sending a man to Banteer to await the Tralee-bound train. Both trains passed the ambush position on time, night after night, but there was no party of military on board.

On the night of 10 February, the Volunteer at the Rathcoole end reported six soldiers on board, with uniforms, but without arms or ammunition, whilst the officer commanding the Dooneen company, who had charge of the Millstreet end, reported the arrival of the train there later with six armed Tommies aboard. It was evident that the rifles and equipment had been hidden beneath the seat of the carriage whilst the train was passing through Rathcoole and Banteer stations. As the days were now lengthening, the battalion commander and the O/C of the column decided, that unless something turned up the next night, the column would be withdrawn and some other method adopted to capture the troops who were known to be getting through by train. On the night of 11 February the column took positions as usual at 6.30 p.m. (it was then nearly dark.)

They were in position about twenty-five minutes when the seven o'clock train was heard approaching from Rathcoole. There was tension amongst the members of the battalion. Would the waiting prove fruitless as on the other nights of the week, or would there be a fight? These were the thoughts uppermost in every man's mind. The engine sounded a long and shrill whistle while nearly a mile off. This was the pre-arranged signal, in case a party of the enemy was aboard the train. It caused intense excitement amongst the Volunteers. Shotguns and rifles were loaded and held at the ready. A bicycle lamp which had lain covered by a sack on the side of the rails, was uncovered and placed in position between the rails, its bright light shining in the direction of the oncoming train. The train slowed up and stopped as it approached the ambush position, the rear of the engine just over the bicycle lamp. As it had travelled a few yards further than was anticipated, the column moved up into fresh positions. The commandant then called out loudly to the military to surrender to the Irish Republic. For answer a rifle shot rang out in the still night air. The column was ordered to open fire on the carriages containing the military. For about fifteen minutes the calmness of the night was broken by the crack of rifle, revolver and shotgun fire, above the din of which could be heard the groans of the wounded 'Tommies'. The slopes of the cutting were lit up by oil torches prepared in advance by the column and thrown down outside the carriage in which the military were travelling when the fight began. The positions of the soldiers were clearly shown up by the torches, whilst the attackers were covered by the darkness. The fight was one-sided from the outset, and the British duly surrendered. Fourteen soldiers came out; one other was dead, and practically all were wounded. The column collected the rifles and seven hundred rounds of ammunition. Just at the surrender, a man in the uniform of a British soldier left the train a few carriages back from where the armed men were situated. He advanced up the slope with his arms above his head, towards the column and asked for 'a rifle to fight for Ireland'. It was then noticed that he was an unarmed Munster Fusilier who spoke with a strong Kerry accent. Needless to state, his request was not granted. It transpired, however, that when he reached his native Kerry he discarded the foreign uniform, joined the Volunteers, fought bravely for Ireland and is today hale and hearty, living somewhere round Tralee. When the military had been disarmed they were put back on the train, which moved off for Millstreet station. Some civilians on the train shouted 'Up the Republic' to the column, who answered with a parting cheer. The column did not suffer any casualty.

TUREENGARRIFFE AMBUSH

TUREENGARRIFFE AMBUSH, WHICH took place on 28 January, resulted in serious losses to the enemy. Major-General Holmes was shot dead and six staff officers were wounded. Tureengarriffe is a wild, rocky district midway between Kingwilliamstown and Scartaglin, County Kerry. It was known that officers of the British army had gone west and the IRA waited at this place for two days to intercept them on their return. A trench had been cut across the road and the driver of the first car seemed to sense trouble ahead and tried to jump his powerful car over it, but failed. A challenge from the IRA instantly rang out; the military party got into action and put up a desperate resistance. It was only when General Holmes was shot dead and practically all the other officers wounded that they surrendered. Seán Moylan, who was in charge of the ambushing party of North Cork and East Kerry men, had the wounded attended to by the First Aid corps, and conveyed in a passing motor car to Castleisland. One of the cars was badly damaged and was destroyed; but the other was driven off by the IRA in the Kingwilliamstown direction. On the following days enraged parties of Black and Tans swept into the village, but the inhabitants had wisely fled into the hills. Three houses were bombed and burned. One belonged to Mr Timothy Vaughan – whose son, Captain Dan Vaughan, afterwards became TD for North Cork. He was at this time a prominent man in the IRA. The others belonged to Mr T. O'Sullivan, post office and general drapery, and the residence of the late Willie McAuliffe.

Men from Rathmore took part in the Tureengarriffe ambush. On the Sunday following the engagement, lorries with crown forces swooped down on Knocknagree. They opened fire with machine guns on some youths who were playing football in a field. A boy named Kelliher was killed and two others were wounded. This dastardly act was undoubtedly intended as a reprisal for Tureengarriffe.

CLONBANIN AMBUSH

ABOUT 4.30 P.M. on 4 March 1921, the North Cork column, which had its headquarters at Lackadota, two miles south of Millstreet, mobilised and got ready to move against the Tans stationed in the town. A messenger arrived from Seán Moylan, who was commandant of the Newmarket battalion area. Arising from the message, plans were altered, and cars were procured to take the men of the column as far as Drishanebeg. There they fell into marching formation and proceeded across the Blackwater by Keale Bridge. Taking to the fields, they went via Derinagree to Clonbanin. When the column was passing through Derinagree, an old man and his wife emerged from a cabin. Their faces reflected the joy they felt in their honest Irish hearts at seeing the fighting soldiers of Ireland. As the rearguard passed, the woman could not restrain herself longer. She shouted: 'I suppose ye have the mischief done last night?'

'Yes,' they assured her, 'you will hear of it bye and bye.'

This was within half a mile of the ambush position.

As the column arrived, other men already in position gave word that the military were approaching from the east in lorries. The column could now see, from the shelter of a fence, three lorries with military pass along the road beneath them, only a field distant. They passed on towards Kerry without a shot being fired.

Some days previous IRA intelligence had reported that a top rank military officer had left Buttevant barracks and proceeded to inspect the troops in Kerry. As the Williamstown–Castleisland road had previously proved fatal to an RIC officer of high rank when he and his escort were ambushed at Tureengarriffe by Seán Moylan's column, it was surmised that the apparently safer Mallow–Killarney road would be used by this officer on his return journey. Two days previously the Newmarket and East Kerry columns had lain in ambush at the 'Bower,' between Rathmore and Barraduff. Owing to the possibility of information having reached the British, the officers in charge decided to abandon that position. They then took up a new one on the same road in County Cork. Clonbanin was selected as the most suitable place. It is about six miles from Kanturk, where a party of military were stationed, and about the same distance from Millstreet, which had a very strong garrison of Black and Tans as well as members of the Royal Irish Constabulary. Mines were laid during the night, and as the British convoy was passing through next morning the batteries connected to these were switched on, but failed to explode. Consequently, the Tommies passed through unmolested and utterly oblivious of their narrow escape from disaster. As soon as the military had passed on towards Killarney, scouts were posted on the hillsides for miles on the Kerry side, whilst the columns from Newmarket, Millstreet, Charleville and East Kerry were provided with breakfast, after which they again took up positions. Newmarket and Charleville held the northern side of the road. The East Kerry column, commanded by the late Humphrey Murphy, and a section of the Millstreet unit took positions south of the, road. A section of the Millstreet men occupied the haggard of Mark O'Shaughnessy where they placed a Hotchkiss gun, manned by the late Bill Moylan and the late Denis Galvin. The Kerry column was on its flank. The remainder of the Millstreet men occupied a position away from the ambush, covering the roads from Kanturk in order to prevent reinforcements from that direction.

About 3 p.m. the signallers announced five military lorries coming from the Killarney direction. A few minutes afterwards the leading lorry drove into the ambush. As it was passing Shaughnessy's Hotchkiss gun opened fire on it. A little further on the same lorry was engaged by the columns on the northern side of the road, and having exchanged six or eight shots, was brought to a stand-still. About two minutes' silence followed, until the remainder of the convoy, which consisted of another lorry about a hundred yards ahead of a touring car, which was followed at a distance of about fifteen yards by a Rolls Royce armoured car, arrived. Another lorry about a hundred yards behind brought up the rear. All vehicles drove right into the ambush position.

The silence was broken by two rifle shots fired in quick succession, and the touring car immediately swerved across the road, apparently out of control. The armoured car collided with the rear of the tourer, and the driver, attempting to push on, got the armoured car bogged in the soft dyke on the side of the road. In the meantime the Hotchkiss engaged the second lorry with deadly effect, and heavy rifle fire was concentrated on all vehicles from both sides of the road. To the shout of 'surrender' from the IRA a voice from the touring car was heard to reply: 'To hell with surrender! Give them the lead!' Immediately a tall man in officer's uniform was seen to leap from the car. He made a dive for cover on the north side of the road but never reached there, as a bullet from an ambusher's rifle blew out his brains. So fell Brigadier-General Cummins, the first British general to take prisoners as hostages on his lorries. That day at Clonbanin his party carried a hostage who escaped during the fighting.

Apparently the occupants of the armoured car suffered initial shock and surprise, as almost five minutes elapsed from the moment that the tourer was fired on before the car's Vickers gun went into action, and even then the firing was wild for some time. On the battle raged, man for man, the trained and specially picked soldiers of England against the raw and badly armed Volunteers of the IRA columns. Above the crack of the rifle and the rattle of the Vickers and Lewis guns which were used by the military, could be plainly heard the moans of the dying and wounded soldiers. The IRA Hotchkiss gun went out of action early in the fight, and our rifles had to fight the Vickers in the armoured car as well as the Lewis gun and opposing rifles. The rifle fire from the roadway gradually grew weaker, until about an hour-and-a-half from the opening of the battle, not a military rifleman dared to fire a shot, though the Vickers gun in the armoured car swept the hedge tops with a leaden hail. It was clear that the military must have suffered heavily, and it was equally obvious that as the armoured car, although stationary, held a position which dominated the road through the full length of the ambush position (about a quarter of a mile long), its capture was out of the question. So the IRA gradually retired, unscathed, leaving thirteen of the enemy dead and fifteen wounded.

Tureengarriffe, Clonbanin, and the train ambush – the latter the only successful one of its kind in the Anglo-Irish War – struck a severe blow at the British military prestige in Munster, and caused consternation in the minds of its highly-ranked officers. They realised that not alone did the King's Writ no longer function, but that His Majesty's direct military communications between Cork and Kerry were completely severed. Worse still, all attempts to restore them were hopeless.

THE CAMPAIGN IN WEST KERRY

BACK IN 1913, Castlegregory was feeling the stir of nationalism in common with the rest of Kerry and Ireland, and this portion of the Dingle Peninsula, which three years later was to become so prominent in connection with the German gun-runner, the *Aud*, was putting in quiet but intensive preparations for the fight which lay ahead.

And when the fight came, the men of this West Kerry battalion were in the thick of every ambush from Kelly Height to Lispole, displaying courage and initiative of a high order which won for them the calculated fear and respect of their opponents in the field. When the split came between the Redmondite and National Volunteers, seven left the ranks of the Nationals at a Killiney parade, and James ('Fox') Kennedy, with the help of Tralee gunsmith, Mr Edwards, secured the arms for the fighting force left by smuggling fourteen shotguns to the peninsula from Tralee.

In common with many other places, Castlegregory struggled along through the Volunteer split until events rushed fast and furious to the fateful week of Easter 1916. On that weekend, to be precise, on Easter Monday morning, Jim Kennedy, Tadhg Brosnan, Seán Brosnan, Abel Mahony, Mick McKenna (Maharabeg), Mick Duhig and Dan Shea were arrested. It will not be invidious to specially mention among these the beloved, rugged figure of Tadhg Brosnan, that natural born leader of a people who have always pined for freedom. 'Tadhg', as he is so affectionately known to the people of Castlegregory, is still spoken of there with hushed reverence. He was their leader in all things, their father and adviser, their dauntless soldier and fighter, their uncrowned king. It is claimed, and not without sound reasons, that Tadhg Brosnan was the first man in Ireland to refuse to recognise the British courts here when he was sentenced to twenty years' imprisonment for his pre-1916 Volunteer activities. Treating the British general and his court martial with cool contempt, Tadhg defied the might of the British forces and went proudly to his jailers to come out twelve months later and be accorded a welcome with Austin Stack and Tom Ashe that will forever remain in the hearts of the beholders and be passed onto their children and children's children for fireside retelling. Tadhg Brosnan himself and the men already mentioned were responsible for the formation of the Volunteer companies in Castlegregory. Cloghane, Ballyduff, Maharees, Aughacasla and Camp which comprised the battalion.

On the release of the prisoners in 1917, training and organising went on with fresh impetus, and when the battalion eventually took the field, no better fighting material was available. First offensive came with the disarming of three RIC and the wounding of one at Killiney Cross. Tadhg Brosnan, Jerh Dowling, Pat O'Donnell, J.G. O'Donoghue and Dan Jeffers took part. About the same time, plans were laid for the taking of Castlegregory barrack, and these were completed when the barrack was evacuated. In February 1920, the battalion decided to attack Camp barrack. All the battalion companies and Tralee companies co-operated by cutting the Tralee–Camp road at Annagh and isolating the area from telephonic communication by cutting trees and telegraph wires. When the attack on the barrack started, military and police in Tralee were confused and believed the attack to be on the Ballyheigue barrack. Meanwhile, at Camp, the Volunteers, after an hour's fight, blew a hole in the barrack gable wall and the defenders evacuated it. Sergeant McDonagh, RIC, was wounded in the face. The Volunteers had no casualties. Some time after this success, it was decided to cut off supplies to Cloghane by attacking the convoy from Kilmore. At Ballyduff, a party of twelve

Volunteers ambushed the convoy and killed two policemen and wounded one, as well as capturing a lorry.

One of the biggest feats of the battalion was to force the evacuation of Cloghane barrack. This, from its situation, was perhaps one of the most difficult barracks in the country to take, covering as it did all approaches from the surrounding countryside. Land mines formed part of the defences, and any attacking force would have met death at every step. But the cutting off of their regular supplies, together with the widespread activities of the Volunteers, caused a midnight evacuation by the occupying enemy forces, and the Volunteers marched in without firing a shot. Well prepared for the minefield, they dismantled and removed the deadly explosives. It is interesting to note that some of these mines were subsequently used to blow up a lorry at Annascaul and a bridge at Mallow.

Further successful attacks were made on RIC patrols on Conor Hill before the coastguard station at Brandon was burned and Verey lights, guns and field-glasses captured. Then came another big engagement with Tans at Annascaul, in collaboration with Dingle and Tralee units. This engagement had for its object the capture of a military lorry conveying supplies to Dingle. The waiting Volunteers allowed the lorry, with thirteen soldiers, to proceed to Tralee, and on the return journey mined the road and opened fire on the lorry. A two-hour fight raged before the military, with half a dozen wounded, surrendered and the lorry was set on fire. A passing motor car was commandeered by the Volunteers and the wounded enemy, after getting first-aid, were sent to Dingle Hospital. Another car was procured and the prisoners were taken to within a short distance of Dingle when they were released. This attack had a tragic sequel next day, when a thirty-year-old, well-known and popular Annascaul man, Mr Patrick Kennedy, brother of Mr T.P. Kennedy, Kerry county accountant, was foully murdered. At an inquest on the victim of Britain's baffled rage and hate the following verdict was returned: 'That the cause of death was shock and haemorrhage as a result of a bullet wound inflicted by a British soldier, without cause, provocation or justification, and they (the jury) desired to express in the most emphatic manner their utter abhorrence of the callous crime, and demanded the arrest and trial of the soldier who fired the fatal shot, as well as the investigation into the conduct of the officers under whose command the soldier was acting.'

The story of the shooting of Patrick McKenna, as unfolded at the inquest, will be read in the pages that follow, as well as the court martial of two Annascaul men charged with the attack on the military lorry.

The Castlegregory battalion companies were on service again soon afterwards at Lispole ambush, the story of which is told elsewhere. Captured on that occasion by the British were several Volunteers and prompt counter-action by their comrades, led by Tadhg Brosnan, Paddy Cahill and Pat Neill, of Cloghane, helped to rescue the captured men. They next moved over to Glenbeigh and were in on the railway station attack on military patrols which resulted in the capture of a valuable machine gun. Counter measures by the enemy resulted in the Brosnan homestead being levelled to the ground.

During the fateful Easter weekend, 1916, the battalion was standing by awaiting instructions, and unaware of the drama being played out on the ocean three miles from them, when the *Aud* was waiting for the pilot who did not come.

SHOOTING OF PADDY KENNEDY
OF ANNASCAUL

THE SHOOTING OF Paddy Kennedy of Annascaul, caused great resentment among the people of Kerry who rallied in thousands for the funeral. They came from Ballylongford and Ballybunion, from Tralee and Castlegregory and Dingle. Over 2,000 Volunteers,

Cumann na mBan and general public marched to the burial place two miles away, with a tricoloured coffin preceded by bands. Over the grave shots were fired.

Dr J. O'Connell, district coroner, held an inquest at Annascaul at which the following jury was sworn: Messrs John Cahillane (foreman). John Counihan, James Sheehan, M.M. O'Donnell, Eugene Courtney, Robert T. Moriarty, Daniel O'Connell, John M. O'Donnell, Patrick Brosnan, M. Kennedy, Thomas Ashe, Denis Moriarty, Patrick T. Flahive, John O'Brien, Patrick Sullivan, Thomas Sheehy.

Mr D.J. Browne, solicitor for the next-of-kin, in addressing the jury at the outset, said he would produce conclusive and unimpeachable evidence to show that Patrick Kennedy was deliberately, foully and cruelly shot without the slightest provocation or excuse, and that the inhuman and callous crime was committed by the army operating in the country with the pretended object of the welfare of the people. The high placed civil and military authorities who devised and organised the plans by reason of the instructions to the troops were as much, if not more, responsible in the eyes of the world for the death of this man. Deceased was a farmer and publican, and by his quiet and admirable manner, earned the respect of his fellow countrymen. Referring to the attack on the military lorry on 18 August, the day before Kennedy's death, and the subsequent treatment given to captives when they were supplied with every comfort and motored to their quarters in Dingle, the following two days, said Mr Browne, provided a striking commentary on the methods employed by the British army. On 19 August, the village of Annascaul and surrounding districts were deluged with the army of the British forces. Houses and people were searched indiscriminately: shots were fired from rifles and machine guns, and every method employed to strike terror into the hearts of the people. The evidence proposed to be produced was then outlined and Mr Browne said the dead man's body had been looted of everything but his Rosary beads. Some time ago, he continued, they saw in the press an announcement that military committing acts of that kind would meet with considerable punishment, but he awaited the results of that order with sceptical curiosity. The 'punishment' which would be imposed on the assassin in this case would be speedy promotion in the ranks.

The coroner said he had been informed that the military would not be represented at the inquest, nor would they produce the soldiers or police implicated. Mr T.P. Kennedy, brother, identified the remains, and Dr Ferris gave evidence of death wounds on deceased. John Mannix, a seventeen-year-old schoolboy, living at Gurteens, said he was saving hay with deceased when they heard shots. With John Kennedy and John Hannifin they walked in single file along a bohereen and after a few minutes a shot rang out. After the shot he heard somebody call out 'Hands up!' There was a soldier standing with a rifle in his hands about ten yards away. The soldier was joined by a man in military uniform and policeman's cap who, when he came up and saw the dead man, said, 'Good man, Mick.' More soldiers came up, and witness and John Kennedy were given permission to go for a priest. They had proceeded about a hundred yards when a volley of shots rang out from an armoured car parked on the main road, and they had to turn back.

In reply to a juryman, Mannix said he could identify the soldier with the rifle, and the coroner told the same juryman he had requested the military to produce this man. Other witnesses gave corroborative evidence, and Mr Browne directed the attention of the jury to a denial by the military authorities that a boy going for the priest was fired on. He asked for a verdict to give the lie to this denial. The jury returned a verdict of wilful murder, and expressed abhorrence at the brutal and callous crime.

WORK OF A KILLARNEY INTELLIGENCE OFFICER

by TORC

'I MUST BE off now, this is the general.' This laconic remark made unwittingly by a British intelligence officer to a Killarney hotel porter spelt disaster for some high-ranking British officers and their men during the Anglo-Irish struggle. It was the lever that set in motion the machinery for the now famed Clonbanin ambush, for the intelligence officer did not know that the braided hotel porter, standing beside him was the 'eyes and ears' of the republicans in Killarney.

John Keogh, of the International Hotel, sought more than just visitors on his daily rounds to Killarney railway station, and he got more, as many a republican has lived to appreciate. He was having a friendly chat with Lieutenant Sherwood when some armoured vehicles and fast army cars came to a standstill outside the Great Southern Hotel. The date was 2 March 1921, and the time, to be precise, four-twenty-five. The IRA were after the 'big guns' of the British army and John flashed a mental wink as he watched Sherwood join a general and a major on the hotel steps. That was the frame of the story and the assembling job was up to John. Here is what he did: contacted local IRA officers and had word sent to brigade headquarters of the 'game' that was to be 'bagged'; metaphorically got inside the steel curtain of the Great Southern Hotel by meeting the manager of the hotel canteen, a friend named Rogers; learned that the 'big noises' would be around for three days and on the third day depart for Buttevant; passed this news onto headquarters; informed Tommy McEllistrim and Seán Moylan that the general and major would be travelling in a blue-coloured car. That was that – the ground was tilled.

Three days later when General Cummins and Major Melleney and their armoured entourage were on the road back they ran into a hail of gunfire just outside the little Cork village of Clonbanin. When the smoke had cleared away General Cummins and Major Melleney and some of their men lay stiff in death. Not alone did the republican attackers retire without a casualty but they had one more than they started with – Maurice Slattery of Milltown, who was riding the British cars as a hostage. The actual engagement is dealt with in detail in that section of *Kerry's Fighting Story* devoted to East Kerry. Memory of the fight often walked in the doors of the International Hotel afterwards in the person of a Black and Tan named Baird who was wont to display a coat bullet-holed in the Clonbannin ambush.

Now a splendid job of work that brought praise from Michael Collins. A crippled boy named Crowley was foully done to death by a few British fiends in Bantry. Not long after the crime and on the same day a motor car pulled up at the International Hotel, Killarney. A captain and two Royal Irish Constabulary men were soon drinking at the hotel bar. John Keogh 'sniffed' around, unobtrusively, examined some parcels which the men had deposited in the office, found guns among the contents. Seeking the car number he found the plate cleverly covered with cow dung. John removed the dung, took the number of the car, checked up on it and found that it belonged to the scene of the hideous crime, Bantry. The information was given to Fr Joe Breen who took it to headquarters in Dublin. The occupants of the car were deemed to be the murderers. Shortly after they were shot at and wounded at Bantry.

John also put the boys on the trail of the two Black and Tans who were shot dead at Ballybrack station. Chivalry there was too, amid the slaughter. But for the astuteness of John Keogh an innocent visitor might have one night lost his life amid the grandeur of Flesk Castle. The IRA were hot on the heels of the notorious and elusive Captain O'Kelly, Britain's chief intelligence officer, in the south of Ireland. Information came through that O'Kelly was to arrive on a particular day at Flesk Castle. A visitor did pass through its doors on the date in question but, according to an arrowed photograph (the arrow pointed to O'Kelly) in the pocket of John Keogh the visitor was not O'Kelly. John saw the visitor and as quickly as possible got word to the waiting guns that lurked around the castle. An innocent life was saved.

Recall the time British uniforms were worn by the IRA in the daring rescue of leading republicans from Mountjoy. Well, let me tell you that John Keogh intercepted a parcel of British officers' uniforms at Killarney and sent them to an address in Dublin named by the late Charlie Daly. Put two and two together and you get four.

The story is not without a humorous paragraph. Take the Polish-Jew commercial traveller of a Belfast firm who came under the eagle eye of John. The 'boys' were tipped off about the presence of this 'funny fish' but a laughable incident forestalled their investigations. Transacting business over the counter of the post office this Polish-Jew (according to Polish custom, John says) sprinkled some bottled scent over the lady inside the counter. The lady did a half-faint at this unorthodox behaviour 'thinking it was vitriol that had been thrown on her'. The police and the medical profession were called in, the 'stuff' analysed and a scent verdict returned. The Polish-Jew overcome with some anxiety or emotion could not be seen for dust taking his heels out of Killarney.

John pays special tribute to some post office officials at Killarney, notably the late Tommy Carey junior, who, he said, intercepted many an important letter that proved an invaluable aid to the 'boys'.

Claimed to be the one and only instance of an interchange of prisoners took place just before the Truce when at a meeting between the commanding officers of the military in Killarney and brigade O/C, IRA, Jack Shanahan, the Castleisland chemist, a prisoner in the Great Southern Hotel, and a British major in farmhouse captivity, were released simultaneously. John had been responsible for the arrest of the British major at Ballybrack station.

John Keogh recalls with pride: The infant days of the movement in 1914 when Pádraig Pearse, Seán T. O'Kelly, Mickey Crowe, and many of 'the leading lights' attended the great Oireachtas in Killarney; 'The meetings were held in Room 25,' he reverently recalls; his many meetings with Austin Stack who, when travelling to Dublin, used invariably take the night mail. On such occasions, John used scout the train to see if the Tralee detectives McKenna or Kneazer were on board. His sad meeting with Austin Stack at Killarney station in 1916 when Stack was in the grip of military on his enforced journey to Spike Island; his even sadder farewell to Tommy McInerney, Con Keating and comrades on the day of the shocking tragedy of Ballykissane; the arrival and departure of the noble Roger Casement on his journey to a patriot's grave in the land of the tyrant. The time the conscription meeting in Killarney was smashed up and the resultant dismissal of employees at Muckross; the arrival at the Great Southern Hotel of the German spy, Lody, where he was taken prisoner and conveyed to the Tower of London for execution. Tipping off Piaras Béaslaí and sending car to take him out of Castleisland before the police could get hands on him.

Those are but a few of the incidents that crowded John Keogh's life during the troubled times. If ever an intelligence officer deserved the name John did.

TRALEE FIANNA ÉIREANN AT WAR

by T.M.

No MERE ACCOUNT of routine scout work is the story of the Tralee Fianna Éireann. It is an integral part of the history of the entire resistance movement in the town, during the Anglo-Irish War. Boys of the Fianna, all of them in their 'teens, stood shoulder-to-shoulder with the men of the Republican Army in many big engagements. They fought bravely; some died leaving to the survivors the rich legacy of their inspiring example of courage and self-sacrifice. The re-organisation of the Fianna took place simultaneously with the re-birth of the Republican Army, in 1917. In Tralee a *sluagh* was formed in each Volunteer area, and the members worked in the closest co-operation with the IRA. The work of organisation was completed by the end of the year 1917; and among the brigade staffs formed at a Fianna Convention in the Mansion House, Dublin, in 1918, was one for Kerry. The following officers were then appointed:

> Brigade O/C, Miko Leary; adjutant, Thomas O'Connor; quarter-master, Billy Myles; intelligence officer, Tadhg P. Kennedy, who held the same rank with the Volunteers.

In 1918, the following officers were appointed to the Tralee battalion: battalion O/C, Miko Leary; vice-O/C, Paddy Daly; adjutant, Patrick

P. Hanafin; intelligence officer, Patrick O'Connor. The officers attached to 'A' company, comprising the Boherbee sector of Tralee, were as follows: O/C, William Griffin; first lieutenant, Thomas Kerins; second lieutenant, Christy Grady; adjutant, Daniel Sullivan; quartermaster, Maurice Kerins. The strength of the company was one hundred and nine. The officers attached to 'B' company, comprising the Strand Street sector were as follows: O/C, Thomas Hussey; first lieutenant, Denis Healy; second lieutenant, Gerald Ryle; adjutant, James Sullivan; quartermaster, Michael Moriarty. The strength of the company was one hundred and twenty. The officers attached to 'D' company, comprising the Rock Street sector of the town were as follows: O/C, Patrick Ryan; first lieutenant, James Barrett; second lieutenant, Daniel Horgan; adjutant, Christy Teahan; quartermaster, Jack Carmody. The strength of the company was one hundred and twenty.

During the year 1917 the Fianna was mostly occupied by the work of re-organisation. Training proceeded intensively, and the boys were engaged in intelligence operations. In addition to which they also carried out most of the stencilling, distribution and publication of literature dealing with Dáil Éireann bonds. During these early days they were also taken up with scouting and outpost work, and participated in the capture of arms and ammunition from British military at Tralee railway station, in October 1918.

When the terror of the Black and Tans was loosed in all its fury, in 1920, the Tralee Fianna showed that the years of intensive training were not wasted. The brigade O/C, Miko Leary, together with his adjutant, Thomas O'Connor, and quartermaster, Billy Myles, fought in the ambushes at Castlemaine and Lispole. The same three Fianna officers, with Patrick O'Connor, participated in the attack on a Black and Tan contingent at Glenbeigh, on 26 May 1920, when nine rifles and a machine gun were captured from the enemy. Miko Leary was also a member of the party which attacked Fenit barracks in June 1920. The assault on this barracks began at midnight, and, in the course of the attack Volunteers had to climb the walls of the building and get onto the roof which they intended to smash. All the while the besieged Royal Irish Constabulary fired at them from windows and loopholes. Whilst the attack was in progress a British gunboat anchored in Fenit Bay fired one shell which was believed to have exploded harmlessly on Ballyheigue strand. Nevertheless, reinforcements from the gunboat compelled the attackers to retire; but dawn showed that the barracks was completely gutted, and of no further use to the enemy.

The following list of activities in which members of the Tralee Fianna participated conveys the idea of the importance of the work undertaken by the organisation: (1) The attack on Sergeant Sullivan, KC, at Oakpark, in January 1920. This action was taken as a result of insulting references by Sullivan to the heroic Bishop O'Dwyer of Limerick. The KC was not molested very seriously. (2) Attack on Camp barracks, in February 1920. (3) Burning of the Custom House documents, in Tralee, on 3 April 1920. (4) Removal and destruction of military water waggon from Dingle train, at Tralee. (5) Capture of eleven rifles from British military in July 1920. (6) Burning of the furniture of Captain Wynne, RM in July 1920. (7) Hold-up and capture of police car at Edward Street, Tralee, July 1920. (8) Attack on British forces in Tralee on November Eve, 1920, culminating in the capture and shooting of two members of the Royal Irish Constabulary. (9) Ambushes at Lispole, Tubrid, Glenbeigh and Castlemaine. (10) Special scouting duty connected with the shooting of Major McKinnon, the notorious Auxiliary commander, at the Tralee golf links, on 15 April 1921.

Not all Tralee Fianna activities are listed above, but sufficient are mentioned to show that not alone was the organisation an invaluable adjunct to the IRA but, in addition, that it was also a first-class fighting unit in its own right. During the period of the Truce a special section of the Tralee Fianna was attached to the republican Police doing protective duty, guarding banks, investigating robberies and attending republican courts as witnesses. The Fianna assisted in repelling the onslaught of the Black and Tans who broke the Truce in Tralee, in January 1922, and ran amuck in the town. Following this incident units of the Fianna were constantly on day and night duty.

The following members of the Kerry Fianna were presented with watches by Éamon de Valera, then the president of the Irish Republic, for distinctive services given during the Anglo-Irish War: Miko Leary; Thomas O'Connor; Billy Myles (killed in action during the Civil War, at Annagh, Tralee); Paddy Daly, then battalion O/C; William Butler, company O/C Ballyroe; Patrick O'Connor, 'D' company, Tralee battalion. The president also presented a silver cup to the Tralee battalion for being the outstanding Fianna in Ireland.

BRITISH TRUCE-BREAKERS IN TRALEE

by VOLUNTEER

THE ADVENT OF the truce on 11 July 1921, brought an uneasy peace to Tralee. Black and Tans and Auxiliaries still strutted belligerently through the streets in which men of the flying columns were also seen openly for the first time in many years. There were tense moments when 'wanted men' of both sides looked each other in the eye for the first time ever and hands clenched on gun butts as they passed each other in the town. It needed but the smallest spark to blow the lid off the powder keg and unleash the dogs of war to a fresh conflagration which could easily become general overnight. To prevent such occurrence, in January 1922, the leader of the IRA in Tralee telephoned the local British commander requesting that he control indiscriminate actions by the Black and Tans and Auxiliaries under his command. A mocking laugh from the Britisher preceded his intimation that matters would continue as they were so far as the occupying British forces were concerned. The stage was thus set for a long-threatened incident which eventually did take place in Edward Street, some days later when a group of Fianna boys, amongst them Michael Mullaly and the late Percy Hannafin, came suddenly face to face with a group of Black and Tans who had a Crossley tender drawn up near Benner's Garage. Guns were drawn in a flash and a fusillade of shots rang out. Percy Hannafin was immediately struck on the head by a revolver bullet but his comrades blazed away at the enemy, two of whom fell one fatally wounded. The Fianna boy, Michael Mullaly, was also wounded before the firing ceased. Volunteers dashed immediately to the scene of the shooting and succeeded in having Percy Hannafin safely removed by lorry to the home of Sandy O'Donnell, at The Kerries, Tralee. As his wound did not respond to medical treatment he was rushed to Cork about a week later, where he died some days afterwards. Michael Mullaly, the other wounded Fianna boy recovered.

The already critical situation in the town worsened a few days later when a particularly rowdy element of Black and Tan reinforcements arrived. From the moment they set foot in Tralee it was the object of these hooligans to stir up all possible trouble. Citizens were openly molested in the streets in which indiscriminate shooting and instances of people being beaten were common occurrences. On the night of 22 January these Black and Tans lost all control and, breaking out of their barracks fully armed, ran berserk through the streets, shooting in all directions. They came charging down Ballymullen, poured into Castle Street, shouting, shooting wildly, and assaulting any unfortunate people who happened to be in their way. In Castle Street, particularly, the Black and Tans let loose the full fury of their venom, and people emerging from St John's church following evening devotions were met by a hail of bullets. Fortunately, only one person was wounded. The Tans next entered the Picturedrome where the performance was held up whilst the patrons were unceremoniously bundled into the streets. So far it had been a pleasant party for the Black and Tans and followed their customary line of terror against defenceless civilians. Lit up with drink, however, they had forgotten that matters then differed from pre-Truce days in so far as there were many armed IRA men in the town.

Furthermore, just before the enemy succeeded in breaking out of barracks, news of their intention reached local Volunteers who quickly organised a force, and within a short time of the Tans reaching the streets there was a veritable pitched battle in progress. During the Truce the battalion's arms were stored in O'Rourke's premises in Boherbee, and on the night of the outbreak, 'A' company from this street turned out to a man to combat the most recent exhibition of Black and Tan terrorism. German rifles, which the battalion had recently secured, were issued to the men, who were seriously handicapped by being unfamiliar with the use of these weapons. Nevertheless, the Black and Tans quickly found that their latest escapade was turning out far from being the anticipated picnic against defenceless townspeople and that they had now to deal with an armed and organised force more than willing to make a fight of it. Arms were issued and Volunteers came dashing from all centres to take up their positions at different strategic points.

Armoured cars emerged from the British barracks and lorry loads of troops rattled their way through the town. At this stage the British were beset on every side and raked by revolver and rifle fire. They remained in positions in Castle Street and Denny Street and showed no inclination to advance towards Boherbee, then known as 'The Dardanelles'; or towards Strand Street or Rock Street from the approaches to which the IRA subjected them to heavy fire. The din of battle was terrific and the scene was far more terrifying than anything which had taken place before the Truce. Verey lights lit the sky on the Clash side of Boherbee, and in the centre of the town the yells of the drunken soldiery added to the uproar. Eventually, the British broke and fleeing down Denny Street, they managed to get across 'The Green' to the safety of their barracks. Their casualties were never known, as they took their dead and wounded with them. It was afterwards rumoured that some Black and Tans were buried in quick-lime in the jail. The IRA suffered no losses.

Tension mounted and mobilisation orders were issued to the town companies and to all units from the surrounding districts. Next night every strategic point was occupied by the IRA who patiently and eagerly awaited some fresh movements by the Black and Tans.

But the British, finding discretion the better part of valour, remained within the comparative safety of their barrack walls. They had learned their lesson, so much so that some days later they meekly acceded to the demand of republican officers who presented themselves at British headquarters in the town and demanded the immediate release of two Volunteers, 'wanted men' who had been arrested in the streets some days previously. Several prominent Black and Tans and Auxiliaries cleared out of town long before the main British evacuation took place. None the less, tension continued until the last of the British forces had left Tralee.

BRITISH WARSHIP ENGAGED IN KENMARE BAY

by ONE WHO WAS THERE

THE PRESENCE OF British warships and sloops off the south-coast of Ireland in the early autumn of 1922 caused a good deal of anxiety to the IRA units who had them under observation. If the British had contented themselves with staying a few miles out to sea their action might not have excited more than passing comment but when they came inshore, took soundings, engaged in mapping and generally behaved as if they had a perfect right to do everything they liked, including the landing of a party of Marines, matters took on a different complexion.

This was the situation on 27 September 1922, when the Kerry No. 2 brigade headquarters, IRA in the Railway Hotel, Killarney, were asked for a direction by the local officer in charge at Kenmare as to what action he should take in the event of a party of British Marines attempting to force a landing in Kenmare Bay. A party who had already come in at Lackeen pier, near the coastguard station, was ordered off by Captain O'Hegarty and the fact communicated to Brigade Commandant John Joe Rice at Killarney. He immediately made up a party of two machine gunners (Johnny O'Connor and Moss Galvin) and twenty riflemen and dispatched them in Crossley tenders to Lackeen under the command of Johnny O'Connor. They arrived about 4 p.m. and took up position along the Lackeen road facing the bay and HMS *Barrington* riding at anchor directly opposite the coastguard station. The small fighting force of Irishmen decided that the challenge of Empire should be accepted and a signaller was ordered to the tower of the coastguard station to get into communication by semaphore with the hostile warship. The IRA officers demanded by what authority British naval units were in Kenmare and requested an explanation of the attempted landing. Equally terse came the British reply demanding the authority of those on land to prevent the landing and the movement of British Marines in Kenmare bay.

This exchange of messages took place in full sight of the crowded deck of HMS *Barrington* and the IRA fighting section. English men and Irish men stared at each other across the narrow stretch of water. The English seamen made gestures of defiance at the Irish men who dared question their right to come and go on the waters and soil of Ireland. Besides this by-play there was intense activity on the British ship. Marines were seen rushing to battle stations, the fore and aft guns being cleared for action under cover of the crowd on the deck. Noticing the move on the part of their opponents the IRA machine gunners, acting on the principle, that twice is he armed who has his quarrel just, but thrice is he armed who gets his blow in first, sprayed the decks of the warship with several pans of ammunition. The riflemen added their quota and for twenty minutes there was merry hell on board HMS *Barrington*. The Marines were unable to bring their guns into action. Sailors and Marines dived for cover and stayed there while a leaden hail raked their ship from stem to stern. Not until one of the IRA machine guns became jammed did the lull occur that enabled the Britishers to get to their deserted guns. When they got moving the answer to the IRA challenge was prompt and devastating. Boom! boom!! boom!!! The British lion was roaring. Shells burst along the Lackeen road. The sea-wall went up in a shower of stones and dust, all of it except the four feet behind which an IRA machine gunner was vainly trying to right a jam.

Believing that the coastguard station was the centre of the attack HMS *Barrington* trained her guns on it, and plastered it with showers of exploding steel. One shell landing plumb on the steps leading to the coastguard station swept four of them right through the building and deposited them well to the rear. That is just by way of indicating the calibre of the guns brought into play. For all the IRA present it was their baptism of shell fire and they got it on the grand scale. They stuck gamely to their ground despite the nerve-shattering ordeal of shell fire at close range, and vigorously replied with their now almost ineffective weapons.

After an hour of bombardment on one side and of rattling machine gun and rifle fire on the other HMS *Barrington* sheered off, out of effective range of the IRA guns. From there she let the coastguard station have it good and plenty. Shell after shell crashed into it until it was completely demolished. The surrounding country side was also sprayed with bursting shells, likely cover in woods and thickets receiving large donations of destructive metal. Alarmed by the loud and frequent explosions, the shrieking of shells, the atmosphere of ruthlessness, the people thought that every inch of ground was being swept clear of every living and standing thing, by flying and bursting steel. It seemed as if the British were not to be satisfied until they had laid waste that strip of Irish soil from which defiance had been hurled at them.

When night fell the British warship drew out to the open sea, leaving behind it a levelled coastguard station, a churned-up roadway, shell holes and shattered trees, but miraculously no casualties. How her own personnel fared under the barrage of machine gun and rifle fire that swept her crowded decks was never learned. She steamed for Berehaven, where medical aid was requisitioned.

The consternation and panic that followed the first burst of fire from the land was evident from the momentary loss of control on board HMS *Barrington*. She spun round and rocked from side to side as if the wheel had been deserted or the navigator wounded.

In his joy, and anticipating that the vessel would be beached and captured, an optimistic IRA man shouted: 'Is there anybody around here who can man a naval gun?' Twenty minutes later when a section of the wall caved in before a shell, one of his companions coolly supplied the answer: 'There is sure one man around here who can work a naval gun.'

The opening shot from the warship was no less than a mile wide of the target, it was learned later. A man working in a bog hearing the boom naturally stopped and listened. Suddenly the whole of the surrounding country seemed to shake and tremble. Ploughing its way deep into the soft bog, the British shell opened an immense cavity a short distance from where the man was standing. Investigation some time afterwards revealed that an unexploded nine-inch shell had buried itself in the bog. It weighed four cwts.

The IRA detachment which attacked the HMS *Barrington* in Kenmare Bay were commanded by Johnny Connor of Farmer's Bridge, and amongst the others who participated in the engagement were: Jeremiah B. O'Sullivan, Daniel O'Shea, John Connor ('Fox'), Jack Connor, Pa Galvin, Timothy M. Sullivan, Michael Riordan, Paddy Doyle, Pat Shea, Jeremiah Sullivan, Patrick Harrington, Denis Hegarty, Michael Quill, Johnny Connor, Moss Galvin, Dan Griffin, Ned McCarthy, Neilus McCarthy, John Quille, Denis Scannell, Jack Sheehan and Eddie McCarthy.

AMAZING ESCAPE OF MILITARY TRAIN

SHORTLY BEFORE THE Truce a company of the Kerry No. 2 brigade, then billeted at Kilcow, planned an attack on the military train to Castleisland. Rations for the troops in that town came regularly from Tralee to Gortatlea where they were transferred to the Castleisland branch train. The time factor was all important to the operation planned, as the running of the branch train did not permit of large scale mobilisation or mining of the railway. There was only a very short time available in which to accomplish the task. Accordingly, two members of the party quartered at Kilcow, Dan McCarthy and Johnny O'Connor, were ordered to move carefully along the line and to remove some lengths of rail. It was considered that more than two men engaged on this task would excite the notice of the military patrols which covered the territory regularly. When McCarthy and O'Connor arrived at the selected spot they found to their dismay that the spanners provided would not fit the nuts of the fish-plates. There followed two hours of back-breaking work under broiling sunshine, the two men sledge-hammering the rails until eventually they succeeded in detaching twenty-eight feet of line. A little nearer to Castleisland the main body of IRA men waited in ambush. All was carefully prepared and it seemed impossible that the trap could have been better set. Their job completed, McCarthy and O'Connor got under cover and awaited events. In a few minutes the noise of the approaching train could be heard chugging its way towards what appeared must be inevitable disaster. In a matter of minutes it was into the trap, and then to the amazement of the waiting men the train cleared the twenty-eight foot gap in the line, leaving only the guard's van which had broken its coupling. The train dashed for Castleisland when an urgent message was sent to Tralee, and inside a short time a strong force of military was rushed towards the IRA positions. In the meanwhile, however, the attackers, amongst who was Dr Andy Cooney, of Dublin, succeeded in getting safely away.

IN THE FIGHT
WITH CUMANN NA MBAN

by *GRANUAILE*

THE PART PLAYED by the women of Tralee in the fight for Irish freedom was especially meritorious because theirs was a steadfast loyalty to the cause, and generous was their measure of co-operation with the Volunteers; co-operation which made possible the success of many military operations. Behind the scenes and in the open the women of Cumann na mBan went steadily ahead with their allotted task, and many a daring coup by the IRA and defeat of the enemy owed success to the women's solid preparations of the preliminaries. Cumann na mBan will occupy an honoured place in Irish history of which they helped to write such glorious chapters. Almost from the formation of a branch of the Volunteers in Tralee, towards the end of 1913, the women's movement had come into being in the town. Some members dropped off, following the Redmondite 'split' in 1914. The seed from which Cumann na mBan really took root in Tralee was sown on Wednesday night, 25 March 1915, when a group of women met in the Rink and listened to Miss McCarthy, national organiser from headquarters in Dublin, tell of great tasks which lay ahead.

Introduced by Tom Slattery, RDC, Miss McCarthy, who was enthusiastically received, outlined ways by which Cumann na mBan could help the Irish Volunteers, through doing things which the men had neither the time nor the opportunity to do. Thus the men and women of Ireland could work together for the common cause of freedom. The men, said Miss McCarthy, are the setters of example, and the women could not have a better inspiration than the sight of the Kerry Volunteers with rifles not merely for parade, but for active service. Details of the work to be done by Cumann na mBan were outlined, training in first year's ambulance work, making flags for the Volunteers, semaphore signalling and ordinary drill. Tom Slattery's vote of thanks to Miss McCarthy was seconded by Austin Stack, who said that their meeting that night would mark an epoch in the history of the local Volunteer movement. A further meeting of the revived Cumann na mBan was held on Friday night, 26 March, at the Rink. Miss McCarthy attended again and enrolled over sixty ladies. The election of officers and committee resulted as follows: Mrs Madden; Misses Ciss Connor, Chrissie Foley, Chrissie Stokes, M. O'Brien, Hanna Moriarty, Miss Kidney, M. Brosnan, Kattie O'Brien, K. Kennedy, Nellie Hurley, Miss Codd, Mollie O'Donoghue. Honorary secretaries: Nora O'Leary and Nellie Barry. Honorary treasurer: L.A. O'Brien. On Monday evening, the 29 March, there was a large attendance of Cumann na mBan at the Rink to participate in a course of instruction given by Instructor Cotter. The girls drilled in a remarkably creditable manner and were congratulated by the Volunteer officers.

The mounting crescendo of the First World War had then attained a fierce tempo, and Tralee, in common with many other towns, had time for little but the gigantic clash of the nations. It had its quota of men on Flanders' fields and on the other great battle fronts, many of them lured into the imperial khaki by the Saxon's false plea for help to save small nations. Others had gone because their sympathies were all with the British who had their roots thrust deep into the soil of Ireland during their seven hundred years of occupation. Accordingly, there was then, as there is today, a good measure of pro-British feeling in the town, and on such ears the gospel of a free Ireland fell strangely. For some time following its formation the newly organised women's group had a rough passage; its members were regarded with hostility and were sometimes openly insulted. Particularly aggressive towards Cumann na mBan were some of the separationists, as wives of Irish soldiers fighting Britain's battles were known, because of the 'separation' money paid to them by the British government. In spite of these obstacles the women went determinedly ahead with the work, and when the Volunteers assembled in Tralee on Easter Sunday morning, 1916, the women of Cumann na mBan were by their side. They had provided for the needs of the big mobilisation of Kerry's fighting strength on that historic day, and later when the disappointment and disillusionment of the countermanding order were wiped clean by the blood of Ireland's martyred heroes amid the burned ruins of her capital city, those patriotic women travelled the highways and by-ways of the county reorganising and again fanning to flame the spark of rebellion. Amongst the members of the Tralee Cumann na mBan who were active during the early days of the organisation were: Misses Liz Anne O'Brien, Nellie Hurley, Nellie Barry, Katty Barry, Cissie Barry, Kattie O'Brien, Hannah Mullins, 'Bunty' Barrett, Bridget Barrett, Mollie Donoghue, Kattie Shea, Annie O'Shea, Mai Dowling, Madge Kidney, Mai Kidney, Pauline Hassett, Madge Clifford, Madge Reidy, Nellie Commane, Ciss Connor, Nora O'Leary, Mai Costello, Katty Sugrue, Mary Fleming, Mary O'Sullivan, Chrissie Foley, Sarah Shea, Nan Tyndall, Bridie Shea, Mollie O'Brien, Kit Heffernan, Nora Aherne, Dr Quinlan, Mrs Moriarty, NT, Blennerville, Mai Bunyan, Kate McMahon, — O'Shea.

Fast upon the work of reorganisation in 1917 came the threat of conscription, and when the women of the nation rallied with the other national groups which formed the solid phalanx of the opposition, those of Tralee did not lag behind. From Rock Street, Boherbee and Strand Street came patriotic women who helped the Volunteer movement by carrying dispatches, assisting in the elections and organising funds to aid the prisoners' dependants. Those years of hard work and training bore fruit when the Black and Tan war developed, and then the women of Cumann na mBan virtually became the eyes and ears of revolutionary Ireland. From the Boherbee area came Mrs Kennedy who also had been active in previous years; Bride Connor and Nora Connor of the Camp Dairy; Sally Sheehy, Úna Moriarty, the Kidney sisters, Mollie Myles, Sheila Myles, Ciss Maher, Aggie Sheehy, Dolly and Dorothy Hanafin, Hannah O'Connor, Mai Moriarty and Nora Casey. In Rock Street, Nellie Hurley, one of the founders of the movement in the town, was in charge, and amongst her active Volunteers were Miss Mai Moriarty, the Casey sisters, 'Bunty' Barrett, Bridget Barrett, Nora Barrett, Cissie Moriarty, Hanna Kelliher, Mary Fleming, the Power sisters and the Barry sisters. The Strand Street group was organised by Miss Liz Anne O'Brien, assisted by Julia Hassett and Frances Casey. All areas in the town worked together in close co-operation, and when the 'split' followed the Treaty with Britain Cumann na mBan was solid in its adherence to the republican cause. One of the most unselfish and hard-working members of the organisation was Miss Cáit Breen, who now ministers to the sick in one of Kerry's public institutions. It would be impossible to detail a list of the activities of that gallant band in this volume. No other generation produced more patriotic, unselfish or more willing workers in the sacred cause of freedom, for the advancement of which personal loss, victimisation and imprisonment proved but the incentive to greater effort.

Cumann na mBan was a strong, force in Killarney. Although never called upon to do anything spectacular the young Killarney women who joined the ranks did splendid work all along the line for their 'brothers-in-arms' and never once faltered in any job they were given to do. In the early years of the resurgence when the Volunteers were just 'marking time the Cumann na mBan were out in the country and up on the rugged mountains Sunday after Sunday with their field-kitchens dispensing food and drink to the boys doing their manoeuvres. Then when things got hot the Cumann got going properly and did everything from purchasing guns and ammunition to tipping off the Volunteers of impending danger. A notable feature of their activities was intelligence work which proved of invaluable assistance. They still recall with pride and no little amusement a cold winter's morning in 1920 when two badly-wanted republicans almost froze to death on a College Street roof-top while frenzied policemen ransacked the rooms below for 'the birds that had flown'. It was like this: Charlie Daly (whose soldierly and patriotic life was ended by a firing squad in the north), and P.C. O'Mahony (now county secretary), were staying the night in Connie McCarthy's in College Street. They were still reposing peacefully at eight o'clock in the morning when a force of police converged on the house. Cumann member and daughter of the house Hanna Mary McCarthy looking out a window sized up the situation. Quick as wink she roused the two guests and had them climbing through the skylight and onto the roof just as the policemen were hammering on the door. The police, who evidently had had good information, were nothing short of mystified when a search of the house brought failure but they kept it under surveillance for the rest of the day. They were still there when two 'priests' emerged from the house next door and walked calmly out of sight. The Cumann had planned and provided the garb for the escape.

Conveying of dispatches formed an important part of the work of the Cumann and they were never known to fall down on the job. They also organised the supply of food to interned republicans and to those 'on the run' and in this connection special tribute is due to the house of Mrs Twomey of Glebe Place. A special word is also due to Miss Bridget Gleeson of Henn Street, a sterling and self-sacrificing worker in the movement from beginning to end.

Those of the gentle sex in Killarney who showed that they had love of country, spirit, and fight in them were: the Misses Kate and Molly Breen, of High Street; Hanna M. McCarthy, College Street; Bridget Gleeson, Henn Street; Molly and Janie Flynn, Market Place; Molly O'Mara, High Street; Lena Connor, New Street; Lotty Foley, May Foley and Mary Anne Mahony, Market Place; Lalla Carey and Peg Cahill, High Street; Agnes Fleming, Henn Street; Ethel

Woods, Emmet's Terrace; Baby Murphy, High Street; Ciss Mason, New Street; Mary O'Connor, New Street; Nell Brosnan, New Street; Statia Flynn, Mangerton View; Nancy Hurley, Main Street; Maggie Clifford, College Street; Kathleen Spillane, Emmet's Terrace.

Prior to 1921 there could not be said to be any organised Cumann na mBan movement in Listowel. This is not to say, however, that up to then the womenfolk of Listowel did nothing in the furtherance of the cause of national independence or that they took no part in the active struggle. Many of them indeed answered the clarion call, but their work was for the most part individual and uncoordinated. They were unorganised and accordingly, although the will was there in plenty, the maximum use could not be made of their services. During that period there was one amongst them who particularly distinguished herself. In fact she was the guiding spirit and the inspiration of the 'woman-movement' all through the struggle, and was in the forefront of everything connected with the national movement. She was Miss May Murphy (now Mrs Tadhg Brennan). Others who were active before 1921 were Misses Mollie Cremins, Ciss Cahill, Mary Ahern, and Lena and Nora Mullally.

Early in 1921 the 'woman-movement' was placed on a regular footing and was completely re-organised. A definite branch of Cumann na mBan was formed and was attached to the 6th battalion of the Kerry No. 1 brigade. Miss Mollie Cremins (now in the USA) was appointed captain; Miss May Murphy, district council secretary, and Miss Ciss Cahill, treasurer. Other members of the branch were Misses Lena and Nora Mullally, Maisie Mulvihill, Margaret Walshe, Mollie Finucane, Mary Ahern, Julia Boyle, Margaret Barrett, Kathleen O'Connor, Nora Walsh, Marie Dowling and Mrs Bridget Wilmot.

From the time of this reorganisation of the movement until the Truce, the branch rendered valuable assistance to the independence movement. They worked, of course, under the general organisation in

Dublin. Their principal functions consisted of carrying dispatches and arms. They proved a most effective and efficient means of distributing arms to the points where most urgently required. In this connection, Mrs Wilmot deserves special mention. She was employed at the Royal Irish Constabulary barrack in Listowel and hardly a day passed that she did not smuggle out ammunition for distribution to the Volunteers – about ninety rounds of revolver or rifle ammunition at the time. She also succeeded in getting out a number of Mills bombs from time to time. On one occasion she smuggled out two revolvers belonging to two Royal Irish Constabulary men who were later fined £7 10s 0d each for the loss of the weapons. This episode had its humorous side – for Mrs Wilmot; she was escorted out of the barrack by one of the two whose revolvers she had on her. The Royal Irish Constabulary got suspicious of her after a while but a bogus threatening letter from the Volunteers dispelled this. Mrs Wilmot was typical of the Irishwoman who was prepared to risk her life (and those of her children) for the freedom of her country.

Although little spectacular occurred in the Cumann na mBan movement in Listowel, they nevertheless played an effective part in the struggle. They worked secretly and efficiently and the realisation of the dream of seven centuries was the reward which it was their privilege to share with their comrades and colleagues in the 'Army of Liberation'.

Caherciveen branch of Cumann na mBan was founded during the early weeks of 1915. Miss A. O'Rahilly, of the executive council, was instrumental in convening the inaugural meeting which was attended by local clergy and leading citizens. The proceedings took place in an atmosphere of enthusiasm, and appeals for recruits met with immediate response. District organisers were appointed, and, in addition to Caherciveen town, branches were formed in Kimegs, Reenard, Foilmore, Kells, Waterville, Valentia and Mastergeehy. The strength of the Caherciveen town Cumann averaged eighty members from 1915 to the Truce.

Miss M. Ryan, who later became Mrs Dick Mulcahy, and Miss Sheila Humphries, of Dublin, carried out several inspections in the Caherciveen district, during the years immediately following the formation there of Cumann na mBan. They were always loud in their praise of the keenness and efficiency displayed by the members.

Later, during the fight for freedom, the different Cumann in the Caherciveen district gave active assistance to the IRA. They removed arms and ammunition, and provided clothing and provisions for the men of the column. A mobile First-Aid unit was established and skilfully staffed by well-trained members of Cumann na mBan. In those days, too, every district had its quota of young men as unwilling guests of his Brittanic Majesty in British and Irish jails. Contact with these men was maintained by Cumann na mBan who regularly sent gifts of food and clothing to the prisoners.

The officers, with terms of office, of the Caherciveen Cumann were:

Presidents: Nora Bean Diarmuid Uí Chonnaill 1915–1920 and Mrs P. Sugrue (then Mary Frances Sullivan) 1920–1923.

Treasurers: Mary Bride Sullivan, 1915–1919. Mrs D. Connor (then Madge Connor), 1919–1923.

Secretaries: Miss Molly Riordan, 1915–1919; Mrs P. Sugrue, 1919–1920; Miss Mary Ann Curran, 1920–1923.

Captains and drill instructors: Miss Annie O'Connell and Miss Aggie M (now Mrs M. Keane).

District organisers: Miss Molly Fitzpatrick (now Mrs Ml. Kelliher); Miss Molly Riordan, Mrs Madge Daly, Mrs J.J. O'Connell.

Delegates to conventions: Miss Molly Riordan, 1915–1918; Miss Aggie Mangan, 1919–1920.

First-Aid lecturers: Doctor J. Mannix, Doctor J. Prendeville and Nurse Eily O'Connell.

Member for district on executive council: Miss Molly O'Riordan.

INDEX

A

'A' Company 31, 36, 37, 315, 320
'An Seabhac' 45, 46, 47, 167, 187, 193
Abbeydorney 38, 76, 128, 176, 192, 199,
    228, 287, 288, 290, 292
Abbeyfeale 75, 216, 217
Ahern, Jack 215
Ahern, Mary 332
Ahern, William 190
Aherne, J. 76
Aherne, Nora 329
Aherne, Paddy 215
Allen, William P. 37, 68
Allman, Dan 256, 257, 258, 259, 260
Annagh 305, 317
Annascaul 49, 54, 57, 128, 193, 245, 306,
    307, 308
Ardfert 29, 75, 112, 123, 140, 192, 231,
    250, 287, 288
Ardoughter 151, 194
Asdee 192, 284, 285
Asgard 27
Ashe, Gregory 191
Ashe, John 191
Ashe, Thomas 16, 155, 157, 158, 160,
    163, 165, 166, 171, 176, 177,
    178, 179, 305, 308
Ashe Street, Tralee 30, 230, 232, 252
Athea 281, 282, 283, 284
Aud 16, 84, 85, 86, 87, 88, 89, 90, 91, 99,
    103, 132, 133, 134, 140, 147,
    148, 304, 307
Aughacasla 204, 305
Auxiliaries 197, 199, 200, 228, 229, 238,
    246, 248, 251, 252, 253, 267,
    268, 269, 284, 286, 291, 292,
    316, 318, 321

B

'B' Company 31, 36, 37, 315
Bailey (Sergeant Beverley) 84, 123
Baily, James 258, 259, 260
Balfour, Arthur James 184
Ballinalee 199

Ballinsteenig 245
Ballyard 135, 139
Ballybeggan 250
Ballybrack 242, 312, 313
Ballybunion 68, 77, 153, 192, 194, 271,
    273, 274, 307
Ballycarbery 70
Ballycarney 71
Ballycarthy Cross 176
Ballyconry 192, 206
Ballydaly 80, 295
Ballydavid 57
Ballydesmond 255
Ballydonoghue 192, 265
Ballyduff 79, 151, 190, 192, 228, 265,
    266, 277, 278, 286, 305
Ballydwyer 234, 236, 237, 238
Ballyferriter 49, 54, 55, 57, 76, 191
Ballygamboon Cross 135
Ballygarrett 193
Ballygologue 53
Ballyhar 45
Ballyheigue 192, 228, 287, 288, 289, 291,
    305, 316
Ballykissane 113, 123, 139, 142, 143, 147,
    150, 170, 172, 313
Ballyknockea 194
Ballylongford 77, 78, 152, 192, 194, 206,
    265, 271, 272, 273, 274, 281,
    285, 307
Ballymacelligott 29, 30, 31, 38, 44, 78,
    124, 125, 126, 128, 213, 214,
    235, 242, 250, 252, 253, 259
Ballymacquin 290
Ballymullen 32, 96, 97, 229, 319
Ballyoneen 192
Ballyroe 30, 36, 44, 191, 250, 317
Ballyronan 288
Ballyseedy 215
Banna 16, 97, 99, 103, 110, 113, 117,
    119, 120, 138, 140, 147, 160, 177
Banteer 296, 297
Bantry 311
Barnett, Francis 288
Barraduff 255, 294, 300
Barrett, Bridget 329, 330

Barrett, Bunty 329, 330

Barrett, James 315

Barrett, John 192

Barrett, Margaret 332

Barrett, Nora 330

Barry, Cissie 329

Barry, D. 43

Barry, E. 31, 43, 128, 193

Barry, Garrett 193

Barry, Katty 329

Barry, Kevin 228

Barry, Ned 178, 179, 180

Barry, Nellie 43, 328, 329

Barry, P. 43

Barry, Pat 31

Barry, Úna 132

Bartishell, Peter 52, 54

Bawnogue 245

Béaslaí, Piaras 168, 169, 187, 188, 189, 190, 313

Beasley, James 192

Beasley, Maurice F. 194

Beaufort 45, 225, 260, 263

Beckett, Thomas 194

Bedford 53

Beenreigh 290

Begley, P. 60

Begley, Patrick 144, 145, 146

Behan, J. 59

Behan, William J. 190, 191

Belfast 92, 98, 147, 150, 160, 194, 209, 210, 236, 312

Belfast Telegraph, The 236

Berehaven 324

Bernard, Isaac 38

Bernstorff 106

Beverley, Sergeant 84, 103, 109, 110, 111, 117, 118, 119, 120, 123

Black and Tans 11, 18, 22, 52, 160, 174, 197, 198, 199, 200, 216, 225, 228, 239, 242, 243, 245, 246, 248, 251, 253, 255, 261, 262, 263, 266, 267, 268, 269, 271, 272, 273, 274, 277, 278, 280, 281, 283, 284, 285, 286, 287, 290, 291, 292, 293, 294, 295, 299, 300, 301, 306, 311, 312, 315, 317, 318, 319, 320, 321, 329

Bland, William 190

Blennerhassett, Babs 47

Blennerville 28, 36, 329

Blythe, Ernest 29, 48, 53, 55, 57, 58, 59, 68

Boherbee 21, 28, 29, 31, 36, 37, 230, 252, 315, 320, 329, 330

Boland, J. 77, 187

Boland, John 32, 66

Bourchier, T. 215

Bowler, T. 215

Boyle, Julia 332

Boyle, Sergeant 201, 202, 203

Boy Scouts 37, 38, 71

Brandon 306

Breathnach, Micheál 71, 78

Breen, Cáit 330

Breen, David 60

Breen, J. 53, 192

Breen, Jeremiah 194

Breen, Jerry 60

Breen, Joe 30, 33, 34, 131, 133, 135, 311

Breen, Kate 331

Breen, Molly 331

Breen, P. 77

Breen, Patrick 54

Brehig 190

Brennan, C. 194

Brennan, Charlie 28, 29, 30

Brennan, D. 194

Brennan, Joseph 69, 71

Brennan, T. 194

Brien, D. 80

Britten 39, 40

Brixton prison 228

Broder, Christy 281, 282

Broder, Mort 60

Broderick, J. 76

Broderick, J.M. 76

Broderick, Patrick 192

Brophy, Michael 181

Brosna 29, 77, 127, 193, 211, 215, 216, 217

Brosnan, J. 190, 217

Brosnan, Jack 258, 259

Brosnan, Jeremiah D. 192

Brosnan, John 193

Brosnan, M. 328

Brosnan, Nell 332

Brosnan, Patrick 308

Brosnan, Rev. Fr 190

Brosnan, Seán 304

Brosnan, T.P. 190

Brosnan, Tadhg 128, 134, 176, 180, 181, 187, 193, 263, 304, 305, 307

Brosnan, Tom 31

Brouder, J. 76

Brouder, P. 76

Browne, C.J. 67
Browne, Con 69, 176
Browne, D. 192
Browne, D.J. (solicitor) 192, 193, 308
Browne, John 201, 202
Browne, Peter 258, 259
Browne, Robert 203, 267, 270
Brugha, Cathal 161, 168, 195
Buckley, E. 80
Buckley, J. 76
Buckley, Lawrence 54, 190
Buckley, M. 76
Buckley, Paddy 215
Buncurrig 288
Bunyan, Mai 329
Burke, G. 59
Burke, J. 31
Burke, Mick 217
Burke, P. 215
Burke, Paddy 259
Butler, Frank 60
Butler, John 204
Butler, Michael 60
Butler, Pat 60
Butler, William 317
Buttevant 300, 311
Byrne, John 128
Byrne, M. 60
Byrnes, John 237
Byrnes, John (Lieutenant) 125, 126

C

'C' Company 31, 36, 37
Caherciveen 19, 49, 55, 69, 70, 71, 128,
    135, 142, 146, 147, 149, 150,
    153, 161, 170, 176, 177, 188,
    193, 333, 334
Cahill, Ciss 332
Cahill, J. 76
Cahill, J.J. 76
Cahill, Paddy (Castlegregory) 307
Cahill, Paddy J. (Tralee) 36, 121, 124,
    125, 128, 130, 139, 140, 141,
    180, 181, 247
Cahill, Patrick J. 190
Cahill, Peg 331
Cahill, Timothy J. 190
Cahillane, John 308
Callahan, Patrick 191
Callinafercy 146
Camp 191, 194, 204, 305, 316, 330
Cantillon, John 60

Caomhanach, Seaghan Óg MacMur-
    chadha 56
Cappagh 191
Carey, Lalla 331
Carey, Tommy 312
Carmody, Jack 217, 315
Carmody, James 237, 288
Carmody, Maurice 203
Carmody, Michael 281
Carmody, Moss 213, 256, 259
Carmody, P. 192
Carmody, Thomas 77
Carroll, Tim 282
Carrueragh 280
Carson, Sir Edward 26, 27, 72, 73, 74,
    186
Casement, Sir Roger 16, 27, 82, 83, 84,
    94, 99, 103, 104, 105, 106, 107,
    108, 109, 110, 111, 112, 113,
    114, 115, 116, 117, 119, 120,
    121, 122, 123, 125, 130, 131,
    132, 134, 135, 138, 140, 147,
    148, 150, 152, 156, 159, 168,
    172, 177, 313
Casey, Frances 330
Casey, John 190
Casey, Nora 330
Casey, Patrick 191, 288
Casey, Rev. J. 191
Cashel, J. 29
Castlegregory 78, 128, 134, 176, 180,
    181, 187, 191, 193, 204, 263,
    304, 305, 307
Castleisland 29, 49, 66, 67, 68, 69, 77, 80,
    96, 128, 158, 176, 188, 190, 193,
    213, 214, 215, 234, 235, 236,
    237, 255, 263, 264, 299, 300,
    313, 325, 326
Castlemaine 155, 200, 261, 262, 263,
    315, 316
Castle Street, Tralee 31, 229, 230, 319,
    320
Causeway 228, 231, 287, 288, 290, 291
Chapeltown 192
Chapman, John 69
Charleville 301
Childers, Erskine 27
Chotah 27
Christensen, Adler 106, 108
Churchill 287
Citizen Army 120
Clahane 194
Clahanelinehan 70, 71

Clancy, Peadar 198, 214
Clan na Gael 82
Clare 93, 97, 98, 100, 156, 179, 181
Clarke, James 192
Clarke, Thomas J. 108, 172
Clieveragh 53
Clifford, D. 60
Clifford, D.J. 60
Clifford, J.C. 49
Clifford, Madge 329
Clifford, Maggie 332
Clifford, T.J. 60
Clifford, Thomas 288, 291
Clifford, W. 60
Cloghane 191, 305, 306, 307
Clogher 203
Clonbanin 300, 301, 302, 303, 310, 311
Clune, Conor 198
Codd, Miss 328
Coffey, D. 60
Coffey, J. 60
Coffey, Jim 257, 259
Coffey, S. 59, 60
Coffey, W.T. 60
Coilagurteen 285
Coilbwee 284, 286
Coilbwee Bog 280
Collins, B.C. 75
Collins, Con 67, 78, 80, 100, 119, 120,
        121, 127, 135, 140, 150, 160,
        168, 169
Collins, D. 76
Collins, D.D. 76
Collins, E. 60
Collins, J. 76, 216
Collins, J. (junior) 192
Collins, J.J. 76
Collins, J.M. 67
Collins, James 78
Collins, John 67
Collins, M. 76
Collins, Michael 173, 179, 185, 196,
        198, 311
Collins, P. 76
Collins, T. 80
Collins, W. 76
Commane, Nellie 329
Connell, Cornelius 77
Connell, Michael 217
Connolly, James 108, 120, 123, 135, 140,
        172
Connolly, Seán 172
Connor, Bride 330

Connor, Ciss 328, 329
Connor, Davie 217
Connor, Jack 325
Connor, Jerry 217
Connor, John 259, 325
Connor, Johnny 211, 213, 215, 325
Connor, Lena 331
Connor, Madge 334
Connor, Mossie 47
Connor, Nora 330
Connor, P. 212, 213, 214, 215, 217
Connor, Thomas 237
Connor, Tim 217
Connor, Timothy T. 190
Connor, Tom 259, 263
Conor Hill 306
Conroy, J. 187
Conroy, Jack 229
Conroy, John 194
Conscription 175, 181, 182, 185, 186
Considine, Constable 202, 203
Conway, John 241
Coolard 281
Coolecross 296
Cooney, Andy 326
Cooper, Daniel 190
Cooper, Madge 47
Corcoran, Cornelius 194
Cordal 29, 67, 68, 78, 80, 128, 190, 213,
        214
Cork 42, 46, 93, 96, 97, 98, 124, 127, 135,
        139, 167, 179, 180, 181, 182,
        196, 199, 200, 204, 209, 210,
        219, 220, 226, 228, 238, 240,
        273, 293, 295, 299, 300, 301,
        303, 311, 319
Corkery, D. 54
Corobeg 71
Corridan, J. 76
Costello, Mai 329
Costelloe, Patrick 194
Cotton, A.W. 57, 68, 92, 128, 133
Coughlan, Seán 78
Counihan, James 128
Counihan, Jim 45
Counihan, John 308
Counihan, M. 60
Cournane, M. 43
Cournane, P. 43
Cournane, T. 43
Courtney, D. 81
Courtney, Eugene 308
Courtney, J.J. 190

Courtney, P. 46, 49
Craughdarrig 78
Crean, Diarmuid 28, 30, 67, 187, 192
Crean, Tom 204
Cregan, Con 215
Cregan, Ned 215
Cremins, Mollie 332
Cremmins, James 192
Cronin, Christy 213, 215
Cronin, D.B. 259
Cronin, D.P. 78
Cronin, Jeremiah F. 78
Cronin, Jerry 263
Cronin, John 212, 215
Cronin, John (Ballymacelligott) 256, 259
Cronin, John (Knockanure) 79
Cronin, John J. 190
Cronin, Michael 213
Cronin, Patrick 78, 259
Crosbie, Maurice Talbot 29, 31
Crowe, Mickey 313
Crowley, Fred 80
Crowley, James 187, 188, 192, 193
Crowley, Jeremiah 295, 296
Crowley, W 60
Crozier, General 198, 199
Cuan 54
Cumann na mBan 16, 43, 123, 125, 177,
        193, 291, 308, 327, 328, 329,
        330, 332, 333, 334
Cummins, General 302, 311
Curraheen 192, 263
Curran, John (Dingle) 54, 191
Curran, John (Ventry) 80, 81
Curran, Mary Ann 334
Currans 29, 68, 69, 78, 128
Curtayne, Tom 80
Curtin, L. 67
Cycle Corps 68, 92, 97

D

'D' Company 31, 36, 37, 315, 317
Dáil Éireann 170, 174, 176, 195, 196,
        220, 315
Daily News 18, 239, 241
Dalton, Patrick 274, 281, 282, 283
Daly, C. 31
Daly, Charlie 212, 217, 312, 331
Daly, Denis 135, 170, 177
Daly, F. 194
Daly, J.T. 80
Daly, John 78

Daly, M.M. 60
Daly, Madge 334
Daly, Paddy 314, 317
Daly, Tom 212
Danaher, R. M. 209
Deane, Eugene 191
Deane, John 194
Dee, Cornelius (Con) 281, 282, 283, 284
Dee, J. 60
Deenihan, Patrick 78
Defence of the Realm Act 36, 43, 53, 75,
        98, 169, 209
de Marsillac, M. 240
Dennehy, D.T. 80
Dennehy, J. 80
Dennehy, Michael 194
Dennehy, T. 187, 191
Dennehy, Thomas 230
Denning, Constable 202, 203
Denny Street, Tralee 30, 37, 38, 39, 249,
        320
Derinagree 300
Derk 267, 268
Derrinadaffe 74, 75
Derrymore 271
de Valera, Éamon 135, 136, 178, 179,
        182, 183, 185, 195, 196, 233, 317
Devane, P. 54
Devlin, Joseph 43, 182, 241
Devoy, John 82, 88, 105, 114
Diggins, J. 60
Dillon, Captain 75
Dillon, John 43, 56, 182
Dillon, Rev. Michael 192
Dineen, William 79, 194
Dingle 29, 49, 54, 55, 56, 57, 58, 59, 123,
        124, 128, 155, 176, 177, 181,
        187, 188, 191, 193, 228, 245,
        304, 306, 307, 308, 316
Dodd, W.W. 60
Donoghue, Donnacadh 263
Donoghue, Mollie 329
Donoghue, Tim 259
Donovan, Timothy 192
Dooneen 296, 297
Dowling, Captain 75
Dowling, Instructor 29
Dowling, Jack 238
Dowling, Jerh 305
Dowling, Mai 238, 329
Dowling, Marie 332
Dowling, William 237
Downey, Jeremiah 193

Downey, P. 60
Doyle, J. 60
Doyle, M. (Captain) 38
Doyle, Michael 128
Doyle, Paddy 325
Doyle, W. 60
Driscoll, Pat 111, 112
Drishanebeg 296, 300
Dromavalla 147
Dromdarlough 194
Dromerrin 284
Dromore 193
Drummond, D. 43
Drummy, William 69, 128
Duagh 53, 72, 73, 74, 75, 192, 193, 267,
        268, 269, 270, 281, 282, 284
Dubháin, Pádraig 189, 190
Dublin 26, 28, 30, 32, 34, 35, 36, 38, 44,
        46, 51, 67, 79, 92, 93, 96, 97, 98,
        100, 104, 105, 107, 108, 109,
        110, 113, 119, 120, 121, 123,
        124, 126, 127, 129, 130, 131, 132,
        133, 135, 138, 139, 140, 146,
        147, 149, 150, 151, 152, 153,
        154, 155, 158, 159, 160, 161,
        163, 167, 168, 169, 170, 171,
        172, 173, 174, 178, 182, 184,
        195, 196, 198, 200, 206, 208,
        214, 215, 234, 236, 311, 312,
        313, 314, 326, 327, 333, 334
Duffy, J. 60
Duggan, Johnny 211, 213, 215
Duhig, Michael 128, 304
Dunne, John 128, 194
Dunquin 55
Dysert 255

E

Edward Street, Tralee 41, 252, 316, 318
Egan, Michael 182
Evans, G. 60
Evans, M. 60
Evans, T.G. 79

F

'F' company 169, 170, 171, 173
Fahy, Frank 176, 177
Fahy, J. 31
Fallon, Constable 201, 202, 203
Falvey, C. 43
Farmer, William 38, 128

Farmer's Bridge 36, 212, 213, 232, 256,
        325
Farranfore 194, 255
Farrell, John 204
Fealy, D. 193
Fenit 36, 82, 88, 93, 94, 96, 97, 109, 122,
        123, 132, 133, 134, 135, 139,
        140, 218, 289, 290, 315, 316
Fernane, Garrett 29
Ferris, Rev. 49, 61, 309
Fianna Éireann 36, 43, 52, 92, 218, 314
Figgis, Darrel 27
Findlay, M. de C. 106
Finglass 81
Finn, Dan 34, 128
Finucane, D.J. 189, 190, 191, 192
Finucane, Mollie 332
Finucane, Pat 75
Finuge 52, 206, 284
Firies 45, 128, 190
Fitzgerald, C.J. 190
Fitzgerald, Desmond 29, 54, 57, 67, 80,
        81
Fitzgerald, Dick (Richard) 48, 49, 50, 52,
        129, 189, 190, 191
Fitzgerald, Francis 78
Fitzgerald, J. 76
Fitzgerald, John T. 194
Fitzgerald, Michael (Ballyroe) 191
Fitzgerald, Michael (Camp) 191
Fitzgerald, P. 76
Fitzgerald, Paddy 217
Fitzgerald, Paddy Paul 263
Fitzgerald, Thomas (Castleisland) 128
Fitzgerald, Thomas (Tarbert) 193
Fitzgerald, William 192
Fitzgibbon, Seán 27, 100
Fitzpatrick, J. 60
Fitzpatrick, Molly 334
Fitzpatrick, T. 59
Flaherty, D. 193
Flaherty, John 79
Flaherty, John (Cappagh) 191
Flahive, Patrick T. 308
Flavin, D.J. 192, 207, 209
Flavin, F. 80
Flavin, M.J. 187
Fleming, Agnes 331
Fleming, C. 46
Fleming, J. 43
Fleming, Jackie 179
Fleming, John M. 193
Fleming, Mary 329, 330

Fleming, Maurice 43
Fleming, Michael 193
Fleming, Thomas M. 190
Flesk Castle 312
Flynn, F. 59
Flynn, J.W. 76
Flynn, Jack 263
Flynn, James 60
Flynn, Janie 331
Flynn, John 75, 259
Flynn, Maurice 134, 191
Flynn, Michael 204, 205
Flynn, Molly 331
Flynn, Patrick 194
Flynn, Statia 332
Flynn, Timothy 60
Flynn, W. 60
Flynn, W.P. 76
Foilmore 333
Foley, B. 60
Foley, Chrissie 328, 329
Foley, Daniel 191
Foley, James 60
Foley, John (Coolbane) 60
Foley, John (Tralee) 180, 181, 194
Foley, Lotty 331
Foley, M. (Killorglin) 60
Foley, M. (Tuogh) 60
Foley, May 331
Foley, Michael 60
Foley, Stephen 59
Foley, Thomas 61, 191
Foley, Tim 61
Foley, Tom 180, 181, 194
Fossa 45
Foylemore 71, 78
French, Lord 184, 185, 196
Frongoch 154, 173
Fuller, Stephen 288

G

Gaelic Athletic Association (GAA) 16,
      154, 156, 158
Gaelic League 45, 71, 76, 92, 152, 155,
      156, 159, 167, 168, 172
Gale 284
Gallivan, Jim 60
Galvin, Denis 301
Galvin, Michael 278, 279, 281
Galvin, Mortimer 192
Galvin, Moss 211, 213, 215, 259, 322,
      325

Galvin, Pa 325
Gavan Duffy, George 131
Geaney, John 67
Gilligan, T. 43
Gleesk 71
Gleeson, Bridget 190, 331
Gleeson, Edward J. 52, 53, 75, 208, 209
Glenaneenta 126, 127
Glenbeigh 65, 78, 177, 194, 217, 218,
      219, 307, 315, 316
Glenesrone Wood 216, 217
Glenflesk 45
Glin 194
Gneeveguilla 294
Golden, John 60
Golden, P. 60
Goodwin, Frank 128
Goodwin, J. 128
Gorman, Mary 110, 111, 112
Gortaglanna 274, 281, 282, 284
Gortatlea 201, 202, 203, 211, 212, 325
Gortdromagowna 280, 282
Gortdromasillahy 278, 280
Gortglass 128
Grady, Christy 315
Grady, James 78
Granville, Michael 191
Greenwood, Sir Hamar 225, 231, 236,
      238, 241
Griffin, Cors. 288
Griffin, Dan 325
Griffin, David 79, 217
Griffin, David J. 128
Griffin, F. 59
Griffin, G. 190
Griffin, James 288
Griffin, Martin 204
Griffin, Maurice 71, 128
Griffin, Michael 204, 205
Griffin, Pat 60
Griffin, T. 60
Griffin, Thomas P. 190
Griffin, William 31, 315
Griffith, Arthur 175, 182, 185, 195, 233
Guiney, D. 77

H

Hackett, Martin 194
Haig, Major 27
Hanafin, Dolly 330
Hanafin, Dorothy 330
Hanafin, Patrick P. 314

Hannafin, Percy 318, 319
Hannifin, John 309
Hannifin, Pat 60
Hanrahan, J.M. 192
Harnett, D.B. 76
Harnett, J.D. 76
Harnett, J.J. 76
Harnett, M.L. 76
Harnett, Maurice 77
Harnett, P.J. 76
Harnett, R.C. 75
Harrington, Joe 141
Harrington, John 61
Harrington, Patrick 325
Harris, Maud 31
Harris, Timothy 190
Hartigan, J.P. 60
Hartigan, Rev. Fr 190
Hartnett, Mossie 215
Hartnett, Philip 217
Hassett, Julia 330
Hassett, Pauline 329
Hawley, Tommy 242, 243, 244
Hayes, James 54
Hayes, Jeremiah 237
Hayes, Maurice 194
Hayes, P. 77, 192
Headford 194, 200, 255, 256, 257, 258,
      259, 260
Headley's Bridge 127
Healy, Con 31
Healy, D. 31, 38
Healy, Dan 259
Healy, Daniel 128, 180, 181
Healy, Dave 256
Healy, Denis 315
Healy, J. 60
Healy, Michael J. 69, 71
Healy, Thomas 191
Healy, Tim 157, 182
Healy, W. 59, 60
Heaphy, Garrett 194
Heard, County Inspector 207
Hearn, Chief Constable 112
Heffernan, John 60
Heffernan, Kit 329
Heffernan, P. 60
Hegarty, Denis 194, 325
Hegarty, John 194
Hennessy, James 79
Herlihy, J. 236, 237
Herlihy, Jack 215, 259
Herlihy, John 259

Herlihy, William 237
Hickey, Ellen 191
Hickey, J.C. 80
Hickey, James J. 190
Hickey, L. 80
Hickey, Sheamus 293
Higgins, Pat 31
Hill, J. 46
Hill, M. 206
Hillee, Rev. C. 191
HMS *Barrington* 323, 324, 325
Hobbs, Dan 179
Hobson, Bulmer 120
Hoffman, Frank 232
Hogan, Eugene 263
Hogan, Michael 36
Hogan, P.J. 128
Holly, John 194
Holmes, Major-General 299
Horan, David 217
Horan, Ned 181, 193
Horgan, Daniel 315
Horgan, E. 60
Horgan, Maurice 189
Horgan, Pat 45, 46
Horgan, T. 46
Horgan, Timothy 190
Horgan, Willie 47, 52
Houlihan, J. 60
Houlihan, J.J. 60
Houlihan, James 266
Houlihan, Seán 266, 267
Houlihan, Willie 266
Howth 27, 30, 70, 109, 119
Hoy, Hugh Cleland 113
Humphries, Sheila 334
Hurley, Nancy 332
Hurley, Nellie 328, 329, 330
Hussey, Thomas 315
Hutchinson, Clifford 236

I

Inch 191
Inchequinn 194
Inishtooskert 82, 87, 88, 103, 134
Irish Independent 106, 238, 282
Irish Parliamentary Party 16, 32, 33,
      40, 61, 169, 170, 179, 182, 184,
      186, 188
Irish Republican Brotherhood (IRB) 82,
      92, 130, 169, 175, 179
Irish Times 26

Islandanny 74, 75
Iveragh 55, 56, 71, 149, 150

J

Jeffers, Dan 193, 263, 305
Jephson, Annie 104
Johnson, J. 60
Johnson, Jim 60
Johnson, M. 60
Johnson, Michael 60
Johnson, Tom 182
Johnson, Tom (Dungeel) 60
Jones, G. 236
Jones, Servelus 128
Joy, James J. 60, 193
Joy, P. 60
Joy, W. 59, 60

K

Kane, J. 60
Kane, Thomas 60
Kanturk 301
Kavanagh, J. 54
Kavanagh, Jeremiah 191
Keale Bridge 300
Keane, Daniel 194
Keane, Jeremiah 192, 193
Keane, John 207
Keane, M. 67
Keane, T.J. 76
Kearney, John 288
Kearney, P.T. 190
Kearns, J. 60
Keating, Con 146, 147, 149, 150, 170, 172, 173, 313
Keel 79, 191, 242
Kelliher, D.P. 80
Kelliher, Hanna 330
Kelliher, Jeremiah 67, 69
Kelliher, M.J. 80
Kelliher, T. 190, 194
Kells 71, 177, 333
Kelly, Thomas 193
Kelly, Timothy 61
Kenmare 51, 189, 256, 322, 323, 325
Kennedy, J. 60
Kennedy, James 128
Kennedy, James ('Fox') 304
Kennedy, John 309
Kennedy, K. 328
Kennedy, M. 59

Kennedy, Patrick 193, 306, 308
Kennedy, Tadhg P. 36, 306, 309, 314
Kennedy, William 54
Kennelly, James 274
Kennelly, P. 60
Kennelly, P.D. 192
Kennelly, Thomas 274
Kenny, James 191, 207
Keogh, John 310, 311, 312, 313
Kepple, Dodo 179
Kerins, Maurice 315
Kerins, Seán 190
Kerins, Thomas 315
Kerry Head 88, 134, 287, 288
Kerryman, The 9, 11, 12, 15, 20, 23, 36, 39, 40, 42, 62, 65, 66, 72, 81, 100, 128, 189
Kidney, Madge 329
Kidney, Mai 329
Kiely, J. 215
Kilcara 72, 193
Kilcow 325, 326
Kilcummin 193
Kilelton 52
Kilflynn 79, 192, 287, 288, 291, 292
Kilgarvan 194
Killarney 30, 38, 44, 45, 46, 47, 48, 49, 50, 51, 52, 54, 67, 68, 69, 75, 77, 79, 96, 122, 123, 129, 153, 159, 168, 175, 176, 188, 189, 190, 193, 194, 225, 242, 255, 256, 258, 294, 300, 301, 310, 311, 312, 313, 322, 330, 331
Killeentierna 190
Killehan 70
Killorglin 19, 59, 60, 61, 62, 65, 66, 139, 142, 144, 147, 170, 177, 191, 219, 228, 261, 262
Killovarnogue 147
Kilmore 194, 305
Kilmorna 73, 192, 278, 279, 280, 281, 282
Kilmoyley 287, 288, 291
Kilquane 255
Kiltomey 79
Kimego 70
Kimegs 333
Kinard 155, 176, 177, 191, 245
King, Thomas 74
King's Own Scottish Borderers 27, 30, 35, 222
Kingwilliamstown 299
Kirby, J. 193

Kissane, M. 60
Kneazer, Constable George 181, 313
Knight, H. 67
Knockanure 79, 206, 279, 282, 285
Knockeen 193
Knocknagoshel 29, 190
Knocknagree 80, 299
Knocknaroor 194
Knockpogue 286
Knockreigh 194

L

Lacey, Jim 217
Lackeen 322
Laide, Jeremiah 67
Laide, John 202
Laide, Richard 201, 202
Landers, Michael 36
Landers, Patrick 53, 128, 206, 208
Lane, J. 76
Lane, P. 60, 76
Langford, John 60
Langford, Ned 60
Larkin 37, 68, 280
Lartigue 68
Lawlor, David 288
Lawlor, Jack 176
Lawlor, Michael 176, 288
Lawlor, P. 31
Lawlor, Tom 79
Lawlor, William 209
Leahy, Daniel 194
Leahy, E.C. 76
Leahy, E.J. 52, 53, 54
Leahy, J. 77
Leahy, Ned 68
Leahy, Timothy 193
Leahy, Tommy 215
Leane, D.H. 192
Leane, Maurice 288
Leary, D. 80
Leary, Jeremiah 213, 217
Leary, Mick 213, 217
Leary, Miko 263, 314, 315, 317
Leen, Edward 29, 37
Leen, Ml. 288
Leen, William 288
Lenihan, Arthur 126
Lenihan, K. 43
Lenihan, Seán Tadhg Óg 126, 127
Lewes 158, 163
Lillis, J.V. 59

Limerick 30, 42, 46, 47, 93, 96, 97, 98,
     100, 108, 122, 124, 127, 135,
     136, 139, 140, 150, 152, 158,
     159, 197, 215, 216, 217, 281,
     316
Linehain, T. 60
Linehan, Denis 191
Lispole 54, 55, 57, 155, 176, 177, 191,
     242, 243, 244, 245, 304, 307,
     315, 316
Listellick 30, 36, 38, 191
Listowel 20, 49, 52, 53, 68, 71, 72, 74,
     75, 77, 96, 100, 129, 176, 181,
     188, 192, 193, 194, 206, 207,
     208, 209, 210, 220, 222, 223,
     225, 240, 265, 266, 267, 270,
     271, 275, 276, 279, 280, 281,
     282, 283, 287, 290, 332, 333
Listowel, Lord 206, 207
Listry 45
Lixnaw 75, 77, 79, 151, 192, 266, 269,
     275, 276, 292
Lloyd George, David 181, 184, 185, 186,
     189
Logue, Cardinal 183
Loinasnic, M. 76
Long, D. 190
Long, Jeremiah 190
Longford 9, 156, 178
Looney, Patrick 61
Loop Head 110, 289
Lynch, Diarmuid 156
Lynch, Fionán 167, 168, 169, 170, 171,
     172, 173, 174, 176, 177, 178,
     187, 188, 193
Lynch, J. (Rev.) 78
Lynch, James 192, 209
Lynch, John 167, 177
Lynch, Tommy 229
Lynch, William 75
Lyne, D. 60
Lyne, Denis 190
Lyne, Pat 60
Lyne, T. 46
Lyons, Jerry 281, 282, 283
Lyons, Patrick 192
Lyre 194

M

MacColuim, Fionán 167
MacDiarmada, Seán 141
Macken, Francis 153

MacNeill, Eoin 32, 34, 35, 48, 49, 50, 53, 55, 67, 69, 77, 120
Macready, General 200, 231
MacSwiney, Terence 228
Madden, Mrs 328
Maguire, Michael 75
Maharabeg 304
Maharees 128, 134, 305
Maher, Ciss 330
Mahon, Bryan 185
Mahony, Abel 128, 304
Mahony, Berty 217
Mahony, D. 29, 31, 77
Mahony, Daniel (Castleisland) 193
Mahony, Daniel (Cloonacurrig) 190
Mahony, G. 48
Mahony, Jack 31, 217
Mahony, Jim 217
Mahony, Mary Anne 331
Mahony, Michael 78
Mahony, Ned 217
Mallow 160, 199, 296, 297, 300, 306
Manchester Guardian 239
Mangan, Aggie 334
Mangan, D. 48, 60
Mangan, E. 60
Mangan, J. 46, 49
Mangan, John 61
Mangan, M.E. 187
Mangan, Michael 79
Mangan, P. 61
Mangan, William 61
Mannix, John 309
Mannix, John (Dr) 334
Mara, J. 76
Markievicz, Countess 92
Marshall, H.J. 193
Martin, Constable 217
Martin, Dr Conor 192
Martin, Fr 80
Martin, Hugh 18, 239, 240
Mason, Ciss 332
Mastergeehy 80, 168, 333
Maunsell, Michael 204, 205
McAlister, R. 237
McAuliffe, David 217
McAuliffe, J. 76
McAuliffe, Jim 217
McAuliffe, Willie 299
McCabe, J. 194
McCann, John 82
McCarthy, Charles 60

McCarthy, Connie 331
McCarthy, Daniel 215, 217, 326
McCarthy, David 213, 214, 215, 217, 259
McCarthy, Denny 217
McCarthy, Eddie 212, 213, 215, 325
McCarthy, G. 49
McCarthy, Hanna Mary 331
McCarthy, Jack 60
McCarthy, John 111, 112
McCarthy, Martin 217
McCarthy, Miss 327, 328
McCarthy, Myra T. 167, 173, 174
McCarthy, Ned 325
McCarthy, Neilus 259, 325
McCarthy, T 54
McCarthy, T.J. 128
McCarthy, W. 49
McCarthy, Willie 276
McCrohan, John 31
McDermott, Seán 98, 99, 133, 135, 168, 169, 171, 172, 173
McDonagh, Thomas 171, 172
McDonnell, Dr 187
McDonnell, Jack 31
McDonnell, James 67
McDonnell, M. (Rev.) 237, 238
McDonnell, Michael 203
McEgan, Michael 288
McElligott, E. 78, 192
McElligott, M.P. 66, 67
McElligott, Michael 270, 287
McElligott, Michael Robert (Bob) 267, 270
McElligott, William 53
McEllistrim, Thomas 125, 126, 128, 212, 213, 214, 215, 256, 257, 258, 259, 264, 311
McEnery, D. 76
McEvoy, Úna 47
McGaley, Jack 43
McGaley, John 180
McGarrity, Joe 105
McGillycuddy, Denis 60
McGillycuddy, John 60
McGillycuddy, Timothy 60
McGoey, Joe 132
McGrath, Patrick 31, 288
McGrath, Rev. J. 191
McGuinness, Joe 179
McInerney, Tommy 145, 313
McKee, Dick 198
McKenna, Detective Sergeant 181, 265

McKenna, Jack 52, 53, 176, 193, 207,
        208, 209, 210
McKenna, Michael 128
McKenna, Mick 304
McKenna, Patrick 288, 307
McKenna, W. 60
McKenna's Fort 117, 119
McKeon, Seán 199, 200
McKinnon, Major 248, 249, 250, 251,
        252, 253, 267, 268, 270, 316
McLeish, George 179
McMahon, Edward 191
McMahon, Jeremiah 192
McMahon, Kate 329
McMahon, Matthew 28, 36
McMahon, Michael 263
McMahon, Mona 179
McMahon, Pat 75
McMahon, Thomas 128
McSweeney, Jeremiah 202
McSweeney, William 128
Meaney, C.J. 296
Meenascarthy 204
Melinn, Joe 36, 37, 43, 128, 176, 179,
        191
Melleney, Major 311
Meredith, James Creed 27
Millstreet 30, 80, 293, 295, 296, 297, 298,
        300, 301
Milltown 187, 191, 223, 224, 225, 261,
        263, 311
Milroy, Seán 44
Minard 245
Molloy, District Inspector 207, 210
Moloney, E.P. 76
Moloney, J. 75, 76
Moloney, P. 76
Moloney, Patrick 193
Monahan, Charlie 139, 147, 150
Monteith, Robert 84, 94, 99, 100, 103,
        104, 107, 108, 109, 110, 111,
        117, 118, 119, 120, 121, 122,
        123, 124, 125, 126, 127, 130,
        131, 140, 141
Moore, J. 54
Moore, T.C. 59
Moore, Thomas 52, 71
Moran, John 54, 77, 192
Morgan, Jim 193
Morgan, Tadhg 45
Moriarty, Cissie 330
Moriarty, D. 59, 61

Moriarty, D.J. 77
Moriarty, Denis 308
Moriarty, Edward 69
Moriarty, Hanna 328
Moriarty, James 128, 176
Moriarty, John 61, 79
Moriarty, Jonathan 54
Moriarty, M. 60
Moriarty, M.J. 128
Moriarty, Mai 330
Moriarty, Michael 128, 176, 315
Moriarty, P. 43
Moriarty, Robert T. 308
Moriarty, T. 128
Moriarty, Úna 330
Moriarty, W.J. 60
Morley, Cornelius 193
Moroney, John 194
Moroney, M. 60
Moroney, Michael 194
Moroney, Pat 61
Morris, J. 60
Mortell, Drill Instructor 52
Mountcoal 193
Mountjoy jail 178, 180, 228, 312
Mountmahon 217
Moybella 194, 274
Moyderwell, Tralee 31, 120, 123, 138,
        140, 180, 252
Moylan, Bill 301
Moylan, J. 31
Moylan, Seán 299, 300, 311
Moynihan, A.J. 194
Moynihan, Mary 191
Moynihan, P. 80
Moynihan, P.J. 190
Moyvane 206
Muckross 313
Mulally, Michael 209
Mulcahy, Paddy 215
Mullally, Lena 332
Mullally, Nora 332
Mullaly, Michael 318, 319
Mullins, Hannah 329
Mullins, J. 31
Mullins, William 120, 123, 128, 138,
        176, 180, 181
Mulquin, John 192
Mulvihill, Dan 77
Mulvihill, Edward 192
Mulvihill, John 151
Mulvihill, Maisie 332

Mulvihill, Michael 151
Mulvihill, Michael C. 192
Mulvihill, Roger 77
Murder Gang 267, 268, 270, 277
Murphy, Baby 332
Murphy, Batt 190
Murphy, Bride 31
Murphy, Con 295
Murphy, Daniel 60
Murphy, Denis 295
Murphy, Edward 209
Murphy, Humphrey 213, 215, 216, 217, 301
Murphy, May 332
Murphy, Michael 194
Murphy, P. (Captain) 80
Murphy, Pat 79
Murphy, Patrick 191
Murphy, T.T. 80
Murphy, Thomas 54, 209
Myles, Billy 263, 314, 315, 317
Myles, Jerry 263
Myles, Michael 79
Myles, Mollie 330
Myles, Sheila 330
Myles, Thomas 27

N

Nagle, Garrett 60
Nagle, George 60
Nagle, John 60
Neeson, Seán 179
Neill, Pat 307
Neill, Tom 31
Neligan, P.J. 54
Newmarket 300, 301
Newtownsandes 192, 193
Ní Chonaill, Máire 168
Ní Mhuirthuile, Treasa 168
Nolan, Jeremiah 190
Nolan, John 194
Nolan, Maurice 288
North Kerry Column 267, 275, 284

O

Ó Annrachán, Peadar 167
O'Brien, D.J. 60
O'Brien, J. 59
O'Brien, J. (Rev.) 192
O'Brien, John 308
O'Brien, Joseph 128

O'Brien, Kattie 328, 329
O'Brien, Liz Anne 43, 328, 329, 330
O'Brien, M. 328
O'Brien, M.W. 60
O'Brien, Michael 53
O'Brien, Michael (Manchester) 37, 68
O'Brien, Mollie 329
O'Brien, Thomas 75
O'Brien, W.B. 79
O'Brien, W.M. 59
O'Brien, William 56, 155, 182
Ó Cathail, Pádraig S. 103
Ó Cathasaigh, Seán 190
Ó Cearbhaill, Seán 76
O'Callaghan, A. 78
O'Callaghan, J. 78
O'Callaghan, Richard 192
O'Callaghan, T. 60
O'Carroll, Mce. 288
O'Carroll, William 192
O'Casey, Seán C. 45, 46, 47, 49
O'Connell, Annie 334
O'Connell, D. 76
O'Connell, D.J. 78
O'Connell, Daniel 308
O'Connell, Denis 60
O'Connell, Denis J. 69, 177, 193
O'Connell, Diarmuid 170
O'Connell, Dr 134
O'Connell, Eily 334
O'Connell, J. 71, 76, 78
O'Connell, J.D. 177, 187, 191, 203
O'Connell, J.J. (Constable) 204
O'Connell, Jeremiah 78, 79
O'Connell, John 191
O'Connell, M. 76
O'Connell, Michael 53
O'Connell, Morgan 50, 51
O'Connell, Mortimer 170, 173, 174, 177
O'Connell, P.J. 36
O'Connell, T. 76
O'Connor, Arthur 60
O'Connor, Brian 67, 128
O'Connor, Charles 60
O'Connor, Commander 55
O'Connor, D. 60
O'Connor, D.M. 80
O'Connor, Daniel 190
O'Connor, David 215
O'Connor, Denis 31
O'Connor, Éamonn 30, 31, 33, 34, 35, 36, 37, 43, 230
O'Connor, Edward 288

O'Connor, Hannah 330
O'Connor, J. 60
O'Connor, J.J. 191
O'Connor, J.K. 190
O'Connor, James 288
O'Connor, Jerry 263
O'Connor, Jim 217
O'Connor, John J. 190
O'Connor, Johnny 256, 257, 258, 322, 326
O'Connor, Kathleen 332
O'Connor, Kerry 29
O'Connor, M. 76
O'Connor, Mary 332
O'Connor, Maurice 128
O'Connor, Michael 128
O'Connor, Michael (Dr) 192, 193, 209
O'Connor, Michael J. 34, 36, 48, 50, 67, 69, 128, 176
O'Connor, Michael P. 192
O'Connor, Mortimer 128, 192
O'Connor, Murty 76
O'Connor, P. 75
O'Connor, Patrick 150, 151
O'Connor, Patrick (Tralee) 315, 317
O'Connor, Rita 43
O'Connor, Simon 229
O'Connor, T.P. 225, 226, 231
O'Connor, T.T. 67, 128
O'Connor, Terence 193
O'Connor, Thomas 314, 315, 317
O'Connor, Timothy 190
O'Connor, Timothy Matt 193, 215, 217
O'Connor, W. (Abbeyfeale) 76
O'Connor, W. (Tralee) 31
O'Connor, William D. 75
O'Connor, William H. 66, 67, 176, 190, 214
O'Doherty, Floss 170, 172, 173, 174, 177
O'Doherty, M. 59
O'Donnell, Francis 192
O'Donnell, J. 76, 128
O'Donnell, J.P. 128, 135, 139, 187, 191
O'Donnell, John 191
O'Donnell, John M. 308
O'Donnell, M.M. 308
O'Donnell, P. 76
O'Donnell, Pat 305
O'Donnell, Sandy 319
O'Donnell, Tom 17, 32, 33, 34, 35, 36, 38, 42, 43, 56, 57, 58, 59, 61, 62, 66, 111, 187
O'Donoghue, D. 60

O'Donoghue, G.M. 49
O'Donoghue, J.G. 305
O'Donoghue, M. 60
O'Donoghue, Mollie 328
O'Donoghue, N. 47
O'Donoghue, N.F. 49
O'Donoghue, Tom 128
O'Donovan Rossa, Jeremiah 38
O'Duffy, Eoin 15, 22
O'Dwyer, Bishop 158, 316
O'Dwyer, William 54
O'Flaherty, Fr 79, 127
O'Flynn, P. 59
O'Grady, Thomas 194
O'Grady, William 75
O'Hanlon, James 192
O'Hegarty, Captain 322
O'Hegarty, Diarmuid 170
O'Hegarty, P.S. 169
O'Herlihy, D.J. 190
O'Keeffe, Dan 80
O'Keeffe, Francis J. 193
O'Keeffe, Frank T. 193
O'Keeffe, J.M 77
O'Keeffe, T. 76
O'Kelly, Captain 312
O'Kelly, J.J. (Sceilg) 176
O'Kelly, Seán T. 313
O'Leary, Daniel 60
O'Leary, J. 215
O'Leary, Jeremiah 190
O'Leary, Jim 60
O'Leary, John 189
O'Leary, M. 43
O'Leary, Molly 47
O'Leary, Mort 134
O'Leary, Nora 43, 328, 329
O'Leary, P.J. 80
O'Leary, Thomas 288
O'Leary, William 288
O'Mahony, Daniel 60, 66, 67, 69, 128, 215, 217
O'Mahony, P.C. 331
O'Mara, Molly 331
O'Meara, Eugene McGillicuddy 29
O'Meara, Tim 259
O'Neill, D. 60
O'Neill, D.J. 60
O'Neill, E. 60
O'Neill, J.J. 60
O'Neill, Lawrence 182
O'Neill, Patrick 194
O'Rahilly, A. 333

O'Rahilly, The 28, 51, 124, 136, 137, 151, 153
O'Regan, P. 60
O'Reilly, Jack 128, 153
O'Riordan, B. 60
O'Riordan, D.J. Canon 53
O'Riordan, M. 60
O'Riordan, Molly 334
O'Riordan, P. 59, 60
O'Riordan, T. 60
O'Shaughnessy, Mark 301
O'Shea, Alexander 194
O'Shea, Annie 329
O'Shea, Daniel 128, 325
O'Shea, David 61
O'Shea, G. 49
O'Shea, George 288
O'Shea, J (Keel) 79
O'Shea, J. 46, 60
O'Shea, J.E. 187
O'Shea, J.P. 60
O'Shea, James 193
O'Shea, James J. 69, 71, 177
O'Shea, John Francis 128, 193
O'Shea, Pat 134, 135
O'Shea, Patrick J. 49, 52, 59, 134, 135, 190, 193
O'Shea, Sheelagh 190
O'Shea, T. 60
O'Shea, Tim 190, 191
O'Shee, Poer 222, 224
O'Sullivan, Charles 52, 192
O'Sullivan, Con 61
O'Sullivan, D. 191
O'Sullivan, D.C. 59
O'Sullivan, D.M. 60
O'Sullivan, Daniel 61
O'Sullivan, Dan P. 259
O'Sullivan, David 77
O'Sullivan, Denis 78
O'Sullivan, Donal 78, 190
O'Sullivan, E. 29
O'Sullivan, Eugene 75, 77, 79
O'Sullivan, Eugene (Rev. Bro.) 190
O'Sullivan, Gearóid 168, 169, 172, 173, 174
O'Sullivan, Humphrey 194
O'Sullivan, J. 49, 60
O'Sullivan, J.J. 54
O'Sullivan, James 74, 190
O'Sullivan, Jeremiah 190
O'Sullivan, Jeremiah B. 325
O'Sullivan, John 60

O'Sullivan, Mary 329
O'Sullivan, Maurice 61, 217
O'Sullivan, Michael 60
O'Sullivan, Michael J. 45, 46, 47, 48, 60, 189
O'Sullivan, Morty 176
O'Sullivan, P.T. 60
O'Sullivan, T. 194
O'Sullivan, T.D. 187, 192, 209
O'Sullivan, Tim 128
O'Sullivan, Timothy 143, 144, 145
O'Sullivan, Ulick 78
O'Sullivan, William 75
O'Sullivan, William D.F. 45
Oakpark 30, 36, 251, 316
Oates, Bernard 204

P

Parnell, Charles Stewart 186
Partridge, W.T. 39, 40, 120, 135, 140, 141
Pattison, Rev. Canon 52, 53
Pearse, Pádraig 33, 38, 93, 132, 133, 136, 151, 172, 177, 313
Pearse, Willie 177
Percy, J.C. 51
Picturedrome 29, 319
Pierce, John 288
Pierce, Michael 288, 291
Plunkett, Count 179, 195
Plunkett, Joseph 83, 88, 131, 135
Pollard, H.P. 236
Portmagee 128, 193
Potally 31
Power, D. 60
Power, Patrick 191
Prendergast, John 190
Prendeville, Denny 212, 213, 217
Prendeville, J. 217
Prendeville, J. (Dr) 334
Prendeville, Jack 217
Prendeville, Jim 217
Prendeville, Patrick 191
Provisional Committee 33, 34, 35, 67, 69, 77, 119
Purtill, John 29

Q

Quill, Michael 325
Quille, Denis 53
Quille, John 325
Quinlan, Michael 179, 329

Quinlan, P. 31
Quinlan, P.J. 176
Quirke, Denis 194

R

Rael, John 176
Rath 37, 44, 155, 202
Rathass 191
Rathbeg 193
Rathcoole 296, 297
Rathduane 80, 295
Rathea 206, 268, 269, 270
Rathmore 79, 80, 150, 190, 193, 194,
224, 256, 293, 294, 295, 299, 300
Rearden, Dick 217
Reardon, Mick 31
Redmond, John 16, 32, 33, 34, 35, 37, 38,
40, 41, 43, 50, 55, 56, 57, 61, 70,
76, 106, 111, 169, 170
Redmondite Volunteers 19, 32, 35, 40,
42, 47, 53, 54, 55, 56, 57, 59, 61,
65, 66, 67, 69, 70, 71, 74, 75, 76,
77, 78, 79, 81, 304, 327
Reenard 71, 128, 149, 170, 333
Regan, James 181
Regan, John 194
Regan, L. 43
Reid, George 31
Reidy, Denis J. 67
Reidy, John 69
Reidy, Madge 329
Reidy, Michael 128
Reidy, Moss 31
Reidy, P. 43
Reidy, Paddy 215
Reidy, Tim 79
Reilly, Constable 112, 154
Rice, John 192
Rice, John Joe 322
Richmond barracks 127, 129, 154, 160
Ring, Eugene J. 70, 177
Ring, Timothy 128
Riordan, C.D. 76
Riordan, J.D. 76
Riordan, Jerome 177
Riordan, Michael 325
Riordan, Molly 334
Riordan, P.D. 76
Riordan, Patrick 193
Robinson, Joseph 92
Roche, David 190
Roche, J. 31

Roche, James 215
Roche, M. 76
Roche, W. 60
Rock Street, Tralee 28, 31, 36, 180, 181,
191, 218, 229, 230, 241, 315,
320, 329, 330
Rooney, W. 81
Royal Irish Constabulary (RIC) 39, 43,
44, 47, 67, 78, 96, 97, 98, 121,
127, 140, 141, 144, 152, 175,
196, 197, 211, 212, 214, 216,
221, 222, 224, 225, 226, 236,
237, 238, 248, 255, 265, 266,
267, 272, 273, 274, 276, 281,
282, 283, 286, 288, 289, 290,
291, 292, 293, 295, 300, 301,
305, 306, 311, 316, 333
Russell, Tom 181
Ryan, Fr 120, 140
Ryan, Patrick 315
Ryan, T. 76
Ryle, Gerald 315
Ryle, Maurice P. 28, 75
Ryle, Pat 31

S

Sandicock, Detective Inspector 113
Scanlan, J. 31
Scanlon, John 79
Scannell, Daniel 194
Scannell, Denis 325
Scannell, Michael D. 190
Scannell, P. 76
Scannell, P.M. 76
Scannell, T. 60
Scartaglin 67, 68, 80, 128, 190, 211, 212,
213, 214, 215, 255, 299
Scollard, Garrett 76
Scott-Hickie, Colonel 52
Scottish Borderers 27, 30, 35, 222
Scully, John 54
Scully, Paul 194
Shanahan, Jack 259, 313
Shanahan, Michael 237
Shanahan, R.E. 67
Shannow Bridge 292
Sharry, John 193
Sharry, Patrick 209
Shea, Bridie 329
Shea, Dan 304
Shea, J. 31
Shea, Kattie 329

Shea, Pat 259, 325
Shea, Sarah 329
Sheahan, Jack 284, 285, 286
Sheehan, C. 59
Sheehan, D. (Dr) 191
Sheehan, Donal 147, 150
Sheehan, Jack 325
Sheehan, James 308
Sheehan, M. 60
Sheehan, P. 60
Sheehan, Pat 60
Sheehan, Patrick 288
Sheehan, W. 194
Sheehy, Aggie 330
Sheehy, John 61
Sheehy, John J. 75, 192
Sheehy, John P. 193
Sheehy, Morgan 209
Sheehy, Pat (Duagh) 75
Sheehy, Pat (Tralee) 31
Sheehy, Sally 330
Sheehy, Thomas 75, 308
Shine, Cornelius 190
Shortis, Patrick 153
Shouldice, Seán 170
Shronderagh 194
Shronebeg 190
Sinn Féin 16, 19, 40, 42, 50, 51, 57, 66,
    71, 146, 148, 161, 168, 175, 177,
    179, 181, 182, 184, 185, 186,
    187, 188, 189, 192, 193, 195,
    196, 197, 206, 207, 210, 220,
    222, 223, 229, 232, 253, 254
Skinner, Jeremiah 43
Slattery, Edward 192
Slattery, J.P. 190
Slattery, Jerome 28
Slattery, John 192
Slattery, Maurice 311
Slattery, Ned 31
Slattery, Thomas 28, 67, 128, 187, 191,
    230, 327
Smith, F.E. 115
Smyth, Gerald Bryce Ferguson 222, 223,
    224, 225, 226
Sommers, I. 79
Spicer, George 117, 118, 119
Spicer, Hanna 31, 118, 119, 120
Spillane, Dominick 194
Spillane, Kathleen 332
Spillane, Michael 45, 46, 48, 50, 51, 52,
    193, 204, 205
Spillane, Patrick 189, 190

Spillane, Timothy 129, 204
Spindler, Karl 83, 84, 85, 86, 87, 88, 89,
    90, 99, 101, 132
Spring, Henry 50, 128, 190, 191
Springmount 217
Stack, Austin 16, 17, 28, 30, 31, 36, 38,
    43, 44, 49, 67, 76, 77, 93, 95, 100,
    118, 119, 120, 121, 122, 127, 128,
    130, 131, 133, 134, 135, 139, 140,
    150, 158, 159, 160, 161, 162, 176,
    177, 178, 185, 187, 188, 191, 192,
    193, 194, 305, 313, 328
Stack, Eyre 192
Stack, James 193
Stack, M. 76
Stack, Ml. 288
Stack, Thomas 75
Stackpoole, Philip 194
Stagmount 190
Stokes, Chrissie 179, 328
Strand Street, Tralee 28, 29, 30, 31, 36,
    37, 38, 44, 67, 125, 180, 228, 315,
    320, 329, 330
Strangeways prison 160, 195
Sugrue, Denis 204
Sugrue, Eugene 79
Sugrue, James 53, 129, 206
Sugrue, Joseph 263
Sugrue, Katty 329
Sugrue, P. (Mrs) 334
Sugrue, Patrick (An Seabhac) 193
Sullivan, D. 76
Sullivan, Daniel 263, 315
Sullivan, Denis 259
Sullivan, J. 129
Sullivan, James 315
Sullivan, Jeremiah 71, 325
Sullivan, Jerry 217
Sullivan, Joe 43
Sullivan, John E. 60
Sullivan, John L. 263
Sullivan, Johnny 263
Sullivan, Mary Bride 334
Sullivan, Mary Frances 334
Sullivan, Michael J. 45, 52
Sullivan, Mort 31
Sullivan, Patrick 308
Sullivan, Peter 259
Sullivan, Timothy M. 325
Sullivan, Ulick 60
Supple, Thomas 190
Sweeney, J. 76
Sweeney, William 193

T

Tackaberry, Jack 53
Talbot, John 191
Tarbert 80, 192, 193, 194, 271, 277, 278, 280, 282
Taylor, Joe 194
Teahan, Christy 315
Teahan, M. 60
Teahan, M.J. 79
Teahan, Patrick 61
Theatre Royal 35, 179
Times, The 50, 239, 241
Timoney, John 31
Tooreenamult 190
Tournafulla 215
Tralee 19, 28, 29, 30, 31, 32, 33, 34, 35, 36, 37, 38, 39, 40, 41, 42, 43, 44, 47, 48, 49, 50, 57, 58, 67, 68, 69, 75, 76, 77, 79, 82, 83, 84, 86, 87, 88, 89, 92, 93, 94, 95, 96, 97, 98, 99, 100, 103, 109, 110, 111, 113, 114, 117, 118, 120, 121, 122, 123, 124, 125, 126, 127, 128, 129, 131, 132, 133, 134, 135, 136, 138, 139, 140, 141, 153, 154, 155, 158, 159, 160, 161, 168, 176, 177, 178, 179, 180, 181, 187, 188, 191, 192, 193, 194, 201, 202, 204, 207, 208, 217, 218, 228, 229, 230, 231, 232, 233, 234, 236, 237, 238, 239, 240, 241, 242, 247, 248, 249, 250, 253, 254, 258, 261, 263, 267, 269, 271, 275, 276, 277, 281, 290, 291, 295, 296, 297, 298, 304, 305, 306, 307, 313, 314, 315, 316, 317, 318, 319, 321, 325, 326, 327, 328, 329
Tralee Pipers' Band 38
Troy, Charles 193
Tudor, General 222
Tureengarriffe 299, 300, 303
Twomey, Mrs 331
Tyndall, Nan 329

U

Uí Chonnaill, Nora Bean Diarmuid 334
Ulster Unionists 26
Ulster Volunteers 26, 115
United States of America 31, 82, 83, 88, 94, 95, 105, 106, 108, 113, 114, 115, 132, 152, 156, 160, 161, 178, 185, 196, 233, 239

V

Vale, Joseph 128
Vale, Milly 31
Vale, Pearl 31
Valentia 55, 71, 147, 150, 333
Vaughan, Dan 299
Vaughan, Timothy 299
Ventry 29, 54, 80, 155, 228
Vickers, Sir Arthur 279
Volunteers' Pipe Band 47, 50
Von Papen 88

W

Wakefield Prison 129
Wall, S. 76
Wall, Tommy 230
Walsh, Captain P. 281
Walsh, David 192
Walsh, F. 43
Walsh, Florence 128
Walsh, James M. 192
Walsh, John 192, 194
Walsh, M. 60
Walsh, Matt 31
Walsh, Nora 332
Walsh, P.J. 192
Walsh, Patrick 282, 283
Walsh, R.J. 67
Walsh, Thomas 191
Walsh, Thomas J. 192, 209, 210
Walsh, Tim 236, 237, 238
Walsh, Tom 193
Walshe, Margaret 332
Waterville 81, 167, 168, 333
Whelan, Patrick 124
Williamstown 300
Willis, Brigadier 230
Wilmot, Bridget 332, 333
Wimbourne, Lord 51, 184
Woods, Ethel 331
Woulfe, D. 76
Woulfe, P. 76
Woulfe, T. 76
Wren, Daniel 192
Wren, T. 67
Wrenn, J. 76
Wrixon, Paddy 45
Wynne, Captain 316